LIBRARY OF HEBREW BIBLE/ OLD TESTAMENT STUDIES

431

Formerly Journal for the Study of the Old Testament Supplement Series

AMBIGUITY IN ECCLESIASTES

Doug Ingram

t &t clark

NEW·YORK • LONDON

For my parents,
Edward and Merle Ingram

T & T Clark International, 80 Maiden Lane, New York, NY 10038

T & T Clark International, The Tower Building, 11 York Road, London SE1 7NX

T & T Clark International is a Continuum imprint.

Library of Congress Cataloging-in-Publication Data
Ingram, Doug.
    Ambiguity in Ecclesiastes / Doug Ingram.
      p. cm. -- (Library of Hebrew Bible/Old Testament studies ; 431)
    Includes bibliographical references and index.
    ISBN 0-567-02711-2 (hardcover)
    1. Bible. O.T. Ecclesiastes--Reader-response criticism. 2. Ambiguity in the Bible. I. Title. II. Series.
    BS1475.52.I55 2006
    223'.806--dc22

                           2006001136

Printed in the United States of America

06 07 08 09 10   10 9 8 7 6 5 4 3 2 1

CONTENTS

PREFACE

This book is partly a book written about books written about a book that says of writing books, "Of making many books there is no end" (Eccl 12:12)! My interest in Ecclesiastes was first sparked during my undergraduate days when it struck me how diverse were the interpretations of the book, and the more I read the more I realised that this diversity goes back to the earliest known comments on the book and continues up to the present day (and this remains true as I write this preface in the Autumn of 2003). Moreover, the more I studied the text of Ecclesiastes in depth (and I learned Biblical Hebrew specifically for this purpose!), the more convinced I became that the differences I was encountering in the commentaries, books and articles (and later among my students and colleagues) could be supported from the text itself. This led to Ph.D. research on Ecclesiastes ("The Ambiguity of Qohelet: A Study of the Ambiguous Nature of the Language. Syntax and Structure of the Masoretic Text of Qohelet" [University of Stirling, 1996]) which deepened my conviction that the text of Ecclesiastes is *fundamentally ambiguous by design*. My Ph.D. defended that thesis and I'm very grateful to T. & T. Clark International for the opportunity to redraft my dissertation for publication. I'm particularly grateful to John Jarick for recommending a major rewrite which would make the results of my research more accessible—the Ph.D. dissertation was a defence pure and simple of the thesis and was never intended to be an easy read. I trust the present work will be an interesting and engaging read in its redrafted form. However, by its nature, it engages extensively with a great deal of (especially recent) secondary material on Ecclesiastes in order to demonstrate conclusively that the book continues to be interpreted in diametrically opposed ways, both in terms of the overall "message" of the book, but also in terms of interpretation of specific words, phrases and passages within the book. Some of this appears in the text of my book itself. Much of it is in rather numerous and sometimes quite extensive footnotes. These latter are provided to give substantial evidence for the claims I make about the ambiguity of Ecclesiastes, but are not necessary for grasping the significance of the discussion. I trust, therefore, that the book can be read through with no reference to the footnotes by those for whom that is appropriate;

while those readers who want to follow up on the more detailed argument will find plenty to work on in the text supplemented by the footnotes.

I believe I can detect a sea-change in how Ecclesiastes is read. For me the most interesting aspect of this is that the change is apparent *both* in academic work on the book *and* in popular reading of it. So, for instance, my perception is that when I first started talking about my growing conviction that Ecclesiastes is fundamentally ambiguous (in the late 1980s), I received a rather frosty response from academics and laypeople alike. This has dramatically changed. In conversations now both academics and "normal" readers respond very warmly to my views on the book. Moreover, in recent scholarly work on Ecclesiastes there is a trend in this direction. In addition to remarks in recent commentaries, I would draw particular attention to Gary D. Salyer's *Vain Rhetoric: Private Insight and Public Debate in Ecclesiastes*[1] and also to Mary E. Mills, *Reading Ecclesiastes: A Literary and Cultural Exegesis*.[2] I thank Gary Salyer for making the text of his book available to me several months before it was published.

Thanks are due also to a number of other people without whose support this work would not have materialised. First, my parents, Edward and Merle Ingram encouraged an enquiring mind which was then open to the possibility of finding ambiguity in the Bible. Their support in many ways has been invaluable over many years of study and research and I

1. Gary D. Salyer, *Vain Rhetoric: Private Insight and Public Debate in Ecclesiastes* (JSOTSup 327; Sheffield: Sheffield Academic Press, 2001).
2. Mary E. Mills, *Reading Ecclesiastes: A Literary and Cultural Exegesis* (Aldershot: Ashgate, 2003). In addition, attention might be drawn to Michael V. Fox, *A Time to Tear Down and a Time to Build Up: A Rereading of Ecclesiastes* (Grand Rapids: Eerdmans, 1999); an earlier version of which appeared as *Qohelet and His Contradictions* (Bible and Literature Series 18; Sheffield: Sheffield Academic Press, 1989); L. Wilson, "Artful Ambiguity in Ecclesiastes 1,1–11," and R. W. Byargeon, "The Significance of Ambiguity in Ecclesiastes 2,24–26," both in, *Qohelet in the Context of Wisdom* (ed. A. Schoors; BETL, 136; Leuven: Leuven University Press, 1998), 357–65, 367–72; Eric S. Christianson, *A Time to Tell: Narrative Strategies in Ecclesiastes* (JSOTSup 280; Sheffield: Sheffield Academic Press, 1998); Craig G. Bartholomew, *Reading Ecclesiastes: Old Testament Exegesis and Hermeneutical Theory* (AnB 139; Rome: Editrice Pontificio Istituto Biblico, 1998); and John Barton, *Reading the Old Testament: Method in Biblical Study* (2d ed.; London: Darton, Longman & Todd, 1996 [1984]), which uses Ecclesiastes as the sample text for various reading strategies. I have also recently published a booklet (Doug Ingram, *Ecclesiastes: A Peculiarly Postmodern Piece* [Grove Biblical Series B34; Cambridge: Grove Books, 2004] which briefly explores ambiguity in Ecclesiastes and considers some of the implications for Christian interpretation of the Old Testament.

dedicate this book to them in acknowledgment of the great debt I owe them. My wife, Sue, has had to share her marriage to me with Qohelet, and has done so with amazingly good grace. She has always encouraged me in my research and writing, even when it has meant considerable sacrifices for her. My children, Sam and Jo, have never known life without Qohelet. I thank them for their forbearance, understanding and teasing even when reading and writing have eaten into family holidays. Keith Whitelam also showed considerable forbearance with a Ph.D. student who had far too many "irons in the fire" and progressed much more slowly with his research than he ought to have done. In addition to engendering in me a love of academic study of the Old Testament, Keith's patience, understanding and advice enabled me to finish my doctoral research and provided the impetus to continue study, research and teaching. I am also grateful to colleagues particularly at Lincoln Theological College and St John's College, Nottingham, who provided both the encouragement and the space for research and writing. My students have, with good grace, put up with my boundless enthusiasm for Qohelet who has crept into many a class and conversation where he probably had no right to be. Their responses and comments convince me that my fascination with the ambiguous nature of this strange book is worth sharing more broadly, and so they must take some of the credit or blame for the emergence, at last, of my book ("… and just when *is* the book finally going to be finished, Doug?"). One of these students, Sarah Giles, gave me help with French and German translation. Finally, I wish to express my thanks to Duncan Burns for his expert work on the proofs and his friendly advice. He certainly helped give this book a "final polish."

ABBREVIATIONS

AB	Anchor Bible
AV	Authorised Version
AnBib	Analecta biblica
ASTI	*Annual of the Swedish Theological Institute*
AUSS	*Andrews University Seminary Studies*
AUUSSU	Acta Universitatis Upsaliensis. Studia Semitica Upsaliensia
BDB	*A Hebrew and English Lexicon of the Old Testament*. Francis Brown, S. R. Driver and Charles A. Briggs. Oxford: Clarendon Press, 1907
BETL	Bibliotheca ephemeridum theologicarum lovaniensium
BibInt	*Biblical Interpretation: A Journal of Contemporary Approaches*
BKAT	Biblischer Kommentar: Altes Testament
BT	*The Bible Translator*
BTB	*Biblical Theology Bulletin*
BZAW	Beihefte zur *ZAW*
CBQ	*Catholic Biblical Quarterly*
CR:BS	*Currents in Research: Biblical Studies*
ESV	English Standard Version
EvT	*Evangelische Theologie*
GesK	*Gesenius' Hebrew Grammar*. Edited by E. Kautzsch. Revised and translated by A. E. Cowley. Oxford: Clarendon, 1910
GNB	Good News Bible
GTJ	*Grace Theological Journal*
HAR	*Hebrew Annual Review*
HS	*Hebrew Studies*
HUCA	*Hebrew Union College Annual*
IBS	*Irish Biblical Studies*
ICC	International Critical Commentary
Int	*Interpretation*
JSOT	*Journal for the Study of the Old Testament*
JSOTSup	*Journal for the Study of the Old Testament*, Supplement Series
JB	Jerusalem Bible
JBL	*Journal of Biblical Literature*
JHStud	*Journal of Hellenic Studies*
JNES	*Journal of Near Eastern Studies*
JSS	*Journal of Semitic Studies*
KJV	King James Version

LXX	Septuagint
MT	Masoretic text
NAB	New American Bible
NASB	New American Standard Bible
NEB	New English Bible
NIBC	New International Biblical Commentary
NICOT	New International Commentary on the Old Testament
NIDOTTE	*New International Dictionary of Old Testament Theology and Exegesis.* Edited by W. A. VanGemeren. 5 vols. Grand Rapids: Zondervan, 1997
NIV	New International Version
NJB	New Jerusalem Bible
NJPSV	New Jewish Publication Society Version
NKJV	New King James Version
NLT	New Living Translation
NRSV	New Revised Standard Version
OLA	*Orientalia Lovaniensia Analecta*
OTG	Old Testament Guides
OTL	Old Testament Library
PEQ	*Palestine Exploration Quarterly*
REB	Revised English Bible
RSV	Revised Standard Version
SBLDS	Society of Biblical Literature Dissertation Series
SJT	*Scottish Journal of Theology*
Syr	Syriac
TB	*Tyndale Bulletin*
TD	*Theology Digest*
TEV	Today's English Version
TDOT	*Theological Dictionary of the Old Testament.* Edited by G. J. Botterweck and H. Ringgren. Translated by J. T. Willis, G. W. Bromiley and D. E. Green. 8 vols. Grand Rapids: Eerdmans, 1974–
TLOT	*Theological Lexicon of the Old Testament.* Edited by E. Jenni, with assistance from C. Westermann. Translate by M. E. Biddle. 3 vols. Peabody, Mass.: Hendrickson, 1997
TOTC	Tyndale Old Testament Commentaries
Vg	Vulgate
VS	Verbum salutis
VT	*Vetus Testamentum*
WBC	Word Biblical Commentary
ZAW	*Zeitschrift für die alttestamentliche Wissenschaft*

Chapter 1

WHAT IS AMBIGUITY?

for rhetorical reasons
the narrator chooses to ambiguate
where he could elucidate

—Meir Sternberg[1]

The Old Testament book of Ecclesiastes is ambiguous. It is upon this premise that the following work is founded, and the statement will be defended in the succeeding chapters. However, the statement itself is problematic, perhaps even ambiguous (it is certainly open to more than one interpretation, as I shall demonstrate), and requires further explanation.[2]

1.1. *The Ambiguity of "Ambiguity"*

The explanation should perhaps start by considering what is indicated in my opening statement by the term "ambiguous." Ambiguity describes some indeterminacy[3] of meaning or significance in a word, phrase,

1. Meir Sternberg, *The Poetics of Biblical Narrative: Ideological Literature and the Drama of Reading* (Bloomington: Indiana University Press, 1985).

2. We might note Kevin J. Vanhoozer's statement that, "The status of literary ambiguity, however, is well . . . more ambiguous" (*Is There a Meaning in This Text? The Bible, the Reader and the Morality of Literary Knowledge* [Leicester: Apollos, 1998]).

3. It may, of course, be said that this is a loaded term. However, as will become apparent, when the concept of ambiguity is taken to its logical conclusions, "gaps" or "spaces" or "aporia" are revealed in the text which suggest the kind of "indeterminacy" of which, for example, Wolfgang Iser makes a great deal in his article "Indeterminacy and the Reader's Response," reprinted from *Aspects of Narrative: Selected Papers from the English Institute* (ed. J. Hillis Miller; New York: Columbia University Press, 1971), 2–45, in K. M. Newton, *Twentieth-Century Literary Theory: A Reader* (Houndsmills, Basingstoke: Macmillan, 1988), 226–31. See further, Wolfgang Iser, *The Act of Reading: A Theory of Aesthetic Response* (Baltimore: The Johns Hopkins University Press, 1978), esp. 170–79. Specifically in relation to

sentence or longer piece of written or spoken language, or in any action which could be perceived as an act of communication. The indeterminacy may be because it is unclear what the author of a piece of language or an action intends to convey by it; or because the word(s) or action(s) used allow(s) for more than one meaning in the context—whether or not this is intended by the author, and whether or not it is clear what that author intends to convey; or because the word(s) or action(s) used appear(s) not to give any coherent meaning in the context. In an oft-cited passage in *Seven Types of Ambiguity*,[4] Empson extends the scope of ambiguity in a literary context so far as to include "any verbal nuance, however slight, which gives room for alternative reactions to the same piece of language."[5] By this definition, taken to its extreme limits,

---

Biblical Studies, see the very different responses to indeterminacy in the biblical text expressed by the contributors to *Textual Determinacy: Part One* (ed. Robert C. Culley and Robert B. Robinson; Semeia 62; Atlanta: Scholars Press, 1993), and *Textual Determinacy: Part Two* (ed. Robert B. Robinson and Robert C. Culley; Semeia 71; Atlanta: Scholars Press, 1995). We should note, however, that Massimo Poesio implicitly makes a distinction between "ambiguity" and "indeterminacy" when he writes, "The dictionary definition of the terms AMBIGUITY and AMBIGUOUS try to capture the intuition that an expression is ambiguous if 'it has multiple meanings.' The need for a more precise definition is seen once one begins to consider the differences between ambiguity and VAGUENESS or INDETERMINACY, for example, or to define notions such as HOMONIMY and POLYSEMY" ("Semantic Ambiguity and Perceived Ambiguity," in *Semantic Ambiguity and Underspecification* [ed. Kees van Deemter and Stanley Peters; CSLI Lecture Notes 55; Stanford, Calif.: CSLI Publications, 1996], 159–201 [161]). A similar distinction is made in Shlomith Rimmon, *The Concept of Ambiguity: The Example of James* (Chicago: The University of Chicago Press, 1977), 19–20.

4. Cited, e.g., in Terry Eagleton, *Literary Theory: An Introduction* (Oxford: Blackwell, 1983), 52; Martin Gray, *A Dictionary of Literary Terms* (York Handbooks; Harlow, Essex: Longman, 1984), 15; Elizabeth Freund, *The Return of the Reader: Reader-Response Criticism* (New Accents; London: Methuen, 1987), 44.

5. William Empson, *Seven Types of Ambiguity* (London: The Hogarth Press, 1991 [1930]), 1. A student at St John's College, Nottingham, Jonathan Tallon, provided me with these suggestions for "seven types of ambiguity" (in a letter ahead of a research seminar on "Ambiguity in Ecclesiastes and the World"; I acknowledge my debt to Jonathan whose examples I have used often since): (1) Intentionally ambiguous, but favouring one interpretation to those in the know. E.g., a reference for a bad employee: "you will be very fortunate if you can get this person to work for you"; (2) Unintentionally ambiguous, but obviously intended to carry one meaning. E.g., "I've not never done no harm to nobody"; (3) Originally clear, but ambiguous through loss of context and/or over time. E.g., What are *urim* and *thummim*? Or hieroglyphics until the Rosetta stone?; (4) Intentionally ambiguous, and without meaning, in order to reveal the reader's mind. E.g., Rorschach ink blots;

all language (and, by extension, any action[6]—but henceforth we shall restrict our discussion to ambiguity in language) could be considered ambiguous because it is always possible to extort different "meanings" (or perhaps "significances"—I shall consider the importance of these two terms below) from a word or collection of words according to the predilections of the reader or hearer.[7] It is for this reason that Empson has

(5) Unintentionally ambiguous, because the text is self-contradictory owing to the author(s) ineptitude or lack of clarity of thought. E.g., some student essays?; (6) Intentionally ambiguous, because the author wishes to appeal to different sections of community. E.g., Tony Blair's position on the Euro? And other ways in which politicians position themselves; (7) Coherently ambiguous (intentionally OR unintentionally), so that radically different answers or intentions can account completely and satisfactorily for all the text or information, despite contradicting each other.

It is something along the lines of (7) that particularly concerns us in this work, although, as we will see, I do not believe that any reading can "account completely and satisfactorily for all the text or information" in Ecclesiastes.

6. Indeed, Page extends the sense of ambiguity even further when she writes, "*Ambiguity* as I shall use it enlarges 'double meaning' to polyvalence, that is, the way in which anything may be interpreted or evaluated in a variety of ways according to one's point of view, intention, practice or culture. Even a rock in the remotest jungle is ambiguous in this sense, since it may be analysed geologically, mined, climbed, depicted, act as a tribe's totem or a home for plants and animals, and will be seen differently in each case" (Ruth Page, *Ambiguity and the Presence of God* [London: SCM Press, 1985], 13). This would, no doubt, fall into Fox's category of "omnipresent indeterminacy. Of the sort that permeates and burdens language itself—in other words, the unsurprising imperfection of all communication," which he says "belongs to the realm of psycholinguistics rather than literary interpretation," adding, "Inevitable, undirected indeterminacy is like background static in the airwaves, which is not relevant to the understanding of a symphony we happen to hear on the radio. Nor (to extend this analogy to reader reception) does the tone-deafness of some listeners show that the orchestra hasn't turned up" (Michael V. Fox, "The Uses of Indeterminacy," in Robinson and Culley, eds., *Textual Determinacy: Part Two*, 173–92 [173]).

7. Page acknowledges, "The endeavour to entertain Ambiguity [*sic*] is vertiginous, for one ambiguous instance has to be explained by something else which is itself ambiguous, unfinished, open to interpretation. So nothing can be finalized. Taken seriously, it leaves no firm rock on which to stand, no perduring order on which to rely" (*Ambiguity*, 35). From the perspective of developing systems to cope with ambiguity in Natural Language Processes in the area of, e.g., Artificial Intelligence, Green argues, "As has been often noted, practically any word can be used to denote an almost limitless variety of kinds of objects or functions." She adds, "The idea that what a word can be used to refer to might vary indefinitely is clearly unsettling. It makes the fact that we (seem to) understand each other most of the time something of a miracle" (Georgia M. Green, "Ambiguity Resolution and Discourse Interpretation," in Deemter and Peters, eds., *Semantic Ambiguity*, 1–26 [10]).

been accused of using the term "ambiguity" in a confusingly loose manner so that it fails to convey anything sufficiently concrete to be of critical value.[8] But it is also for this reason that *Seven Types of Ambiguity*, despite being written from an "intentionalist" perspective, has attracted the attention of literary critics who seek to free language from authorial intention and allow it to function as an autonomous entity. For the same reason, the book has also been utilised by those for whom the reader is the final authority in determining, and perhaps even creating, the "meaning" of a text. Thus Culler regards Structuralism as the logical extension of Empson's work:

> William Empson's *Seven Types of Ambiguity* is a work from a non-structuralist tradition which shows considerable awareness of the problems of literary competence and illustrates just how close one comes to a structuralist formulation if one begins to reflect on them.[9]

Eagleton, on the other hand, suggests that *Seven Types of Ambiguity* opens the door to a reader-oriented approach to literature:

> Empsonian ambiguities . . . can never be finally pinned down: they indicate points where the poem's language falters, trails off or gestures beyond itself, pregnantly suggestive of some potentially inexhaustible context of meaning. Whereas the reader is shut out by a locked structure of ambivalences, reduced to admiring passivity, "ambiguity" solicits his or her active participation. . . . It is the reader's response which makes for ambiguity, and this response depends on more than the poem alone.[10]

---

8. See, e.g., F. W. Bateson, *English Poetry: A Critical Introduction* (London: Longmans, 1950), 180, and Rimmon, *The Concept of Ambiguity*, 16–26. This is also an accusation levelled by James Smith in a review for *Criterion* in July 1931—an article which Empson addresses in the Preface to the second edition (and subsequent editions) of *Seven Types of Ambiguity*.

9. Jonathan Culler, *Structuralist Poetics: Structuralism, Linguistics and the Study of Literature* (London: Routledge & Kegan Paul, 1975), 125–27 (125).

10. Eagleton, *Literary Theory*, 51–52 (52). But see the discussion in Rimmon, *The Concept of Ambiguity*, 11–16. She maintains that, "'Ambiguity' should first be distinguished from the multiplicity of subjective interpretations given to a work of fiction," explaining that "The essential difference between this phenomenon and ambiguity proper is that while subjectivity of reading is conditioned mainly by the psyche of the reader, ambiguity is a fact in the text—a double system of mutually exclusive clues" (p. 12). She adds: "An ambiguous work . . . is characterized by a highly determined form, limiting the text's plurality by its organization of the data into two opposed systems which leave little or no room for further 'play'" (p. 13). In exploring ambiguity in Ecclesiastes I am seeking "ambiguity [that] is a fact in the text," but I do not share Rimmon's confidence in so clearly separating text and reader. Moreover, as noted above, I consider ambiguity to arise as a result of

1.2. *The Meaning of "Meaning"*

I asserted above that ambiguity is some indeterminacy of meaning, but the word "meaning" is itself highly ambiguous. The question of where the meaning of a piece of language is to be found has exercise the minds of literary critics[11] ever since the emergence of New Criticism in the 1920s and 1930s.[12] Is meaning to be found in the intention of the author

indeterminacy in the text, albeit that this may arise because of two or more "determined" readings.

11. And increasingly of biblical critics. The book edited by John Barton, *The Cambridge Companion to Biblical Interpretation* (Cambridge: Cambridge University Press, 1998), provides a useful introductory overview. Vanhoozer's *Is There a Meaning in This Text?* is, to my mind, a fascinating study of the subject. The work of David J. A. Clines (see, e.g., *On the Way to the Postmodern, 1968–1998*, vols. 1 and 2 [JSOTSup 292/293; Sheffield: Sheffield Academic Press, 1998]), and Stephen D. Moore (see, e.g., *Poststructuralism and the New Testament* [Minneapolis: Fortress, 1994]) offers intriguing examples of the application of postmodern literary perspectives on "meaning" to Biblical Studies, as do recent volumes of the *Semeia* journal. See also the books edited by A. K. M. Adam, *Handbook of Postmodern Biblical Interpretation* (St Louis, Mo.: Chalice, 2000), and *Postmodern Interpretations of the Bible: A Reader* (St Louis, Mo.: Chalice, 2001); David Jobling, Tina Pippin and Ronald Schleifer, eds., *The Postmodern Bible Reader* (Oxford: Blackwell, 2001); and The Bible and Culture Collective's *The Postmodern Bible* (New Haven: Yale University Press, 1995). On the application of theories of "meaning" to hermeneutics, see, e.g., James W. Voelz's *What Does This Mean? Principles of Biblical Interpretation in the Post-Modern World* (2d ed.; St Louis, Mo.: Concordia) for an introductory work, and the work of Anthony C. Thiselton for a deeper engagement (e.g. *New Horizons in Hermeneutics: The Theory and Practice of Transforming Biblical Reading* [Grand Rapids: Zondervan, 1992]). Recent books on Ecclesiastes which have been much influenced by postmodern approaches to literature are Salyer's *Vain Rhetoric*, and Mills's *Reading Ecclesiastes*. Barton's *Reading the Old Testament* uses Ecclesiastes as its example as it explores different methods of studying the Bible right up to the postmodern era.

12. See, e.g., C. K. Ogden and I. A. Richards, *The Meaning of Meaning* (New York: Harcourt, 1923). I. A. Richards's *Principles of Literary Criticism* (New York: Harcourt, 1924) had a major impact on the formation of what came to be known as "New Criticism," along \with the works of T. S. Eliot, such as *The Use of Poetry and the Use of Criticism* (London: Faber & Faber, 1933). However, the label was fixed with the publication of J. C. Ransom's *The New Criticism* (Norfolk, Conn.: New Directions, 1941). It is noteworthy that commentators seem to be uncertain whether to include Empson, who was a pupil of Richards, among the ranks of New Critics. Freund compares Richards and Empson in a section of her book entitled "Regulating and Deregulating Meaning: Richards and Empson" (*The Return of the Reader*, 42–49), while Eagleton argues that "in the opposition between [Empson's] 'ambiguity' and New Critical 'ambivalence' we find a kind of early pre-run of the debate between structuralists and post-structuralists" (*Literary Theory*, 53).

or artist who created the piece of language; in the work itself; in the response of the audience; in the world or universe from which the work derives and/or from which the reader derives; or in some combination of two or more of these? A diagram drawn by Abrams in *The Mirror and the Lamp*[13] has become the standard way of representing the four objects of critical investigation in a "work of art" (see Fig. 1):

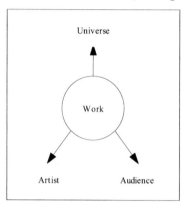

Figure 1

1.2.1. *Authorial Meaning*

If the artist is viewed as the source of meaning, a piece of language is regarded as the medium through which the author communicates to the audience. Meaning is, in Husserl's terms, an "intentional object" and is permanently fixed by the author at the time of writing. The task of the critic is then to determine what the author intended at the time of writing, and if this is hindered by the ambiguity of the text, the author can be said to that extent to have failed in communicating her or his intention. In the case of the Bible this issue is further complicated by the notion of divine inspiration whereby the author may in some fashion and to some greater or lesser degree be regarded as conveying the intention of another Author, namely, God.[14] If the authority of the author in determining the

13.   M. H. Abrams, *The Mirror and the Lamp: Romantic Theory and the Critical Tradition* (repr., New York: W. W. Norton, 1958 [orig. pub. 1953]), 6. See Barton's discussion of this diagram and what it represents in John Barton, "Classifying Biblical Criticism," *JSOT* 29 (1984): 19–35.

14.   See particularly in this regard Walter C. Kaiser, Jr., *Toward an Exegetical Theology: Biblical Exegesis for Preaching and Teaching* (Grand Rapids: Baker Book House, 1981), 108–14, where he explores the concept of the *sensus plenior* in biblical texts. Of course, many other writers also explore this concept, and there is a huge amount of literature on the nature of Scripture and the concepts of "revelation"

meaning of a biblical text is denied, does this necessarily also deny the authority of the Author?[15] In this case "authorial" intention and "Authorial" intention may need to be considered separately, and it may be that the question of Authorial intention should still be regarded as something worth examining even if the author is no longer seen as dictating meaning. This is an important factor in consideration of biblical literature in general and Qohelet in particular, especially when the identity of its author is so vague. Of course, such considerations also raise the highly pertinent question of whether the Bible as a specifically religious work is not a special case which ought to be excluded from the general field of literary criticism (although as *literature* it would be a proper object of such study[16]). The intentions of such an Author are not my immediate

and "the word of God": see, e.g., Avery Dulles, *Models of Revelation* (New York: Doubleday, 1983); Terence E. Fretheim and Karlfried Froehlich, *The Bible as Word of God: In a Postmodern Age* (Minneapolis: Fortress, 1998); Robert Gnuse, *The Authority of the Bible: Theories of Inspiration, Revelation and the Canon of Scripture* (New York: Paulist Press, 1985); John Goldingay, *Models for Scripture* (Grand Rapids: Eerdmans, 1994); and Donald K. McKim, ed., *The Authoritative Word: Essays on the Nature of Scripture* (Grand Rapids: Eerdmans, 1983).

15. Although for Barthes the term "Author" is not directly applied to God, the results of his "Death of the Author" undoubtedly have theological consequences: "Once the Author is removed, the claim to decipher a text becomes quite futile. To give a text an Author is to impose a limit on that text, to furnish it with a final signified, to close writing. . . . In precisely this way literature (it would be better from now on to say *writing*), by refusing to assign a 'secret', an ultimate meaning, to the text (and to the world as text), liberates what may be called an anti-theological activity, an activity that is truly revolutionary since to refuse to fix meaning is, in the end, to refuse God and his hypostases—reason, science, law" (Roland Barthes, *Image, Music, Text* [London: Fontana, 1977], 146). See further Vanhoozer on "the Author" (*Is There a Meaning in This Text?*, especially Chapters 2, 5, 7).

16. The "General Introduction" to Robert Alter and Frank Kermode's *The Literary Guide to the Bible* (London: Fontana, 1987), 1–8, succinctly argues the case for studying the Bible as literature. Alter and Kermode readily admit that their aims "are not theological," and that they "do not seek to duplicate the work of traditional historical scholarship." Rather there has been "a revival of interest in the literary qualities of these texts" over the past couple of decades, such that "Professional biblical criticism has been profoundly affected by it; but, even more important, the general reader can now be offered a new view of the Bible as a work of great literary force and authority, a work of which it is entirely credible that it should have shaped the minds and lives of intelligent men and women for two millennia and more." "It is this view of the Bible," they add, "that the present volume seeks to promote" (pp. 1–2). There is now a burgeoning literature on the Bible/Old Testament as "literature": see, e.g., David J. A. Clines, "Story and Poem: The Old Testament as Literature and as Scripture," in his *On the Way to the Postmodern*, 1:225–38;

concern in this book, but I shall have cause in due course to reflect on ambiguity in relation to this Author and the "text" (i.e. the world) this Author has created.

A major proponent of an author-oriented approach to meaning in literature (who readily admits the influence of Husserl's philosophy of meaning[17]) is Hirsch, who rigorously defends "the stable determinacy of meaning,"[18] where the meaning of a work is identical with what the author meant by it at the time of writing. While Hirsch contends that "The reader should try to reconstruct authorial meaning,"[19] he also allows that a literary work may "mean" different things to different readers at different times. However, this variable "mean"-ing he labels not as "meaning" but as "significance":

> while meaning is a principle of stability in an interpretation, significance is a principle of change. Meaning-for-an-interpreter can stay the same although the meaningfulness (significance) of that meaning can change with the changing contexts in which that meaning is applied.[20]

This is an important distinction which is evidently valid to some extent. Eagleton, for example, refers to a reading of Macbeth which shows its relevance to nuclear warfare: while Macbeth may bear such a "meaning" for a late twentieth-century audience, this is not what Shakespeare would have "meant" by it, and this distinction might be represented by asserting that the "meaning" of Macbeth may have this particular "significance" for a twentieth-century audience (or, now, a twenty-first-century

---

Robert Alter, *The World of Biblical Literature* (London: SPCK, 1992); John Dancy, *The Divine Drama: The Old Testament as Literature* (Cambridge: Lutterworth, 2001); Paul R. House, ed., *Beyond Form Criticism: Essays on Old Testament Literary Criticism* (Winona Lake, Ind.: Eisenbrauns, 1992).

17. See E. D. Hirsch, *The Aims of Interpretation* (Chicago: The University of Chicago Press, 1976), 79 n. 2.

18. Ibid., 1.

19. Ibid., 8. From a rather different perspective (studies in the processes of Natural Language Processing), Green, in "Ambiguity Resolution and Discourse Interpretation," 23–24, concludes her discussion by saying, "I have argued, and I hope, demonstrated, that resolving ambiguities that arise from the fact that grammars provide more than one interpretation for certain words, or more than one structure for sequences of certain constituent types, frequently boils down to the familiar pragmatic problem of determining what motivates any linguistic act in the first place." However, she goes on to state, "The chief requirement for such an enterprise is to reject the simplistic view of linguistic expressions as simple conduits for thoughts, and model natural language use as action of rational agents who treat the exchange of ideas as a joint goal."

20. Ibid., 80.

audience.[21] Thus the work takes on a significance which Shakespeare could not have intended.[22]

1.2.2. *Textual Meaning*

For the New Critics the intentions of the author are of no importance: as Wimsatt and Beardsley argue in the best-known piece of New Critical writing, "The Intentional Fallacy," "The poem[23] is not the critic's own and not the author's (it is detached from the author at birth and goes about the world beyond his power to intend about it or control it)."[24]

21. Eagleton, *Literary Theory*, 67–70.
22. Fox, whose recent commentary on Qohelet (but not the most recent; cf. Michael V. Fox, *Ecclesiastes* [The JPS Bible Commentary; Philadelphia: The Jewish Publication Society, 2004] has an important bearing on this study, follows Hirsch's line of reasoning. In his article "Job 38 and God's Rhetoric" (in *The Book of Job and Ricoeur's Hermeneutics* [ed. John Dominic Crossan; Semeia 19; Chico, Calif.: Scholars Press, 1981], 53–61 [53]), Fox argues: "The primary task of exegesis is ascertaining the text's meaning, which is to be identified with the authorial intention. . . . My main concern in approaching a text is essentially the same as that of traditional literalist exegesis: to ascertain the meaning of the text, which is to say, the authorial intention. Following E. D. Hirsch, I would apply the term 'meaning' only to the authorial meaning. All other understandings are better termed 'significances.'" See also the opening paragraph in M. V. Fox and B. Porten, "Unsought Discoveries: Qoh 7:23–8:1a," *HS* 19 (1978): 26–38. Fox and Porten's comment that "otherwise there is no limit to the meanings one can read into the text and the author will have failed to communicate *his* meaning" (p. 26, their emphasis) is telling. Longman, who has recently published a commentary on Ecclesiastes that contrasts very sharply with Fox's, argues similarly: "If literature is an act of communication, then meaning resides in the intention of the author. The author has encoded a message for the readers. Interpretation then has as its goal the recovery of the author's purpose in writing. . . . Our interpretation is correct insofar as it conforms to the meaning intended by the author" (Tremper Longman III, *Literary Approaches to Biblical Interpretation* [Foundations of Contemporary Interpretation 3; Leicester: Apollos, 1987], 64–65). Vanhoozer makes a great deal of the distinction between "meaning" and "significance": he says, e.g., "the Word of God for today (significance) is a function of the Word of God in the text (meaning), which in turn is a witness to the living and eternal Word of God in the Trinity (referent). The meaningfulness of the Bible is thus a matter of the Spirit's leading the church to extend Scripture's meaning into the present; in this way it displays its contemporary significance" (*Is There a Meaning in This Text?*, 423).
23. "Poem" is used, as Robey points out, as "short-hand . . . for a literary work of art" (David Robey, "Anglo-American New Criticism," in *Modern Literary Theory: A Comparative Introduction* [ed. Ann Jefferson and David Robey; 2d ed.; London: B. T. Batsford, 1986 (1982)], 73–91 [81]).
24. W. K. Wimsatt and M. C. Beardsley, "The Intentional Fallacy," in *The Verbal Icon: Studies in the Meaning of Poetry* (ed. William K. Wimsatt and Monroe

According to New Criticism, the text itself is the source of meaning regardless of what may have been intended by the author, and regardless of the response of the reader. The task of the literary critic is to deploy a scientific or objective technique (as opposed to the subjectivism of author- or reader-oriented approaches) because meaning is embodied in the text and is "wholly accessible to anyone with a knowledge of the language and culture to which the text belongs."[25] Thus Wimsatt and Beardsley write:

> We enquire now not about origins, nor about effects, but about the work so far as it can be considered by itself as a body of meaning. Neither the qualities of the author's mind nor the effects of a poem upon a reader's mind should be confused with the moral quality of the meaning expressed by the poem itself.[26]

There is evident validity in this argument too: there is no *a priori* reason why the author should be more qualified than any other critic (and the author is in any case less likely to be an impartial critic) to assess the meaning "embodied" in a piece of language.[27] The meaning of language is a social matter, and no individual may ascribe an objective meaning to a piece of language unless it can be determined scientifically by any other competent individual within that society, regardless of whether or not he or she created that piece of language ("moulded" may be a better term—the point is precisely that it is not creation *ex nihilo*), and regardless of what his or her intentions may be.

A major philosophical difference between Hirsch and the New Critics is that Hirsch, following Husserl, views meaning as pre-linguistic: meaning is intended and then captured in language, while for the New Critics, more in line with Heidegger's philosophy, language pre-exists meaning and meaning cannot exist apart from language.[28] Thus for Hirsch

C. Beardsley; repr., London: Methuen, 1970 [1954]), 3–18. This article (which first appeared in the *Sewanee Review* in 1946), and "The Affective Fallacy" (also found in *The Verbal Icon*, which first appeared in the *Sewanee Review* in 1949), provide a theoretical basis for the New Critical attack on the notion of expressive criticism. See further Raman Selden and Peter Widdowson, *A Reader's Guide to Contemporary Literary Theory* (3d ed.; New York: Harvester Wheatsheaf, 1993), 16–18.

25. Robey, "Anglo-American New Criticism," 81.

26. Wimsatt and Beardsley, *The Verbal Icon*, 87.

27. An excellent example of this is provided by Eco's debate with Culler, Rorty and Brooke-Rose about his own novels, especially *Foucault's Pendulum* (see Stefan Collini, ed., *Interpretation and Overinterpretation: Umberto Eco* [Cambridge: Cambridge University Press, 1992]).

28. The concept of the *logos* comes to mind here, and, in theological terms, particularly the beginning of the Fourth Gospel. Discussion of the philosophical and

the author conveys *her or his* meaning through the medium of language, and the critic's task is to unwrap that intentional meaning (and, it may be argued, once the meaning is found the text becomes obsolete, like the wrapping on a parcel). However, for New Criticism, language is the meaning (and so the text never becomes obsolete), and the critic's task is to discern the *public* meaning that is embodied in the piece of language itself. It should be noted, however, that from both perspectives there is a definitive meaning to be uncovered, a truth or reality which it is the critic's task to seek. In an author-oriented approach, the "truth" to be sought is specifically the authorial intention: this is the "reality" which the critic seeks to uncover, however poorly the author may have succeeded in conveying it. In the New Critical approach to the text, the "truth" to be sought is the meaning the words have for the society in which they function: the critic's task is to discover what is "signified" by the "signifiers"[29] of which language is composed, and this elucidates society's understanding of reality rather than the author's. Structuralists take this a step further by asserting that the "signifiers" are totally arbitrary designations of "signifieds,"[30] and the critic's task is then to uncover the *system* (or structure) of the language which uses these words, rather than attempting to determine meaning as such. I shall consider Structuralism in a little more detail later.

In the case of both Hirsh's approach and that of New Criticism, ambiguity can be adjudged successful or otherwise precisely to the

theological implications of this word is clearly beyond the scope of this study, but the notion of "logocentrism" forms an important aspect of consideration of Deconstruction (and its rejection of logocentrism must have theological implications) which will be mentioned briefly below. See, e.g., Jonathan Culler, *On Deconstruction: Theory and Criticism After Structuralism* (UK ed.; London: Routledge & Kegan Paul, 1983 [1982]), 99–111; Christopher Norris, *Deconstruction: Theory and Practice* (New Accents; London: Methuen, 1982), 29–31; Ann Jefferson, "Structuralism and Post-Structuralism," in Jefferson and Robey, *Modern Literary Theory*, 92–121 (112–19).

29. As is well known in literary circles, the "signifier" is the word, or sound-image, and the "signified" is the concept which that word names. Together the signifier and signified make up the linguistic "sign" which is used in a language to express the concept. Thus, as Hawkes explains, "The structural relationship between the concept of a tree (i.e. the *signified*) and the sound-image made by the word 'tree' (i.e. the *signifier*) thus constitutes a linguistic sign, and a language is made up of these: it is 'a system of signs that express ideas'" (Terence Hawkes, *Structuralism and Semiotics* [New Accents; London: Methuen, 1977], 25).

30. Onomatopoeia is an obvious exception to the *total* arbitrariness of signifiers—but even onomatopoeia is culturally determined and does not represent an absolute link between signifier and signified.

extent that it assists or inhibits comprehension of the meaning of a piece of language. From these perspectives, "ambivalence" is a much more comfortable concept because it is clear that different and even opposing attitudes may be displayed by one piece of language. The difference between "ambivalence"—whereby meanings can still be fixed, albeit that the meanings so fixed may be in opposition—and "ambiguity"—whereby, I have suggested, there is some indeterminacy of meaning—is very important in this study.[31] Thus, for example, the root חכם is clearly important in Ecclesiastes and it might appear that words derived from this root ("wise," "wisdom," etc.) would merit consideration. However, significant as these words undoubtedly are, I would argue that the book displays an *ambivalent* attitude to wisdom:[32] readers do, I believe, have a fair idea of what is conveyed by the words "wise," "wisdom," and so on,[33] but discover that at times wisdom is treated as a decidedly negative concept,[34] whereas at other points it is praised and striven for.[35] Hence,

31. For a rather different perspective on the difference between ambiguity and ambivalence, see Rimmon, *The Concept of Ambiguity*, 18–19.

32. See also, e.g., Murphy, who says that "Qoheleth's attitude toward traditional wisdom is ambivalent" (Roland Murphy, *Ecclesiastes* [WBC 23A; Dallas: Word, 1992], lxiii). Mills states that "Here 'wisdom' contains two opposing aspects. There is the wisdom that entails complete mental control of the patterns of human experience and the wisdom that is fleshed out as an accepted lack of the first wisdom mode" (*Reading Ecclesiastes*, 49). However, Bartholomew argues that "Ecclesiastes exhorts Israelites . . . to pursue genuine wisdom. . . . [I]t is an exhortation to be truly wise" (Bartholomew, *Reading Ecclesiastes*, 263).

33. Whybray notes that "The word wisdom (*ḥokmāh*) has a number of somewhat different connotations in the Old Testament. But behind them all is the idea of the possession of knowledge: a practical knowledge which confers the ability to achieve success" (R. N. Whybray, *Ecclesiastes* [OTG; Sheffield: Sheffield Academic Press, 1989], 66). Crenshaw initially appears to disagree when he says of *ḥokmāh*, "This word has a wide range of meanings"; but he continues, "*Ḥokmāh* itself refers to practical knowledge, skill, cleverness, guile, insight, general intelligence, and wisdom" (J. L. Crenshaw, *Ecclesiastes* [OTL; London: SCM Press, 1988], 72), which seems not to differ greatly from Whybray.

34. E.g. "For in much wisdom is much vexation" (1:18); "Then I said to myself, 'What happens to the fool will happen to me also; why then have I been so very wise?'" (2:14); "For what advantage have the wise over fools?" (6:8); "Do not be too righteous, and do not act too wise; why should you destroy yourself?" (7:16); "Again I saw that under the sun the race is not to the swift, nor the battle to the strong, nor bread to the wise, nor favour to the skilful; but time and chance happen to them all" (9.11); "Dead flies make the perfumer's ointment give off a foul odour; so a little folly outweighs wisdom and honour" (10:1).

35. E.g. "Then I saw that wisdom excels folly as light excels darkness. The wise have eyes in their head, but fools walk in darkness" (2:13–14); "Better is a poor but wise youth than an old but foolish king" (4:13); "It is better to hear the rebuke of the

discussion of wisdom would not contribute greatly to a study of the ambiguous nature of Ecclesiastes because the difficulty is not so much that it is difficult to pin down its "meaning" as that readers find "different and even opposing attitudes" towards it. By contrast, הבל is an eminently suitable word for such a study precisely because its "meaning" is so difficult to pin down—it is, in short, highly ambiguous.

1.2.3. *Readerly Meaning*
The concept of ambiguity, as opposed to ambivalence, lends itself very readily to a reader-oriented approach to literature precisely because ambiguity describes indeterminacy of meaning which permits, even requires, the reader to determine meaning—one of the "gaps of indeterminacy" of which Iser writes.[36] Indeed, for a piece of language to be "ambiguous" rather than just "ambivalent" (although, due to the ambiguous nature of "ambiguity," both cases are covered by the term "ambiguous") there must be the possibility of different readings of that piece of language. It may be that such ambiguity has little effect on the *overall* understanding of a work, as in the case of a pun, which is the simplest example of ambiguity. On the other hand, a complete work may be ambiguous and susceptible to more than one reading: this is the case with Ecclesiastes.[37]

---

wise than to hear the song of fools" (7:5); "Wisdom gives strength to the wise more than ten rulers that are in a city" (7:19); "All this I have tested by wisdom; I said, 'I will be wise,' but it was far from me" (7:23); "Wisdom makes one's face shine, and the hardness of one's countenance is changed" (8:1); "Whoever obeys a command will meet no harm, and the wise mind will know the time and way" (8:5); "The quiet words of the wise are more to be heeded than the shouting of a ruler among fools" (9:17); "If the iron is blunt, and one does not whet the edge, then more strength must be exerted; but wisdom helps one to succeed" (10:10); "Words spoken by the wise bring them favour, but the lips of fools consume them" (10:12). However, in both the negative and more positive uses of חכם, once the context is taken into account along with the complexities of the Hebrew in some cases, there is more ambiguity than is apparent in these quotes out of context.

36. See, e.g., Iser, "Indeterminacy and the Reader's Response." The reader's "choice" between different readings is a key element for Rimmon, though she argues that it is a choice between "determined" readings (*The Concept of Ambiguity*, 17).

37. The literature on Henry James's *The Turn of the Screw* provides a good example of diametrically opposed readings of the same ambiguous work. See also the discussion in Rimmon, *The Concept of Ambiguity*, 116–66. Rimmon observes that "Henry James's *The Turn of the Screw* yields two 'finalized' hypotheses: *a*, It is a story about evil children who secretly communicate with the ghosts of two corrupt servants but whose souls are saved by the courageous governess who fights the ghosts off (major statement: 'The children communicate with ghosts' or 'There are real ghosts at Bly'); *b*, It is a story about a mad governess who has hallucinations

Reader-oriented theories of literature are hugely varied, but have in common a focus on the reader as, to a greater or lesser extent, determinant of meaning. The range of reader-oriented approaches to literature falls roughly on a line from Jauss's Reception Theory, through Iser's theory of indeterminacy (Iser being counted among both the Reception Theorists and the Reader-Response critics), to the Reader-Response criticism of Stanley Fish (although one might consider separately the burgeoning literature in Biblical Studies on ideological and cultural approaches to the text[38]).

1.2.3.1. Hans Robert Jauss. Jauss is concerned with how a piece of language is perceived by different audiences, from the original audience right up to the present time—for a literary work

> is not an object that stands by itself and that offers the same view to each reader in each period. It is not a monument that monologically reveals its timeless essence. It is much more like an orchestration that strikes ever new resonances among its readers and that frees the text from the material of the words and brings it to a contemporary existence.[39]

and who destroys the children by subjecting them to her hysterical vagaries about ghosts which they have never seen (major statement: 'The children do not communicate with ghosts' or 'There are no real ghosts at Bly')" (p. 10).

38. See, e.g., Tina Pippin, ed., *Ideological Criticism of Biblical Texts* (Semeia 59; Atlanta: Scholars Press, 1992), and J. Cheryl Exum and Stephen D. Moore, *Biblical Studies/Cultural Studies: The Third Sheffield Colloquium* (Gender, Culture, Theology 7; Sheffield: Sheffield Academic Press, 1998). Specifically on Ecclesiastes, see Mills, *Reading Ecclesiastes*; Dianne Bergant, *Israel's Wisdom Literature: A Liberation–Critical Reading* (Minneapolis: Fortress, 1997), 108–23; Elsa Tamez, *When the Horizons Close: Rereading Ecclesiastes* (Eng. ed.; Maryknoll, N.Y.: Orbis, 2000 [orig. pub. 1998]); Eric S. Christianson, "Qoheleth the 'Old Boy' and Qoheleth the 'New Man': Misogynism, the Womb and a Paradox in Ecclesiastes," and Carole R. Fontaine, "'Many Devices' (Qoheleth 7.23–8.1): Qoheleth, Misogyny and the *Malleus Maleficarum*," both in *Wisdom and Psalms* (ed. Athalya Brenner and Carole Fontaine; A Feminist Companion to the Bible, 2d Series; Sheffield: Sheffield Academic Press, 1998), 109–36 and 137–68; Anthony R. Ceresko, *Introduction to Old Testament Wisdom: A Spirituality for Liberation* (Maryknoll, N.Y.: Orbis, 1999), 91–114; Carole R. Fontaine, "Ecclesiastes," in *The Women's Bible Commentary* (ed. Carole A. Newsom and Sharon H. Ringe; London: SPCK, 1992), 153–55. In addition, see the three essays on the same text, Eccl 3:1–8, in *Return to Babel: Global Perspectives on the Bible* (ed. John R. Levison and Priscilla Pope-Levison; Louisville, Ky.: Westminster John Knox, 1999)—Elsa Tamez, "A Latin American Perspective," 75–80; Francois Kabasele Lumbala, "An African Perspective," 81–86; and Choan-Seng Song, "An Asian Perspective," 87–92.

39. First presented as his inaugural address at the University of Constance in 1967 under the title, "What Is and For What Purpose Does One Study Literary

It is clear from the title of his essay "Literary History as a Challenge to Literary Theory,"[40] as well as the seven theses he proposes in that essay, that Jauss's purpose is to place historical concerns at the centre of literary studies. There are three different aspects to such a literary history. First, no reading occurs in an "informational vacuum" but rather is always set against the background of the "horizon of expectations"[41] of any particular reader, and this horizon is the result of the reader's literary experience (theses 1 and 2). Thus, whenever a literary work is read,

> [it] awakens memories of that which was already read, brings the reader to a specific emotional attitude, and with its beginning arouses expectations for the "middle and end," which can then be maintained intact or altered, reoriented, or even fulfilled ironically in the course of reading according to specific rules of the genre or type of text.[42]

Secondly, a work is written within a certain horizon of expectation, and reconstruction of this horizon "allows one to determine its artistic character by the kind and the degree of its influence on a presupposed audience"[43] (theses 3 and 4). Such an historical undertaking enables later readers to discern the questions that the text originally addressed, and thus

> The philological question of how the text is "properly"—that is, "from its intention and time"—to be understood can best be answered if one foregrounds it against those works that the author explicitly or implicitly presupposed his contemporary audience to know.[44]

History?," this now famous (or "notorious" according to Robert C. Holub, *Reception Theory: A Critical Introduction* [New Accents; London: Routledge, 1984], 53) address is the basis upon which most commentaries of Jauss's reception theory are based (e.g. Edgar V. McKnight, *The Bible and the Reader: An Introduction to Literary Criticism* [Philadelphia: Fortress, 1985], 75–78; Ian Maclean, "Reading and Interpretation," in Jefferson and Robey, eds., *Modern Literary Theory*, 122–44 [132–35]; Jeremy Hawthorn, *Unlocking the Text: Fundamental Issues in Literary Theory* [London: Edward Arnold, 1987], 119–21). However, Holub (*Reception Theory*, 53–82) maintains that Jauss moved his position considerably from the theses set out in this address.

40. Hans Robert Jauss, "Literary History as a Challenge to Literary Theory," in Newton, ed., *Twentieth-Century Literary Theory*, 221–26.

41. The concept of "horizon of expectations," drawn from Gadamer, is the acknowledged "methodological centrepiece" of Jauss's theory upon which it largely stands or falls. However, Holub argues that "The trouble with Jauss's use of the term 'horizon' is that it is so vaguely defined that it could include or exclude any previous sense of the word. In fact, nowhere does he delineate precisely what he means by it" (*Reception Theory*, 59).

42. Jauss, "Literary History," 223.

43. Ibid., 223.

44. Ibid., 225.

Thirdly, to understand fully a literary work the reader should consider how it fits into its "literary series." Literature has its own evolving history which affects and is influenced by general history, and it is the critic's task to explore how literary and general history interact (theses 5–7):[45]

> The gap between literature and history, between aesthetic and historical knowledge, can be bridged if literary history does not simply describe the process of general history in the reflection of its works one more time, but rather when it discovers in the course of "literary evolution" that properly *socially formative* function that belongs to literature as it competes with other arts and social forces in the emancipation of mankind from its natural, religious, and social bonds.[46]

Jauss's essay makes it clear that Abram's diagram, which I reproduced above, is insufficient as a representation of the possible sources of meaning in a piece of language. Hawthorn offers a more comprehensive alternative (see Fig. 2):[47]

---

45. Bartholomew argues that "there is a close relationship between the history of the interpretation of Ecclesiastes and that of hermeneutics. Modernity and its hermeneutical legacy were obviously particularly influential in the interpretation of Ecclesiastes, and yet at the end of the twentieth century there is no agreement about the message of Ecclesiastes. . . . [I]f we are to get a better understanding of Ecclesiastes then it is important to explore the relationship between hermeneutics and the reading of Ecclesiastes more closely" (*Reading Ecclesiastes*, 266). John F. A. Sawyer seeks to explore the interpretation of Isaiah throughout Christian history so as to determine how interpretation has been influenced by "general history"; see Sawyer's *The Fifth Gospel: Isaiah in the History of Christianity* (Cambridge: Cambridge University Press, 1996). See also Yvonne Sherwood, *A Biblical Text and its Afterlives: The Survival of Jonah in Western Culture* (Cambridge: Cambridge University Press, 2000). In a rather different vein, Keith W. Whitelam explores how on the one hand history has influenced scholarly understandings of "the history of Ancient Israel" and how on the other hand the way in which "the history of Ancient Israel" has been portrayed has impacted upon events in modern Israel/Palestine in recent times; see Whitelam's *The Invention of Ancient Israel: The Silencing of Palestinian History* (London: Routledge, 1996).

46. Jauss, "Literary History," 226, his emphasis.

47. Hawthorn wisely warns, "Like all such models this one has to be used with care if we wish to avoid being—in the words of George Eliot—ensnared by our metaphors. It is, for instance, potentially misleading to separate 'literary context' from 'socio-historical context,' as the former is actually an aspect of the latter and inseparable from it. We can also posit that both the author and the literary and socio-historical contexts are in a sense 'in' the text as well as standing outside and apart from it" (*Unlocking the Text*, 8–9).

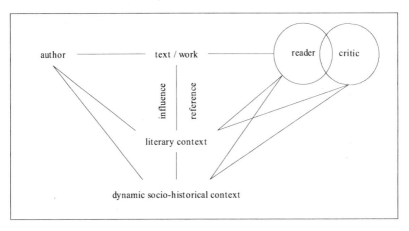

Figure 2

The "universe," in Abrams's model, is more fully represented here by "literary context" and "dynamic socio-historical context," which might be equated with Jauss's "literary history" and "general history." Moreover, in Hawthorn's diagram we no longer find the "work" at the centre with the other elements in orbit around it, rather there is a complicated network of interactions between the various elements. This better encapsulates the meaning of a piece of literature in terms of Reception Theory because meaning derives from the interaction in the text between the original horizon of expectation and the reader's horizon of expectation according to the place of text, author and reader in literary and general history (see Fig. 3):

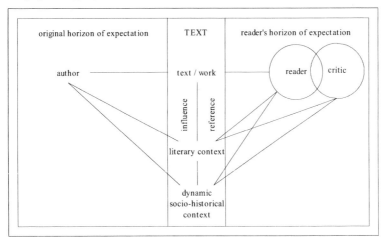

Figure 3

1.2.3.2. *Wolfgang Iser.* Meaning, then, is determined not by the author alone, nor by the reader alone, nor even by the text itself, but by the interaction of these three factors at any one moment in history (both literary and general).

By contrast with Jauss, Iser focuses his attention more sharply on the reader. For him meaning is specifically an effect which is experienced by the reader:

> If texts actually possessed only the meaning brought to light by inter-pretation, then there would remain very little else for the reader. He could only accept or reject it, take it or leave it. The fundamental question is, however, what actually does take place between text and reader? . . . [I]t must be pointed out that a text can only come to life when it is read, and if it is to be examined, it must therefore be studied through the eyes of the reader.[48]

However, readers at not at liberty to create meaning at their whim because it is precisely the skeleton of *determination* in a text which constitutes the potential for readers to produce meaning as they flesh out the bare bones by filling in the spots of *indeterminacy* in the text, what Iser calls "concretization"[49] or "actualization." Hence meaning is not to be found either in the reader or in the text, but emerges in the process of interaction between the two: the reader is constrained by the possibilities offered by the text, but is nonetheless free to "pin down the oscillating structure of the text to some specific meaning"[50] according to his or her reaction to it:

> the meaning of the text does not reside in the expectations, surprises, disappointments or frustrations that we experience during the process of gestalt-forming.[51] These are simply the reactions that take place when the gestalten are disturbed. What this really means, though, is that as we read, we react to what we ourselves have produced, and it is this mode of reaction that, in fact, enables us to experience the text as an actual event. We do not grasp it like an empirical object; nor do we comprehend it like a predicative fact; it owes its presence in our minds to our own reactions, and it is these that make us animate the meaning of the text as a reality.[52]

We should note that Iser's "concretization" is radically different from Hirsch's "significance," because for Hirsch meaning exists in the text

---

48. Iser, "Indeterminacy and the Reader's Response," 226–27.

49. Both "spots of indeterminacy" and "concretization" are terms Iser borrows from Roman Ingarden, although both take on a slightly different meaning for Iser. See, e.g., *The Act of Reading*, 170–79.

50. Iser, "Indeterminacy and the Reader's Response," 228.

51. "Gestalt" in this context refers to the structure of a literary work.

52. Iser, *The Act of Reading*, 128–29.

and takes on different significances for different readers, but for Iser there is no meaning in a text until the reader fills in the gaps of indeterminacy in order to produce some concrete meaning.[53] However, although Iser's concept of "meaning" is very different from Hirsch's, he does argue for a distinction between "meaning" and "significance" in terms highly reminiscent of Hirsch: "The significance of the meaning can only be ascertained when the meaning is related to a particular reference, which makes it translatable into familiar terms."[54]

1.2.3.3. *Stanley Fish.* It is on the issue of determinacy and indeterminacy that Fish disagrees most strongly with Iser, as is clear from Fish's article "Why No One's Afraid of Wolfgang Iser,"[55] and Iser's response, "Talk Like Whales."[56] Fish maintains that Iser's theory "falls apart because the distinction on which it finally depends—the distinction between the determinate and the indeterminate—will not hold."[57] The judgment that something is determinate or indeterminate is part of the process of interpretation and reveals more about the presuppositions of the reader than about the text:

> The distinction itself is an assumption which, when it informs an act of literary description, will *produce* the phenomena it purports to describe. That is to say, every component in such an account—the determinacies or textual segments, the indeterminacies or gaps, and the adventures of the reader's "wandering viewpoint"—will be the products of an interpretive strategy that demands them, and therefore no one of those components can constitute the independent given which serves to ground the interpretive process.[58]

Thus, while Jauss considers meaning to arise from the interaction of past and present horizons of expectation, and Iser maintains that meaning is produced as the reader, guided by the determinate schemata of the text, fills in the spots of indeterminacy, for Fish meaning is located in the

---

53. For a rather different view on "filling the gaps," see Rimmon, *The Concept of Ambiguity*, 45–51.

54. Iser, *The Act of Reading*, 151–52.

55. Stanley Fish, "Why No One's Afraid of Wolfgang Iser," *Diacritics* 11, no. 1 (1981): 2–13; reproduced in extended form in his *Doing What Comes Naturally: Change, Rhetoric, and the Practice of Theory in Literary and Legal Studies* (Oxford: Clarendon, 1989), 68–86.

56. Wolfgang Iser, "Talk Like Whales," *Diacritics* 11, no. 3 (1981): 82–87. Freund discusses this debate under the sub-title "The Indeterminacy of Reader-Response Criticism" (*The Return of the Reader*, 148–51); Holub considers it in a section entitled "Determinacy and the Fish–Iser Debate" (*Reception Theory*, 101–6).

57. Fish, *Doing What Comes Naturally*, 74.

58. Ibid., 77, his emphasis.

reader alone. He does away altogether with any notion of an objective work of literature and argues that everything in the text—grammar, form and meaning—is simply the result of interpretation. The consequence of this line of reasoning is that there is no distinction between different literary texts as such, the distinction is only in the interpretative approach to these texts:

> The notions of the "same" or "different" texts are fictions. If I read *Lycidas* and *The Waste Land* differently (in fact I do not), it will not be because the formal structures of the two poems (to term them such is also an interpretive decision) call forth different interpretive strategies but because my predisposition to execute different interpretive strategies will *produce* different formal structures.[59]

Fish is therefore unperturbed by Wimsatt and Beardsley's "Affective Fallacy":

> The Affective Fallacy is a confusion between the poem and its *results* (what it *is* and what it *does*). . . . It begins by trying to derive the standards of criticism from the psychological effects of the poem and ends in impressionism and relativism. The outcome . . . is that the poem itself, as an object of specifically critical judgment, tends to disappear.[60]

His argument is precisely that the poem "is" only in the sense of what it "does" when it is interpreted, and that there is no "poem itself, as an *object* of specifically critical judgment" (my emphasis). This implies that there is actually nothing that could be pinned down and labelled as the "meaning" of a text because the text means only what is experienced by the reader, "and that experience is immediately compromised the moment you say anything about it."[61] Perhaps, then, "meaning" is an inappropriate term to apply to literary texts, as Fish himself suggests—although he continues to refer to it frequently!

When a readerly approach to literature is taken to this extreme it may be that the term "ambiguity" also ceases to convey anything of critical value. Certainly if "meaning" is an inappropriate term to apply to literary texts, "ambiguity" is too. Further, if the distinction between "determinacy" and "indeterminacy" is lost, so too is the distinction between the

---

59. Stanley Fish, "Interpreting the *Variorum*," in Newton, ed., *Twentieth-Century Literary Theory*, 235–40 (237), reprinted from *Critical Inquiry* 2 (1976): 478–85.

60. In the Appendix to *Self-Consuming Artifacts: The Experience of Seventeenth-Century Literature* (Berkeley: University of California Press, 1972), entitled "Literature in the Reader: Affective Stylistics," Fish specifically addresses the questions raised by the Affective Fallacy. Indeed, one of his sub-titles is "The Affective Fallacy Fallacy."

61. Fish, *Self-Consuming Artifacts*, 425.

terms "unambiguous" and "ambiguous": either everything is ambiguous because there is nothing that can be tied down as the meaning of a piece of language, or nothing is ambiguous because all meaning in a piece of language arises from the reader's interpretative experience. Perhaps what a text may achieve is to highlight some of the ambiguities in the reader's interpretative strategy rather than revealing *its* ambiguities. Applied to the case of Ecclesiastes, we would then have to conclude that the book is not *itself* ambiguous, but that a study of secondary material (Fish's *variorum* in the essay "Interpreting the *Variorum*" which addresses this issue) would reveal the ambiguities in the different approaches to it. It is true that a comparison of different readings of Ecclesiastes reveals a great deal about the presuppositions of the readers, and that the book appears to "mean" very different things depending on the interpretative strategy of the reader.[62] However, this is not solely the result of interpretation: there is something in "the marks on the page" which enables different readers to experience the text differently, and my claim is that the particular "marks on the page" of which Ecclesiastes is made up encourage different responses more than other "marks on the page" (in the Old Testament or elsewhere) precisely because of their ambiguity. The point is that readers are experiencing "it" differently, and Fish's theory gives no explanation of what "it" might be: "if intention, form, and the shape of the reader's experience are simply different ways of referring to (different perspectives on) the same interpretive act, what is that an interpretation *of*? I cannot answer that question."[63] He maintains that nobody else can answer the question either, but acknowledges that "formalists try to answer it by pointing to patterns and claiming that they are available independently of (prior to) interpretation."[64] However, he

---

62. Thus, e.g., Crenshaw says, "It may be in the last resort Qoheleth is a mirror which reflects the soul of the interpreter" (J. L. Crenshaw, "The Shadow of Death in Qoheleth," in *Israelite Wisdom: Theological and Literary Essays in Honor of Samuel Terrien* [ed. J. G. Gammie et al.; Missoula, Mont.: Scholars Press, 1978], 205–16 [51]), and "Research into the book also shows that it reflects the interpreter's world view. That is why, I think, opinions vary so widely with regard to such basic matters as Qohelet's optimism or pessimism, his attitude to women, and his advocacy of immoral conduct" (Crenshaw, *Ecclesiastes*, 47). Bolton makes a similar remark about Job: "something very important which is so often made too little of: that the history of comments on the book of Job exhibits more of the commentators than of the text itself as sense and reference" (F. J. Bolton, "The Sense of the Text and a New Vision," in Crossan, ed., *The Book of Job and Ricoeur's Hermeneutics*, 87–90 [87]).

63. Fish, "Interpreting the *Variorum*," 479, his emphasis.

64. Ibid., 479.

goes on to point out that "These patterns vary according to the procedures that yield them," and this is amply illustrated in the formalist
approaches to Ecclesiastes which seem to reveal hugely varying patterns
and structures in the book. Nonetheless, "the marks on the page" remain
and readers are constrained by them however they organise them, so that
their readings must take them into account if those readings are to offer
anything which can be recognised as an interpretation *of Ecclesiastes*. It
is with Fish's stated thesis that "the proper object of analysis is not the
work but the reader"[65] that I take issue, because if the focus is on the
reader alone there ceases to be any real interpretation of a work, because
there ceases to be anything which we can elucidate as "meaning." This
does not necessarily suggest that Fish is wrong, what it does indicate is
that I have set myself a different task—perhaps that I have adopted a
different interpretative strategy.

1.2.4. *Reality and Meaning*

Of the four elements in Abrams's diagram—artist, work, text and universe—the only one I have not yet explicitly addressed is the last, the
"universe." The "universe" contains the concepts or realities or "things-
in-the-world" that we term "signifieds," which are named by the sounds
or words or "marks on the page" that we term "signifiers." Thus the concept of a tree, in Hawkes's example,[66] is the thing in the "universe" which
is "signified" by the word, or "signifier," "tree." This "universe," which
we might also label "reality," is divided by Longman into "historical
events" and, of particular relevance here, "theological ideas," and we
might also include in the term the "dynamic socio-historical context" in
Hawthorn's diagram or my adaptation of that diagram.[67] In the author-,
text- and reader-oriented approaches to meaning which we considered
above (with the exception of Fish who in this regard is very close to
Structuralism and Deconstructionism, and ought properly to be counted
among the post-Structuralists), meaning is in some way a reflection of
the "universe." Whatever the source of meaning, be it authorial intention
or textual form or reader's experience, it is worked out in relation to
some concept of "reality."

   For Husserl, whose philosophy Hirsch follows in his author-oriented
approach to literature, language is an activity used to give names to
meanings which we already possess. The language of a literary work,

---

65. Fish, *Self-Consuming Artifacts*, 4.
66. Hawkes, *Structuralism and Semiotics*, 25.
67. Longman, *Literary Approaches*, 18. See also Barton, "Classifying Biblical
Criticism," 23–25.

therefore, is simply the *expression* of a fixed meaning, and the task of criticism is to immerse itself in the "world" of the text and to reproduce as accurately as it can the meaning that it finds there. Thus "Criticism is not seen as a construction, an active interpretation of the work which will inevitably engage the critic's interests and biases; it is a mere passive reception of the text."[68]

However, if language is but a vehicle of meaning which can be passively absorbed, there must be some other source in which meaning resides and which gives to the phenomena the author records a meaning which the reader can receive. Husserl posits a system of universal "essences," along similar lines to Plato's "forms," which are given their meaning by a transcendental subject. These essences constitute part of the deep structure of human consciousness and it is such structures that Husserl's philosophy of Phenomenology claims to lay bare.[69]

---

68. Eagleton, *Literary Theory*, 59.

69. See Edmund Husserl, *The Idea of Phenomenology* (The Hague: Nijhoff, 1964). Neither Plato nor Husserl equate this super-ego with God, but it is clear nonetheless how such an approach to religious literature could be appropriated by biblical criticism if God is the Transcendental by which and in which the meaning of biblical texts is to be found. If God pervades the deep structures of human consciousness, perhaps a text's meaning can be passively received by the reader without reference to the human author of the text, and perhaps even beyond that author's human ability to intend. The result of this line of reasoning, regardless of how we define the transcendental subject, is that meaning moves from the author to the "Author." This raises the much-debated issue of the Bible as "the Word of God," whereby through these human words (produced by human "authors") God (as "Author") is perceived in some sense to communicate with people. Barr writes of "the belief, which most Christians surely hold, that in some way the Bible comes from God, that he has in some sense a part in its origin, that there is a linkage between the basic mode through which he has communicated with man and the coming into existence of this body of literature," although he also notes "the range of meaning of which the term 'Word of God' is capable" (James Barr, *The Bible in the Modern World* [reissue, London: SCM Press, 1990 (1973)]). This is helpfully discussed at some length in Goldingay, *Models for Scripture*. See also Fretheim and Froehlich, *The Bible as Word of God*, and Vanhoozer, *Is There a Meaning in This Text?*, 44, and his following discussion. Later in the book, Vanhoozer asks, "Is the Bible objectively the Word of God, or does it only become the Word of God when the Holy Spirit enables hearers and readers to receive it as such?," raising questions *both* about "Authorial" intent *and* about the role of the "spirit-enabled" reader in allowing God's "word" to be heard (pp. 409–11)—though, notably, he refers to the latter as "significance": "The meaningfulness of the Bible is thus a matter of the Spirit's leading the church to extend Scripture's meaning into the present; in this way it displays its contemporary significance" (p. 423).

Where for Husserl language is the vehicle for a pre-existent meaning, for Heidegger—as also for the New Critics—it is language which pre-exists, because without language, he argues, we cannot conceive of meaning. As Eagleton explains,

> Heidegger does not think of language primarily in terms of what you or I might say: it has an existence of its own in which human beings come to participate, and only by participating in it do they come to be human at all. Language always pre-exists the individual subject, as the very realm in which he or she unfolds; and it contains "truth" less in the sense that it is an instrument for exchanging accurate information than in the sense that it is the place where reality "un-conceals" itself, gives itself up to our contemplation.[70]

"Meaning," in this respect, is reality as revealed by language—albeit a historical, existential "reality" rather than Husserl's ahistorical transcendent "reality." Meaning, then, is not truly found in the text *itself*, but in the "reality" which it reveals. Moreover, the Author is reintroduced through the back door as Heidegger's contingent "Being" (*Dasein*), which is our experience of the world in which we live.[71] This contingent Being could not be equated with the God of orthodox theology, but it may be relevant to interpretation from the perspective of Process Theology.[72]

Jauss's Reception Theory is greatly influenced by Gadamer's approach to hermeneutics. Gadamer, who was a student of Heidegger (who, in turn, was a student of Husserl—a pertinent observation because a thread of phenomenology can be traced through all three[73]), developed Heidegger's concept of a contingent *Dasein* and insists on the historical nature of literary meaning.[74] As opposed to the New-Critical exclusion of readerly input, Gadamer (and Jauss) insists that new meanings arise as

70. Eagleton, *Literary Theory*, 63.
71. See Martin Heidegger, *Being and Time* (New York: Harper, 1962), and *Poetry, Language and Thought* (New York: Harper & Row, 1971).
72. For views on Process Theology and the Old Testament, see William A. Beardslee and David J. Lull, eds., *Old Testament Interpretation from a Process Perspective* (Semeia 24; Chico, Calif.: Scholars Press, 1982). In their "Introduction" Beardslee and Lull write: "A theory of interpretation may center upon one or more of several factors in the interpretive process: the world of reality with which the text deals, the author, the form of the text or the nature of language, and the reader of the text would be classical examples. . . . Most Old Testament interpretation from a process perspective has concentrated upon the first of these possible centers and has dealt primarily with a reconceptualizing of the transcendent God of the Old Testament in the direction of the process God of persuasion" (pp. 1–6 [1]).
73. See, e.g., "Phenomenology: Husserl, Heidegger and Gadamer," in Selden and Widdowson, *A Reader's Guide*, 51–52.
74. See Hans Georg Gadamer, *Truth and Method* (London: Sheed & Ward, 1975).

the literary text passes from one cultural or historical context to the next, because it "says" different things as the reader addresses different questions to it. Nonetheless, these different meanings which the reader perceives are still related to the historical horizon of the reader; and the reader's horizon is part of a continuing tradition connecting the past and the present. Hence, as the reader interacts with the "reality" of this tradition, the "universe" continues to be an important factor in the meaning of a text.

Similarly, the "determinate schemata" in Iser's theory reflect a reality which constrains readers as they fill in the gaps of indeterminacy to produce meaning. Iser addresses this issue specifically when, after identifying literature with fiction, he asserts, "fiction is a means of telling us something about reality,"[75] and adds that his approach focuses "on two basic, interdependent areas: one, the intersection between text and reality, the other, that between text and reader, and it is necessary to find some way of pinpointing these intersections if one is to gauge the effectiveness of fiction as a means of communication."[76] This is the very point at which Fish's abnegation of Iser's distinction between determinacy and indeterminacy strikes. In true post-Structuralist style, he challenges the legitimacy of Iser's assertion that there is a determinate world to which the language of the text refers:

> the larger theory that stands behind Iser's pronouncements on merely literary matters [is] the theory by which the world is "given" in a way that the world of literary (read fictional) works are not. It is only if the world —or "reality"—is itself a determinate object, an object without gaps that can be grasped immediately, an object that can be perceived rather than read, that *in*determinacy can be specified as a special feature of literary experience.[77]

Fish maintains that perception of the world, or reality, is always mediated by an interpretative strategy every bit as much as understanding of a literary text: in effect "reality" is simply another text to be interpreted, and is no more a source of meaning than is any other text.

1.2.5. *The Structure of Meaning*
Structuralism shares Heidegger's (and Gadamer's) view of language as productive of meaning, but goes a step further (perhaps drawing

---

75. See Rimmon's discussion of mimetic and nonmimetic "ways of accounting for the functions and significance of a given literary phenomenon" (*The Concept of Ambiguity*, 227).

76. Iser, *The Act of Reading*, 53–54.

77. Fish, *Doing What Comes Naturally*, 78, his emphasis.

Heidegger's philosophy to its logical conclusion) by severing the link between language and reality. One of the basic tenets of Structuralist literary criticism is the assertion that the link between the signifier and the signified is totally arbitrary. The meaning of a word (and by extension of a whole text) is therefore determined not by its arbitrary connection with reality or our conception of reality, but solely in relation to other words—that is to say that meaning is not "substantial" but "relational." Structuralism, as its name suggests, is concerned less with the elucidation of meaning than with explanation of the structures which produce meaning.

There are two planes on which the relationship between words can be determined, the "syntagmatic" and the "paradigmatic" (or "associative"). The "syntagmatic" dimension explores how a word (or phrase, or sentence, or paragraph, or chapter, etc.) relates to other words (phrases, sentences, paragraphs, chapters, etc.) in a given text (or how a text relates to other texts within a given language)—what is often described as the "horizontal plane."[78] We might consider the sentence

> The cat sat on the mat.

In this sentence, "cat" obtains its meaning from its relationship with "the," which informs the reader that a particular cat is in mind; "sat," by which we know the action it performed; and "on," "the" and "mat," which together tell us where this action was performed by "the cat." It could still at this stage be argued that we know the meaning of all these words because of their connection with "reality": we know what mats and cats look like, and we can conceive of definiteness and "on-ness." But according to Structuralism this is a misconception. Our understanding of these words comes rather from their "paradigmatic" relationship with other words in the overall structure of language (a "synchronic" as opposed to a "diachronic" perspective)—what is often termed the "vertical plane." Thus we know what the word "cat" means in relation to and by its difference from other words such as "dog," "horse," "cow," and so on. This is one particular "code," which could be called the "animal code," and other codes could be indicated for each of the other words in the phrase. (See Fig. 4 opposite.)

Of course, this is grossly over-simplified. For example, "the" could also be "my," "Bob's" and "that" all at the same time; "cat" is distinguished from the other animals in the above code because it is distinct from most of them, but it could also be the source of a sub-code of

---

78. See, e.g., Culler, *Structuralist Poetics*, 13, and Hawkes, *Structuralism and Semiotics*, 26–28.

hyponyms which might include "lion," "kitten" and "tom-cat"; "cat" could also be part of a code of "things-which-might-have-sat-on-the-mat," which might include "stool," "book," and so on, and which would subtly change the meaning of "sat"; "cat" is also defined in terms of its relation to such words as "hat" or "bat" (and "sat" and "mat," of course) and "car" or "can"—and so we could go on through all the words in the sentence.

paradigmatic syntagmatic					
The	cat	sat	on	the	mat
a	dog	lay	under	a	table
one	man	settled	below	one	roof
my	bear	reclined	against	my	chair
your	elephant	stood	above	your	shed
Bob's	lion	lounged	in	Bob's	grass
this	monkey	sprawled	over	this	bed
that	frog	crouched	beside	that	road
etc.	etc.	etc.	etc.	etc.	etc.

Figure 4

Thus each word is part of a veritable web of relationships with other words. Moreover, this is what may be called a "major-pattern sentence"[79] whose meaning is little changed by adjusting one word, for example from

The cat sat on the mat

to

The cat sat on the table

or

The dog sat on the mat.

But the words in a "minor-pattern sentence," which bear a specific meaning apart from the semantic structure of the string of words, relate to one another differently so that the meaning may be totally altered if one word is changed. Compare, for example, the phrase,

Not on your life

with

Not on your bed!

79. See Peter Cotterell and Max Turner, *Linguistics and Biblical Interpretation* (London: SPCK, 1989), 191.

We might represent these relationships in this way:

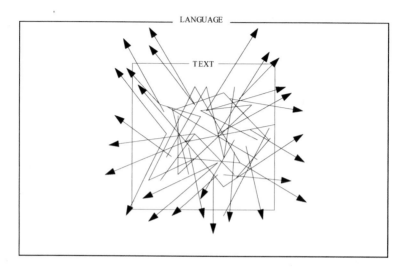

Figure 5

What this indicates is that the text is part of a closed system which is totally independent of the material world. The meaning of the text is therefore to be derived solely in terms of the inter-relations of the constituent parts of that closed system without any reference to the "real" world. The role of the literary critic then becomes that of analysing this system to discover its rules and conventions, to discern the network of relations that produce meaning. Texts come to have relevance only as instances of the overall structure of language.[80]

80. In terms borrowed from Saussure's theory of linguistics, explained in his book, Ferdinand de Saussure, *Cours de Linguistique Générale* (Paris: Payot, 1922; Eng. trans. Wade Baskin, *Course in General Linguistics* [New York: Philosophical Library, 1959]), the "instance" is termed *parole*, and the "overall structure" is termed *langue*. Hawkes explains these terms using an illustration deriving from Saussure: "The distinction between *langue* and *parole* is more or less that which pertains between the abstract language system which in English we call simply 'language', and the individual utterances made by speakers of the language in concrete everyday situations which we call 'speech'. Saussure's own analogy is the distinction between the abstract set of rules and conventions called 'chess', and the actual concrete games of chess played by people in the real world. The rules of chess can be said to exist above and beyond each individual game, and yet they only ever acquire concrete form in the relationships that develop between the pieces in individual games" (*Structuralism and Semiotics*, 20–21).

What this means in practice is that that the meaning of the text, which is usually sought by the reader, is ignored in favour of the structures of language, so that, as is commonly acknowledged, "structuralism is a calculated affront to common sense."[81] Olsen, in a book entitled, *The Structure of Literary Understanding*, criticises Structuralism on precisely these grounds when he asserts that "One objection to the view of the literary work as a semantic 'structural' unit is that this is simply not the way the reader sees it or understands it."[82] This is also apparent in biblical structuralist criticism. A striking example is Jobling's analysis of Gen 2–3 where Greimas's "actantial schema"[83] is used as the basis of analysis (see Fig. 6). Jobling proposes an actantial scheme for "getting a man to till the earth," as shown in Fig. 7.

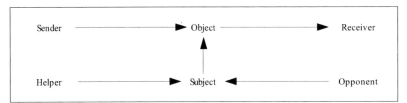

Figure 6

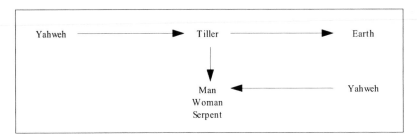

Figure 7

81. Eagleton, *Literary Theory*, 96.

82. Stein Haugom Olsen, *The Structure of Literary Understanding* (Cambridge: Cambridge University Press, 1978), 19.

83. On Greimas's "actantial schema," see A.-J. Greimas, *Structural Semantics* (trans. D. McDowell, R. Schleifer and A. Velie; repr. Lincoln: University of Nebraska Press, 1983 [1966]); Ronald Schleifer, *A. J. Greimas and the Nature of Meaning: Linguistics, Semiotics and Discourse Theory* (London: Croom Helm, 1987); Mieke Bal, *Narratology: Introduction to the Theory of Narrative* (2d ed.; Toronto: University of Toronto Press, 1997 [1995]), 195–208; Hawkes, *Structuralism and Semiotics*, 87–95; Culler, *Structuralist Poetics*, 75–95. On Greimas and Biblical Studies, see Longman, *Literary Approaches*, 33–37.

However, he admits that,

> If one were to ask the average person literate in the Bible what happens in
> Gen. 2–3, the answer would probably be "the fall" and "the origin of sexu-
> ality and marriage" (i.e. 2:18–25), in that order of importance. *No one
> senses that the text is about enabling vegetation by finding a gardener!*[84]

In fact, for the average reader such a rendering of this passage is sheer
nonsense.[85]

Another example we might consider, which is particularly relevant to
this study, is Loader's conclusion to his *Polar Structures in the Book of
Qohelet*, in which he says, "The conclusion of this study is that the
literary face of the Book of Qohelet is determined by its polar structures,
while the tension in these patterns can be explained by the overlapping of
chokmatic and religio-historical developments."[86] He offers the scheme
shown in Fig. 8 to illustrate his conclusion, explaining "I have argued
that (iii) is the cause of (ii), which in turn is the cause of (i). The relation
between these is constantly shown and confirmed by (iv)."[87]

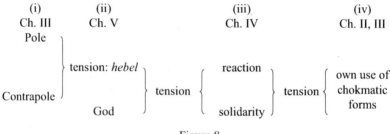

Figure 8

We might note, however, that Loader simplifies this considerably
for his commentary,[88] and this may serve to support Longman's argument that Structuralist criticism tends to be "obscurantist."[89] In his

84. David Jobling, *The Sense of Biblical Narrative: Structural Analyses in the
Hebrew Bible* (2 vols.; JSOTSup 7, 39; Sheffield: Sheffield Academic Press, 1986),
2:27, my emphasis.

85. A further example would be Polzin's summary of the message of Job with
this mathematical type formula: $F_x(a):F_y(b)=F_x(b):F_{a-1}(y)$ (Robert Polzin, *Biblical
Structuralism: Method and Subjectivity in the Study of Ancient Texts* [Philadelphia:
Fortress, 1977], 75).

86. J. A. Loader, *Polar Structures in the Book of Qohelet* (New York: de Gruyter,
1979), 132.

87. Ibid.

88. J. A. Loader, *Ecclesiastes: A Practical Commentary* (trans. John Vriend;
Text and Interpretation; Grand Rapids: Eerdmans, 1986 [orig. pub. 1984]).

89. Longman, *Literary Approaches*, 49.

commentary, Loader concludes, "Over and over in the book we saw one pole of thought in tension with another."[90] The outcome, and the message of the book, is then represented with the diagram in Fig. 9.

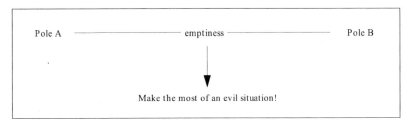

Figure 9

Barton, however, maintains:

> At first sight one would have little hesitation in describing Loader's very original work as structuralist; and he himself stresses its interest in "text-immanent" features rather than in the extrinsic, historical questions with which traditional biblical methods deal. His "polar structures" are clearly an *avatar* of the structuralists' "binary opposition," and his charts are a familiar part of structuralist equipment. Nevertheless, it seems to me only in a very qualified sense that we can call this a structuralist study. . . . In spite of its structuralist terminology it does not depend in any way on a characteristically structuralist view of literature; and it strikingly fails to share the structuralist indifference to authorial intention and to the historical circumstances of composition. It is not necessarily the worse for that: but it is not structuralism in the strict sense. It merely adds structuralist ideas to the historical-critical tool-box.[91]

This directly contradicts Jefferson's view that "Structuralism is revolutionary because it can be adopted only as an alternative and not as an addition to traditional academic habits. It cannot be incorporated as a handy extra methodological tool to be resorted to when all else fails."[92] However, Loader's book does illustrate how Structuralism may be used in conjunction with other literary techniques to explore the text in greater depth. While Structuralist Criticism, in its strict sense, is simply the

---

90. Loader, *Ecclesiastes*, 132.

91. Barton, *Reading the Old Testament*, 130–31. Barton goes on to offer his own "structuralism-as-theory" treatment of the book. He says, "we could sketch a treatment of Ecclesiastes that adhered more closely to the pure structuralist gospel without offering a new *interpretation* of it at all. We could begin by merely stating the data with which any interpretation whatever has to cope, and then analysing what the process of interpretation involves" (Barton's emphasis).

92. Jefferson, "Structuralism and Post-Structuralism," 92.

study of structures and does nothing to elucidate "meaning" in literature, the "close reading" of the text that it involves, its emphasis on paradigmatic as well as syntagmatic study, and the attempt to discern structure in the relation of a text's constituent parts, all make a Structuralist approach to the text worthwhile because it may assist the interpreter to discern possibilities for meaning. In this sense it may well be used as a "handy extra methodological tool."

1.2.6. *The Deconstruction of Meaning*

One of the greatest benefits of Structuralism for literary criticism is the development of new literary theories in reaction to it. Deconstruction is one of the most intriguing of these developments. In its most basic form (as proposed by Derrida[93]), Deconstruction, like Structuralism before it, denies both authorial intention and reader response a role in determining the meaning of a text—the statement for which Derrida is probably best know is "*Il n'y a pas de hors-texte*" ("There is nothing outside the text"). Deconstruction presupposes Structuralism, but where Structuralist Criticism confidently builds up structures and systems, Deconstructionist Criticism overturns them by showing their internal contradictions. As Culler writes,

> Deconstruction arrives in the wake of structuralism to frustrate its systematic projects . . . [it] shatters their "faith in reason" by revealing the uncanny irrationality of texts and their ability to confute or subvert every system or position they are thought to manifest. Deconstruction, by these lights, reveals the impossibility of any science of literature or science of discourse and returns critical inquiry to the task of interpretation.[94]

Deconstruction is, then, the ultimate in exclusively *text*-based literary criticism because it seeks to explore *all* the implications of the text on their own merit, and employs the presuppositions underlying the text to thwart its own purposes. It is, in this regard, the logical result of the task which the New Critics set themselves: disinterested study of the text itself.

---

93. Gray suggests that "Many of the ideas of deconstruction originate in three books by the French philosopher Jacques Derrida, all of which were published in France in 1967 and have been translated into English with the following titles: *Speech and Phenomena* (1973), *Of Grammatology* (1976) and *Writing and Difference* (1978)" (*A Dictionary of Literary Terms*, 61). Rorty maintains that Derrida and de Man are the two people who give prestige to Deconstruction (Richard Rorty, "The Pragmatist's Progress," in Collini, ed., *Interpretation and Overinterpretation*, 89–108 [101]). Rorty himself is more in line with Fish, and describes himself as a "pragmatist."

94. Culler, *On Deconstruction*, 219.

As a philosophy, Deconstruction examines the hierarchies that make up social structures and indicates how these hierarchies can be reversed and how the social framework (or the "deep structures" of society which Structuralism claims to disclose) is disrupted as a result. Derrida draws attention to some simple examples of these hierarchies: "good before evil, the positive before the negative, the pure before the impure, the simple before the complex, the essential before the accidental, the imitated before the imitation."[95] He then argues that all metaphysicians "from Plato to Rousseau, from Descartes to Husserl" have proceeded on the basis that the first term in each opposition is "simple, intact, normal, pure, standard, self-identical," and the second a "derivation, complication, deterioration, accident, etc." But if these hierarchies are reversed, the whole system that is founded on them is called into question. Culler employs the example of "cause and effect" to illustrate how such a reversal is achieved:

> If the effect is what causes the cause to become a cause, then the effect, not the cause, should be treated as the origin. By showing that the argument which elevates cause can be used to favour effect, one uncovers and undoes the rhetorical operation responsible for the hierarchization and one produces a significant displacement. If either cause or effect can occupy the position of origin, then origin is no longer originary, it loses its metaphysical privilege.[96]

When applied to literature, Deconstruction involves showing how a text undermines the philosophy it asserts by reversing the hierarchical oppositions on which its arguments rely. Rather than seeking unity in the

---

95. Jacques Derrida, *Of Grammatology* (trans. Gayatri Chakravorty Spivak; Baltimore: The Johns Hopkins University Press, 1976), 236. Other hierarchies in our society which might be very interesting to explore further include male/female (to which Culler devotes a very interesting and provocative section of his book [*On Deconstruction*, 43–64], and which Jobling also touches on although with considerably less force than Culler [*The Sense of Biblical Narrative*, 2:40–43]), white person/ black person, employed/unemployed, heterosexual/homosexual, etc. Clines gives a list of "some classical binary oppositions" in his *On the Way to the Postmodern*, 1:85. In relation to Ecclesiastes, Sneed "explores instances of *différance* in his text, places where the text resists mastery and reveals its own Otherness against Qohelet's intentions (Mark Sneed, '[Dis]closure in Qohelet: Qohelet Deconstructed,' *JSOT* 27 [2002], 115–26 [115]). Sneed starts his conclusion with these words: "Qohelet indeed does a service to wisdom by deconstructing traditional dichotomies like wisdom/folly and righteousness/wickedness. However, both his radicalism and conservatism are demonstrated in his alternative to these: the fearing God/not fearing God dichotomy" (p. 125).

96. Culler, *On Deconstruction*, 88.

text—which is the usual goal of exegesis, of Ecclesiastes as much as of any other text—Deconstruction probes the text to tease out the stress points where it will burst open and reveal readings which contradict the supposed ground of the text. In Johnson's words, it is "the careful teasing out of warring forces of signification within the text."[97] By focusing on these points in the text, Deconstruction allows the text to speak with several contradictory voices rather than trying to squeeze all its constituent parts into one univocal reading as previous literary theories have done. It explores all the logical implications of the language used in the text, and to achieve this Derrida asserts that "the motif of homogeneity, the theological motif par excellence, is what must be destroyed."[98] Also, where interpretation generally attempts to determine what is the core of the text and tends to rely on distinctions between the central and the marginal, the essential and the inessential, deconstruction reverses these hierarchies so that the implications of the whole of the text are allowed to speak out, regardless of their relation to the supposed core.[99]

In this sense Deconstruction is also a logical progression from the study of ambiguity in literature, because it seeks to explore the implications of "any verbal nuance, however slight, which gives room for alternative reactions to the same piece of language."[100] It also shows the futility of a solely text-based approach to meaning in literature: by drawing out all the implications of the language of a literary work (at least

97. Barbara Johnson, *The Critical Difference* (Baltimore: The Johns Hopkins University Press, 1980), 5.

98. Jacques Derrida, *Positions* (trans. Alan Bass; Chicago: University of Chicago Press, 1981), 64.

99. Clines's chapter, "Deconstructing the Book of Job," is an example of the application of Deconstruction to Biblical Studies. Clines relates the practice of deconstruction to readerly concerns when he says, "When a text has been deconstructed, what happens next? This is a question not often raised by professional deconstructionists, who tend to believe in a never-ending spiral of deconstructions, but it is a pressing question for many other readers, who cannot bear too much dizziness and nausea" (David J. A. Clines, *What Does Eve Do to Help? And Other Readerly Questions to the Old Testament* [JSOTSup 94; Sheffield: JSOT Press, 1990], 106–23 [121]). He suggests: "What sustains a book's life beyond its deconstruction is its rhetoric, that is, its power to persuade beyond the bounds of pure reason, its ability to provoke readers into willing its success even beyond its deserts." See also J. D. Crossan, *Cliffs of Fall: Paradox and Polyvalence in the Parables of Jesus* (New York: Seabury, 1980); P. D. Miscall, *The Workings of Old Testament Narrative* (Philadelphia: Fortress, 1983); G. Aichele, Jr., *The Limits of Story* (Philadelphia: Fortress, 1985); and Robert Detweiler, *Derrida and Biblical Studies* (Semeia 23; Chico, Calif.: Scholars Press, 1982).

100. Empson, *Seven Types of Ambiguity*, 1.

this is the goal—it is, however, an impossible undertaking), Deconstruction reveals endless possibilities for the meaning of a piece of language[101] and makes clear the need for an interpretative strategy to fix something that can usefully be described as the "meaning" of a text. In other words, if it is meaning we seek, the text itself is not enough to provide that meaning.

Essentially, Deconstruction, like Structuralism, is a philosophical discipline that explores the philosophical systems on which social structures are built: Structuralism seeks to elucidate these systems, while Deconstruction seeks out the flaws to show how these systems are self-contradictory. The end results of both disciplines are therefore philosophical rather than literary in the same way that psychoanalytical and Freudian theories of literature tend to psychological ends, and Marxist theory tends to socio-economic or political ends. Of course, the same criticism could be leveled at historical criticism (to say nothing of feminist criticism, liberation criticism and various other ideological approaches to biblical texts, and also, one may suppose, many Christian and Jewish reading strategies[102]): Does it tell us more about history and society than it does about the text?

---

101.   Culler argues that Deconstruction "stresses that meaning is context bound —a function of relations within or between texts—but that context itself is boundless: there will always be new contextual possibilities that can be adduced, so that the one thing we *cannot* do is to set limits" (Jonathan Culler, "In Defence of Overinterpretation," in Collini, ed., *Interpretation and Overinterpretation*, 109–23 [120–21], his emphasis).

102.   In "Possibilities and Priorities of Biblical Interpretation", Clines asks "whether feminist criticism and ideological criticism are, properly speaking, *interpretational* at all". He goes on, "Perhaps we should be sharply distinguishing between the acts of *interpretation*, which seek only to represent the text, to exegete it and explicate it, to rehearse it in words other than its own, to understand it—but *not* to critique or evaluate it—and, on the other hand, acts of *criticism*, which judge the text by a norm outside itself. If a feminist or some other ideological criticism takes its point of departure from an ethical or intellectual position that lies outside the text, one that may indeed by deeply hostile to the text, its goal cannot be mere *understanding*, mere *interpretation*" (*On the Way to the Postmodern*, 1:46–67 [66–67], his emphasis). In "The Pyramid and the Net: The Postmodern Adventure" he adds, "We do not discount the project of exegesis; we might even sometimes, though not on principle, regard it as foundational. But it is the point of departure for more grown up questions about texts, for questions that go beyond mere *meaning*. The trouble with *meaning* as the goal for the study of texts is that it restricts the scholar to recapitulating the message of the text. . . . At the very least, the critic in a postmodern age will need to be asking, What does this text do to me if I read it?" (*On the Way to the Postmodern*, 1:138–57 [153], his emphasis). However, in another article

But, again like Structuralism, Deconstruction can be "a handy extra methodological tool," provided it is part of a broader methodology which enables the reader to make sense of the text. Its probing into the presuppositions on which the text is based gives insight into what the ground of the text is, and even if these hierarchies are finally re-established, a greater understanding will have been achieved of how they operate and what alternatives might be possible. Moreover, the plurivocity of the text which Deconstruction reveals opens the text to the possibility of different readings and prepares the way for a reader-oriented approach to the text.

1.3. *Interpretative Strategy: Meaning and Ambiguity*

It should be clear from the above discussion that the meaning of "*meaning*" can no longer (if it ever could) be taken for granted. Nor, it seems, can it be taken for granted that the literary critic's task is to elucidate the meaning of literary texts: arguments about what a literary critic *ought* to do will, no doubt, continue for a long time (probably as long as literary criticism is practised[103]), as also will arguments about what are *proper* goals of biblical criticism.[104] However, my aim in this book is specifically

---

in this same volume, Clines acknowledges that "as an exegete, I behave for all the world as if the indeterminacy of texts had never been heard of," adding, "I think that in interpretation scholars are *essentially the servants of the text* (as I am when I am writing my commentary on Job). It is our business to *unfold, explain, represent, annotate, rehearse the text, thinking the authors' thoughts after them*, so to speak. In critique, on the other hand, the scholar is measuring the text by a standard outside the text" ("Varieties of Indeterminacy," in *On the Way to the Postmodern*, 1: 126–37 [133–34], my emphasis). Clearly for Clines there is a very significant difference between the disciplines of "biblical exegesis" or "interpretation" and "biblical criticism." I'm not convinced that the two can be so easily disentangled.

103.   Although some scholars seem to suggest that postmodernism is "the end of literary criticism." See, e.g., William V. Spanos, "Breaking the Circle: Hermeneutics as Dis-closure," in Newton, ed., *Twentieth-Century Literary Theory*, 196–202 (199), and Culler's criticism of Rorty in "In Defence of Overinterpretation," 117–20.

104.   See, e.g., the conclusion in Barton, *Reading the Old Testament*, 237–46, where he states, "Over and over again biblical critics seek *correct* methods, *prescriptive* answers to the question how we may read the Old Testament, *successful* procedures and techniques that will process the text and extract from it the answers that we *ought* to be looking for. In so far as biblical criticism belongs to theory, perhaps there must be some concern for norms and rules; and of course secular literary criticism is far from lacking in prescription and legislation! Yet in our discussion it has emerged that problems with methods almost always begin at the point where they cease to be descriptive and tentative and become rigid and doctrinaire: where codified intuition starts to be counter-intuitive in its results. The basic flaw, I

to study possibilities for interpretation of Ecclesiastes, not necessarily with the aim of finding a single unified meaning, but rather with the goal of exploring the range of possible meanings of the book indicated by close examination of key words and, significantly, of the way these words have been understood by recent commentators and writers on the book of Ecclesiastes. The particular emphasis will be on the ambiguous nature of these key words, and how this ambiguity encourages readers to play an active role in determining meaning. This is a new approach to Ecclesiastes, although, as shall be noted in the next chapter, an increasing number of writers are noting the ambiguous nature of the book, and this is especially true of Salyer's recent book, *Vain Rhetoric*. My purpose is not to deny the value of previous approaches, but rather to explore how the active involvement of the reader in the production of meaning might increase our appreciation of this difficult, yet fascinating part of the Old Testament. Indeed, interaction with a large number of different readings of Ecclesiastes will be an important element in my study of ambiguity in Ecclesiastes—whether or not readers are convinced that I have demonstrated that Ecclesiastes is fundamentally ambiguous, there can be no doubt that this biblical book has been read in markedly different ways throughout its history, and especially among scholars over the last twenty or so years. Rather than attempting to squeeze Ecclesiastes into a univocal mould, as has mostly been done previously (though Mills's *Reading Ecclesiastes* provides a striking exception), I will explore something of its plurivocity, because it does seem that any univocal reading strains under the pressure of other voices crying out to be heard. My intention is to demonstrate that this book, more than most biblical books, is susceptible to different readings depending on the approach of the reader— specifically because key elements of the text (and much else, I believe) are ambiguous. I hope to provide sufficient evidence to indicate that this is a deliberate technique adopted by the author, though, of course, the possibility cannot be ruled out that some of the ambiguity results from editorial activity, errors in the transmission of the text and the difficulty of trying to interpret the text at some two thousand and more years distance, with relatively little knowledge of its cultural setting.

have suggested, is the belief that the question 'How should we read the Old Testament?' can be answered" (p. 246, his emphasis). On the impact of postmodern reading strategies on biblical criticism, see Terence J. Keegan, "Biblical Criticism and the Challenge of Postmodernism," *BibInt* 3, no. 1 (1995): 1–14. See also the articles by David J. A. Clines, "Methods in Old Testament Study" (pp. 23–45), "Possibilities and Priorities of Biblical Interpretation," "Varieties of Indeterminacy" and "The Pyramid and the Net," in volume 1 of his *On the Way to the Postmodern*.

However, while there is a greater focus on the role of the *reader* than is usual in biblical interpretation in general (though undoubtedly this is changing) and study of Ecclesiastes in particular,[105] both *author* and *universe* will also be considered as important in determining the meaning of the *text*. The reason why this approach has been adopted is because this is how readers usually address the book: they come to the text with the express purpose of discovering what *it* means—but they also come to it with their interpretative strategies already in place, and this affects their reading whether they like it or not, and whether they realise it or not; they also seek to discover what the author intended when she or he wrote the text, and how that meaning relates to the universe as they know it, and—so far as they can determine—as the author knew it. To this end, Ecclesiastes will be read as it is found in its canonical form. This does not deny the value of historical-critical approaches to the Bible, nor does it imply an acceptance of Childs's (or the various other recent forms of) canonical criticism. Rather it acknowledges the fact that historical criticism is an endless task which produces few definitive results, and the reader or commentator can never be one hundred per cent certain of the origin and development of any biblical text, least of all Ecclesiastes. The issue of editorial additions to, or emendations of, the text will be considered from time to time, however, because it may appear to any reader that some parts of the text seem unlikely to have come from the hand of the "implied author" of the bulk of the text. But this can be, and often is, an easy way to avoid tackling certain tensions in the text and for the most part I will study the text of Ecclesiastes as it is found in *BHS*: I shall explore how difficult passages *might* be understood—even when they appear to be grammatically incorrect or semantically incoherent or incomplete—rather than searching for possible emendations. It is noteworthy that there are a number of such passages whose interpretation has an important bearing on how the whole book is understood: it is also noteworthy that commentators have translated such passages very differently depending on their understanding of the book as a whole. This is a key element in the ambiguity of Ecclesiastes.

In the reading of any text some parts of that text will be foregrounded and others marginalised, and perhaps my approach is similar to Deconstruction insofar as I shall explore the margins to show how centralising

---

105.   But see Edwin M. Good, "The Unfilled Sea: Style and Meaning in Ecclesiastes 1:2–11," in Gammie et al., eds., *Israelite Wisdom*, 59–73, and Mills, *Reading Ecclesiastes* (who explores "What contributions to the profile of an autobiographical self [i.e. Qohelet] are made by readers who watch and listen from different cultural positions" [p. 102]), and Salyer, *Vain Rhetoric* (in which he has a section entitled, "Sharing the Loom with the Author: Readers as Co-Authors of Meaning", 54–61).

the margins of one reading may produce a very different reading where the central aspects of the first reading themselves become marginalised. However, I intend to demonstrate that in Ecclesiastes what is centred and what is marginalised depends very largely on the interpretative strategy of the reader,[106] and that the ambiguity of the text encourages the reader to choose what should be central and what should be marginal.[107]

I do not accept that Ecclesiastes can be read however the reader wants to read it. The reader is, I believe, constrained by what can be discerned from the text of authorial intention, and also by the structure and determinate schemata within the text.[108] Fish is right to argue that the structures we find and the determinate schemata we reveal—and also, no

---

106.   Fish would maintain that such is the case with any text (and Clines's "Varieties of Indeterminacy" provides an interesting example focusing on "The Lord is my shepherd" [pp. 127–29]): if that were true, my case still stands on the grounds that the *process* of foregrounding and marginalising may be more obvious to the reader in Ecclesiastes than it is in other texts. From this perspective ambiguity has particular interest because it helps the reader to appreciate the process that occurs all the time in reading: if the reader perceives a word, phrase, sentence, paragraph, chapter or complete text as ambiguous, he or she may also be aware of the processes whereby she or he decides how to resolve the ambiguity. McKnight addresses this issue when he writes: "Readers assume that a text makes sense as a linguistic and literary unit and intuitively use their linguistic and literary competence in the process of actualization. When ambiguity arises, a reader becomes conscious of the process that is being followed. . . . In the processing of the text, then, the reader will discover that the text (intentionally and unintentionally) does not (indeed, *cannot*) make explicit all that must be known to make sense of the text" (Edgar V. McKnight, *Post-Modern Use of the Bible: The Emergence of Reader-Oriented Criticism* [Nashville: Abingdon, 1988], 223–24, his emphasis).

107.   Mills argues, "It has been stated in these last two chapters that Qoheleth's textual voice, his autobiographical 'I', can be interpreted both from culturally central sites and from the margins. Whereas the search from the centre looks to the sameness of a modern selfhood with that of the ancient autobiographer, that which concerns itself with borders looks to the otherness already present in Qohelet's account of his experience of the social world of existence. . . . [I]n explorations of the 'Qoheletic self' commentators cannot decide which of his voices is central and which marginal, and cannot therefore be sure of the meaning of his key term *hebel*" (*Reading Ecclesiastes*, 134–35). See Rimmon's discussion on "the existence of mutually exclusive sets of clues" (*The Concept of Ambiguity*, 51–58).

108.   To this extent I agree with Eco when he says, "What I want to say is that there are somewhere criteria for limiting interpretation" (Umberto Eco, "Interpretation and History," in Collini, ed., *Interpretation and Overinterpretation*, 23–43 [40]). He states that "the internal textual coherence controls the otherwise uncontrollable drives of the reader" (Umberto Eco, "Overinterpreting Texts," in Collini, ed., *Interpretation and Overinterpretation*, 45–66 [65]).

doubt, the authorial intention we discern—will all depend to some extent on the way we approach the text, or the questions we address to it. Nonetheless, there are marks on the page, and they do more readily lend themselves to certain patterns than to others, and they do reflect certain "realities" or aspects of the universe more than others, so that a reader has the right to expect an interpretation to reflect certain textual, realistic and authorial norms. However, there are undoubtedly possible interpretations relevant to a twenty-first-century reader which could not have been intended by the author some two thousand years and more previously. For this reason, the distinction between "meaning" and "significance" may be employed to distinguish between the meanings which are in some sense embodied in the text, and the significances which arise as a later reader gives voice to those meanings in terms which are appropriate to his or her own situation. Nonetheless, it must be realised that latent meanings in the text can *only* ever bear meaning for the reader as they are given a contemporary significance, and hence the distinction between meaning and significance is not always so easily drawn. By meaning, then, I shall indicate that which a reader may discern of what *could* have been meant by the author—so far as we can determine from the text itself in conjunction with our knowledge of the possible provenance of the book (by which I acknowledge my debt to historical criticism). Latent meaning is given voice as the *reader* addresses the *text* from her or his unique perspective, but also within the constraints placed upon her or him by what she or he can discern of what the *author* might have intended— in this instance, as indeed in most others, mostly from the text itself.[109]

109.   The opening words of the Conclusion to Robert Morgan with John Barton, *Biblical Interpretation* (The Oxford Bible Series; Oxford: Oxford University Press, 1988), sub-titled, "Texts, Authors, and Readers" (pp. 269–71), offer a useful summary of the approach, or interpretative strategy, I have adopted: "A text has no life of its own. It 'lives' only as an electric wire is alive. Its power originates elsewhere: in a human author. There is another point of comparison: however powerful the author's act of creation, the text lies impotent until it also comes into contact with a human reader. Only then can the human power, imagination, and intellect carried by the marks on a page strike a light, communicate warmth, or give a nasty shock. The medium itself is important, and determines how much of the source's power is communicated. Old wires can give unreliable service and cause accidents. But it is the source that gives the wire its potential for illumination or destruction. Without this, there is no live wire. Once this is present, however, those at the receiving end are in control. It is they who decide what to do with the powerful resource they possess—whether and how to use it. They have all power in their hands. . . . [However,] for all the emphasis which literary criticism now places on the reader, common sense continues to look for the grammatical meaning of the text, on the assumption that this usually corresponds to the intention of the writer. Even after

Of the various approaches to the meaning of literary texts whichI considered above, the method used in this book is probably closest to the Reception Theory/Reader Response Theory of Wolfgang Iser.[110] It assumes that there is something in the text which to some extent determines meaning, and this is largely the result of authorial activity. However, the reader is required to actualise this meaning, and in so doing fills in the indeterminacies of the text according to his or her interpretative strategy (consciously and, mostly, unconsciously). In the case of Ecclesiastes, the reader is given a major role because so much of the text is indeterminate due to its ambiguities.

"Ambiguity" will be understood as those aspects of the text—be it a word, phrase, sentence, or longer piece of text, including the whole book (though my particular focus is on individual words and one particular phrase)—whose indeterminacy requires the reader to fill in the meaning in order for a coherent reading to be produced. However, the scope of this ambiguity will be limited precisely by what I can discern of the determinate schemata in the book. Thus only those ambiguities will be considered important which require the reader's active participation in the production of a coherent reading of the whole book—although more minor ambiguities will be noted in passing. This means that I have chosen to define "ambiguity" in a way that is useful to the purposes of my study and meaningful to those who read it, and perhaps by so doing I may be accused of restricting the ambiguous nature of the term "ambiguity."[111] Of course, I have also chosen to pin down the meaning of

two generations of emphasizing the text at the expense of the author, the natural instinct is to ask what the speaker or writer intended."

110. See also Salyer's treatment of Iser, *Vain Rhetoric*, 90–108.

111. I certainly use the term more restrictively than, e.g., Page, who says, "I propose to use Ambiguity, capitalized to indicate the whole metaphysical view, as an umbrella term for the three [diversity, change, polyvalence], and for the conditions which they create." As a result, she argues that "*Everything* we experience—humanity and its artefacts, animate and inanimate nature—is ambiguous" (*Ambiguity and the Presence of God*, 13, 35, her emphasis). My usage is also more restrictive than Empson, who maintains: "I propose to use the word in an extended sense, and shall think relevant to my subject any verbal nuance, however slight, which gives room for alternative reactions to the same piece of language" (*Seven Types of Ambiguity*, 1). My usage is, however, more expansive than that of Rimmon, who applies the following four criteria: "1. An ambiguous expression has two or more distinct meanings operating in the given context. 2. The meanings of an ambiguous expression are not reducible to each other or to some common denominator, nor are they identifiable with each other or subsumable in a larger unit of meaning which they conjoin to create or in which they are reconciled and integrated. 3. The meanings of an ambiguous expression are mutually exclusive in the context, in the sense that if

"meaning" so that it fulfils a useful purpose and also can clearly be understood by those who read this book. On both counts there may be those
who would find me culpable, but I plead my case on the grounds that
unless these terms are carefully defined they may cease to serve any
useful critical purpose, rather signifying whatever the interpreter wants
them to signify regardless of how they are understood by his or her
readers.

There is one aspect of ambiguity which I have only just begun to
explore that offers fascinating insights into how readers/hearers understand ambiguous language: this is the processes of disambiguation
involved in Natural Language Processing for automated responses.[112]
These studies bring a certain rigour to study of ambiguity which could
bear considerable fruit in literary studies. However, my purpose here is
not at all "disambiguation" because I believe that Ecclesiastes is ambiguous *by design* precisely to engage the reader in the process of creating or
discovering meaning, not just in the text of Ecclesiastes, but in the world
it reflects also. Just how natural language processing systems would cope
with such widespread deliberate ambiguity remains uncertain, though it
seems reasonable to assume that it would rather confute the drive for
disambiguation. Another aspect of ambiguity which is likely to be much
more fruitful in relation to Ecclesiastes is the ambiguity associated with
"metaphor."[113] In this respect, Miller's book *Symbol and Rhetoric in
Ecclesiastes*[114] makes a significant contribution, and I should like in the

one applies, the other cannot apply, and vice versa. 4. Hence, an ambiguous expression calls for choice between its alternative meanings, but at the same time provides
no ground for making the choice. The mutually exclusive meanings therefore coexist
in spite of the either/or conflict between them" (*The Concept of Ambiguity*, 17).

112.   So far as I can tell, the "key text" to date in this field is Graeme Hirst,
Semantic Interpretation and the Resolution of Ambiguity (Studies in Natural Language Processing; Cambridge: Cambridge University Press, 1987). However, I
found much more useful for study of ambiguity in Ecclesiastes, van Deemter and
Peters, eds., *Semantic Ambiguity and Underspecification*.

113.   Thus, e.g., in a chapter entitled, "Metaphor and Symbol," Ricoeur argues,
"real metaphors are not translatable. Only metaphors of substitution are susceptible
of translation which could restore the literal significance. Tension metaphors are not
translatable because they *create their meaning*. This is not to say that they cannot be
paraphrased, just that such a paraphrase is infinite and incapable of exhausting the
innovative meaning" (Paul Ricoeur, *Interpretation Theory: Discourse and the
Surplus of Meaning* [Fort Worth: Texas Christian University Press, 1976], 52, his
emphasis).

114.   Douglas B. Miller, *Symbol and Rhetoric in Ecclesiastes: The Place of
Hebel in Qohelet's Work* (Atlanta: Society of Biblical Literature, 2002).

future to explore in much greater depth how the concept of metaphor might enhance our understanding of Ecclesiastes.[115]

One further approach to ambiguity in Ecclesiastes that might prove fruitful is the comparison of this text with other acknowledged ambiguous texts. The ambiguity in Henry James's *The Turn of the Screw* would make this novel an eminently suitable candidate for such comparison because it, too, has generated a wealth of commentary characterised by diametrically opposed conclusions about its "meaning." I am fascinated by Rimmon's stated aim in relation to this work (among others written by James), to undertake a

> detailed demonstration of the irresolvability of the ambiguity of these works, in the hope that such a demonstration will stop the endless debates among critics, debate motivated by a compulsion to choose between mutually exclusive hypotheses, when the very phenomenon of ambiguity makes such choice impossible and undesirable.[116]

This seems to me to be a reasonable aim in relation to Ecclesiastes also.

---

115.   David H. Aaron's book, *Biblical Ambiguities: Metaphor, Semantics, and Divine Imagery* (Leiden: Brill, 2001), really does not engage at all with ambiguity as I have defined it here. Rather it is about metaphor, which often involves an element of ambiguity, as the following statement by Aaron demonstrates: "Virtually all theorists accept that metaphor functions by means of indirect meaning, which is only rarely univocal. As more than one meaning is usually possible, the interpretive process requires us to rule out some senses as irrelevant to the speaker's meaning, while accepting others (or perhaps one) as most relevant" (p. 7). It is precisely the indeterminacy of metaphor that particularly interests me, and I warm to Aaron's assertion that "religions must address, in some manner, the problem of our world's ambiguities" (p. vii). This, I believe, is the role that Ecclesiastes fulfils. (I don't, though, go along with Aaron's reading of ambiguity in Ecclesiastes: "Qohelet, too, is entangled in a world of ambiguity [with which I agree]. He concentrates on the fact that one does not know what, if anything, will influence the future. The ambiguity which derives from our limited understanding of the world's purpose is accepted and used to undermine all attempts at bypassing its implications. The work argues that one had no choice but to fabricate meaning out of thin air [with which I do not agree!]. Or, to put it in more theoretical terms: all theology which posits a 'meaning' to the universe is nothing other than reader's meaning" [p. 198]). See also William P. Brown, *Seeing the Psalms: A Theology of Metaphor* (Louisville, Ky.: Westminster John Knox, 2002); unfortunately Brown does not employ this "theology" to any great extent in his various work on Ecclesiastes: *Character in Crisis: A Fresh Approach to the Wisdom Literature of the Old Testament* (Grand Rapids: Eerdmans, 1996); *Ecclesiastes* (Interpretation; Louisville, Ky.: John Knox, 2000); "'Whatever Your Hand Finds to Do': Qoheleth's Work Ethic," *Int* 55, no. 3 (2001): 271–84.

116.   Rimmon, *The Concept of Ambiguity*, xi–xii.

Chapter 2

AMBIGUITY IN ECCLESIASTES

the rhetoric of ambiguity
which rampages throughout the book

—Gary Salyer[1]

2.1. *Contrasting Interpretations of the Book*

With the possible exception of the Song of Songs, the book of Ecclesiastes (or Qoheleth) is unique in the Old Testament in having been interpreted in a variety of ways, some of these in direct opposition to others. In the past hundred years, for example, it has been described, on the one hand, as "Das Hohelied der Skepsis" ("the quintessence of scepticism") by Heinrich Heine, while at the other end of the scale Franz Delitzsch considered it to be "Das Hohelied der Gottesfurcht" ("the quintessence of piety"). Earlier this century M. Jastrow Jr. gave his commentary on it the title "A Gentle Cynic" and, more recently, H. W. Hertzberg has gone so far as to describe it as "die ershütternsdte messianische Weissagung, die das Alte Testament aufzuweisen hat" ("the most staggering messianic prophecy to appear in the Old Testament"). These quotations draw attention to the extremes of opinion held as to the book and its contents.

> It should not be thought, however, that this variety of opinion is merely the result of the critical scholarship of the 19th and 20th centuries. It might be said that the book of Ecclesiastes has divided scholarly opinion throughout its existence, and the controversy which accompanied the inclusion of the book in the Jewish canon (c.100 A.D.) a summary of which accompanied the inclusion of the book in the Midrashim and Talmud, simply underlines this. This division among the Rabbis throws into relief just where the problems of interpretation lie; in effect one side is saying that the orthodox and pious statements in the book modify and control the unorthodox, while the other side claims that the scepticism is of the essence of Qoheleth and remains over against the pious statements to be found there.

---

1. Salyer, *Vain Rhetoric*, 255.

Thus Salters[2] sums up what many commentators had previously and a number have since observed about the history of interpretation of Ecclesiastes.[3] And the controversy continues unabated, as commentaries and other books and journal articles on Ecclesiastes continue to appear which present very different, often diametrically opposed, interpretations of the book. Ogden is representative of a number of commentators when he claims of Ecclesiastes:

> Its thesis, then, is that life under God must be taken and enjoyed in all its mystery. . . . Qoheleth's purpose, then, may be defined as calling on the next generation to ponder deeply the kinds of life issues to which there seem to be no complete answers, while at the same time holding firm, and positively accepting, life as God gives it.[4]

2. R. B. Salters, "Exegetical Problems in Qoheleth," *IBS* 10 (1988): 44–59 (44).

3. See also George A. Barton, *Ecclesiastes* (ICC; Edinburgh: T. & T. Clark, 1912), 18–31; James L. Crenshaw, "Qohelet in Current Research," *HAR* 7 (1983): 41–56; K. J. Dell, "Ecclesiastes as Wisdom: Consulting Early Interpreters," *VT* 44 (1984): 301–29; Christian D. Ginsburg, *Coheleth, Commonly Called Ecclesiastes* (New York: Ktav, 1970), 30–245; Robert Gordis, *Kohelet: The Man and his World; A Study in Ecclesiastes* (3d ed.; New York: Ktav, 1968), 3–7; S. Holm-Nielsen, "On the Interpretation of Qoheleth in Early Christianity," *VT* 24 (1974): 168–77; idem, "The Book of Ecclesiastes and the Interpretation of it in Jewish and Christian Theology," *ASTI* 10 (1975–76): 38–96; David A. Hubbard, *Ecclesiastes, Song of Solomon* (Dallas: Word Books, 1991), 21–33; Roland Murphy, "Qohelet Interpreted: The Bearing of the Past on the Present," *VT* 32 (1982): 331–37; idem, *Ecclesiastes*, xlviii–lvi; idem, "Recent Research on Proverbs and Qoheleth," *CR:BS* 1 (1993): 119–40. Gordis (*Kohelet*, 4) comments, "Koheleth himself would have seen in all the time and ingenuity spent on the interpretation of his tiny masterpiece one more example of the futility of human effort. For there is scarcely one aspect of the book, whether of date, authorship or interpretation, that has not been the subject of wide difference of opinion."

4. Graham Ogden, *Qoheleth* (Readings: A New Biblical Commentary; Sheffield: Sheffield Academic Press, 1987), 14–15. Other recent books displaying a fairly positive interpretation of Ecclesiastes include Bartholomew, *Reading Ecclesiastes*; Ellen F. Davis, *Proverbs, Ecclesiastes, and the Song of Songs* (Westminster Bible Companion; Louisville, Ky.: Westminster John Knox, 2000); Kathleen A. Farmer, *Proverbs and Ecclesiastes: Who Knows What is Good?* (ITC; Grand Rapids: Eerdmans; Edinburgh: Handsel Press, 1991); Daniel C. Fredericks, *Coping with Transience: Ecclesiastes on Brevity in Life* (The Biblical Seminar 18; Sheffield: JSOT Press, 1993); Duane A. Garrett, *Proverbs, Ecclesiastes, Song of Songs* (The New American Commentary; Nashville: Broadman Press, 1993); Norbert Lohfink, *Qoheleth* (trans. Sean McEvenue; A Continental Commentary; Minneapolis: Fortress, 2003); Iain Provan, *Ecclesiastes, Song of Songs* (The NIV Application Commentary; Grand Rapids: Zondervan, 2001); Graham S. Ogden and Lynell Zogbo, *A Handbook on Ecclesiastes* (UBS Handbook Series; New York: United Bible Societies, 1997); Tamez, *When the Horizons Close*. R. N. Whybray (*Ecclesiastes* [Grand Rapids:

On the other hand, Crenshaw is one of many who adopt an opposing position: he writes,

> Life is profitless; totally absurd. This oppressive message lies at the heart
> of the Bible's strangest book. Enjoy life if you can, advises the author, for
> old age will soon overtake you. And even as you enjoy, know that the
> world is meaningless. Virtue does not bring reward. The deity stands
> distant, abandoning humanity to chance and death.[5]

Eerdmans; London: Marshall, Morgan & Scott, 1989]) is somewhat more cautious in his approach, but might still be included among those who view the book "positively." Murphy is quite clear that "Qoheleth loved life" (*Ecclesiastes*, lxix), but shares Whybray's caution. For example, on the issue of the repeated "call to enjoyment" Murphy argues that "Qohelet is not expressing a verdict about values in life, and expressions like these are not a positive recommendation. They are a concession to human nature" (p. lx). Miller (*Symbol and Rhetoric in Ecclesiastes*) also basically views Ecclesiastes as a positive book and, for example, on the issue of the "call to enjoyment" argues that "Qohelet's exhortations to enjoy life, to be wise, and to find good in one's work are not secondary to his main concern. . . . They are not half-hearted, wishful thinking, later additions to the book, or inconsistencies in Qoheleth's thought. . . . Nor are they ways to avoid the reality that life is actually totally absurd. . . . Rather, they, along with the fear of God, are at the center of Qoheleth's rhetorical program—lifestyle elements which he has been commending as gifts from a benevolent, if mysterious deity" (p. 174).

5.   Crenshaw, *Ecclesiastes*, 23. Other recent works which adopt a fairly negative approach include William H. U. Anderson, *Qoheleth and its Pessimistic Theology: Hermeneutical Struggles in Wisdom Literature* (Lewiston, N.Y.: Edwin Mellen, 1997); Christianson, *A Time to Tell*; Fox, *A Time to Tear Down* (although this is less negative than his earlier book, *Qohelet and His Contradictions*); Tremper Longman III, *The Book of Ecclesiastes* (NICOT; Grand Rapids: Eerdmans, 1998) (though it is *Qohelet's* words he views negatively, these being modified by the words of the epilogist who gives the book its definitive meaning); Diethelm Michel, *Untersuchungen zur Eigenart des Buches Qohelet* (Berlin: de Gruyter, 1989); Dominic Rudman, *Determinism in the Book of Ecclesiastes* (JSOTSup 316; Sheffield: Sheffield Academic Press, 2001); Salyer, *Vain Rhetoric*; and Choon-Leong Seow, *Ecclesiastes: A New Translation with Introduction and Commentary* (AB 18C; New York: Doubleday, 1997). Jacques Ellul (*Reason for Being: A Meditation on Ecclesiastes* [Grand Rapids: Eerdmans, 1990]) certainly should not be included in this category, but neither should his "Meditation on Ecclesiastes" be termed "positive." Ellul is prepared to go along with those scholars who "call Qohelet a 'skeptic,' because he gleefully demolishes values and illusions" (p. 28), but he has no time for Crenshaw's perspective. Ellul writes of Crenshaw, "He has just one end in view: to contrast Qohelet's skepticism with all the traditional values of Yahwism. How trite!" I think Mary E. Mills (*Reading Ecclesiastes*) would come into the "negative camp," but it is rather difficult to tell because she presents a variety of different readings with little attempt to evaluate these readings or to indicate whether she herself considers the book a negative or positive work. Huwiler also gives a rather negative reading of

Again, we might contrast as further representative examples the article by Cochrane entitled "Joy to the World: The Message of Ecclesiastes,"[6] with Walsh's "Despair as a Theological Virtue in the Spirituality of Ecclesiastes";[7] or Knopf's "The Optimism of Koheleth,"[8] with Forman's "The Pessimism of Ecclesiastes."[9] Among very recent scholarly works on Ecclesiastes, we might compare Mills's "plurality of readings" approach which presents on equal terms two main "voices" in the book, one positive and one negative,[10] with Lohfink's univocal and much more positive interpretation (both 2003);[11] or Rudman's focus on the deterministic and decidedly negative nature of Ecclesiastes[12] with Provan's

Ecclesiastes in R. Murphy and E. Huwiler, *Proverbs, Ecclesiastes, Song of Songs* (NIBC; Carlisle: Paternoster, 1999). Brown contends: "Arguing over whether Ecclesiastes is either optimistic or pessimistic is sort of like trying to determine whether Stravinsky's *The Rite of Spring* is happy or sad. Such profound works cannot be shackled to simple categories" (Brown, *Ecclesiastes*, 10).

6. A. C. Cochrane, "Joy to the World: The Message of Ecclesiastes," *The Christian Century* 85 (1968): 27–35. See also R. N. Whybray, "Qoheleth, Preacher of Joy," *JSOT* 23 (1982), 87–98.

7. J. T. Walsh, "Despair as a Theological Virtue in the Spirituality of Ecclesiastes," *BTB* 12 (1982): 46–49.

8. C. S. Knopf, "The Optimism of Koheleth," *JNL* 49 (1982): 195–99.

9. C. C. Forman, "The Pessimism of Ecclesiastes," *JSS* 3 (1958): 336–43. See also E. F. F. Bishop, "A Pessimist in Palestine," *PEQ* 100 (1968): 33–41, and, more recently, Anderson's *Qoheleth and Its Pessimistic Theology*. Even more recently, Salyer has written of Qohelet, that his "legacy in the Canon is that of being the preeminent pessimist, thoroughly renowned for his 'melancholy'" (*Vain Rhetoric*, 124).

10. As noted above, it is very difficult to pin down what Mills herself actually thinks about Ecclesiastes, though the following sentence seems to suggest a more negative reading: "Although God is consistently equated with the cosmic order, dealing out each person's portion of good and bad fortune, the gap between humanity and divinity is unmistakable and the relationship between universal order and human activity is problematic, linguistically contained within the view that all is *hebel*" (*Reading Ecclesiastes*, 7–8). I will say more about the "two voices" she describes later.

11. For example, Lohfink argues that "Qoheleth analyzes human existence as being in the time that is given only in the now that accompanies human living and that for individuals ends at death. It can be experienced as happiness. It is more than a falling into nothingness, because in its individually specific form it originates in the eternity of God, who transcends this world and yet is always at work in each event. His action is perfect." He states that Qoheleth describes the world using an "image of an eternal cycle structuring the cosmos [which] is not, as almost all commentators suggest, an image of despair, but rather is completely positive" (*Qoheleth*, 15–16).

12. Rudman maintains that "the joyful imperative is the one positive conclusion that Qoheleth reaches during his investigation into 'what was that good for

very positive and explicitly Christian approach (both 2001);[13] or Brown's reading of Ecclesiastes as "the notebook of a resigned cynic,"[14] with Tamez's view that the book strives for "The utopia of everyday enjoyment"[15] (both 2000); or Christianson's somewhat negative examination of Ecclesiastes as a narrative which elucidates the "central figure who searches for relief from his absurd condition,"[16] with Bartholomew's positive portrayal of the book as "an ironic exposure of an empiricistic epistemology"[17] (both 1998); or Anderson's description of Qohelet's "utter existential despair,"[18] with Seow's view that Qohelet's "ethic ... is about acceptance and joy"[19] (both 1997); or Longman's assertion that Qohelet

humankind, that they should do under the heaven all the days of their life' (2:3)" (*Determinism*, 127).

13. Provan describes Qohelet's message in these terms: "Understand that God exists. The universe we inhabit comes from his hand and comes to us as a gift. Our lives are a gift, offered for a short period and then taken back once again. Embrace life for what it is, rather than what you would like it to be. Live it out before God, reverencing and obeying him. This is the pathway on which joy lies, even though puzzlement and pain will also be found there, and there are never guarantees about how things will turn out" (*Ecclesiastes, Song of Songs*, 41).

14. Brown, *Ecclesiastes*, 17. Brown also states that "The heart of Qoheleth's messages is, thus, bracketed by cosmos and extinction, by weariness and death" (p. 15).

15. Tamez explains, "The utopia of everyday enjoyment is a viable, humanizing way of repudiating the present but at the same time living it by a contrary logic. That is, to live as human beings who feel that they are alive, in a society that does not allow them to live because of its demands for productivity and efficiency" (*When the Horizons Close*, 25).

16. Christianson, *A Time to Tell*, 258.

17. Bartholomew states, "Ecclesiastes is crafted by a wisdom teacher as an ironical exposure of such an empiricistic epistemology which seeks wisdom through personal experience and analysis without the 'glasses' of the fear of God" (*Reading Ecclesiastes*, 263).

18. Anderson, *Qoheleth and Its Pessimistic Theology*, 196. Anderson argues that "the book reveals a person who was in a great deal of turmoil over the way life is. His pessimism was as a result of life's experiences which he found painful—and a God who is unwilling to aid the plight of humanity in a consistent and fair way. The essence of pessimism lies in a sense that change for the better is impossible—which may indicate a faith crisis on the part of the author" (p. 193).

19. Seow argues, "his ethic requires radical change—not of social and political structures, but of attitude toward everything that humanity may want: material possessions, wisdom, esteem, and passion. As emphatic as Qohelet is about the good of joy when one has it, his ethic is not so much about joy as it is about acceptance and spontaneity. . . . God is related to humanity, and God has given humanity the possibilities of each moment. Hence people must accept what happens, whether good or bad. They must respond spontaneously to life, even in the midst of uncertainties,

describes "a life full of trouble" where "death was the end of the story,"[20] with Ogden and Zogbo's claim that "Qoheleth seems to sense that there is something beyond death, at least for the wise"[21] (both also 1997); and so on![22]

2.1.1. *The Centre and the Margins*
There seems little doubt that there are elements in Ecclesiastes that readily lend themselves to a more positive reading, but equally some parts of the book that seem to demand a more negative interpretation. Perhaps, then, it is as Whybray suggests, that

> Depending on the relative weight placed by interpreters respectively on the negative and positive sides of statements [in Ecclesiastes], a whole range of assessments of Qoheleth's outlook, from one of extreme pessimism and despair to one of courageous faith and radiant optimism has been made by ancient and modern scholar alike. . . . Whether he was a pessimist or an optimist, therefore, will remain a matter of opinion.[23]

Murphy takes this a step further when he argues,

> If there is one feature that is common to *all* periods in the history of the interpretation of Ecclesiastes it is that of selective emphasis. In *Scepticisme Israélite* Johannes Pedersen concludes from his brief resume of history of exegesis (with particular attention to J.D. Michaelis and Ernest Renan) that "very different types have found their own image in Ecclesiastes, and it is remarkable that none of the interpretations mentioned is completely without some basis. There are many aspects in our book; different interpreters have highlighted what was most fitting for themselves and their age, and they understood it in their own way. But for all there was a difficulty, namely that there were also other aspects which could hardly be harmonized with their preferred view." This observation is true of other ages and interpreters as well. If the trend of the patristic writers

and accept both the possibilities and limitations of their being human" (*Ecclesiastes*, 58–60).

20. Longman, *The Book of Ecclesiastes*, 34. Longman asks, "What is the theological message of Qohelet's autobiography?," and answers, "Life is full of trouble and then you die."

21. Ogden and Zogbo, *A Handbook*, 6.

22. I have chosen to list selected books in English published since the submission in 1995 of my Ph.D. dissertation, "The Ambiguity of Qohelet: A Study of the Ambiguous Nature of the Language, Syntax and Structure of the Masoretic Text of Qohelet." In that study I examine the diverse interpretations of Ecclesiastes as a whole and each section within it up to 1995. It fascinates me that the diversity I observed then has continued since, and confirms me in my belief that Ecclesiastes is fundamentally ambiguous and hence open to different interpretations.

23. Whybray, *Ecclesiastes*, 28.

and most medievals was to find in the book a doctrine to abjure the world, later emphases were equally selective, such as fear of the Lord (Eccl 12:13), and enjoyment of life (שׂמחה *simḥâ*), the vanity of the world in the perspective of one who believes in a blessed immortality, or the issue of the greatest good (*summum bonum*). Or sometimes the book was interpreted in a pious vein as an expression of Solomon's "conversion." These directions appear over and over again, and they are the inevitable expression of the tensions that exist in the book itself and also within the interpreters.[24]

This accords with my belief that what is "centred" and what is "marginalised" in Ecclesiastes depends very largely on the interpretative strategy of the reader.[25] Thus while one reader centres the positive aspects of the book and marginalises (or in some way seeks to explain away) those aspects which are in tension with such a reading, another reader will find negativity to be the central characteristic of the book, and will read the more positive elements in the light of this[26]—perhaps regarding them as traditional views to be opposed, or as tinged with irony, or deleting them as "pious glosses."[27] Thus, for example, on the one hand Provan notes "the more troubled and gloomy tone in Ecclesiastes, which marks out significant sections of the book and has so often grasped the attention of readers to the exclusion of the other material," arguing that:

> The parts of Qohelet's discourse that have this tone are best understood, in my opinion, only in relation to the obviously hortatory passages, which

24. Murphy, *Ecclesiastes*, lv, his emphasis.

25. Mills notes that "commentators cannot decide which of [Qohelet's] voices is central and which marginal" (*Reading Ecclesiastes*, 135). Crenshaw writes, "Research into the book also shows that it reflects the interpreter's world view. That is why, I think, opinions vary so widely with regard to such basic matters as Qohelet's optimism or pessimism, his attitude to women, and his advocacy of immoral conduct" (*Ecclesiastes*, 47). Ellul takes this a stage further when he asserts, "Qohelet's book does not reveal its message when a single method of interpretation is used. It presupposes biases, and invites the reader to have them, too!" (*Reason for Being*, 196).

26. Lohfink helpfully notes that "In synagogues the book of Qoheleth is read during the celebration of the Feast of Booths, no doubt because of its invitation to rejoice. Thomas à Kempis took the first sentence in the book—*vanitas vanitatum, omnia vanitas*—as an invitation to despise all earthly things and to desire only the otherworldly. And he was not alone in this. Christian piety has heard mostly this message in the book for over a thousand years" (*Qoheleth*, 1).

27. Salyer observes: "Alongside the 'pessimistic Qoheleth,' there is also the 'pious Qoheleth' for many readers. How the two stand side by side in the reading history of this book is truly an astounding feature of the tradition" (*Vain Rhetoric*, p. 4).

he directs at his hearers in the hope of leading them to think and live in a certain way. They are designed to gain a hearing for Qohelet's more positive advice by dispelling false consciousness about the world and by undermining false dreams and hopes.[28]

Figure 10

That is to say, the negative aspects of the book constitute the "dark" background against which the "bright" and positive advice that Qohelet has to offer can be seen the more starkly. Like Rubin's picture (see Fig. 10),[29] the darkness at the margins functions to set off the brightness in the foreground. On the other hand, of the passages that some critics "interpret as offering a positive view toward life," Longman maintains that:

> It is more in keeping with the book as a whole to understand these passages as they have been taken through much of the history of interpretation, that is, as a call to seize the day (*carpe diem*). In the darkness of a life that has no ultimate meaning, enjoy the temporal pleasures that lighten the burden. . . . If we isolate Qohelet's statements from the context of the entire book, it is possible to interpret some of them as positive. . . . However, reading Qohelet's statements about God in context leads one to side with those scholars who characterize Qohelet's God as distant, occasionally indifferent, and sometimes cruel.[30]

28. Provan, *Ecclesiastes, Song of Songs*, 38.

29. See the discussion of this, but especially of the rabbit and the duck illusion in Rimmon, *The Concept of Ambiguity*, ix–xii and passim.

30. Longman, *The Book of Ecclesiastes*, 34–35. Salyer seems to take something of a middle road when he says, "The call to enjoyment halts the narrative progression of Qoheleth's presentation at key junction points in his argument, effectively functioning as a reading interlude for the implied reader. Undoubtedly, it softens the pessimistic blows which pummel the reader's consciousness" (*Vain Rhetoric*, 121).

In this case, the dark aspects of the book are the foreground and the light aspects form the marginal material which serves as background. Thus, like Rubin's illustration, the dark foreground is the sharper because it is set against so light a background.

Such "tensions"[31] or "contradictions"[32] or "incongruities"[33] or "voices"[34] in the book have long been recognised, and have been explained in various ways (helpfully summarised by Fox[35]), but I would contend that these tensions are an important factor in the ambiguity which is a key feature of the book. Mills helpfully presents these as "two narrative moods": she explains that

> the narrator [i.e. Qohelet] produces a social commentary which is pessimistic in tone, because the first and very strong line of commentary in the text is that of *hebel*. This term offers mystery, ambivalence and

31. Huwiler presents two conclusions Qohelet arrives at, which are in tension: "life has no meaning, but it can still be enjoyed. There is a possibility of joy, but it exists only within the context of human limitations and the ultimate limitation, death" (Murphy and Huwiler, *Proverbs, Ecclesiastes, Song of Songs*, 159).

32. Ellul argues: "instead of applying the principle of noncontradiction to this text, we must read and understand it on the basis of the principle of contradiction, which is the key to its mode of thinking" (*Reason for Being*, 40). Fox states: "Qoheleth is not so much contradicting himself as *observing* contradictions in the world. To him they seem to be *antinomies*, two equally valid but contradictory principles. He does not resolve these antinomies, but only describes them, bemoans them, and suggests how to live in such a refractory world" (*Time to Tear Down*, 3, his emphasis). Rimmon maintains: "In life we cannot allow equal tenability to contradictories, and although we sometimes realize that the information we have is insufficient for choice, choice itself always seems imperative. Art, on the other hand, makes the coexistence of contradictories possible. Indeed, the creation of ambiguous works is one of art's ways of solving the problem of contradictories—solving it not by choice but by an articistic dramatization of their coexistence" (*The Concept of Ambiguity*, 234).

33. Davis asserts that "Ecclesiastes is in its entirety a book of incongruities" (*Proverbs, Ecclesiastes, Song of Songs*, 159).

34. See Murphy, "Recent Research," 129. Perry reads Ecclesiastes as a dialogue between two voices, one positive and one negative (T. A. Perry, *Dialogues with Kohelet* [Pennsylvania: The Pennsylvania State University Press, 1993], esp. 33–48), and Mills argues very similarly, stating that "The voice of pessimism expresses an alienation from the social world of family and status, from the tradition that society has a deep value, expressed through the established social norms of an elite society. The voice of optimism reasserts the ongoing significance of that traditional lifestyle of the household of a rich man" (*Reading Ecclesiastes*, 29).

35. Fox, *Qohelet*, 11–12. In *A Time to Tear Down*, Fox's first chapter, "On Reading Contradictions," 1–26, sets out different ways in which such contradictions have been explained, both in ancient times and modern.

potential lack of meaning as a social commentary on life. But the reader then comes to passages where this viewpoint appears to be challenged by a second line, which encourages readers to engage more optimistically with events. . . . The second narrative voice undermines the first and shows it to be less than totally reliable. . . . [T]he reader finds a choice opening up between two apparently opposing "Qohelets."[36]

However, this makes the book "ambivalent" rather than truly "ambiguous": it speaks with two contradictory voices and the reader might then choose between two determinate readings by centring one voice and marginalizing the other[37]—like Rubin's illustration, the dark elements are *either* foreground or background, and correspondingly the bright elements are *either* background or foreground.[38] That is, the reader chooses whether Qohelet displays a positive or negative attitude to life. But I believe the book is much more ambiguous than this suggests, because not only can the book as a whole be read in different ways, many key words and passages within the book (indeed, a high percentage of all the passages in the book) may be read in quite different ways. So, it is not simply the case that there are (determinately) positive (or "light") elements and (determinately) negative (or "dark") elements in Ecclesiastes whereby the reader chooses (consciously or unconsciously) to centre certain elements and marginalise other elements in order to produce a reasonably coherent positive or negative reading of the book over all;[39] rather, much of the book is "indeterminate" in the sense that it may *either* be understood positively *or* be read negatively (although there will always remain those parts of the text "at the margin" of either reading which deconstruct it) depending on the "meaning" brought by the reader to the gaps which the text's ambiguity creates.

36. Mills, *Reading Ecclesiastes*, 27. This bears marked similarities to Perry's "Presenter" and "Kohelet" (*Dialogues with Kohelet*, passim). Later Mills argues, "There is no longer any need to make 'of two voices, one', for instance. Qohelet's contradictory voices can stand as different. Qohelet is an 'I' whose self hood is inherently fragmented and whose conscious voice is under pressure from other internal voices, those of his own others" (*Reading Ecclesiastes*, p. 101).

37. Though it should be noted that while Mills (*Reading Ecclesiastes*) does discuss such centring and marginalising a number of times (e.g. pp. 128, 134–35), and does present these two distinct and somewhat determinate voices, she also refers to the "ambiguity" of the book (e.g. pp. 30, 35, 98, 102) and its "plurivocity" (e.g. p. 101). Perhaps there is here some tension in her approach to Ecclesiastes.

38. But for a different approach, see Rimmon, *The Concept of Ambiguity*, 9–10.

39. See Rimmon's discussion of "The Equilibrium of Singly Directed Clues" and "Doubly Directed Clues" (*The Concept of Ambiguity*, 52–58).

2.1.2. *The Rhetoric of Ambiguity*

It is nothing new to note that there is ambiguity in Ecclesiastes—most modern commentators indicate many points of ambiguity in the text[40]—but I want to take this further and suggest that studied ambiguity is a primary feature of the book, what Salyer describes as a "rhetoric of ambiguity."[41] Farmer goes some way in this direction when she argues,

> How is it possible for one small book to generate such opposite and contradictory theories about its meaning? One important reason is the ambiguity of the thematic word *hebel*. . . . Ecclesiastes has been understood in radically different ways by different readers in part because the thematic metaphor "all is *hebel*" is fundamentally ambiguous.[42]

It is certainly the case that for readers of Ecclesiastes today the word הבל (rendered "vanity" in the NRSV) is ambiguous. It is also clear that הבל is a, if not *the*, key word in the book. But it appears (as I shall demonstrate in a later chapter) that the word, rather than being a key that unlocks "the meaning" of Qohelet, is one of many places in the book where a space is created which the reader is required to fill in.[43] Reed recognises something of this (although her own reading of the book is actually rather unadventurous) when she describes Ecclesiastes as "a biblical text that is unexpectedly pertinent to the postmodern age." She continues,

> The intention is not to synthesize but to create space in which to play between the deconstruction of gender-based metanarratives of freedom and justice and the hope of social transformation. . . . The primary condition that qualifies a reading of the text of Ecclesiastes in the postmodern context of feminism is its thematic statement of vanity.[44]

40. See, e.g., Wilson, "Artful Ambiguity in Ecclesiastes 1,1–11"; Byargeon, "The Significance of Ambiguity"; and Antoon Schoors, "Qoheleth: The Ambiguity of Enjoyment," in *The Bright Side of Life* (ed. Ellen van Wolde; *Concilium* 2000, no. 4; London: SCM Press), 35–51.

41. Salyer explains: "What I mean by 'rhetoric of ambiguity' is a literary design which frustrates the reader in such a way that the 'whole truth' is never disclosed in any satisfactory way. The reader is left suspended in a state of literary limbo regarding the text's final meaning. An ambiguous text is characterized by the enduring and resolute presence of multiple interpretations which seem equally justifiable" (*Vain Rhetoric*, 126–27). Later he describes Qohelet as "the master of ambiguous language" (p. 131).

42. Farmer, *Who Knows What is Good?*, 142, 146.

43. Salyer states, "the opacity created by the use of *hebel* has created a definite sense of ambiguity regarding the book's overall theme. . . . In short, readers have a problem isolating which connotation in such a lively tensive-symbol is the salient aspect that succinctly sums up the overall meaning of the work" (*Vain Rhetoric*, 256).

44. E. D. Reed, "Whither Postmodernism and Feminist Theology," *FT* 6 (1994): 15–29 (18–19). I am, however, unconvinced by her assertion that "The text of

While Reed seeks "space" for a feminist reading, others use the aporia that Ecclesiastes provides in accordance with their own more or less optimistic or pessimistic readings. My contention is that the book readily lends itself to such varied readings because the ambiguity of many key words, phrases and passages—and indeed of the book as a whole, demands that the reader plays a significant part by filling in the gaps to create meaning.[45]

In the following chapters I will examine a number of key words in the book (קהלת, הבל, ירתון, עשׂה/עמל, טוב and the expression תחת השׁמשׁ) to demonstrate that all these key words are fundamentally ambiguous, and in the process many passages in Ecclesiastes will be briefly discussed, and their ambiguity demonstrated also. Having shown conclusively that the book as a whole has been, and continues to be, interpreted in markedly different ways, I will now give an example of a significant passage in the book which is variously interpreted. The passage is the introductory section, 1:4–11. (1:1–3 will not be discussed at this point because it will be treated in depth later as we consider the key words within these verses.)

Ecclesiastes is a *locus classicus* of anti-foundational thinking" (p. 29). She contends that "In many ways the text is the most densely woven anti-foundationalism and eclecticism that we can encounter. His views contrast radically with previous wisdom teaching, for example the book of Proverbs in which ethical and speculative knowledge accord prosperity and honour to the righteous" (p. 21). In fact, while Ecclesiastes does pose some very probing questions, similar questions are raised elsewhere, if not, perhaps, with the same force. Moreover, the margins of Reed's reading must contain those parts of the book where traditional wisdom is asserted, e.g., 3:17; 8:12, 13; 11:9b; 12:13, 14. Nonetheless, the idea that Ecclesiastes is a text that is particularly appropriate to postmodernity bears some consideration.

45.   There are hints of this in R. E. Murphy's article, "On Translating Ecclesiastes," *CBQ* 53 (1991): 571-79, where he says, "My modest purpose is to designate and discuss some key passages, especially in chap. 7, where the translation is simply dubious or the interpretation ambiguous. . . . If an ambiguity occurs, it is to be resolved by an evaluative choice among several possibilities. . . . But another important factor is the previous construal of the translator, whether this be a construal of the book as a whole or in part" (pp. 571–72). Bartholomew devotes considerable attention to the issue of gaps in Ecclesiastes, asking, "Why is it that the gaps in Ecclesiastes have not been attended to?" He answers: "The answer lies in the failure of commentators to take the *literary* nature of Ecclesiastes seriously" (*Reading Ecclesiastes*, 254, his emphasis). However, he goes on to argue, "Chapter twelve of Ecclesiastes is fundamental to the book in the answer it gives as to how the gaps should be filled, namely by remembering one's creator" (p. 268). I would be inclined to go along more with his observation earlier in the book that "The failure of twentieth century scholars to reach any kind of consensus about its meaning could indicate radical textual indeterminacy" (p. 49).

2.2. *A Sample Text: Ecclesiastes 1:4–11*

2.2.1. *The Passage in Context*

The poem in 1:4–11 is clearly a significant part of Ecclesiastes[46] because it occurs so early in the book, and how it is understood may have a considerable bearing on how the rest of Qohelet's words are read. Moreover, the way readers interpret vv. 2–3 will also bear on their understanding of this poem, but, as I shall show later, these verses are open to quite different interpretations. Salyer writes:

> After inviting the reader through the doorway to Qoheleth's consciousness in verses 1:2–3, the frame-narrator proceeds to give a short guided tour of the narrator's world in 1:4–11. With these verses the reader's initiation into the requisite values needed to appreciate the narrator's counsel becomes complete. In this poem the reader begins to form a *Gestalt* of the narrator's character. Nothing so characterizes a person like their worldview. By enabling the reader to see the world through Qoheleth's eyes, the implied author begins to characterize the narrator by employing the strongest means possible.[47]

However, there are also important questions about how these verses relate to what follows: 1:12 looks like an introduction and while 1:12–2:3 is full of key words, expressions and themes that appear in the book as a whole, these are largely absent from 1:4–11. The style of the poem is also quite different from the rest of the book, as is the case for the poem on old age and death in 12:1–7.[48] (Of course it may well be significant

---

46. Although there is some debate about where the poem starts: some commentators take vv. 3–11 together (e.g. A. B. Caneday, "Qoheleth: Enigmatic Pessimist or Godly Sage?," *GTJ* 7 [1986]: 21–56 [34]; Robert Davidson, *Ecclesiastes and the Song of Solomon* [The Daily Study Bible; Louisville, Ky.: Westminster John Knox, 1986], 10–12; Fox, *A Time to Tear Down*, 163–69; Garrett, *Proverbs, Ecclesiastes, Song of Songs*, 284–88; Murphy and Huwiler, *Proverbs, Ecclesiastes, Song of Songs*, 180; Murphy, *Ecclesiastes*, 5–10; A. Schoors, "La structure litteraire de Qoheleth," *Orientalia Lovaniensia Analecta* 13 [1982]: 91–116; Tamez, *When the Horizons Close*, 35–37), others vv. 2–11 (e.g. Dianne Bergant, *Job, Ecclesiastes* [Old Testament Message 18; Wilmington, Del.: Michael Glazier, 1982], 231; Brown, *Ecclesiastes*, 212–18; Michael A. Eaton, *Ecclesiastes* [TOTC; Leicester: InterVarsity, 1983], 50; Loader, *Ecclesiastes*, 19; Longman, *The Book of Ecclesiastes*, 58–59; A. G. Wright, "Additional Numerical Patterns in Qoheleth," *CBQ* 45 [1983]: 32–43 [34]) and some treat the whole of 1:1–11 as a unit (e.g. Ellul, *Reason for Being*, 38; H. C. Leupold, *Exposition of Ecclesiastes* [Grand Rapids: Baker Book House, 1952], 25). Seow treats 1:2–11 as: thematic statement (v. 2) + poem (vv. 3–8) + prose commentary (vv. 9–11) (*Ecclesiastes*, 111–17).

47. Salyer, *Vain Rhetoric*, 262.

48. So, for example, while Qohelet's words are presented in the first person (a point that is discussed in some depth by Christianson (*A Time to Tell*), Mills

that within the *inclusio* formed by 1:2 and 12:8, the book begins and
ends with poems whose language is markedly different from what comes
in between—we start with a poem about cycles in nature and in the
human realm, and end with a poem about a cataclysmic [apocalyptic-
type?] disaster that strikes nature and humanity.[49]) The question then
arises whether 1:4–11 should be read as the words of Qohelet, or of the
frame narrator. Thus, for example, Christianson states, "the introductory
passage of 1:3–11 (although its narrative form is, on the surface, impersonal) *can only be* the words of Qoheleth that were just introduced,"[50]
while Longman maintains, "Two textual signals *make it certain* that we
are not hearing Qohelet's voice yet."[51] Salyer acknowledges that "the text
is somewhat vague as to who exactly is speaking here, the frame-narrator
or Qoheleth," and concludes, "Perhaps we should designate this as an
example of ambiguous narration."[52]

2.2.2. *Interpretation of the Passage as a Whole*

Fox represents many commentators when he writes of 1:4–11, "This
poem characterizes nature as an endless round of pointless movement, a

---

(*Reading Ecclesiastes*) and Salyer (*Vain Rhetoric*)—but, perhaps surprisingly, not
picked up in Philip R. Davies, ed., *First Person: Essays in Biblical Autobiography*
[The Biblical Seminar 81; London: Sheffield Academic Press, 2002]), the poems in
1:4–11 and 12:1–7 use no first person terms at all.

49. Thus, for example, Brown writes: "Qoheleth's own discourse is framed by
1:2–11 and 12:1–8. The former opens with the sage's thesis statement regarding the
pervasiveness of 'vanity,' and the latter concludes almost verbatim (1:2; 12:8). The
former offers a comprehensive picture of cosmic weariness and repetition that is also
reflected in the course of human affairs, a cosmology without creation. The climax
of the sage's reflections concludes with a no less encompassing picture of death's
encroachment upon the living, extinguishing even the celestial lights (12:2), a creation without continuance. *The heart of Qoheleth's message is, thus bracketed by
cosmos and extinction*, by weariness and death" (*Ecclesiastes*, 15, my emphasis).
Fredericks refers to "the three main poems in his speech, 1:4–11, 3:1–8, 12:2–7," of
which he says, "Each deals with transience and cyclicity" (*Coping with Transience*,
24).

50. Christianson, *A Time to Tell*, 46, my emphasis. This is the view of the majority of commentators.

51. Longman, *The Book of Ecclesiastes*, 58, my emphasis. Longman explains:
"The first is the appearance of 'Qohelet said' in v. 2. . . . Second, and perhaps more
importantly, 1:12 bears a likeness to the opening phrase found in the genre of
Akkadian autobiography. . . . Only after that verse may we be certain that Qohelet
himself is speaking" (pp. 58–59). Ogden and Zogbo simply say, "Whether it is a
poem he has written himself or one he is quoting is difficult to answer" (*A Handbook*, 25).

52. Salyer, *Vain Rhetoric*, 263.

rhythm that engulfs human generations as well,"[53] but Lohfink presents the contrary view, arguing:

> The greatest difficulty for modern readers of this poem is that our spon-
> taneous reaction, in the face of its continuous assertion of the eternal
> return of the same, is to judge that this is a negative and depressing
> message. If we cannot break free of this prejudice, then we simply miss
> the entry point into the poem. The poem praises the cosmos as glorious
> and eternal in this image of cyclic return.

Earlier in his commentary, Lohfink commented, "This image of an eternal cycle structuring the cosmos is not, as almost all commentators suggest, an image of despair, but rather it is completely positive."[54]

Perhaps, then, Murphy is right to assert that "The understanding of this passage depends in large part on the general construal placed upon verses and groups of verses within it, and indeed on the construal of the entire book."[55] I have considered "the construal of the entire book" above, now I will look briefly at those parts of this particular passage that engender ambiguity.

The passage is ambiguous at the beginning, in the centre and at the end. The ambiguity at the beginning and end is similar: the word דור in v. 4 might refer either to human generations or to natural eras,[56] while ראשנים[57] and אחרנים[58] in v. 11 could refer either to people past and future or to things or times past and future. הדברים in v. 8, at the centre of this section, ties in with this ambiguity because it could be translated "things," referring back to the cycles in nature described in vv. 4–7, or "words," indicating the human response to what is described in the earlier verses.

---

53. Fox, *Ecclesiastes*, 61. Brown states: "Activity abounds; everything is in perpetual motion, like a hamster in a wheel, but no destination is reached. This display
of endless cosmic exertion is all for naught. . . . The perdurability of creation amounts
to nothing; it simply reflects the static nature of a creation forever locked in the same
wearying courses." Brown contrasts the view of creation in Ecclesiastes and Pss 19
and 104, arguing that "For the sage, 'the heavens are telling' only the absurdity of
life" (*Ecclesiastes*, 23–25).

54. Lohfink, *Qoheleth*, 40, 14. Provan reads in this poem, "a threefold response
of human wonder to the threefold exposition of creation's workings. . . . Creation is
a vast and intricate reality, which escapes the grasp of human beings in speech, sight,
and hearing; we are unable to find the words for it, and all our looking at it and listening to it cannot comprehend it" (*Ecclesiastes, Song of Songs*, 55).

55. Murphy, *Ecclesiastes*, 9. Ogden and Zogbo are non-committal in this
instance: "Qoheleth points to the circular motion and flow in nature, and *he wonders*
about people and their place in such a world" (*A Handbook*, 25, my emphasis).

56. See D. N. Freedman and J. Lundbom, "דור, *dôr*," *TDOT* 3:169–81 (174).

57. See BDB, 911b.

58. See BDB, 30b–31a.

2.2.3. *Ecclesiastes 1:4*

Crenshaw explains the issue in relation to דּוֹר in this way:

> The word *dor*, an appropriate choice because of its ambiguity, suggests both nature and people. The primary sense here is probably the former: the generations of natural phenomena. But the other nuance must also be present, lending immense irony to the observation that the stage on which the human drama is played outlasts the actors themselves.[59]

Many commentators acknowledge this ambiguity but most choose the latter sense of the word. דּוֹר is a common word in the Hebrew Bible where both senses appear often, but it is used only in 1:4 in Ecclesiastes so that there are no other occurrences in the book with which to compare it. However, as 1:3 is about humanity, the most obvious progression might be to view דּוֹר as a reference to human generations, contrasting their constant changing with the durability of the earth. This may be the reader's first impression, but as we read on we discover that vv. 4–7 address the cyclical nature of the four ancient elements of the universe: earth, wind, fire (sun) and water. In view of this, דּוֹר . . . וְדוֹר might be understood to refer to the cycles of nature in contrast with the steadfastness of the earth on which these cycles take place.[60] This ties in well with what may be the original meaning of the root, "moving in a circle."[61] It is also possible that no contrast is intended, that the *waw* should be read as "and" rather than "but" to express the constancy לְעוֹלָם of these cycles that take place on the earth. After discussing the various possibilities for interpretation of this verse, Longman simply states, "It is difficult, if not impossible, to adjudicate these issues."[62] Perhaps the best solution is to acknowledge the ambiguity of the word and see it as a link between the human element in v. 3, and again in vv. 8–11, and the natural elements in vv. 4–7.[63]

The terms הלך and בא also contribute to this ambiguity. The reader may connect them with the cycles of nature, or read them as euphemisms

---

59. Crenshaw, *Ecclesiastes*, 62. Longman says: "James Crenshaw is probably correct in saying that *dôr* has both human and natural cycles in mind. It is impossible to be dogmatic one way or the other" (*The Book of Ecclesiastes*, 68).

60. See especially G. S. Ogden, "The Interpretation of *dôr* in Ecclesiastes 1:4," *JSOT* 34 (1986): 91–92.

61. See BDB, 189; *DCH* 2:428–30 (428); and Freedman and Lundbom, *TDOT* 3:169. However, Gerleman states that "Opinions regarding etymology are divided, esp. concerning whether *dôr* is associated with the 'circle' concept" (G. Gerleman, "דּוֹר, *dôr* generation," *TLOT* 2:333–35 [333]).

62. Longman, *The Book of Ecclesiastes*, 67.

63. See further the discussion in Fox, "Qohelet 1:4"; Ogden, "The Interpretation of *dôr*"; and Whybray, "Ecclesiastes 1:5–7."

for death and birth as appears to be the case in 5:14–15 (Eng. 5:15–16) and 6:4:[64]

5:14 כאשר יצא מבטן אמו ערום ישוב ללכת כשבא ומאומה לא־ישא בעמלו
שילך בידו:

5:15 וגם־זה רעה חולה כל־עמת שבא כן ילך ומה־יתרון לו שיעמל לרוח:

6:4 כי־בהבל בא ובחשך ילך ובחשך שמו יכסה:

In 1:4 they are used in reverse order and could convey the sense of one generation dying and another being born to take its place and thus continue the cycle of generations. In this case ודור בא might be read, "*but* a(nother) generation is born."

The ambiguity is maintained by the word הארץ which usually refers to the physical earth,[65] but may also, by extension, indicate the people of the earth, that is, humanity.[66] Thus Fox, arguing against the majority of commentators, says, "The key to understanding this verse lies in recognizing that *haʾareṣ* here does not mean the physical earth, but humanity as a whole—'le monde' rather than 'la terre.'"[67] Elsewhere Fox maintains that "There is no other way in biblical Hebrew to express the concept of humanity as a unit; בני אדם signifies people as individuals."[68] ארץ is used thirteen times in Ecclesiastes, and only eight of these clearly refer to the physical earth.[69] Of the remaining five, 5:8 (Eng. 5:9) is a difficult verse to interpret, but the translation "humanity" makes at least as good sense of the verse as does "earth"; in 7:20 "humanity" would also fit the context well, especially in consideration of the prefixed ב rather than על; 10:16–17 seem to refer to the people of the land; which leaves the verse we are considering here.

Ambiguity also enshrouds the following word, לעולם. This word occurs only in the nominal form in the Old Testament[70] and appears well

---

64. הלך (e.g. in Ps 39:14; Job 10:21; 14:26) and בא (e.g. in Ps 71:18) do occur elsewhere as euphemisms for death and birth, but not together. See BDB, 234a, 98a. Ironically, both words can also mean the opposite!

65. Good suggests that it might also mean "underworld" ("The Unfilled Sea," 64). Cf. Magnus Ottosson, "ארץ, *ʾerets*," *TDOT* 1:388–405 (399–400).

66. See BDB, 76a; *DCH* 1:392a.

67. Fox, *A Time to Tear Down*, 166. He adds: "Good examples of this usage are Gen 11:1; 1 Kgs 2:2; and Ps 33:8."

68. Fox, "Qohelet 1:4," *JSOT* 40 (1988): 109.

69. See 3:21; 5:1 (Eng. 5:2); 8:14, 16; 10:7; 11:2, 3; 12:7.

70. Though BDB lists another two roots, one of which appears as a verb meaning "to conceal." It is debated whether or not this latter root ("conceal") is used in Eccl 3:11: Whitley argues that it is this root (Charles F. Whitley, *Koheleth: His Language and Thought* [BZAW 148; Berlin: de Gruyter, 1979], 32–33), and G. Barton maintains that "The context *compels* us to render it 'ignorance,'" which he derives from the root meaning "conceal" (*Ecclesiastes*, 105–6). נעלם in 12:14 is from this root.

over four hundred times. Its meaning is well established as a long period of time either in the past or in the future.[71] Thus it is used of ancient time,[72] ancient people,[73] ancient gates,[74] the long dead,[75] and so on, as well as indefinite futurity in phrases such as עבד עולם,[76] עד לעולם,[77] עולם אשירה[78] and הודה לעולם.[79] But a problem arises in trying to assess whether the word can bear the sense of the eternal, of something beyond our conception of time.[80] Certainly the majority of its occurrences are in connection with some aspect of God's character or of his dealings with his people. For example, it is used of divine existence,[81] of many others of God's attributes,[82] of his covenant,[83] of his promises,[84] of the Messianic dynasty,[85] and of the relationship between God and his people.[86] However, commentators are divided over whether or not these occurrences convey the notion of "the eternal."[87] Ogden, for example, suggests that עולם in Ecclesiastes "accord[s] with the general Old Testament usage, that is as a reference to the "eternal" dimension."[88] On the other hand, Whybray asserts that "*ʿolam* does not mean 'eternity'" because this

---

71. See BDB, 761b–62a, and H. D. Preuss, "עוֹלָם, *ʿôlam*; עָלַם, *ʿālam*," *TDOT* 10:530–45.

72. E.g. Isa 63:11; Amos 9:11; Mic 5:1; 7:14; Mal 3:4.

73. E.g. Isa 44:7; Jer 5:15.

74. E.g. Jer 6:16; Ps 24:7, 9; Job 22:15.

75. E.g. Ezek 26:29; Ps 143:3; Lam 3:6.

76. Deut 15:17; 1 Sam 27:12; Job 40:28.

77. Exod 21:6; Lev 25:46.

78. Ps 89:2; cf. Pss 52:10; 115:18; 145:1, 2.

79. Pss 30:13; 44:9; 52:11; 79:13.

80. See, e.g., J. Barr, *Biblical Words for Time* (London: SCM Press, 1962), 82–104.

81. E.g. Gen 21:33; Deut 32:40; Isa 40:28.

82. E.g. אהבה, Jer 31:3, etc.; חסד, Isa 54:8, etc.; כבוד, Ps 104:31; אמת, Ps 117:2, etc.; צדק, Ps 119:142; עצה, Ps 33:11.

83. E.g. Gen 9:16; Exod 31:16; Isa 24:5, etc.

84. E.g. 2 Sam 7:13; Isa 40:8; Ps 133:3, etc.

85. Isa 9:6; Pss 45:7; 110:4, etc. Of course it is a moot point whether these and other such verses refer to some kind of divinely instituted figure, or to a purely human institution.

86. E.g. Isa 57:16; Ps 45:18; 1 Chr 29:18, etc.

87. Thus Jenni argues, "The Eng. Translation 'eternity' used in the heading is inappropriate for a number of Old Testament passages with *ʿôlām*, and, even when it seems appropriate, it may not be permitted to introduce a preconceived concept of eternity, burdened with all manner of later philosophical or theological content" (Ernst Jenni, "עוֹלָם, *ʿôlam*, eternity," *TLOT* 2:852–62 (853). See also Anthony Tomasino, "עוֹלָם," *NIDOTTE* 3:345–51 (346).

88. Ogden, *Qoheleth*, 55.

is "a concept foreign to Old Testament thought and certainly to that of Qoheleth."[89] This is too big an issue to address in depth here, so I will focus on its occurrences in Ecclesiastes in particular.

עולם occurs seven times in this book (not including נעלם in 12:14, which is from a different root). Here in 1:4 it may accord with the meaning we discussed above of indefinite existence in the future—whether "eternal" or not. This is also the sense in 2:16. In 1:10 the notion is of a long period of time in the past. 3:14 accords with the majority of occurrences in the Old Testament in referring to activities of God enduring לעולם, whether that means for the indefinite future or for eternity. 9:6 and 12:5 are particularly noteworthy because they refer to what happens (12:5) and what does not happen (9:6) after death, although this too could presumably refer to either the indefinite future or eternity.[90] There is considerable debate over the precise meaning (or necessary emendation) of עולם in 3:11. In short, the sense of the word, and the possibilities for disagreement over its meaning, in the Old Testament in general, appear also in Ecclesiastes.

2.2.4. *Ecclesiastes 1:5–7*

The main question in relation to vv. 5–7 is whether these three verses are to be read negatively, indicating the monotony of these endless cycles in nature, or positively, as a description of the constancy or reliability of nature. Crenshaw writes of these verses, "This poem characterizes nature as an endless round of pointless movement,"[91] but Whybray states, "These examples are *not* intended to show the futility of these phenomena, but only their regularity . . . the reader is implicitly invited to regard their activity with wonder and admiration."[92] Taken in isolation, they could be read either way since there is no clear indication within them of how they are to be interpreted—they are in fact quite neutral. Fox implicitly acknowledges this when he argues, "*After reading 1:2*, 1:4–7 cannot be a celebration of the glorious stability of the natural order."[93] However, the difficulty here is the ambiguity of the term הבל: What is it that we are

---

89. Whybray, *Ecclesiastes*, 40.

90. Of particular interest in this respect is Dan 12:2–3 which reads:

ורבים מישני אדמת־עפר יקיצו
אלה לחיי עולם ואלה לחרפות לדראון עולם: ס
והמשכלים יזהרו כזהר הרקיע
ומצדיקי הרבים ככוכבים לעולם ועד: פ

91. Crenshaw, *Ecclesiastes*, 61.

92. R. N. Whybray, "Ecclesiastes 1:5–7 and the Wonders of Nature," *JSOT* 41 (1988): 105–12 (105), my emphasis.

93. Fox, *A Time to Tear Down*, 163, my emphasis.

looking for in these natural processes? If הבל means "breathlike" or "ephemeral" it would actually form a sharp contrast with the endlessly repeating cycles of nature. Does this mean, then, that some such interpretation of הבל as "absurd" or "futile" should be adopted instead? Not necessarily, as the author may intentionally have followed 1:2 with these verses so as to raise the question in the reader's mind: If the cycles of nature are so constant, what does it mean to say that "all is *hebel*"? Besides, it is not at all clear that it makes any more sense to say that these natural cycles are absurd or futile than it does to say that they are ephemeral.

The word שואף illustrates well the ambiguity of 1:5–7.[94] It occurs only here in Ecclesiastes, and the root from which it derives is used on only seven other occasions in the Old Testament. Of these seven, two[95] suggest panting from weariness, and five[96] panting with desire.[97] Either could apply here, giving a negative or positive reading of the verse. Crenshaw reads the word in the first way: "Instead of picturing a vigorous champion who easily makes the daily round, he thinks of strenuous panting to reach the destination. Having arrived, an exhausted sun must undertake the whole ordeal again."[98] By contrast, Whybray opts for the second: "The positive sense is the more appropriate here: the sun pants eagerly towards its next appearance."[99] Perhaps it would be best to agree with Ogden on this point when he says,

> Whether this movement is wearying or bears a sense of eagerness and longing is not a question to be settled unequivocally, as "panting" is used in both senses in the Old Testament (cf Ps 56:2; Isa 42:14). Unfortunately our text leaves us without clear guidance as to which view approximates

94. But *BHS* suggests that שואף should probably be read שב אף. On a literary level this seems to make good sense. If it is combined with the other emendation of this verse suggested by *BHS*, deletion of the last three words, the verse would be nicely balanced, would retain the sense of circularity, and would follow on well from v. 4. However, it has no textual support, and שואף is in keeping with the author's use of words which allow for different nuances.

95. Isa 42:14; Jer 14:6.

96. Jer 2:24; Ps 119:131; Job 5:5; 7:2; 36:20.

97. See BDB, 983b. BDB places Eccl 1:5 in the "weariness" category; by contrast Fredericks says, "Even the sun pants with anticipation to return from whence it came" (D. C. Fredericks, "שאף," *NIDOTTE* 6:11).

98. Crenshaw, *Ecclesiastes*, 63. Brown says, "in Qoheleth's eyes, the sun gasps for breath from its enervating circuits" (*Ecclesiastes*, 24).

99. Whybray, *Ecclesiastes*, 41. Provan writes, "The sun rises and sets as it always has, only to 'hurry' (lit. 'gasp, pant,' in its eagerness and speed to fulfill its mission) back to its starting point and rise once again in the new morning" (*Ecclesiastes, Song of Songs*, 55).

to Qoheleth's. Only for those who, for other reasons, adopt the view that Qoheleth's basic position is a pessimistic one, is it clear that the sun grows weary of this constant round.[100]

And, presumably, the same argument holds true for an optimistic reading. The *zaqeph* cantillation over מְקוֹמוֹ in the Masoretic text does nothing to aid interpretation, and in fact it is the first of a number in Ecclesiastes which seem to occur at inappropriate points in the verse.

2.2.5. *Ecclesiastes 1:8*

Verse 8 is a key verse in terms of negative or positive readings of 1:4–7.[101] The way this verse is understood will have a major bearing on the interpretation of the earlier verses—but it is far from clear how it is to be read.[102] The difficulties start with the word הדברים. In the light of the preceding verses, כל־הדברים might be read as referring to the cycles of nature and translated as "all things."[103] But the recurrence of the root דבר a few words later with the sense of "speak" serves to cast doubt on this initial understanding. Does הדברים relate back to the "things" described in the earlier verses, or does it relate to the "words" that a man is unable to speak? The commentators are divided on the issue, with Whybray, for example, contending that we should read "things,"[104] while Fox argues for the translation "words."[105] Precisely the same issue arises over the singular דבר in v. 10, which also precedes a verb connected with speaking, אמר. Perhaps in both cases the word is intended to be ambiguous. In v. 8 this would allow it to serve as a link between the cycles of nature

100. Ogden, *Qoheleth*, 31. Ogden and Zogbo assert, "Whether the poet thinks that the sun actually grows weary from all this activity, or whether it is 'panting' with eagerness, becomes a matter for interpretation" (*A Handbook*, 28). Similarly, Longman states, "Context and the overall message of the book will determine one's understanding" (*The Book of Ecclesiastes*, 69). This accords with the fourth of Rimmon's conditions for establishing ambiguity: "an ambiguous expression calls for choice between its alternative meanings, but at the same time provides no ground for making the choice" (*The Concept of Ambiguity*, 17).

101. Thus, for example, Longman argues: "This verse is pivotal in establishing the pessimistic tone of this section of the text" (*The Book of Ecclesiastes*, 71).

102. Rudman observes: "there is considerable ambiguity evident in the MT of v. 8a . . . and this has led to widely differing translations and interpretations by modern commentators. . . . The general confusion of latter-day exegetes is mirrored by that of the Versions" (*Determinism*, 80).

103. For discussion of the meaning of דבר, see, for example, BDB, 180–84; Frank Ritchel Ames, "דבר," *NIDOTTE* 1:912–15; G. Gerleman, "דָּבָר, *dābār*, word," *TLOT* 1:325–32; W. H. Schmidt, "דָּבַר, *dābhar*," *TDOT* 3:84–125; *DCH* 2:397–411.

104. Whybray, *Ecclesiastes*, 44.

105. Fox, *Qohelet*, 171.

described in 1:5–7 (or 1:4–7), and the human sphere which is the focus of the rest of v. 8 and perhaps also vv. 9–11.

The word יְגֵעִים also raises difficulties. The root occurs twice more in Ecclesiastes (10:15; 12:12) and another 45 times elsewhere in the Hebrew Bible. However, only three times does it occur as an adjective,[106] if indeed the word is an adjective in this verse—it could also be a participle.[107] The root bears the meaning "toil, grow or be weary,"[108] and it is usually the latter sense which is understood here, the sense the root also bears in 10:15 and 12:12. Thus it might be rendered "weary" or "wearied" or perhaps "wearying"[109] or possibly by extension (though there appears not to be a biblical precedent) "wearisome."[110] However, some commentators argue that the sense of toil or hard work is what is being considered here. For example, Whybray says, "In the present context it makes good sense to take the phrase 'All things are *yege ʿim*' as referring to the ceaseless 'toil' or busy activity of the natural phenomena."[111] In this case the word here might be rendered "hard-working" or perhaps "busy." There are, then, a number of possible translations of the first clause of this verse:

All things are weary[112]
All things are wearying

106. Here in Eccl 1:8, and Deut 25:18; 2 Sam 17:2.

107. Ogden argues against the majority (see also Seow, *Ecclesiastes*, 109) when he asserts that it is more likely here to be a participle than an adjective (*Qoheleth*, 32).

108. BDB, 388.

109. Thompson argues, "In Eccl 1:8 *yāgēaʿ* modifies all things (NIV, preferable to NAB, all speech), not describing all things themselves as weary, but rather naming the tiring effect of the unchanging cosmos" (David L. Thompson, "יגע," *NIDOTTE* 2:400–402 [401]). By contrast, Rudman states, "There is no evidence of which I am aware, either in biblical or postbiblical Hebrew, that the adjective can express the idea of *causing* weariness" (*Determinism*, 81, his emphasis).

110. Whybray (*Ecclesiastes*, 39) argues that "wearisome" is an inappropriate translation here (see also Provan, *Ecclesiastes, Song of Songs*, 54–55). This correlates with Hasel's assertion that "The basic verbal meaning of the root *ygʿ* may properly be defined as 'be/become weary' in the objective sense of bodily fatigue, e.g., 'be/become weak, weary, exhausted,' rather than in the subjective psychological sense of 'be/become weary of something.'" He continues, "The statement in Eccl 1:8a can be translated literally: 'All words are wearying.' The active aspect of *yāgēaʿ* thus indicates that it is not the words that are weary; they 'weary' those who speak and hear them" (G. F. Hasel, "יגע," *TDOT* 5:385–93 [388–89]). However, Seow argues that "the distinction 'weary' (being worn out) and 'wearisome' is one made in English, not Hebrew" (*Ecclesiastes*, 109).

111. Whybray, *Ecclesiastes*, 39.

112. So, e.g., Garrett, *Proverbs, Ecclesiastes, Song of Songs*, 287. According to Perry, Kohelet states, "All things are weary," and the Presenter replies, "things that a person cannot say!" (*Dialogues with Kohelet*, 58).

All things are wearisome[113]
All things are busy[114]
All words are weary[115]
All words are wearying[116]
All words are wearisome[117]

It makes a considerable difference to the sense of the verse which of these is chosen.[118]

The next clause of 1:8 also causes problems. Its translation is clear enough, but what its relevance is in the context is much less clear. It seems to link in with the second half of the verse because of its similarity in structure and content:

איש לדבר   לא־יוכל
עין לראות   לא־תשבע
אזן משמע   ולא־תמלא

113. So, for example, Murphy, though he concedes, "The meaning of יגעים, 'wearisome,' is not assured" (*Ecclesiastes*, 5–6). Longman translates, "All things are wearisome beyond words," explaining: "Literally, *beyond words* is 'a man is not able to say.' The sense of the statement is that the weariness of all things is so mind-boggling that it exceeds human ability to describe it" (*The Book of Ecclesiastes*, 60, 71).

114. Provan argues: "Certainly a statement that 'all things are hard at work' fits the context much better as a summary of verses 4–7 than the statement 'all things are weary'" (*Ecclesiastes, Song of Songs*, 55). Lohfink translates: "All things are constantly restless" (*Qoheleth*, 39); Hubbard suggests, "All things are full of labor" (*Ecclesiastes, Song of Solomon*, 48, 51).

115. Fox translates: "Words are all weary," arguing that "The *debarim* that are weary are not the 'things' mentioned—the world, sun, wind, and rivers. *Dabar* is nowhere used of physical entities. Rather, it is *words* that are weary, too feeble to communicate. These are Qohelet's words, of course, and he is weary. Repetition and routine wear one down" (*A Time to Tear Down*, 163, 167).

116. Seow translates: "All words are wearying," arguing, "in every instance through the rest of Ecclesiastes, *dĕbārîm* (5:2; 6:11; 7:21; 10:14) and *dibrê* (1:1; 9:17; 10:12,13; 12:10 [×2],11; cf. 5:1; 9:16) always mean 'words.' The meaning 'words' is confirmed by the parallel line that has *lĕdabbēr* 'to speak' (v 8b) and the association with the activities of the eye and the ear (v 8c)" (*Ecclesiastes*, 109).

117. Loader explains the line thus: "All human words are wearisome—just wearisome" (*Ecclesiastes*, 21). Brown writes: "The NRSV translation 'all things' in verse 8 can also mean 'all words.' As 'all things are wearisome,' from the cosmic to the mundane . . . so all language remains inadequate to express the ineffable, namely, experience itself. However, plentiful, words only add to the weight of weariness" (*Ecclesiastes*, 25).

118. Ogden, for example, says: "The thought expressed in this verse by *yegēʿîm*, translated 'weariness,' is for many commentators that which brings to the poem its tired and negative attitude towards the cycles within nature. We need to clarify its meaning, for apart from *yegēʿîm*, the text gives no other reason for adopting such a negative view" (*Qoheleth*, 31–32).

But it is no easier to determine precisely what the last two clauses of the verse refer to, and whether they are a negative or a positive judgment. It may be that the first part of the verse is a negative conclusion to the preceding verses: because of the endless drudgery of the cycles in nature everything is weary. In this case these three phrases might link this weariness to the human sphere: people are too weary to be able to speak and they achieve no satisfaction no matter how much they see and hear. On the other hand, the first phrase may be neutral, describing the busyness of nature as portrayed in the earlier verses. In this case the following three phrases might be paraphrased: "speech cannot capture it all, nor can the eye see it all, or the ear hear it all." A third option is to see the first two clauses of the verse as more closely linked to each other: "all words are weary so that a man cannot speak." This might be read negatively to mean that even speech is weary or wearisome, or positively to mean that there is so much activity that speech wearies in the telling and still fails to express it all.

The matter is further complicated by the inappropriateness of each clause. The first clause is, strictly speaking, untrue: people are able to speak, and, moreover, the first half of v. 10 relates words which have been spoken. שׂבע is an unusual verb to use in connection with the sight of the eye because it refers to one's literal appetite for food, or to other "appetites" which people seek to satisfy: it is in this latter sense that the root is used in connection with the eye again in 4:8. It is perhaps noteworthy that שׂבע occasionally seems to bear the sense of being wearied by something,[119] but nowhere else does it take the preposition ל.[120] מלא is also an unusual verb to use with reference to the ear because the ear cannot actually be "filled" with what it hears. Of course, this is all metaphorical language which, by its nature, involves a degree of ambiguity. However, in this context I believe the ambiguity of the individual words and expressions is used to good effect in order to create an ambiguous passage.

If the three human senses referred to in this verse balance the three natural elements described in the preceding verses, it seems probable that something similar is being asserted about the senses to what is said in vv. 5–7 about the natural elements. Whatever the implications, these earlier verses indicate the endless repetition in nature: the sun never stops rising and setting; the wind never stops changing its direction; the rivers never stop flowing into the sea, which in turn never fills up. To take the

---

119. Cf. Isa 1:11; Hab. 2:16; Ps 123:3, 4; Job 7:4; Prov 28:19.
120. It takes מן- in Eccl 6:3 and in Isa 66:11; Ezek 32:4; Ps 104:13; Job 19:22; Prov 14:14.

last first, because the word מלא is used both of the sea and the ear, the implication may be that just as water constantly flows into the sea but never fills it, so sounds constantly flow into the ear but it is always ready to hear more—or it is never satisfied with what it does hear.[121] The previous clause might then indicate that as the wind moves round and round but is always ready to blow, so the eye is always on the move but its ability to see is never exhausted—or it is never content with what it sees. The word שואף in relation to the sun in v. 5 is then highly appropriate because panting is of course associated with the mouth which also produces words. Moreover, if the mouth is panting, be it from exhaustion or from eagerness, its ability to produce words would be greatly reduced —but is it excitement[122] or drudgery[123] it wants to express?

Alternatively, the two halves of this section may be antithetical: the sun, the wind and the rivers carry on their proper roles in perpetuity, but a man (*sic*) wants more. He is fed up with talking, seeing and hearing, and wants something new. However, nature indicates that there is nothing new. Moreover, while people come and go, the earth stands forever. This antithesis comes out most clearly in the contrast between the earth in v. 4 and the people who are not remembered in v. 11: the earth continues forever, but generations of people come and go and those who come after bear no memory of those who went before.

2.2.6. *Ecclesiastes 1:11*

This assumes, of course, that v. 11 refers to people. But just as דור and הארץ in v. 4 are ambiguous, so too are ראשנים and אחרנים in v. 11, because they could refer either to former and later "generations" or to former and later "things" or "times." Again the commentators are divided on the issues, with Fox, for example, arguing for "things" (or "events"),[124]

121. So, e.g., Brown, *Ecclesiastes*, 26.

122. Provan makes reference to "a threefold response of human wonder to the threefold exposition of creation's workings in verses 5–7" (*Ecclesiastes, Song of Songs*, 55).

123. Brown argues: "As the eye and ear cannot get enough, so the mouth cannot spew out enough, unable to communicate anything of lasting value, let alone anything new" (*Ecclesiastes*, 26). Rudman interprets in line with his deterministic reading of Ecclesiastes: "Just as the human generations, sun, wind and rivers follow a path that is set for them, and from which they cannot deviate, so human action is tightly circumscribed by the deity" (*Determinism*, 74).

124. Fox, *Qohelet*, 173. In *A Time to Tear Down*, Fox specifically disagrees with Crenshaw, "*Rišonim* and *ʾaḥăronim* refer not to earlier and later generations (as Crenshaw says), but to earlier and later events, since the issue in this passage is not whether people are remembered but whether events are" (p. 169).

while Crenshaw reads the verse as a reference to "generations."[125] The issue is often decided by reference to the fact that the usual impersonal form is the feminine plural,[126] which would suggest that the masculine here refers to people.[127] Even if Ecclesiastes could be depended upon for adherence to grammatical norms (and the singular היה associated with the plural עלמים in v. 10 is just one of many grammatical anomalies in the book[128]), this would not be decisive. Both singular[129] and plural,[130] definite and indefinite, of אחרון and ראשׁון are used with reference to people and to things or periods of time. While it is true that the closest parallels, where ראשׁונים[131] and אחרונים[132] are used without any accompanying noun, refer to people, it would be grammatically correct to render the words either as "those people who" or "those things which" came before and will come after. Moreover, it is possible on the one hand that the sense of "ages" past and present carries over from עלמים in the previous verse; or on the other hand that, in the light of 1:4, an allusion is being made to the expression דור אחרון, which occurs a number of times in Psalms, with the clear meaning "former *generation*,"[133] and the parallel expression דור ראשׁון in Job 8:8. Of course, this might serve to compound the ambiguity rather than help to resolve it.

There may also be an allusion to the use of אחרון and ראשׁון in Second and Third Isaiah, referring usually to former and latter *things*, but also to people and to God.[134] If this is the case, it adds a certain touch of irony to

---

125. Fox, *Ecclesiastes*, 68. See also, e.g., Seow, *Ecclesiastes*, 111. Whybray reckons the issue unimportant: "these phrases could equally well be rendered 'former/later men [*sic*]' or 'former/later ages'; the general point is unaffected" (*Ecclesiastes*, 46).

126. See, e.g., Isa 42:9; 43:9, 18; 46:9.

127. See, e.g., Gen 33:2; Lev 26:45; Deut 19:14; Ps 79:8; Job 18:20. This is the line taken, for example, by Ogden and Zogbo (*A Handbook*, 36).

128. Subject and verb seem not to agree in number in 1:10, 16; 2:7, 9; 10:1, 12; and not to agree in gender in 7:7; 10:15.

129. Compare, e.g., Prov 31:25 and Neh 8:18 with Ps 48:14 and Deut 29:21; and Job 8:8 and Gen 40:13 with 2 Sam 19:21 and Num 21:26.

130. Compare, e.g., Isa 41:4 with 2 Chr 9:29; and Ps 79:8 with Deut 4:32.

131. Lev 26:45; Deut 19:14; Ps 79:8.

132. Isa 41:4 and possibly Job 18:20.

133. Pss 48:14; 78:4, 6; 102:19. See also Deut 29:21.

134. Isa 41:4, 22, 27; 42:9; 43:9, 18, 27; 44:6–7; 46:9; 48:3; 61:4; 65:16, 17. The discussion of former and latter things is an important element in the way Clements and Childs treat Isaiah. See, e.g., R. E. Clements, "Beyond Tradition-History," *JSOT* 31 (1985): 95–113, and B. S. Childs, *Introduction to the Old Testament as Scripture* (London: SCM Press, 1979), 311–38. See in more detail, Benjamin D. Sommer, *A Prophet Reads Scripture: Allusion in Isaiah 40–66* (Stanford, Calif.: Stanford

Eccl 1:4–11 because several times in Isaiah Yahweh declares that he will
do a new thing,[135] while Eccl 1:9–10 clearly states that there is nothing
new (at least not "under the sun"). There is also an emphasis in Second
Isaiah on remembering the former things, but Third Isaiah declares,

> . . . the former troubles are forgotten
> and hid from my eyes.
> For behold, I create new heavens and a new earth;
> and the former things shall not be remembered
> or come to mind. (Isa 65:16–17[136])

2.3. *Ambiguity in Ecclesiastes 1:1–11*

The ambiguity of Eccl 1:4–11 operates on a number of levels:

(1) First, there is the question whether דור and הארץ in v. 4, and
הראשנים and האחרנים in v. 11 refer to people or things/eras in nature.
This means that the passage is enclosed by ambiguity. A related question
concerns the translation of הדברים in v. 8: does it indicate "things" in
nature or human "words," presumably the words referring in some way
to the cycles of nature described in the first half of the passage. This
means that there is also ambiguity at the centre of the passage. The
ambiguity at this level is a literary device which enables a particularly
close connection between the description of nature in vv. 4–7 and the
human realm which is the subject of vv. 8–11: the two halves merge into
each other at the centre, and the beginning and end of the passage use
terms which have a double meaning allowing them to relate to *both*
humanity and to the cycles of nature. In terms of interpretation, therefore,
there is no need to choose one or other sense of these words, but rather
their plurivocity should be acknowledged, and allowed to resonate
throughout the passage. Translation, of course, is another matter.

(2) The second level of ambiguity relates to the connection between
the two halves of the section: What is the human response in the second
half to the repetition and circularity portrayed in the first half? Two
diametrically opposed interpretations can be sustained, dependent largely
on how v. 8 is understood. Either the cycles in nature are regarded as
dependable phenomena producing a bustle of activity which will keep
any individual and endless generations occupied all their lives—even

University Press, 1998); Patricia Tull Willey, *Remember the Former Things: The
Recollection of Previous Texts in Second Isaiah* (SBLDS 161; Atlanta: Scholars
Press, 1997).
  135. E.g. 42:9; 43:19; 48:6.
  136. Cf. Ps 79:8.

though nothing is actually new, it just fades from one individual or collective memory to be rediscovered by another (of course, new and more efficient ways of doing things are discovered or invented, but nonetheless people and nature continue basically unchanged). Or alternatively humanity is viewed as caught up in one of a series of endless, monotonous cycles from which there is no escape—and there is not even any continuing memory of people after they die. The ambiguity at this level reflects reality: the cycles of nature are observable phenomena to which people respond in their own way. On the one hand, the provisions of nature can be gratefully accepted,[137] and, in the best traditions of scientific research, its predictability can be utilised to best effect. On the other hand, one can succumb to despair at the monotony of nature which fails to provide for the inexhaustible greed of humanity which seeks gratification of desires beyond the grasp of life "under the sun." We might reflect that ironically such greed has created in recent years something that is genuinely and horrifically new and unprecedented—the human capacity to halt forever the cycle of human generations. But even then, the sun would continue shining, even if its rays didn"t reach the earth; the wind would continue to blow, even if its patterns were greatly altered; and water would continue to fall from polluted clouds and collect in rivers incapable of supporting life, which in turn would flow into seas that would not only never be full of water, but possibly would never again be full of living creatures and plants.

(3) The third level of ambiguity concerns the relation of this passage to the rest of Ecclesiastes: What purpose does 1:4–11 serve in the book, and is it to be read as Qohelet's own words or the words of the "frame narrator?" It is not at all clear how it relates either to the preceding verses, or to those which follow it. It might be an illustration of the statement in v. 2 that הבל הבל, but we have already noted the difficulties involved here because of the ambiguity of the word הבל. If הבל means something like "ephemeral," the constantly repeating cycles of nature stand in contrast to this ephemerality, but perhaps human achievements could be described in this way, particularly if nothing new is achieved nor any memory left of them. On the other hand, if הבל indicates absurdity or futility, it again seems an inappropriate description of the cycles of nature which are not obviously either futile, as they do serve to maintain the balance of nature, or absurd, as there is nothing inherently unreasonable

---

137. See, for example, Lohfink's comment on v. 9: "There is nothing melancholy about this statement. It is a shout of joy: behind the ephemeral moment shines eternal permanence" (N. Lohfink, "The Present and Eternity: Time in Qoheleth," *TD* 34 [1987]: 236–40 [238]).

about them.[138] It might be possible to describe human activity in this way if people fail to achieve satisfaction in their speech or from what they see and hear, and if what they do is only what has been done before and they are not remembered for it. But the link is not obvious.

1:4–11 might relate to the question, מה־יתרון לאדם בכל־עמלו שיעמל תחת השמש, posed in 1:3. Again, the first half of the poem describing the cycles of nature seems to bear no connection with this question except for the first four words which could indicate that generations come and go, perhaps implying that nothing of any lasting value can be achieved. However, this seems a decidedly tenuous link. The most pertinent part of the passage is the statement in v. 9 that אין כל־חדש תחת השמש, particularly because of the use of the key expression תחת השמש. Also the repeated assertion in v. 11 that no memory is retained of former people/things may bear on the question. But again the link is somewhat tenuous. Moreover, the use of איש in v. 8 raises questions about the relation of this passage to v. 3 where האדם is used. In fact, איש occurs only eight times in Ecclesiastes (1:8; 4:4; 6:2 [×2], 3; 7:5; 9:15 [×2])—compared with 49 occurrences of אדם—and most of these seem to refer to a specific man as opposed to humanity in general.[139] Indeed, a very similar phrase to this one appears in 8:17, but in that verse האדם is used, לא יוכל האדם, and there is no apparent reason why איש is used here instead.

The link between 1:4–11 and the following verses is just as uncertain. 1:13 picks up from v. 9 the theme of "what is done," which may form an *inclusio* to a section running from 1:12 to 2:3, but the expression תחת השמים is used instead of תחת השמש. Another possible link may be the allusion to Solomon in 1:12. This would be particularly ironic in the light of v. 11, which not only states that future generations forget those who went before, but expresses these sentiments using the very words used to sum up Solomon's deeds in 2 Chr 9:29:

ושאר דברי שלמה הראשנים והאחרונים הלא־הם כתובים על־דברי נתן הנביא
ועל־נבואת אחיה השילוני ובחזות יעדי [יעדו] החזה על־ירבעם בן־נבט:

But again it is difficult to see how the passages bear on each other: How does 1:1–3 affect 1:4–11, and how does it in turn affect 1:12–2:3? These three sections seem rather to be juxtaposed with no obvious

---

138. Whybray argues: "These examples are not intended to show the futility of these phenomena, but only their regularity. . . . Not a word is said about their futility: on the contrary, the reader is implicitly invited to regard their activity with wonder and admiration" ("Ecclesiastes 1:5–7," 105).

139. See 6:2 (×2), 3; 9:15 (×2). Note that 4:4 and 7:5 are more like the usage here, although the proverbial form of 7:5 may explain its use there. The plural אנשים is used twice, both times to refer to specific men.

attempt to establish a connection between them. However, 1:4–11 does establish a pattern that is followed throughout the book, more or less explicitly. The first half pictures the way things are on earth, while the second half explores the implications for human life—in an ambiguous fashion so that readers are forced to draw their own conclusions.

2.4. *Conclusion*

Wilson explores the possible interpretations of this passage in an article entitled "Artful Ambiguity in Ecclesiastes 1,1–11," and he explains the ambiguous nature of the passage well when he proposes

> That the purposeful use of ambiguity is a way of reminding the reader that wisdom observations usually reflect part, not all, of the truth. In other words, what is being asserted from one viewpoint might need to be qualified by other perspectives. The effect of this ambiguous opening section is that the reader is warned to tread carefully. The same words can indicate both the regularity of nature and the apparent pointlessness of human activity. Both interpretations pass the wisdom test of ringing true to the sage's experiences and observations of the world. Reality is much richer than either insight stretched so far as to exclude the other. The use of ambiguity thus does not mean that the text fails to communicate its message, but rather implies that the message is more complex that [*sic*] it appears at first.[140]

I believe Wilson is correct to argue that the ambiguity in 1:1–11 is "purposeful" and "artful" and conveys a much more complex "message" than either a "black" or a "white" (or, better, "dark" or "bright") reading which ignored the ambiguous nature of the text and tried to squeeze it into a univocal mould could possibly capture. Good, writing about 1:2–11, also observes that "statements are often ambiguous, patent of more than one possible meaning." He goes a stage further than Wilson when he writes,

> Ambiguity itself is a stimulus to expect a consequent, though one may be split among several possible expectations. Or the stimulus may be the beginning of a pattern or series of statements, which we expect to continue or, conversely, to close. The possibilities of the kinds of tendency to respond or of expectations are many, and their illustration in Qoh 1:2–11 will show several. If the hypothesis works, if the meaning of the passage (or meanings, if there are several) is to be found not simply in its unified "message" but in the very process by which the passage makes its linear way, then the style *is* the meaning, and perceiving the process as it unfolds is the interpretation.[141]

140. Wilson, "Artful Ambiguity in Ecclesiastes 1,1–11," 364.
141. Good, "The Unfilled Sea," 62, his emphasis.

However, it is my contention that the kind of ambiguity which Wilson and Good explore is by no means restricted to the opening section of Ecclesiastes, but is a key rhetorical tool employed by the author which, as Salyer puts it, "rampages throughout the book."[142] Indeed, the exercise I have undertaken in relation to 1:4–11 (indicating the points of ambiguity and demonstrating the varied responses of the commentators to individual words, phrases, verses and the passage as a whole) could be repeated for much of Ecclesiastes. Thus, with the exception of his use of the word "absurdity," I agree with Salyer's comment:

> The implied author has consciously constructed a text which would recreate the same sense of *hebel* at a literary level that one often experiences in real life. . . . The rhetorical effect of the text's various gapping techniques and strategies of indirection is to recreate in the reader life's penchant for absurdity and ambiguity.[143]

---

142. Salyer, *Vain Rhetoric*, 255.

143. Ibid., 18. Here again, though, I would not use "absurdity" in this context. I agree here with de Beauvoir when she writes, "The notion of ambiguity must not be confused with that of absurdity. To declare that existence is absurd is to deny that it can ever be given a meaning; to say that it is ambiguous is to assert that its meaning is never fixed, that it must be constantly won. Absurdity challenges every ethics; but also the finished rationalization of the real would leave no room for ethics; it is because man's condition is ambiguous that he seeks, through failure and outrageousness, to save his existence. Thus, to say that action has to be lived in its truth, that is, in the consciousness of the antinomies which it involves, does not mean that one has to renounce it" (Simone de Beauvoir, *The Ethics of Ambiguity* [New York: Citadel, 1976], 129). I believe Qohelet would go along with de Beauvoir.

Chapter 3

קהלת IN ECCLESIASTES

3.1. *The Superscription*

Most commentators view the first verse of Ecclesiastes as a late addition. In fact, Barton goes so far as to say, "The title, ch. 1:1, 'The words of Qoheleth, son of David, king in Jerusalem,' may readily be granted *without controversy* to be the work of an editor."[1] Many have suggested that it was added by the final editor as a claim to Solomonic authority, thus granting the work credence it would not otherwise have had.[2] However, the verse has functioned as part of the book for many generations and is certainly part of Ecclesiastes as it has come down to us in its canonical form. Moreover, it is quite possible that the author of this work deliberately wrote this "heading" in the style of the headings given to other, probably older, and usually prophetic, works. Longman acknowledges this possibility, but dismisses it very readily:

> The most natural reading of the superscription in wisdom and prophetic literature is that it was added by a second, subsequent hand. It is not impossible that the author or speaker wrote the superscription, referring to himself in the third person, but the only reason to argue in this direction is to defend a rather mechanical view of biblical inspiration that insists only one author stands behind a single book. In my view, this superscription is the work of the frame narrator.[3]

Now, I agree that "this superscription is the work of the frame narrator," but not that this indicates "a second, subsequent hand" (and out of no desire to "defend a rather mechanical view of biblical inspiration"!). Rather, in this verse the author of the whole book of Ecclesiastes uses the words of the frame narrator to introduce us to the main character of the

---

1. G. Barton, *Ecclesiastes*, 44, my emphasis. So, for example, Whybray simply states, "Like some other Old Testament books, Ecclesiastes has been provided *by an editor* with a title identifying the author" (*Ecclesiastes*, 26, my emphasis).

2. This is discussed, for example, by Crenshaw, *Ecclesiastes*, 57, and Loader, *Ecclesiastes: A Practical Commentary*, 19.

3. Longman, *The Book of Ecclesiastes*, 57.

book, Qohelet, whose words make up almost everything we read within the *inclusio* formed by 1:2 and 12:8. I will explain this in more detail below.[4]

Whether or not this verse was added later as a heading or title, it already introduces a sense of enigma to the book and raises a number of issues.[5] Of crucial importance is the question, "Who is קהלת?" Ecclesiastes 1:1 states that he is בן־דוד, but there is no reference elsewhere to a son of David by this name. However, the term בן can refer to a more distant descendant, or even a person related in some other way, for example as a disciple or pupil,[6] and the plural, בני־דו[י]ד, is used elsewhere in the Hebrew Bible with such an extended sense.[7] While 4:8 and 5:13 (Eng. 5:14) use the word בן with the literal sense "son," בני ("my son"), in 12:12, בן־חורים ("of noble birth"), and the expression בני־האדם for people (1:13; 2:3, 8; 3:10, 18, 19, 21; 8:11; 9:3, 12) show that it is also used often in an extended sense in Ecclesiastes.

---

4. But at this point I readily acknowledge the influence of Michael V. Fox, Eric S. Christianson and Gary D. Salyer on my reading of these roles in the book (see Michael V. Fox, "Frame-Narrative and Composition in the Book of Qohelet," *HUCA* 48 [1977]: 83–106, and *A Time to Tear Down*, 363–77; Christianson, *A Time to Tell*; and Salyer, *Vain Rhetoric*). I agree with Salyer's assessment that Fox's article "marks a quantum leap forward for the understanding of how the use of third-person discourse affects the book's implied reader" (p. 211).

5. Charles F. Melchert notes: "From the opening line of the text, reader-learners are drawn into a puzzle about the identity of the author that escalates into an enigma about the worth of anything and everything, including reading itself" (*Wise Teaching: Biblical Wisdom and Educational Ministry* [Harrisburg, Pa.: Trinity Press International, 1998], 114).

6. Crenshaw explains: "*Ben-dawid* (son of David) does not necessarily mean one of David's children. In Hebrew usage it can refer to grandchildren or simply to a remote member of the Davidic dynasty. Furthermore, the word *ben* also denotes close relationships of mind and spirit without implying actual physical kinship (sons of the prophets = disciples or guild members; sons of God = servants)" (*Ecclesiastes*, 56). See also H. Haag, "בֵּן, *bēn*," *TDOT* 2:145–65; J. Kühlewein, "בֵּן, *bēn*, son," *TLOT* 1:238–45; Chrys C. Caragounis, "בֵּן," *NIDOTTE* 1:671–77. Ogden and Zogbo maintain that it is "best if the translator can preserve the indirect reference to Qoheleth and use an expression like 'a descendant of David'" (*A Handbook*, 21).

7. Cf. 2 Chr 13:8; 23:3; 32:33; Ezra 8:2. בני־דו[י]ד is used literally of David's sons in 2 Sam 8:18; 1 Chr 3:1, 9; 18:17. Christianson is right that "nowhere in the Old Testament does בן־דוד mean anything other than a biological son of David," but is not quite correct when he adds, "and only once is it other than Solomon (2 Chr 11:18)" (*A Time to Tell*, 129), because in addition to Jerimoth in this verse, both Absalom and Amnon are called בן־דוד in 2 Sam 13:1. Seow gets it right (*Ecclesiastes: A New Translation*, 97).

The next phrase, מלך בירושלם, is usually read as a description of Qohelet: "The words of Qohelet [who is] a 'son of David' [and is] *king in Jerusalem*." This seems to be what is suggested by the pause indicated above דוד, but the sentence divisions in Ecclesiastes do sometimes hinder rather than aid interpretation, and cannot always be relied upon. Moreover, as we have already noted, there is no record of a king in Jerusalem by the name of Qohelet, so we might read the phrase as modifying דוד to give the translation: "The words of Qohelet, a "son" of King David of Jerusalem."[8]

However, it should be noted that there are two roots מלך in the Hebrew Bible: one is associated with kingship, sovereignty, and so on, the other with advice or counsel[9]—although מלך as "king" occurs over 2500 times in the Hebrew Bible, while the noun never has the sense "counsellor" and the verb מלך means "counsel" only once in Hebrew (Neh 5:7, and this is possibly an Aramaic loanword, but is used in the same verse as קהלה[10]), and once in Aramaic (Dan 4:24). Nonetheless, some commentators have made this connection,[11] and Nel points out that "The cognate word in Akk. *malkum* . . . designates an adviser, and not a king."[12] Moreover, if Fox is correct (as I believe he is) that "Qohelet's vocabulary . . . cannot be confined to the usual Biblical usages, especially in his key concepts,"[13] this link should be given due consideration. Certainly this reading ties in better with the description of Qohelet in 12:9–11, where he is described as a wise person and maybe one of a body known as "the wise"—perhaps a group of people employed as state advisers because of their wisdom. It is particularly noteworthy that these verses focus on "words," using דברי three times, and this may specifically allude back to

---

8. Longman notes this possibility, stating, "it is difficult to tell whether the phrase is in apposition to *David* or to the entire phrase *son of David*" (his emphasis), but continues, "The issue is hardly crucial" (*The Book of Ecclesiastes*, 58).

9. See BDB, 572–76; also H.-P. Müller, "מֶלֶךְ, *melēk*," *TDOT* 8:346–88 (352); Philip J. Nel, "מלך," *NIDOTTE* 2:956–65 (965); J.A. Soggin, "מֶלֶךְ, *melek*, king," *TLOT* 2:672–80 (672).

10. In addition, the phrase וימלך לבי עלי in Neh 5:7 is reminiscent of the use of לב in Ecclesiastes.

11. Robert Davidson, for example, states, "The words translated 'king' may indeed mean simply 'counselor'" (*Ecclesiastes and the Song of Solomon*, 7). See also, Soggin, *TDOT* 2:672, and the scholars mentioned there. Some commentators note this possibility but point out that it has not received much support (e.g. Crenshaw, *Ecclesiastes*, 57; Murphy, *Ecclesiastes*, 1; cf. Seow, *Ecclesiastes*, 97; Whybray, *Ecclesiastes*, 34).

12. Nel, *NIDOTTE* 2:965. See also Al Wolters, "מלך," *NIDOTTE* 2:965.

13. Fox, *A Time to Tear Down*, 40 n. 11.

1:1: Who is responsible for the words we read in 1:3–12:7—might it be קהלת the wise "counsellor" or "adviser" of whom we read that he "taught the people knowledge, weighing and studying and arranging many proverbs" (Eccl 12:9)? (I can imagine a reader reaching the epilogue and exclaiming, "Ah, yes! So perhaps that's what מלך in 1:1 means. I didn't think 'king' was quite right somehow!") Reading מלך as "adviser" also accords with the tremendous emphasis on wisdom in the book and Qohelet's claims about his own great wisdom. Wisdom is not mentioned in the introductory verses, but on the three other occasions that precisely the same word, דברי, is used in Ecclesiastes (9:17; 10:12, 13), it is in the context of wisdom and folly.

If Ecclesiastes is read against the background of other biblical literature, in other words if the other books of the Hebrew Bible are, to use Hawthorn's term, its main "literary context," then מלך here is likely to be understood as "king." However, if its context is broader and includes Aramaic texts where מלך is readily understood to mean "adviser," the verse may be interpreted quite differently. It is not sufficient counter-argument to point out that elsewhere in Ecclesiastes the word clearly indicates a king (this probably applies to 8:1, 4; 9:14) because Ecclesiastes displays a propensity for using words with different meanings. Perhaps the word is deliberately ambiguous. If (as is usually suggested—and with which I agree) Solomon's reputation for great wealth and wisdom lies at least behind chs. 1 and 2,[14] it would be appropriate for the reader initially to understand this verse as an allusion to Solomon. However, the reader may in retrospect realise (along with the vast majority of modern

14.   The vast majority of recent commentators refer to the "Solomonic fiction" or "guise" or "royal experiment," although there is some dispute about how long it is sustained. Thus Dominic Rudman, in a book published in July 2001, shares the view held by, among others, Fox and Seow when he refers to "the 'Royal Experiment' in 1:12–2:12" (*Determinism*, 248); Salyer also shares a popular view (held, among others, by Longman and Whybray) when he writes, in a book published by the same publisher a month earlier, of "the King's Fiction" in 1:12–2:26 (*Vain Rhetoric*, 286). However, Christianson (writing for the same publisher three years earlier), maintains that "the guise continually reasserts itself" throughout the book (*A Time to Tell*, 128–48 [148]). Ogden does not specifically address the issue, but refers to the "autobiographical" material in 1:12–3:21 (*Qoheleth*, 34). Crenshaw notes the "prominence of the *royal testament* in 1:12–2:16" (*Ecclesiastes*, 29). I would maintain that there is no clearcut conclusion to the "fiction": at no point is it "dropped" (as, indeed, Fox acknowledges [*A Time to Tear Down*, 153]), but rather the reader is likely to come to the realization at some point that it has not been maintained throughout the book. If one then goes back specifically to find the point at which it ceased, in my opinion the last *clear* reliance on Solomonic tradition is in 2:4–10, but as Christianson rightly points out, there may be hints of it later on.

scholars[15]) that Qohelet is not, in fact, to be equated with Solomon, literal son of David and king in Jerusalem, and seek an alternative interpretation. Such ambiguity would also add an ironic twist to 4:13; 5:8 and 10:16–17:

4:13   טוב ילד מסכן וחכם מִמֶּלֶד זקן וכסיל אֲשֶׁר לאֹ־ידע להזהר עוד׃

5:8   ויתרון ארץ בכל היא [הוא] מֶלֶד לשדה נעבד׃

10:16   אִי־לד ארץ שֶׁמַּלְכֵּד נער וְשָׂרַיִד בבקר יאכלו׃

10:17   אֹשְׁרֵיד ארץ שֶׁמַּלְכֵּד בן־חורים וְשָׂרַיִד בעת יאכלו בגבורה ולא בשתי׃

The opening verse of Proverbs bears some striking resemblances to Eccl 1:1 that raise further questions about the link between Solomon and Qohelet:

Prov 1:1   מִשְׁלֵי שלמה בן־דוד מלך ישראל׃

Eccl 1:1   דברי קהלת בן־דוד מלך בירושׁלם׃

There is sufficient similarity between the verses to cause readers well acquainted with both books (or even well acquainted with the book of Proverbs when reading Ecclesiastes for the first time) to make comparisons between them,[16] while the differences may raise questions in their minds. The first obvious difference between these verses is that Proverbs starts with the word מִשְׁלֵי rather than דברי—but Eccl 12:9 refers to מְשָׁלִים in relation to קהלת, and, as Crenshaw points out, "the epilogue in Eccl 12:9–11 virtually equates the respective words *dibre* and *mesalim*."[17] The second difference is the use of בירושׁלם in Eccl in place of ישראל—but in

---

15. So, for example, Gordis writes, "the view that Solomon is the author has been universally abandoned today" (*Koheleth*, 203). However, Walter C. Kaiser Jr. (*Ecclesiastes: Total Life* [Everyman's Bible Commentary; Chicago: Moody Press, 1979], 24–29), and Garrett (*Proverbs, Ecclesiastes, Song of Songs*, 254–67) are exceptions. Garrett writes: "The use of the name 'the Teacher' indicates that the author is distancing himself from his role as absolute monarch and taking on the mantle of the sage. Both the name 'the Teacher' and the use of third person (frame-narrator) allow him to do this. The device is certainly a literary success. What emerges from Ecclesiastes is not a royal pronouncement but the reflection of a wise man who 'has been' king" (p. 264).

16. G. H. Wilson states: "the striking similarities between the initial superscript of Qohelet and that of Proverbs produce two effects on the reader's understanding of the book of Qohelet and the identity of its author . . . First, the otherwise unidentified author, Qohelet, is here connected with the person Solomon. . . . Second, the addition of such a superscription to Qohelet serves to associate the book with the collection process that produced the divisions marked by similar editorial comments in Proverbs" ("The Words of the Wise: The Intent and Significance of Qoheleth 12:9–14," *JBL* 109 [1984]: 175–92 [179]).

17. Crenshaw, *Ecclesiastes*, 56.

1:12 Qohelet states, אני קהלת הייתי מלך על־ישראל בירושלם. This appears to strengthen the link between Qohelet and Solomon because there were only two kings of Israel in Jerusalem, David and his son Solomon, before the southern kingdom of Judah and the northern kingdom of Israel separated.[18]

However, there are a couple of anomalies in 1:12 that raise questions about how the verse should be read. First, the verb הייתי *may*, as Barton suggests, be "a perfect denoting state,"[19] but the most obvious reading, especially in the light of the way the perfect verb is used elsewhere in Ecclesiastes,[20] is to see it as a verb indicating completed action, "I *was* king," or "I *have been* king."[21] If it were intended clearly to indicate the present tense, either the participial form of היה (or of the verb מלך) could have been used, or an imperfect verb, or, more probably, the verb might have been omitted altogether as in the closest parallel uttered by David in 2 Sam 19:23: אני־מלך על־ישראל. The likely implication of the perfect form of the verb is that the writer is not at the time of writing king over

18. Rehoboam was briefly king over the whole of Israel, but his reign seems to have been from Shechem. When all of Israel apart from the tribe of Judah rebelled against him and adopted Jeroboam as their king, he returned to Jerusalem, there to reign over the southern kingdom of Judah. And, as 1 Kgs 12:19–20 states, "Israel has been in rebellion against the house of David to this day . . . there was none that followed the house of David, but the tribe of Judah only."

19. G. Barton, *Ecclesiastes*, 85. Bo Isaksson explains, "The stative aspect of *hayiti* in 1:12 obviously must not be construed as an actual (cursive) present. It involves at the same time a perfect and a present: 'I have been, and still am'" (*Studies in the Language of Qoheleth with Special Emphasis on the Verbal System* [AUUSSU 10; Uppsala: Almquist & Wiksell, 1987], 50). A good number of commentators follow this line. Seow maintains that "the use of the perfect is in keeping with the narrative style of the west Semitic royal inscriptions" (*Ecclesiastes*, 119; cf. Fox, *A Time to Tear Down*, 171).

20. Antoon Schoors points out, "In Qoh, perfect tense is generally used with reference to past acts or situations; thus very often in the first person, when the author recalls his intellectual activity . . . or when he tells what happened in the past" (*The Preacher Sought to Find Pleasing Words: A Study of the Language of Qoheleth* [OLA 41; Leuven: Peeters, 1992], 172).

21. This point is noted by many commentators: for example, Ogden maintains that it "leaves the impression that the author once was king but now has ceased to reign" (*Qoheleth*, 34); Longman discusses various options, then concludes, "None-theless, normally the verb describes a completed action in the past and is well rendered by the English perfect (*have been*)" (*The Book of Ecclesiastes*, 76). It is often pointed out that rabbinic tradition provided the explanation that the demon Ashmedai usurped the throne from King Solomon because of his sins, so that there was a time when he was not actually king (see E. Levine, *The Aramaic Version of Qohelet* [New York: Sepher-Hermon, 1978], 28, 49).

Israel. Perhaps this is a hint that קֹהֶלֶת is not in fact King Solomon,[22] perhaps even that he makes no pretence at being a king, but is rather an adviser over Israel.

Secondly, the preposition מֶלֶךְ עַל־יִשְׂרָאֵל is also unusual, because, although the construction with עַל does occur a number of times elsewhere,[23] the much more common expression in the Hebrew Bible is just מֶלֶךְ יִשְׂרָאֵל,[24] as, indeed, it is in Prov 1:1 and the two other occasions when exactly the same phrase, שְׁלֹמֹה בֶן־דָּוִד מֶלֶךְ יִשְׂרָאֵל, is used (2 Chr 30:26; 35:3). It is perhaps noteworthy that on the two occasions that the root מלך meaning "to advise" occurs (Neh 5:7; Dan. 4:24), it is followed by the preposition עַל. The matter is further complicated by the use of עַל in the phrase כֹל־אֲשֶׁר־הָיָה לְפָנַי עַל־יְרוּשָׁלַם in Eccl 1:16, because there was only one king "over Jerusalem" before Solomon.[25]

Nonetheless, most commentators throughout the ages have seen in 1:1 (and 1:12, 16) reference to a king in Jerusalem who bore a filial relationship to David, i.e., Solomon, even if the majority of recent scholars have

---

22. This point is made by R. Lux ("'Ich, Kohelet, bin König . . .' Die Fiktion als Schlüssel zur Wirklichkeit in Kohelet 1:12–2:26," *EvT* 50 [1990]: 331–42 [335]). Farmer describes the "use of the completed-action form of the verb" here as a riddle: "It seems much more likely that Qohelet is here playing a role in order to argue a point. He uses the form of a self-introduction to pose a type of riddle. In effect he is saying, 'Given these clues (I was king over Israel in Jerusalem and known for my wisdom), guess who I am?'" (*Who Knows What is Good?*, 154). Garrett turns this around, arguing: "The perfect tense of the verb, 'was,' does not mean that the real Solomon is dead and the author is here speaking in his behalf but that Solomon, the author, is speaking to the reader not as king but as teacher, as is implied in his use of the name 'the Teacher'" (*Proverbs, Ecclesiastes, Song of Songs*, 289).

23. 1 Sam 15:17, 26; 2 Sam 5:3, 12, 17; 12:7; 19:23; 1 Kgs 1:34; 11:37; 14:14; 19:16; 1 Chr 11:3; 14:2; 28:4.

24. Cf., e.g., 1 Sam 26:20; 1 Kgs 15:9; Hos 1:1; 10:15; Amos 1:1; 7:10.

25. This is noted by many commentators. Whybray reckons "Probably this is just a slip: Qoheleth was thinking of the many kings who had reigned in Jerusalem in the period of the kingdom of Judah, and had *temporarily forgotten* that Solomon came very early in the list" (*Ecclesiastes*, 51, my emphasis). Longman refers to this as an "enigmatic expression" which "has led to different interpretations." He argues that there is "a loose association with Solomon, not a strict identification, and therefore, we need not worry about his lack of many royal predecessors" (*The Book of Ecclesiastes*, 83–84). Seow states that Qohelet here is simply adopting "a stock phrase in royal boasts" (*Ecclesiastes*, 124). Kaiser, however, defends Solomonic authorship, maintaining (with Hengstenberg) that "the reference is probably to the line of Canaanite kings who preceded Solomon in Jerusalem, such as Melchizedek (Gen 14:18), Adonizedec (Josh 10:1), and Araunah (2 Sam 24:23)." That, he says "easily cares for the issue" (Kaiser, *Ecclesiastes*, 28).

taken this to be a "literary fiction."[26] However, the point is that, contrary to Whybray's assertion, "there can be *no doubt* that the reference is to Solomon,"[27] when the reader reflects back on this opening verse in the light of what follows, there is considerable doubt about these being Solomon's words. Moreover, the name "Solomon" is never actually used, we have noted a number of factors that sit uneasily with this reading, and there is a viable alternative interpretation. In short, the name or title קהלת aside, there is already much ambiguity in this opening verse of the book, which suggests to me that it may well be from the same hand as the rest of Ecclesiastes.

3.2. *The Word* קהלת

So what about the name or title קהלת? Almost a century ago George Barton stated that "Qoheleth . . . is a crux";[28] around half a century later Gordis wrote, "The name Koheleth remains as enigmatic today as ever before";[29] some years later Whitley asserted, "uncertainty attaches to its precise meaning";[30] more recently Murphy noted that "the meaning of קהלת (*qōhelet*) remains a mystery";[31] and even more recently Davis argued, "It is fitting that the book begins with a puzzle, the author's peculiar name."[32] קהלת has been variously rendered: "the Preacher" (KJV, NKJV, RSV);[33] "the Teacher" (NRSV, NIV, NLT);[34] "the Speaker" (NEB, REB); "the Philosopher" (GNB); "the Quester" (the Message); simply as "Qoheleth" (NJB)[35] or "Koheleth" (NJPSV);[36] and explained as

26. Salyer (*Vain Rhetoric*, 167–93) and Christianson (*A Time to Tell*, 128–72) very usefully discuss this "fiction" and its implications in some depth. Salyer reasons, "Obviously, there must be clues in the text which communicate that a character is performing a fictional role. The major reading clue in the book of Ecclesiastes is the name of the protagonist" (p. 170).

27. Whybray, *Ecclesiastes*, 34.

28. G. Barton, *Ecclesiastes*, 67.

29. Gordis, *Koheleth*, 203.

30. Whitley, *Koheleth*, 4.

31. Murphy, *Ecclesiastes*, 1.

32. Davis, *Proverbs, Ecclesiastes, Song of Songs*, 169.

33. Fox says, "The traditional translation, 'the Preacher,' is reasonable" (*A Time to Tear Down*, 161), but Whybray contends that "The rendering 'preacher' is . . . wide of the mark" (*Ecclesiastes*, 2). Longman, among others, believes that "Qohelet is too untraditional to be located in a religious setting" (*The Book of Ecclesiastes*, 1).

34. Also Garrett, *Proverbs, Ecclesiastes, Song of Songs*, 282. Longman maintains that the translation "Teacher" "has its fatal flaws" (*The Book of Ecclesiastes*, 1).

35. But this explanation is offered in the Preface: "'Qoheleth' means only 'man of the Assembly,' perhaps its speaker or president."

"the Gatherer";[37] "the arguer";[38] "public teacher";[39] "convener of an assembly";[40] "an official speaker in an assembly";[41] "participant in an assembly";[42] "the Sceptic";[43] and so on. The word appears to be a Qal feminine participle from the root קהל, which has the meaning "assemble."[44] It is often explained as a title or office, on the basis of the use of other feminine participles (with or without the article) in this capacity elsewhere in the biblical text (סֹפֶרֶת in Ezra 2:55; Neh 7:57; and הַצֹּבְאִים פֹּכֶרֶת in Ezra 2:57; Neh 7:59).[45] The root is fairly common, but the verb, generally reckoned to be a denominative, appears elsewhere in the Hebrew Bible only in the Hiphil and Niphal. The noun קָהָל ("assembly") is also common, and is distributed throughout most books of the Hebrew Bible.[46] The RSV's "preacher" is derived from the fact that קָהָל often refers to a religious assembly, so that Qohelet is reckoned to be one who addresses such an assembly (hence the Greek, Ἐκκλησιαστής). But its scope is much greater than this, including assembly for evil counsel,[47] for civil affairs[48] and for war;[49] the assembly of the returning exiles[50] and the restored community;[51] a general assembled multitude;[52] and even, in Ps 89:6, of the assembly of angels. Notably, the root is used several times in

---

36. But with a footnote: "Probably 'the Assembler,' i.e., of hearers or of sayings; cf. 12:9–11."

37. Seow, *Ecclesiastes*, 97.

38. Ogden, *Qoheleth*, 27.

39. Fox, *A Time to Tear Down*, 161.

40. Davis, *Proverbs, Ecclesiastes, and the Song of Songs*, 170. See also Longman, *The Book of Ecclesiastes*, 1.

41. G. Barton, *Ecclesiastes*, 68.

42. Provan, *Ecclesiastes, Song of Songs*, 50.

43. Whitley, *Koheleth*, 6.

44. Though Fox argues: "We should not assume that *qōhelet* is the participle of (an unattested) qal of QHL. It is best explained as a noun-from-noun denominative from *qāhāl* 'assembly'" (*A Time to Tear Down*, 161).

45. However, Ellul says, "'Qohelet,' it seems to me, represents neither a title nor a function. Rather, it is a gratuitous designation . . . which has ironic and questioning overtones that the book as a whole expresses" (*Reason for Being*, 18).

46. The root קהל occurs 173 times, with nominal forms occurring 134 times and verbal forms 39 times, 19 in the Niphal and 20 in the Hiphil. These statistics are discussed by H.-P. Müller, "קָהַל, *qāhāl*, assembly," *TLOT* 3:1118–26.

47. E.g. Gen 49:6; Ps 26:5.

48. E.g. Job 30:28; Prov 5:14; 26:26.

49. E.g. Num 22:4; Judg 20:2; 1 Sam 17:47.

50. E.g. Jer 31:8; Neh 7:66.

51. E.g. Ps 149:1; Ezra 10:12, 14; Neh 8:2, 17.

52. E.g. Gen 28:3; 48:4; Prov 21:16.

connection with Solomon, particularly in 1 Kgs 8 (and also in 2 Chr 5–7), and this passage may be alluded to by this unique name.[53]

3.3. *Other Uses of* קהלת *in Ecclesiastes*

The word קהלת is used seven times in Ecclesiastes. Although it has the form of a feminine participle, it seems to act five times as a masculine proper noun (1:1, 2, 12; 12:9, 10).[54] However, once (7:27) it takes a feminine verb, which has prompted many commentators to posit an alternative reading, changing MT אמרה קהלת to אמר הקהלת, a reading underlying ὁ Ἐκκλησιαστής in the LXX. Once (12:8) it occurs as a definite masculine noun. קהלת appears three times in ch. 1, apparently in the guise of King Solomon, once in ch. 7, and three times in ch. 12, where he is described as one of the wise. Thus he appears first in the introduction to the book, he features again in the epilogue, and otherwise his presence is indicated only by the first person address, apart from one mention in the middle of the book as if to remind the reader who is speaking. In 1:2; 7:27; and 12:8 קהלת is used with the verb אמר, but on each occasion the phrase takes a different form:

אמר קהלת	1:2
אמרה קהלת	7:27
אמר הקוהלת	12:8

Either mistakes have crept into the text, as is usually suggested,[55] or this is another literary ploy to draw a veil of mystery over the main character

---

53. While Müller's chart (*TLOT* 3:1120) shows that the noun is fairly evenly spread throughout the Hebrew Bible, appearing in most books, it occurs five times in 1 Kgs 8, and only six times in the rest of the Deuteronomistic History. It is also notable that the noun occurs more often in texts that display a particular cultic interest: thus it is used more in the Chronicler's History than in the Deuteronomistic History, and much more in Ezekiel than any other prophetic book. Müller writes: "in the Chr history (*kol-haq)qāhāl* is the model for the full assembly of the Jewish cultic community convened by the king or the post-exilic leadership for religious purposes in epochal moments in the history of salvation" (p. 1124).

54. Murphy suggests: "Perhaps the best explanation recognizes that the feminine participle indicates an office associated with an assembly and that this term is used secondarily as a proper name" (*Ecclesiastes*, xx). Seow offers the example in English "smith"/"the smith" > "Smith" (*Ecclesiastes*, 96). There are other examples in the Hebrew Bible of masculine names that have a feminine form, for example, מסֹפֶּרֶת in Neh 7:7, which offers a close parallel.

55. In fact, Whybray says of אמרה קהלת in 7:27, "the verb is feminine; but *all commentators agree* that this is an error due to wrong word-division" (*Ecclesiastes*, 126, my emphasis).

of Ecclesiastes.[56] These three verses could indicate either that קֹהֶלֶת is a masculine proper noun, a feminine proper noun or the title of an office (e.g. the assembler,[57] preacher, teacher, speaker, etc.): thus the main speaker in Ecclesiastes could be a man, a woman (although a number of verses in the book appear to indicate that קֹהֶלֶת is a man[58]), or the holder of an office. In view of the web of ambiguities that become ever more entangled in the book, it seems likely that this variation is intentional.

3.4. קֹהֶלֶת *in the Frame Narrative*

A key point to note about all these occurrences of קֹהֶלֶת is that they appear in text that speaks *about* him in the third person, that is, in what is now commonly referred to as the "frame-narrative" of Ecclesiastes. This is a crucial point that has been too little acknowledged until recently because at least 1:1 and 12:9–14, if not also 1:2 and 12:8, were, in my opinion, too readily ascribed to editors.[59] Fox is undoubtedly correct that, at least in the final form of the text, "The body of the book is formally a long quotation of Qohelet's words. The frame narrator presents himself

56. Provan writes: "It is much more likely that the Masoretic word division is the original one, which has survived in spite of the difficulties it has caused many readers. Taken seriously as such, the authorial insertion in 7:27 introduces an element of doubt into our minds about the gender of the speaker, for it makes us ask just how far our firm conviction that he is male arises from the same source as the firm convictions held by others that he is Solomon or that he finished his book around 198B.C.—namely, a failure to distinguish the speaker as he appears (in different guises) in the text from the speaker as he may truly and historically have been in reality. The fact of the matter is that Qohelet is all but completely veiled behind the text of Ecclesiastes, subsumed by 'his' words" (*Ecclesiastes, Song of Songs*, 29).

57. Commentators are divided on whether the "assembling" might be of, say, wisdom and wealth (so, e.g., Seow, *Ecclesiastes*, 97) or only of people (so, e.g., Whybray, *Ecclesiastes*, 2).

58. See שִׁדָּה וְשִׁדּוֹת in 2:8, although the meaning of this expression is uncertain and much debated; 7:26–29 (could a woman possibly have written this, I wonder); 9:9; in addition, of course, to the masculine gender used throughout 1:1–2 and 12:9–10.

59. Whybray asserts: "It is *universally* agreed that this final section of the book is the work not of Qoheleth but of one or more persons who were familiar either with the book in its present form or at least with its contents" (*Ecclesiastes*, 169, my emphasis). Crenshaw, for example, writes: "In my view, the only secondary materials are the superscription (1:1), the epilogues (12:9–11, 12–14), some glosses (2:26a; 3:17a; 8:12–13; 11:9b; perhaps 5:18 [19E] and 7:26b), and possibly the motto (1:2; 12:8)" (*Ecclesiastes*, 48). Gordis contends that "the Epilogue (12:9–14) . . . is manifestly from another hand" and "The first verse, which is really the title, emanates from the editor" (*Koheleth*, 73).

not as the author of Qohelet's teachings or as their editor but as their transmitter."[60] He goes on to explain,

> The book of Qohelet, then, is built of nested levels of perspective, each one with its own time-frame and each encompassed in the next:
> 1. The frame-narrator, who tells about
> 2. Qohelet-the-reporter, the narrating "I," who speaks from the vantage point of old age, and looks back on
> 3. Qohelet-the-observer, the experiencing "I," who undertook the investigation that the book reports.
> Levels 1 and 2 are different persons (different, that is, within the text; the distinction may, however, be fictive). Levels 2 and 3 are different perspectives of the same person. The time-frame of level 1 is the present tense of the speaker in the epilogue; it is the temporal context in relation to which the phrase "Qohelet said" is past tense. The time-frame of the frame-narrator is supposed to be some time after Qohelet lived. The time-frame of level 2 is the one in which Qohelet speaks, when he reflects on his experiments and experiences and reports them. This is the present to which the past tense of certain verbs of observation, cognition, and speaking ("I saw," "I realized," "I said," and the like) is relative. The time-frame of level 3 is the context in which the exploring, experiencing, and cognition took place.[61]

What Fox does not take into account here (nor does Salyer[62]) is how the "Solomonic fiction" fits into this scheme (Christianson comes at the issue from a different perspective—"Solomonic fiction" throughout—and discusses the issues raised in considerable depth[63]). Actually, because 1:1 displays similarities to the superscription to a number of other biblical books (probably intentionally so),[64] and because the remaining third person description is held over to the end of the book, the different "levels" in the book only become apparent when the closing frame narrative is

60. Fox, *A Time to Tear Down*, 365. Fox has been followed in this by a number of modern scholars, including Salyer, Longman and Christianson.

61. Ibid., 366.

62. Salyer, *Vain Rhetoric*, 211–21 (212–13). However, Salyer does take some account of the issues raised when he notes, "the reader of the book of Ecclesiastes may well question whether any reader would trust a narrator who stealthily and reticently utilizes Solomon's ethos and reputation as a mask" (p. 220).

63. That Christianson follows this scheme exactly is clearly demonstrated on p. 69 of *A Time to Tell*. The differences from Fox's position (notably the extent of the "Solomonic fiction" and the authorship of the "frame") are apparent throughout Chapters 2, 4–6, where the "outer borders" and the "Solomonic guise" are discussed in considerable depth.

64. Especially Jer 1:1; Amos 1:1. In Hos 1:1; Joel 1:1; Mic 1:1; and Zeph 1:1 the text starts, דבר־יהוה אשר היה על־; Jonah 1:1 and Mal 1:1 are very similar.

reached[65] (and probably only after a number of readings). This means that at least on a first reading, the reader cannot be sure what the various levels are: for example without the epilogue(s), the reader may assume that 1:1–2 serve simply (as an editorial addition along the lines of other biblical books?) to introduce the words of Qohelet, the putative author of the book (though 7:25 provides a clue that this is not the case); the connection between Qohelet and any literal "son of David" is far from clear; and certainly there is no indication at the start of the book that Qohelet is reflecting back from his old age (which is anyway only an assumption, albeit, I believe, a good one). In fact, it seems to me there are a number of instances where the reader can never be sure. So, for example, we might ask if the passage 1:4–11 comes from the frame narrator or from Qohelet (Qohelet only introduces himself in the first person in 1:12, although his first words are recorded—or perhaps they are summarized— in 1:2). Is 1:12–2:11 intended to be perceived as "Qohelet-as-Solomon" after which point the "Solomonic fiction" is dropped? Does the change to first person halfway through 4:8 hint that יֵשׁ אֶחָד refers to קֹהֶלֶת, and suggest that other such descriptions might be autobiographical? Whose old age is described in 12:1–5 (if this is what these verses are all about!) —is קֹהֶלֶת writing in his own old age, reflecting back on his youth, and, if so, whose death is then pictured in 12:6–7?

Christianson asserts, " In terms of Qoheleth as the frame narrator saw him, [the epilogue] is the most informative text in Ecclesiastes and presents the reader with a well-defined final portrait."[66] In fact, in a number of respects the closing frame is fundamentally ambiguous (which may well be an argument in favour of its authorship being the same as the rest of the book),[67] and it raises as many questions as it answers about קֹהֶלֶת. Scholars remain divided over the question of the authorship of the

---

65. As Christianson says, "with the commencement of the first-person narrative of Qoheleth at 1:12 . . . the reader will inevitably forget (with the possible exception of 7:27) that these are reported words, and will assume that they are being narrated to directly by Qoheleth throughout the rest of the book—until, that is, the epilogue, where the frame narrator appears again" (*A Time to Tell*, 46).

66. Ibid., 99–100.

67. Longman observes: "Within this section we encounter some of the most significant disputes concerning translation and interpretation of the text" (*The Book of Ecclesiastes*, 274). Christianson also states, "The translation and general sense of this section present one of the most difficult tasks to Qoheleth studies" (*A Time to Tell*, 106). Murphy writes: "One may conclude with the ironic but apt observation that it was somehow not fitting that the enigmatic book of Ecclesiastes should come to an end without the subtlety and open-ended character that the epilogue shows" (*Ecclesiastes*, 130).

epilogue(s), but if one holds that the same person wrote the whole book,[68] what attitude does he cause the frame narrator (whether or not the frame narrator is the same as the implied author, or even the author) to take towards Qohelet, and to what effect? Does he commend Qohelet's words to the reader;[69] or defend them against criticism;[70] or does he perhaps intend to guide the reader towards a "proper" interpretation of Qohelet's words;[71] or does he provide an orthodox conclusion to ease acceptance of Qohelet's words;[72] or does he intentionally create tension between Qohelet's words and those of the frame narrator?[73] If these verses are not

---

68. E.g. Salyer, *Vain Rhetoric*, 214–15; Bartholomew, *Reading Ecclesiastes*, 157. Garrett, for rather different reasons, holds the same view, declaring that "treating the conclusion as a secondary epilogue, either as a pious gloss or as part of an emerging canon consciousness, decapitates the entire work" (*Proverbs, Ecclesiastes, Song of Songs*, 345). Seow and Fox both ascribe most of the epilogue to the same writer as the rest of the book, but contend that 12:13b–14 has *probably* been added secondarily (Seow, *Ecclesiastes*, 38; Fox, *A Time to Tear Down*, 95–96, 144). It is notable that both commentators seem hesitant (and, e.g., in "Frame-Narrative," 83, and *Qohelet*, 311, Fox maintains the unity of the whole book, including 12:13–14), and assert that even this last verse and a half are in keeping with the rest of the book: "This addition is not an irrelevant appendage," says Fox, "It is a conclusion that reasonably builds on Qohelet's words" (*A Time to Tear Down*, 144). Davis, however, is saying something different (and, I believe, incorrect) when she writes, "The epilogue is conceivably from his own [i.e. Koheleth's] hand" (*Proverbs, Ecclesiastes, and the Song of Songs*, 226).

69. See, e.g., Seow, *Ecclesiastes*, 392–94. J. Stafford Wright says: "these verses put the imprimatur on the book" ("Ecclesiastes," in *The Expositor's Bible Commentary* [ed. Frank E. Gaebelein; Grand Rapids: Zondervan, 1991], 5:1137–97 [1196]).

70. Gordis argues that the epilogue may be "an apology and defense of the book against such criticisms as *Wisdom of Solomon* chap. 2, contains" (*Koheleth*, 350).

71. Bartholomew notes that the contradictory views expressed in Ecclesiastes set up "gaps," and argues: "Ecclesiastes itself gives us clues as to how the gap between empiricistic skepticism and the *carpe diem* perspective is to be filled.... [T]he epilogue is, I think, crucial in indicating finally how the narrator intends us to fill in the gaps" (*Reading Ecclesiastes*, 253). He continues, "12:13–14 ensures a foolproof reading of Ecclesiastes" (p. 254). Andrew G. Shead writes to "present instead an epilogue which, together with 1:1–2 and 12:8, provides the reader with the book's own key to the message it sets forth" ("Reading Ecclesiastes 'Epilogically,'" *TB* 48, no. 1 [1997]: 67–91 [67]).

72. Fox writes: "The caution the epilogue expresses is a public, protective stance, intended to ease acceptance of Qohelet's pungent words" (*A Time to Tear Down*, 372).

73. Salyer argues: "*both* Qoheleth and the frame narrator are literary creations whose roles dissent because they represent two epistemological poles which were perceived as conflicting by the implied author. Indeed, the implied author of Ecclesiastes created their adversarial and mutually subversive relationship for the

by the same person (still clearly the majority view), are they written by someone (or someones) who approves of Qohelet's words and wishes to aid their acceptance by appending a more orthodox conclusion;[74] or are they written to highlight what the editor thought was important in the book;[75] or perhaps they were written to connect Ecclesiastes to other wisdom literature, especially Proverbs;[76] or are they written by someone who disapproves of Qohelet's words and hopes to subdue the unorthodoxy of the book (perhaps also making a few minor additions elsewhere);[77] or are they perhaps written by someone who fundamentally misunderstood Qohelet's words;[78] or are there two epilogues, one of which commends Qohelet, the other being more critical,[79] possibly one from the writer of the rest of the book and the other the words of an editor?[80]

purpose of exploiting those well-perceived differences in order to say something about the prospects and limitations of all human knowing" (*Vain Rhetoric*, 215–16).

74. See, e.g., Murphy, *Ecclesiastes*, 125–30.

75. Shannon Burkes refers to "the final verses (12:9–14), which sum up for the reader what this particular editor would like one to take away from the work, in case one might be led to the wrong conclusions" (*Death in Qoheleth and Egyptian Biographies of the Late Period* [SBLDS 170; Atlanta: Society of Biblical Literature, 1999], 1).

76. Wilson argues: "It is probable that the editor(s) who appended Qoh 12:9–14 shaped these verses in light of Proverbs 1–9, which already occupied their present position" ("'The Words of the Wise,'" 189). G. T. Sheppard writes: "Qoheleth has been thematized by the epilogue in order to include it fully within a 'canon conscious' definition of sacred wisdom, one that is remarkably similar to that of Sirach and Baruch" ("The Epilogue to Qoheleth as Theological Commentary," *CBQ* 39, no. 2 [1977]: 182–89 [188]). More recently, Brown has written: "This 'epilogue' serves both to confirm the sapiential character of the putative author and to bring his message into the biblical mainstream." He adds, "The epilogist's words significantly qualify Qoheleth's own" (*Ecclesiastes*, 116).

77. Longman argues: "Qohelet's speech is a foil, a teaching device, used by the second wise man in order to instruct his son (12:12) concerning the dangers of speculative, doubting wisdom in Israel" (*The Book of Ecclesiastes*, 38). He asserts later that, "this description of Qohelet's task lacks any honorifics or terms of respect" (p. 277).

78. Melchert writes of 12:12–13: "Here is the voice of a censor warning reader-learners not to take too seriously what has been said in the preceding book. In recommending that everything can be summed up in a one-line wise saying, he either profoundly misunderstands Qohelet's message(s), or else he seeks to mislead reader-learners" (*Wise Teaching*, 135).

79. See, for example, Loader, who maintains: "When we read Ecclesiastes from the perspective of the first redactor, we have before us a different book than when we read it from the standpoint of the second redactor" (*Ecclesiastes*, 135).

80. This is the position that Seow (*Ecclesiastes*, 38) and Fox (*A Time to Tear Down*, 95–96, 144) adopt.

All these possibilities find support among modern scholars, and it is notable that even in the most recent works in English there is disagreement (1) regarding the extent of any secondary additions, from none (Salyer; Provan; Bartholomew), or possibly none (Davis), to 12:13b–14 (Fox; Seow), or 12:9–14 (Brown; Tamez; Huwiler; Burkes; Christianson; Melchert; Ogden and Zogbo); (2) regarding whether there are one (Huwiler; Longman) or two epilogues (Tamez; Fox; Seow; Ogden and Zogbo); (3) regarding whether the message of the book is to be sought in Qohelet's words (Christianson), or in the theology of the frame narrator (Longman), or perhaps in the way the epilogue guides us to "fill in the gaps" (Provan; Bartholomew); (4) regarding whether there is a fundamental incongruity between the frame and Qohelet's words (Brown; Melchert; Longman)—and if there is, whether this is part of the book's message (Salyer), or a "garish, 'establishment-issue' frame" (Christianson)—or whether the epilogue is basically in harmony with the rest of the book (Provan; Huwiler; Fox; Seow).

3.5. Conclusion

I believe I have demonstrated that at least for modern readers (clearly illustrated by the many positions adopted by recent commentators) the name or title קהלת bristles with prickly issues which mean that the word raises many questions for readers and creates gaps that they are required to fill in order to make sense of this enigmatic character and to determine what role he plays in the book of Ecclesiastes. In short, קהלת is highly ambiguous.

Chapter 4

הבל IN ECCLESIASTES

4.1. *The Importance of the Word* הבל

There seems little doubt that הבל is a, if not *the*, key word in the book of Ecclesiastes. Whether or not one accepts that the *inclusio*, הבל הבלים אמר [ה]קהלת הבל הבל, in 1:2 and 12:8 is the work of the writer of what lies within that *inclusio*,[1] few would dispute that it captures well an overriding theme in the book.[2] Moreover, it would seem that how readers understand this word will have a considerable bearing on how they read the book. So, for example, Ogden and Zogbo assert, "There is no doubt that the understanding we have of this word will determine our evaluation of the book and its message."[3] Miller likewise argues that הבל "has correctly been recognized as pivotal to understanding the book of

---

1. Christianson maintains that הבל is "the most critical (and meaningful) word for both Qoheleth *and* the frame narrator" (*A Time to Tell*, 79, his original).

2. As I will discuss below, Whybray argues that the *inclusio* was written by an editor who did not correctly represent Qohelet's views: "the words הבל הבלים . . . , all is הבל' in 1,2, repeated in 12,8, are not those of Qoheleth: they are an editorial interpretation of what was supposed to be the essence of Qoheleth's teaching, placed at the beginning and conclusion of his work to guide the reader to read it in a particular way. It should not be assumed that this is a correct interpretation of his thought" ("Qoheleth as a Theologian," in Schoors, ed., *Qohelet in the Context of Wisdom*, 239–65 [263]). F. Ellermeier expresses a similar view when he writes of the motto: "im allerhöchsten Grade misverständliche Summierung Qoheletscher Aussagen" (*Qohelet*, Vol. 1, part 1 [Herzberg: Jungfer, 1967], 100).

3. Ogden and Zogbo, *A Handbook*, 2. Fredericks expresses the same sentiments when he argues, "any reading of Ecclesiastes is based on one's estimation of this key word" (*Coping with Transience*, 14–15). Salyer describes הבל and יתרון as "the north (*hebel*) and south (*yitrôn*) poles from which the other terms gain their latitudinal and longitudinal bearings." He maintains that "This gives the reader a specific reading grid or lens through which they are to interpret the narrator's observations" (*Vain Rhetoric*, 248). By contrast, Whybray notes, "The precise meaning of *hebel* as used by Qoheleth has been the subject of much discussion . . . and the word has been translated in many different ways," but then adds, "Ultimately this question is a technical one *of secondary importance*" (*Ecclesiastes*, 26, my emphasis).

Ecclesiastes as a whole. . . . [T]he approach taken to הבל dramatically shapes the way the entire book is understood."[4] Crenshaw says about the expression, הכל הבל, "The function of the motto is to guide the reader toward a proper interpretation of Qohelet's words."[5] Similarly, Fox writes, "The book's motto is a thesis that we can expect to see validated by the following monologue, and which by this expectation controls the way we read."[6] But herein lies a problem: if the word הבל is so important (or "pivotal") in "guiding" the reader, in "shaping" our understanding— if not actually "determin[ing] our evaluation of the book and its message," or even "control[ling] the way we read"—the fact that it is understood in different ways by different commentators is bound to result in very varied readings of the book. Farmer reveals that she has perceived the problem when she writes,

> How is it possible for one small book to generate such opposite and contra-dictory theories about its meaning? One important reason is the ambiguity of the thematic word *hebel*. . . . Ecclesiastes has been understood in radically different ways by different readers in part because the thematic metaphor "all is *hebel*" is fundamentally ambiguous.[7]

4.2. *Translation and Interpretation of* הבל

A study of the translations in modern English Bibles already gives some indication of the problem: the NRSV (and the RSV before it, as well as the KJV and the NKJV) uses "vanity";[8] the NEB opts for "emptiness";[9] while

4. Douglas B. Miller, "Qohelet's Symbolic Use of הבל," *JBL* 117, no. 3 (1998): 437–54 (437). For a detailed discussion, see his *Symbol and Rhetoric in Ecclesiastes*.

5. Crenshaw, *Ecclesiastes*, 23.

6. Fox, *Qohelet*, 168. It seems to me that Fox has softened this assertion a little in his more recent book, *A Time to Tear Down*, where—rather than *controlling* the way we read—he writes about the motto giving "strong interpretive guidance": "The book's motto is a thesis that the reader can expect to see validated in the following monologue, and this expectation *channels the interpretation*" (p. 163, my emphasis).

7. Farmer, *Who Knows What is Good?*, 142, 146. Salyer expresses similar senti-ments when he writes, "the semantic opacity of the term *hebel* also adds a great deal of ambiguity to this verse. This compromises its ability to thoroughly direct the reader's understanding of Qoheleth's message and character" (*Vain Rhetoric*, 248).

8. By contrast, Graham Ogden wrote an article entitled, "'Vanity' it certainly is not" (*BT* 38 [1987]: 301–7). Murphy agrees, but renders הבל as "vanity" anyway: "'Vanity' is certainly not the best rendering, but I am using it as a code word in the translation in order to call attention to הבל as it occurs in the book" (*Ecclesiastes*, xxxiii). As we shall see, this is quite a common approach, but it is one thing for scholars to declare their intention to use a "code word," it is quite another to use this word in a translation for general use.

the REB (and the JB/NJB and NJPSV) renders the word as "futility";[10] the NIV (and the New Living Translation) translates with "meaningless";[11] the GNB with "useless";[12] and *The Message* with "smoke."[13] The words "vanity," "emptiness," "futility," "meaningless" and "useless" have *some* similarity in meaning ("smoke" less so), but they are far from being identical. Moreover, if הבל is understood as a key word in the book, the difference in meaning between these words proves to be very important.

The problem is compounded when recent commentaries and studies are taken into consideration. In a book published in 1987, Ogden devotes an appendix to "The Meaning of the Term *Hebel*" and states that

9.   John E. McKenna argues that "Futility, emptiness, ridiculous, incongruous, ironic, illusory, incomprehensible, valueless, nothing, absurd, temporary, all the words that might be employed to bear Qohelet's thought to us, can each be adequate in this or that particular situation in the exploration, but none are adequate in and of themselves to cause us to hear the real nature of the world's relation to its Creator" ("The Concept of *Hebel* in the Book of Ecclesiastes," *SJT* 45 [1992]: 19–28 [22]). Ogden maintains that "It seems abundantly evident from the representative examples of *hebel* which we have investigated that Qoheleth does not mean to claim that life is empty, vain, and meaningless" (*Qoheleth*, 21). For a fascinating discussion of "emptiness" in Ecclesiastes and in Chinese society, see Peter K. H. Lee, "Re-reading Ecclesiastes in the Light of Su Tung-p'o's Poetry," *Ching Feng* 30 (1987): 214–36.

10.   Whybray contends that "it would be wise to reconsider the meaning of the word הבל as unlikely to imply a total rejection of everything in life as futile or valueless . . . "futility" is certainly inappropriate" ("Qoheleth as a Theologian," 251, 264). L. Wilson argues similarly, saying in relation to the word הבל, "This reality is not so much futile, or absurd, or meaningless, but rather it is complex, ambiguous, enigmatic" ("Artful Ambiguity in Ecclesiastes 1,1–11," 362).

11.   Provan, in a commentary specifically on the NIV text, states, "It is certainly true that to translate *hebel* as "meaningless," as the NIV does, causes serious difficulties for the interpretation of the book as a unified work, for even a cursory reading of Ecclesiastes demonstrates that Qohelet does not consider everything 'meaningless'" (*Ecclesiastes, Song of Songs*, 51). Ogden and Zogbo also assert, "we do not agree that *hevel* means 'vain,' 'meaningless,' or 'worthless'" (*A Handbook*, 4). Seow agrees, arguing that Qohelet "does not mean that everything is meaningless or insignificant" (*Ecclesiastes*, 59). Christianson maintains that "Clearly a word is needed that best represents the majority of instances [in which הבל occurs]," but "'Meaningless' (NIV), for example, does not accomplish this" (*A Time to Tell*, 87).

12.   Ogden's article, "'Vanity' it Certainly is Not," also takes issue with the GNB translation (and that of the NIV).

13.   Ellul cites André Chouraqui who translates "smoke of smoke, all is smoke" (*La Bible, traduite et présentée par André Chouraqui* [Paris: Desclée de Brouwer, 1975], 113–14), saying, "I disagree with this interpretation. In the first place, as with 'vapor,' I fail to see the meaning of 'smoke of smoke.' All I see in it is a silly redundancy. . . . I cannot see that this idea has anything to do with Qohelet's content" (*Reason for Being*, 50).

in its occurrences outside Qoheleth, *hebel* means something equivalent to "vanity," "nothingness," "vapour." This is the sense we discover from its uses in Deut 32:21; Isa 57:13; Jer 8:19; 10:8; 51:18; Prov 13:11; 21:6; Ps 78:33, and many others; it addresses the notion of the uselessness, the powerlessness of the idols, and the fruitlessness of much human endeavour.[14]

This concurs with BDB, which gives the meanings of הבל as "1) vapour, breath, *fig* vanity; and 2) *fig* of what is evanescent, unsubstantial, worthless, vanity." However, after a study of the contexts in which this word is found in Ecclesiastes, Ogden comes to the conclusion that, "the term *hebel* in Qoheleth has a distinctive function and meaning: it conveys the notion that life is enigmatic, and mysterious; that there are many unanswered and unanswerable questions."[15] He makes the following suggestions for translation (in a journal article published the same year):

> Our translations of Ecclesiastes will do greater justice to the author's intention if we render the term *hebel* by words such as "enigma," "mystery," and the compound forms in 1:2 and 12:8 as something approaching "everything (about life) is exceedingly enigmatic," or, "there are so many unanswered questions"![16]

Crenshaw, in a study published the same year as Ogden's book,[17] maintains that in Ecclesiastes the word הבל "shows two nuances: temporal ('ephemerality') and existential ('futility' or 'absurdity')."[18] He continues,

---

14. Ogden, *Qoheleth*, 19.

15. Ibid., 22. His understanding of this word is not new: a similar perspective is seen, for example, in the work of W. E. Staples, who wrote as long ago as 1943, "the author does not look upon these things so much as 'vain' as incomprehensible. They are mysteries which are unfathomable to his finite mind" ("The 'Vanity' of Ecclesiastes," *JNES* 24, no. 2 [1943]: 95–104 [104]). Much more recently, Bartholomew has expressed his approval of Ogden's view (*Reading Ecclesiastes*, 166 n. 109). Seow comes to similar conclusion about הבל, arguing that "the activities in the world and their unpredictable consequences are said to be *hebel*. . . . They are unpredictable, arbitrary, and incomprehensible," but he goes on to say, "it is clear that no single English word is adequate to convey the nuances of the Hebrew . . . we will follow the traditional translations . . . and use the term 'vanity' to represent all that *hebel* may mean" (*Ecclesiastes*, 102). Wilson, like Ogden, uses the word "enigmatic" in relation to הבל ("Artful Ambiguity," 362).

16. Ogden, "'Vanity' it Certainly is Not," 307. Ogden and Zogbo suggest, "In the context of the book, and given the situations it describes, *hevel* seems most often to mean 'incomprehensible,' 'enigmatic,' 'mysterious,' 'impossible to understand'" (*A Handbook*, 4).

17. Crenshaw's *Ecclesiastes* was first published in the USA in 1987. I refer in this study to the British edition published in 1988 by SCM.

18. Crenshaw, *Ecclesiastes*, 57.

The first category, breath or vapour, is reinforced by the image of chasing or herding the wind (cf. 2:17). Wind, breath, and smoke are insubstantial when viewed from one perspective. Nevertheless, they are very real, even if one cannot see the wind or take hold of any one of the three. Although Qohelet and the person who wrote the *inclusio* normally prefer the second sense of *hebel*, this preference is not exclusive. Several uses in the book virtually demand the first meaning, that of fleeting appearance and ephemerality.[19]

His own translation of the *inclusio* is, "Utter futility! Everything is futile!"[20] Crenshaw seems to see the meaning of הבל in Ecclesiastes as being much more closely tied to the other uses in the Hebrew Bible than does Ogden.[21]

Fox, in a book published two years later, uses the second word that Crenshaw suggested in his second category above when he translates הבל as "absurd."[22] However, he, like Ogden, maintains that "the use of *hebel* in Qohelet is distinctive,"[23] and he argues that "The *hebel* leitmotif disintegrates if the word is assigned several different meanings."[24] I will discuss Fox's understanding of this word in more detail a little later.

19. Ibid., 58.

20. A few years earlier, Derek Kidner wrote, "In the terms we use today the summing up could be: 'Utter futility . . . utter futility! The whole thing is futile'" (*The Message of Ecclesiastes: A Time to Mourn, and a Time to Dance* [Leicester: InterVarsity, 1976], 22). Bergant also suggests that the word "connotes pointlessness or futility" (*Job, Ecclesiastes*, 231), although, like others, she uses the word "vanity" throughout (but without specifically designating it as some kind of "code word"). Her article, "Vanity (*Hebel*)," *The Bible Today* 22 (1984): 91–92, takes a similar approach (here הבל "bespeaks futility and worthlessness" [p. 91]), and in *Israel's Wisdom Literature*, she maintains that "The word . . . takes on the connotation of futility or absurdity" (p. 110).

21. So also Whybray, who says "the meanings of the word הבל itself do not seem to be substantially different from its meanings elsewhere in the Old Testament" ("Qoheleth as a Theologian," 264).

22. Brown follows this rendering in *Character in Crisis*, 129–34 (which Fox notes in *A Time to Tear Down*, 32), but this is not clear in Brown's more recent commentary, where he refers to the "amorphous quality to the meaning of *hebel* as Qoheleth employs it," saying that it is "difficult to translate consistently" (*Ecclesiastes*, 22). Like others I have mentioned above, he uses "vanity" as a code word for this untranslatable term.

23. Fox, *Qohelet*, 46. In *A Time to Tear Down* he argues that "Qohelet uses a common word in a new way" (p. 27).

24. Fox, *Qohelet*, 36. He expands on this in *A Time to Tear Down*, saying, "If Qohelet were saying, 'X is transitory; Y is futile; Z is trivial,' then the summary, 'All is *hebel*' would be meaningless. Indeed, it would be specious reasoning or a rhetorical device—arguing from disparate categories that share only a multivalent label" (p. 36).

Michel also published a book on Ecclesiastes in 1989, also suggests the word "absurd" (*Absurdität*) as a translation for הבל, and, like Fox, draws attention to the use of the word "absurd" by Albert Camus.[25] However, Michel interprets "absurdity" in terms of "meaninglessness" (*Sinnlosigkeit*), saying, "I therefore suggest rendering הבל in Qohelet as 'absurd,' with the sense of 'meaningless.'"[26] He explains,

> By use of the strange word "absurd," awareness should be raised that the core arguments of Qohelet are of a philosophical nature. Wisdom is based on the conviction that God has placed things in the world, such that wise people should recognise the laws of nature and the meaning of what happens. Qohelet, in contrast to this optimistic way of viewing life, represents the worldview of a skeptic, with the basic theory that people are unable to make sense of what happens under the sun.[27]

This is similar to Barucq, who also translates הבל as "absurd" (*absurdité*), arguing that "it is understood that God controls the meaning, but people do not pierce the mystery of what he does. This leads to the collapse of wisdom."[28] Barucq, however, clearly use "absurd" differently from Fox who responds to Barucq's statement thus:

> While Qohelet would agree with this statement, it is not what he means by the word *hebel*. As I see it, *hebel* designates not the mysterious but rather (and this is a fundamental difference) *the manifestly irrational or meaningless*. To call something *hebel* is an evaluation of its nature. Whether or not there is meaning beyond the visible surface of events, that surface, which is the world as it presents itself to humans, *is* warped.

25. C. B. Peter wrote an article before either of these commentaries came out, directly comparing Ecclesiastes and Camus, and discussing the parallels between "vanity" in Ecclesiastes and "absurdity" in Camus; see Peter's "In Defence of Existence: A Comparison Between Ecclesiastes and Albert Camus," *Bangalore Theological Forum* 12 (1980): 26–43. (Kenneth W. James's article, "Ecclesiastes: Precursor of Existentialists," *The Bible Today* 22 [1984]: 85–90, and N. Karl Haden's "Qoheleth and the Problem of Alienation," *Christian Scholars Review* 17 [1987]: 52–66, make for interesting comparison with this article.) Matthew J. Schwartz takes a different tack when he writes in "Koheleth and Camus: Two Views of Achievement" (*Judaism* 35 [1986]: 29–34), "Koheleth's world is neither meaningless nor absurd, and man may work, learn and be happy" (p. 31). Christianson also reflects on Camus's use of "absurd," and on existentialism more generally (*A Time to Tell*, 81–91, and the Postscript, "Qoheleth and the Existential Legacy of the Holocaust," 259–74).

26. Michel, *Untersuchungen*, 44 (my translation).

27. Ibid., 44–45 (my translation).

28. A. Barucq, *Ecclésiaste* (VS 3; Paris: Beauchesne, 1968), 55–56. Jean-Jacques Lavoie also uses the word *absurdité* (*La pensée du Qohélet: Étude exégétique et intertextuelle* [Quebec: Fides, 1992], 207–25).

Similarly, while *hebel* is a near-synonym of "meaningless," the terms differ insofar as "absurd" is not merely the absence of meaning, but an active violation of meaningfulness.[29]

In another commentary written in 1989, Whybray concurs with the NRSV translation in reading הבל as "vanity."[30] But he suggests that the *inclusio* was written by an editor who did not correctly represent Qohelet's own views:

> Elsewhere Qoheleth never employs this extremely emphatic form of speech, nor does he speak in such a general way of *everything* as "vanity": he applies the word only to specific, clearly defined situations. Consequently it cannot be affirmed with certainty that v. 2 expresses Qoheleth's own thought: the verse is undoubtedly an *interpretation* of his thought, but may well be a *mis*understanding or at least an over-simplification of it.[31]

What, then, can we conclude from a comparison of the translation of the word הבל in these commentaries by Ogden, Crenshaw, Fox, Michel and Whybray (contemporaneous commentators, all, moreover, white American or European scholars, who must share similar "dynamic socio-historical contexts," to use Hawthorn's phrase)—which were published within three years of each other? Perhaps the first thing to note is that the commentators give us four different translations of the word: "enigmatic" (enigma), "futile" (futility), "absurd" (absurdity) and "vanity."[32]

---

29. Fox, *Qohelet*, 36, his emphasis. In *A Time to Tear Down* (p. 34), Fox also notes that Pennacchini "glosses *hebel* as 'absurd,' but he interprets the concept as an assertion of incomprehensibility relative to a cultural climate (p. 496)" (see Bruno Pennacchini, "Qohelet ovvero il libro degli assurdi," *Euntes Docete* 30 [1977]: 491–510). It would appear that the word "absurd" is open to various interpretations also, and therefore ambiguous!

30. Many commentators retain the word "vanity." It seems to me that those who describe it as a "code word" (or similar; so, e.g., Murphy and Seow) have adopted the most useful approach. Simply to offer it as a *translation* is, I believe, no longer (if it ever really was) adequate.

31. Whybray, *Ecclesiastes*, 35, his emphasis. Longman contends that Whybray "goes on . . . rightly to attribute these verses to a second hand, but wrongly to argue that this later editor "misunderstood" or at least "oversimplified" Qohelet's message" (*The Book of Ecclesiastes*, 62). Fox, however, argues, "Of course it is an over-simplification, but that's what summaries are. There is no need to ascribe it to an editor who did not read Qohelet's message quite right. In fact, the motto is best ascribed to the author, who is here paraphrasing Qohelet, who is his creation" (*A Time to Tear Down*, 162).

32. Melchert provides a useful list, divided into eight categories, of different translations offered for הבל (*Wise Teaching*, 117).

Moreover, the word "absurd" seems to be used in two different ways. Crenshaw and Fox agree that הבל (translated as "futile" and "absurd" respectively) is Qohelet's negative assessment of everything (הכל), but while Fox thinks that Qohelet is consistent in his use of the word (which takes on a distinctive meaning in Ecclesiastes), Crenshaw finds two different "nuances" (in line with its use elsewhere in the Hebrew Bible). Fox and Ogden agree that the use of הבל in Ecclesiastes is distinct from the rest of the Hebrew Bible, but while Fox sees it as a negative assessment of הכל, Ogden sees it as a neutral ("enigmatic") term used to describe what is beyond human comprehension. Fox and Barucq both render הבל as "absurd," but they understand absurdity differently, it being a decidedly pessimistic term for Fox, but much less so for Barucq. Whybray agrees with Crenshaw and Fox in seeing הבל as a negative term, but does not agree that Qohelet would use the superlative הבל הבלים.

The problem continues in more recent commentaries and studies. Perhaps the issue can be seen at its sharpest by comparing comments by Longman (1998) and Seow (1997) on the use of הבל in Eccl 1:2. Longman translates הבל as "meaningless" and declares confidently, "The book of Ecclesiastes leaves no doubt about Qohelet's ultimate conclusion— everything is completely meaningless."[33] Seow specifically states that Qohelet "does *not* mean that everything is meaningless or insignificant, but that everything is beyond human apprehension and comprehension."[34] He argues that "In Ecclesiastes itself, the meaning of *hebel* is difficult to determine" and "No single definition . . . works in every case."[35] However,

---

33. Longman, *The Book of Ecclesiastes*, 61. Loader makes an almost identical statement (*Ecclesiastes*, 20). Longman argues (pp. 61–65) that "meaningless" is actually the normal sense of the word elsewhere in the Hebrew Bible, too. Huwiler is a little more circumspect when she states, "The word thus has varying nuances in different contexts within Ecclesiastes. With that understood, 'meaningless' is an appropriate translation, although the careful reader will observe specific instances in which meaning is not entirely the issue" (Murphy and Huwiler, *Proverbs, Ecclesiastes, Song of Songs*, 164). T. M. Moore, in a recent meditation on Ecclesiastes, explicitly follows Longman in the *inclusio* in 1:2 and for most of chs. 1–3, but changes from "meaningless" to "vanity" when he gets to Eccl 4, then uses "vanity" in the *inclusio* 12:8 (*Ecclesiastes: Ancient Wisdom when All Else Fails. A New Translation and Interpretive Paraphrase* [Downers Grove, Ill.: InterVarsity, 2001]).

34. Seow, *Ecclesiastes*, 59, my emphasis.

35. Eugene H. Peterson argues that "various meanings glance off the surface of the word as the context shifts" (*Five Smooth Stones for Pastoral Work* [Grand Rapids: Eerdmans, 1980], 153). Similarly, Webb maintains that "it is like the whole category of things it refers to: rootless, unstable, subject to continuous change" (*Five Festal Garments*, 90).

something of his own understanding of the word comes across when he writes,

> Perhaps it was [the] imagery of a futile pursuit that led the author to use the word *hebel* for matters that are beyond the grasp of mortals—both physically (for the literal meaning of *hebel*) and intellectually (for the figurative use of the word). So the activities in the world and their unpredictable consequences are said to be *hebel*. . . . They are unpredictable, arbitrary, and incomprehensible.[36]

Although this puts a more negative slant on things than is offered by Ogden and Zogbo (1997), it is not so far from their suggested renderings, "incomprehensible," "enigmatic," "mysterious" and "impossible to understand,"[37] or from Wilson's view (1998) that it "is not so much futile, or absurd, or meaningless, but rather it is complex, ambiguous, enigmatic."[38]

Davis (2000) contends that "In Hebrew as in English, 'breath, vapor' (*hevel*) chiefly connotes ephemerality (e.g. Psalm 62:9; Job 7:16), not emptiness,"[39] concluding, "this is the sense it has most often for Koheleth."[40] A similar line is followed by Provan (2001), although he adds that it is not just "the *ephemerality* of reality, from the mortal point of view, that Qohelet has in mind in using *hebel*. It is also the *elusive* nature of reality, that is, the way in which it resists our attempts to capture it and contain it, to grasp hold of it and control it."[41]

Christianson (1998), on the other hand, maintains that "'absurd' is the best expression of Qoheleth's use of הבל. All said, 'absurd' remains the best choice throughout, if for no other reason than that the reader is enabled to perceive the thematic unity of the judgments."[42] Fox (1999) continues to hold to this rendering also, arguing that "The statement 'all is absurd,' unlike the ones produced by other renderings, is true of much more of what Qohelet describes, even in passages where he does not use the formulaic *hebel*-judgment."[43] And Tamez (2000) writes, "I follow

36. Seow, *Ecclesiastes*, 102.
37. Ogden and Zogbo, *A Handbook*, 4.
38. L. Wilson, "Artful Ambiguity," 362.
39. However, Rami Shapiro, in a recent meditation on Ecclesiastes, writes, "The idea that Solomon had been crying, 'Emptiness! Emptiness upon emptiness!' rather than the well-known 'Vanity of vanities!' shook me deeply. Suddenly the whole book of Ecclesiastes changed for me" (*The Way of Solomon: Finding Joy and Contentment in the Wisdom of Ecclesiastes* [San Francisco: HarperSanFrancisco, 2000], 2).
40. Davis, *Proverbs, Ecclesiastes, and the Song of Songs*, 167.
41. Provan, *Ecclesiastes, Song of Songs*, 52, his emphasis.
42. Christianson, *A Time to Tell*, 87.
43. Fox, *A Time to Tear Down*, 42.

Michael V. Fox in believing that the broadest meaning, which embraces almost all the nuances that appear in the book, is 'the absurd' in its oppressive and tragic sense."[44] By contrast, Bartholomew (1998) argues that "Qoheleth is *not* declaring life to be absurd in an existentialist way but shows it to be empirically impossible to grasp";[45] and Clifford (1998) asserts, "To translate every occurrence 'absurd' (in a modern existential sense) is too sweeping."[46] Whybray (1998) contends that "There is no English equivalent for the term הבל as it was used by Qoheleth," argues that "'futility' is certainly inappropriate," but allows that "'Absurd' does not carry the same implication, and probably comes nearer the mark."[47] However, he goes on to say, "the meanings of the word הבל itself do not seem to be substantially different from its meaning elsewhere in the Old Testament: he sees human life as insubstantial, transitory, sometimes senseless or absurd, in the perspective of eternity." In this he stands quite apart from Christianson, who argues: "It seems, then, that Qoheleth used the term quite unconventionally";[48] that there is "a uniquely existential quality of Qoheleth's use of the word";[49] and "Clearly *a* word is needed that best represents the majority of the instances."[50] Van der Wal (1998) is with Whybray on this, asserting, "In my opinion, the term הבל in Qohelet points to different things; I see the following meanings of the word הבל in the Book of Qohelet: it points to the absurdity or vanity of human acting (Qoh 2,11), secondly to the incomprehensibility, the enigma of life (Qoh 3,11), and thirdly it points to the fact that man and things are fading away."[51] Miller's approach (1998) is somewhat more sophisticated when he argues that הבל in Ecclesiastes is a "multi-valent symbol":

> Qohelet develops three major metaphorical senses of הבל: Insubstantiality, Transience, and Foulness. Qohelet structures his argument in order to mold these separate connotations into one multivalent literary symbol. For this reason, he can sometimes use the term in a way that assumes all

---

44. Tamez, *When the Horizons Close*, 34.
45. Bartholomew, *Reading Ecclesiastes*, 166, n. 109, my emphasis. He asserts, "Fox's translation seems to be influenced by modern existentialism and hence in danger of being anachronistic."
46. Richard J. Clifford, *The Wisdom Literature* (Interpreting Biblical Texts; Nashville: Abingdon, 1998), 103.
47. Whybray, "Qoheleth as a Theologian," 264.
48. Christianson, *A Time to Tell*, 82.
49. Ibid., 83.
50. Ibid., 87, my emphasis.
51. A. J. O. Van der Wal, "Unique Statement in Israel's Wisdom Tradition," in Schoors, ed., *Qohelet in the Context of Wisdom*, 413–24 (413).

three metaphors. This occurs most significantly in the framing statements of 1:2 and 12:8 in which Qohelet states that "all is הבל."[52]

Miller's "multi-valent *symbol*" is sufficiently different from a "multi-valent *label*" to avoid Fox's valid criticism: "If Qohelet were saying, 'X is transitory; Y is futile; Z is trivial,' then the summary, 'All is *hebel*' would be meaningless. Indeed, it would be specious reasoning or a rhetorical device—arguing from disparate categories that share only a multivalent label."[53] He argues: "Some things are Insubstantial; others are wrong and Foul; still others are Transient. None of these three metaphors *by itself* applies to *all* of human experience, and yet with this symbol, Qohelet can demonstrate that 'all is הבל' in one way or another."[54] Nonetheless, it seems to me that the outworking of Miller's argument actually leaves him quite close to commentators like Seow and even Ogden, as this comment in a later article (2000) demonstrates: "the declaration that certain things are *hebel* is Qoheleth's assertion of life's limitations and anomalies, not that all of life is meaningless, vain, or absurd."[55]

Melchert (1998) develops the idea of הבל as a metaphor, noting that "once we have established the metaphor itself as a reference point, we must go on to do what most translators do: say what the metaphor means."[56] However, rather than try to pin down the motto, Melchert raises the question:

---

52. Miller, "Qohelet's Symbolic Use of הבל," 452. Clifford uses the same categories when he argues, "*Hebel* characterizes some aspects of life as insubstantial and transient, and other aspects as wrong or repugnant" (*The Wisdom Literature*, 103). Burkes picks up on the concept of insubstantiality, observing: "The main theme that emerges from most of the commentators is that *hebel* signifies what is insubstantial and ephemeral, and while it certainly carries different nuances throughout the text of Qoheleth, these do seem to come closest to its core meaning" (*Death in Qoheleth*, 47). John Jarick uses the phrase "everything is transient," although he offers the rendering "everything is nothing" or "everything is changing" as capturing the essence of the words used in Ecclesiastes ("The Hebrew Book of Changes: Reflections on *hakkol hebel* and *lakkol zeman* in Ecclesiastes," *JSOT* 90 [2000]: 79–99).

53. Fox, *A Time to Tear Down*, 36.

54. Miller, "Qohelet's Symbolic Use of הבל," 454, his emphasis.

55. Douglas B. Miller, "What the Preacher Forgot: The Rhetoric of Ecclesiastes," *CBQ* 62 (2000): 215–35 (233 n. 50). Although in "Qohelet's Symbolic Use of הבל" he does note occasions when, "In these contexts, Fox is correct that Qohelet is seeking to communicate something akin to 'absurdity'," he points out that "Fox insists that הבל is *not* metaphorical" (p. 452 n. 52, my emphasis).

56. Melchert, *Wise Teaching*, 117.

What if this opening affirmation does not seek to be simply accepted or assimilated but seeks to arouse contention among reader-learners and thereby stimulate more testing by their own experience, evidence, and argument—perhaps even discussion? If that were the case, would it not be useful to choose a word that might well be read with different connotations, so as to allow or even encourage various assessments of the assertion itself? Indeed, is that not exactly what has occurred among readers and scholars through the centuries?[57]

He goes on to argue, "The text started a debate about the meaning of life and its various events that continues today. Instead of offering reader-learners a conclusion, suppose the text entices reader-learners to join in exploring conflicting views," concluding with the assertion (which I very much support): "If that were so, another strategy for reading is required,"[58] what Salyer refers to as "The Need for a New Loom."[59]

Salyer (2001), building on Miller's study of the metaphorical function of הבל, takes this a stage further and comes close to my own view when he states, "That Qoheleth has chosen such a polyvalent and fertile term is quite consistent with the rhetoric of ambiguity which operates throughout the book."[60] He maintains that "the opacity created by the use of *hebel* has created a definite sense of ambiguity regarding the book's overall theme," such that "Readers do not understand which of the various nuances of 'breath' is supposed to express the viewpoint of the narrator: the fleeting connotation, the empty connotation, the meaningless or absurd connotation, or some other aspect of the term's root metaphorical meaning."[61] I disagree with his suggestion that "a better way to handle

---

57. Ibid., 118.

58. Ibid., 118. Melchert also asks here, "If the author was seeking to transmit clearly and unequivocally his conclusions, why has he chosen words that are so ambiguous and open textured? Is it possible the author did not intend precision in meaning? If not, might that suggest a different way of reading this text?"

59. Salyer, *Vain Rhetoric*, 380. This is also discussed in I. J. J. Spangenberg, "A Century of Wrestling with Qohelet: The Research History of the Book Illustrated with a Discussion of Qoh 4,17–5,6," in Schoors, ed., *Qohelet in the Context of Wisdom*, 61–91. Both Salyer and Spangenberg note with agreement C. A. Newsom's comment: "scholarly work on Ecclesiastes has remained, with very few exceptions, the province of traditional historical criticism" ("Job and Ecclesiastes," in *Old Testament Interpretation—Past, Present, and Future: Essays in Honor of Gene M. Tucker* [ed. J. L Mays, D. L. Petersen and K. H. Richards; Nashville: Abingdon, 1995], 227–50 [242]).

60. Salyer, *Vain Rhetoric*, 256. Salyer has a wonderful expression here: "the rhetoric of ambiguity which rampages throughout the book" (p. 255). This sums up very well my thesis in this study.

61. Ibid., 256.

the semantic opacity of *hebel* is to allow it to have a dominant meaning (absurd) with a variety of other nuances (fleetingness, meaningless, transitory, futile),"[62] because this loads it with negativity and unnecessarily closes down something of the ambiguity of the word. This aside, Salyer captures something of my understanding of how הבל functions in Ecclesiastes when he says, "the implied author has consciously constructed a text which would recreate the same sense of *hebel* at a literary level that one often experiences in real life. . . . The rhetorical effect of the text's various gapping techniques and strategies of indirection is to recreate in the reader life's penchant for absurdity and ambiguity."[63]

There are a number of commentators (recent and otherwise) who attempt to render the word הבל in a literal rather than a figurative sense—although they tend then to explain in their commentary just what are the (figurative) implications of their literal rendition, at which point they, too, choose how they will interpret the metaphor. Thus Scott (1965) translates Eccl 1:2, "Breath of a breath! (says Qoheleth). The slightest breath! All is breath!," and explains, "The writer's thesis is that everything in man's experience of life in this world ('under the sun' [passim]) is empty of meaning or worth, both in itself and because of its transience."[64] Fredericks (1993) suggests, "Breath of breaths, utter breath, all is breath,"[65] then argues that "the key word in Ecclesiastes means 'temporary' in most cases, as opposed to any more negative meanings like 'empty, futile, vain,' etc."[66] Beal (1998) opts for, "'vapor of vapors,' says Qohelet, 'the whole of it is vapor,'" and continues: "While suggesting the fleeting, transient quality of all creation (from cosmos to polis), then, the vapor also suggests that there are always traces in creation—and in creation's undoing—of an unnameable other who is both caught 'in the fray' and beyond it."[67] Provan (2001) offers the translation, "'The merest of breaths,' says Qohelet, 'The merest of breaths. Everything is a breath,'" but (as noted above) he goes on to explain: "It is not, however, just the *ephemerality* of reality, from the mortal point of view, that Qoheleth has in mind in using *hebel*. It is also the *elusive* nature of reality, that is, the way in which it resists our attempts to capture it and

---

62. Ibid., 254.

63. Ibid., 17–18.

64. R. B. Y. Scott, *Proverbs, Ecclesiastes: A New Translation with Introduction and Commentary* (AB 18; New York: Doubleday, 1965), 209.

65. Fredericks, *Coping with Transience*, 11.

66. Ibid., 94.

67. Timothy K. Beal, "C(ha)osmopolis: Qohelet's Last Words," in *God in the Fray: A Tribute to Walter Brueggemann* (ed. Tod Linafelt and Timothy K. Beal; Minneapolis: Augsburg Fortress, 1998), 290–304 (302).

contain it, to grasp hold of it and control it."[68] And Farmer (1991), along similar lines, renders the second half of the verse, "the most breathlike of all breaths."[69] However, she goes on to argue:

> If the translation preserves the metaphor (as Scott does), the reader is forced to decide in what sense the comparison should be taken. In my opinion it is unfortunate that many modern versions of Ecclesiastes have chosen to take the decision away from the reader. Most translators obscure the metaphorical nature of the original statement and replace the concrete, nonjudgmental phrase ("breath" or "puff of air") with various abstract terms. . . . I would advise readers of the text in English to suspend judgment temporarily on the meaning of the metaphor and to substitute the phrase "breathlike" (or something similar) for every occurrence of the word "vanity" in the RSV. In this way they may allow the text to speak more clearly for itself before they draw interpretive conclusions about its meaning.[70]

Farmer does, nonetheless, seek to explain what "breathlike" might mean: "When we look closely at the ways in which the word is used in other parts of the Old Testament, it becomes clear that the essential quality to which *hebel* refers is lack of permanence rather than lack of worth or value. A breath, after all, is of considerable value to the one who breathes it. However, it is not something one can hang on to for long. It is airlike, fleeting, transitory, and elusive rather than meaningless."[71]

Garrett (1993) notes the difficulty of finding an adequate English word for all the occurrences of הבל in Ecclesiastes (where, he argues, sometimes "vapid" fits well, sometimes "absurd," sometimes, "meaningless"): he then takes Farmer's argument a stage further, arguing,

> One option, of course, is to translate *hebel* with a number of different words in accordance with context. This is legitimate translation procedure; but, as Fox points out, the Teacher is building a case around the word *hebel*. A variety of translations obscure this. It may be that the

---

68. Provan, *Ecclesiastes, Song of Songs*, 52, his emphasis.
69. Farmer, *Who Knows What is Good?*, 143, 152.
70. Ibid., 146. Salyer discusses at some length the metaphorical role of הבל in Ecclesiastes, and concludes that "the two extremes in this particular debate are best summarized by the analyses of Michael Fox and Kathleen Farmer, who accent the vehicle and tenor respectively" (*Vain Rhetoric*, 252). It seems that Salyer has got these terms the wrong way around (he notes later that Fox pays "close attention to the term's extended context, and specifically, the tenor of its various applications" [p. 253]), though I do not believe it is as clearcut as he makes out—as the following discussion should make clear. See Salyer, *Vain Rhetoric*, 250–57, and the literature referred to there.
71. Farmer, *Who Knows What is Good?*, 145.

modern, Christian reader can do no better than to import *hebel* into his or her vocabulary, much as has been done with *agape* and to a lesser extent *koinonia*.[72]

This approach seems to me to have a lot of merit (and is one I will adopt in this study), although the word cannot then function as the key word which "guide[s] our reading," "shapes the way the entire book is understood," "determines our evaluation of the book" or "controls the way we read." It would appear that the word הבל, rather than being the key that unlocks "the meaning" of Qohelet, is actually highly ambiguous and presents a gap of indeterminacy which the reader is required to fill in in order to create meaning. It thus functions as, what Rimmon would call, a "central gap": she writes,

> It is possible to establish a scale of the importance or centrality of gaps in the narratives in which they appear, ranging from the most trivial gaps, through various degrees of importance, to gaps which are so crucial and central in the work as to become its very subject . . . there are gaps which are so crucial and so central as to become the very pivot of the work in which they appear. . . . Gaps which do constitute central mysteries are generally kept open until the end of the narrative, as in detective stories, or even beyond the end, as in "The Figure in the Carpet," *The Turn of the Screw*, and *The Sacred Fount*.[73]

4.3. *The Uses of* הבל

The root הבל occurs a total of 38 times in Qohelet (if we follow the MT), and only 40 times elsewhere (plus eight occurrences of the name Abel,[74] also הֶבֶל) in the Old Testament. Of the latter, it is only once used

---

72. Garrett, *Proverbs, Ecclesiastes, Song of Songs*, 283. Derek Tidball is a good example of a commentator who translates the word in a wide variety of ways: "The phrase 'Meaningless! Meaningless! Utterly meaningless!' comes up thirty times in the book one way or another. He is saying that life, when you look at it hard enough, is 'a whisp or vapour, a puff of wind, a mere breath—nothing you can get your hands on; the nearest thing to zero.' Life is empty, useless, insignificant, zilch! Life is brief and insubstantial. It is frail and unreliable. It is futile and purposeless. It is also cruel and deceptive for it promises much and fails to live up to its promise; offers much but delivers little" (*That's Life! Realism and Hope for Today from Ecclesiastes* [Leicester: InterVarsity, 1989], 12). A number of commentators use a range of words to render הבל, or to capture its meaning or significance in different contexts. Thus Webb, for example, can contend that "it is a mistake to try to nail this word down, as though one 'right' meaning could be found for it in Ecclesiastes" (*Five Festal Garments*, 90).

73. Rimmon, *The Concept of Ambiguity*, 47–48.

74. Gen 4:2 (×2), 4 (×2), 8 (×2), 9, 25.

unambiguously as a noun meaning "breath" or "vapour," in Isa 57:13, where it is used in parallel to רוח. It functions a further 13 times[75] as an adjective or adverb which could be translated "breath-like" or "vapour-like," though different aspects of "breathlikeness" are appropriate in these verses and commentators disagree about the precise implications in each case—as a comparison of Christianson, Fox, Fredericks and Longman makes clear.[76] On another 11 occasions (all within the Psalms and Wisdom Literature[77]) הבל is used as a noun (and might on most occasions reasonably be rendered as "breath"[78]) which forms the basis of a comparison,

---

75. Isa 30:7; 49:4; Jer 10:3, 15; 16:19; 51:18; Zech 10:2; Job 9:29; 21:34; 27:12; 35:16; Prov 31:30; Lam 4:17. These could be read as nouns, but they would still serve much the same function. R. Albertz states: "as the governed noun it should be translated adj. In addition there is an adv. use" ("הֶבֶל, *hebel*, breath," *TLOT* 1:351–53 [351]). Christianson categorises most of these occurrences under the headings, "worthless/false," "no purpose/useless," "futile," "nothing/empty" and "deceptive in appearance," adding also three uses of the word הבליעל in 1 Sam 25:25; 2 Sam 16:7; 1 Kgs 21:13, which he reads as derivative. Longman argues that in many of these cases, "only 'meaningless' is possible" as a translation (*The Book of Ecclesiastes*, 63).

76. See Christianson, *A Time to Tell*, 79–81; Fox, *A Time to Tear Down*, 27–29; Fredericks, *Coping with Transience*, 15–22; Longman, *The Book of Ecclesiastes*, 61–64. See also Albertz, *TLOT* 1:351–53; D.C. Fredericks, "הֶבֶל," *NIDOTTE* 1:1005–6; K. Seybold, "הֶבֶל, *hebhel*, הֶבֶל," *TDOT* 3:313–20; O. Loretz, *Qohelet und der alte Orient: Untersuchungen zu Stil und theologischer Thematik des Buches Qohelet* (Freiburg: Herder, 1964), 218–25.

77. Pss 39:6, 7, 12; 62:10 (×2); 78:33; 94:11; 144:4; Job 7:16; Prov 13:11; 21:6. Some of these could also be read as adjectives, but they would still serve much the same function. Fredericks regards most of these as evidence for the sense of "temporary" outside of Ecclesiastes (*NIDOTTE* 1:1006; and *Coping with Transience*, 18–22), and Fox agrees at least in the cases of Job 7:16; Pss 39:6, 12; 144:4 Prov 21:6 (*A Time to Tear Down*, 28), but Christianson acknowledges this sense of the word only in Job 7:16 (*A Time to Tell*, 80); Longman argues that they mean "meaningless" (*The Book of Ecclesiastes*, 63).

78. Christianson argues that הבל means "breath/vapour" eight times in the Hebrew Bible: Pss 39:6, 7, 12; 62:10; 94:11; 144:4; Prov 21:6; Isa 57:13, and possibly also Ps 78:33 (*A Time to Tell*, 79–80). *DCH* 2 lists eight occurrences also, but agrees on only six of Christianson's list (italicised): *Isa 57:13*; *Pss 39:6, 12*; *62:10*, 10; *144:4*; Job 7:16; *Prov 21:6*. Fox reduces this to four in *A Time to Tear Down*, 27–28: Isa 57:13; Prov 13:11; 21:6 and Ps 144:4—but in *Qohelet* he maintained that this is "a sense apparent only in Isa 57:13 (p. 29; see also Longman, *The Book of Ecclesiastes*, 62). Fredericks says, "*hebel* is used only 3× in its literal sense of 'breath'," in Ps 62:10; Prov 21:6 and Isa 57:13 (*NIDOTTE* 1:1005). Albertz argues for the one occurrence in Isa 57:13 (*TLOT* 1:351). The literal sense of this word is also found in Rabbinic Hebrew, Jewish Aramaic, Mandean, Syriac, Ethiopic and Arabic (see Seybold, *TDOT* 3:313–14; and Gordon H. Johnston, "הבל," *NIDOTTE* 1:1003–5).

thus effecting the notion of "breathlikeness" in another way. There are ten occurrences[79] of nominal forms of הבל which seem to refer to idols or false (vapour-like?) gods, with two occurrences of verbal forms (in identical phrases in 2 Kgs 17:15 and Jer 2:5) immediately following use of the noun, probably indicating that people who followed false (vapour-like?) gods acted in a false (vapour-like?) way. Another three times[80] verbal forms appear: the first is a participle describing what false prophets do; the second is an imperative not to be הבל; and the last is a question posed by Job to his "friends" asking why they have become הבל (and, as in 2 Kgs 17:15 and Jer 2:5, the verb follows the nominal form). The words used in parallel with הבל, and probably therefore serving as near-synonyms, are ריק ("emptiness," Isa 30:7), תהו ("emptiness," Isa 49:4), בהלה ("terror," Ps 78:33), שקר ("deceit," Prov 31:30), לא־אל ("no god," Deut 32:21), רוח ("wind," Isa 57:13), כזב ("lie," Ps 62:10)[81] and צל עובר ("passing shadow," Ps 144:4).[82]

The name "Abel" probably indicates the transience of Abel's life[83]—although it might also be argued that it indicates absurdity, futility or meaninglessness (or something similar). Ellul asserts that the story of Abel should be taken into account when considering the word הבל in Qohelet because:

> When Qohelet read Genesis 4, clearly he knew all the meanings of the word. Abel was mist, breath, or smoke that melts away; his name predicted all the rest of his tragic life. . . . All is vanity, but not just in the

---

79. Deut 32:21; 1 Kgs 16:13, 26; 2 Kgs 17:15; Jer 2:5; 8:19; 10:8; 14:22; Jonah 2:9; Ps 31:7. Albertz states, "When used like a genuine noun it usually has the meaning 'idol'" (*TLOT* 1:351). Christianson agrees with all of these except 2 Kgs 17:15 and Jer 2:5 (*A Time to Tell*, 79; see also *DCH* 1:485). Longman leaves out 1 Kgs 16:13, 26, but adds Isa 57:13; Jer 10:15; 16:19; 51:18, where the context concerns idols even if הבל is not specifically used to designate them. He asserts that "It is absolutely certain that these passages are attributing uselessness or meaninglessness to the idols, not transitoriness" (*The Book of Ecclesiastes*, 63).

80. Jer 23:16; Ps 62:11; Job 27:12.

81. See further, *DCH* 1:485–86.

82. See further, Albertz, *TLOT* 1:351.

83. Seybold argues in relation to the name "Abel," "Since this is the only instance of the name, since it is not explained etymologically (in contrast to the name *Qayin*, 'Cain'), and especially since it is attached to a '"novellistic" figure' [quoting Mowinckel], everything favors the view that the name is intended to signify the breath character of the fleeting life of the victim and, in general, 'the transitoriness or vanity of man [as] a possibility of our common human existence' [quoting Westermann]. In this case Gen 4 (J) contains the earliest occurrence of the word *hebhel* and its meaning as a name does not have to be explained, since it is phonetically motivated and is thus directly present" (*TDOT* 3:315–16).

sense we have detected. Beyond what we have seen, all is Abel: that is, condemned beforehand, just like Abel. Everything bears Abel's name. Here we see an aspect of Qohelet's intransigence: everything that we see as power, grandeur, success—all this belongs in advance to the category of vanity. It is all condemned to disappear, to vanish, without any kind of posterity.[84]

From this brief survey of the occurrences of הבל in the Hebrew Bible two clear semantic threads can be drawn. The first arises from the use of words from this root to describe things as in some way breathlike or vaporous. The second probably derives from this: the use of הבל either specifically to refer to false gods (or, in some cases, possibly false teaching or worthless things more generally), or in contexts where false gods are being described. These are the semantic fields we should bring to bear in consideration of the use of the word in Ecclesiastes. In addition, the words that appear to be used in parallel to הבל should be borne in mind.

The plural noun[85] in its absolute and construct forms is *only* used of false gods[86] (two of these in construct with שוא, meaning "vain" or "empty"). Therefore, although הבל הבלים appears to be "the genitive expressive of the superlative idea,"[87] it is also possible that הבלים is a plural noun meaning "false gods" which is modified by הבל. Psalm 62:10 provides an example of this kind of construction, אך הבל בני־אדם, where the plural noun בני־אדם is described as הבל. Following this reading, the word הבל would also refer to these false gods so that the final clause, הכל הבלים, could be read, "all of them (i.e. the false gods) are *hebel*." An example of this type is found in Ps 94:11, which ends, המה הבל. This gives two possible readings for Eccl 1:2 (using at this stage as general a translation as possible for הבל): "'Supremely vapour-like,' says Qohelet, 'supremely vapour-like, everything is vapour-like'"; or "'False gods are a vapour [or "vapour-like"],' says Qohelet, 'false gods are a vapour—they are all a vapour.'"

84. Ellul, *Reason for Being*, 58. See also Davis, *Proverbs, Ecclesiastes, and the Song of Songs*, 168–69. It seems clear that the author of Ecclesiastes draws on the early chapters of Genesis which makes some kind of link with the name Abel quite possible. See especially, D. M. Clemens, "The Law of Sin and Death: Ecclesiastes and Genesis 1–3," *Themelios* 19 (1994): 5–8.

85. Deut 32:21; 1 Kgs 16:13, 26; Jer 8:19; 10:8; 14:22; Jonah 2:9; Ps 31:7.

86. This is noted by Ellul, *Reason for Being*, 52. He maintains: "we can say that *hebel* in the plural designates idols. Qohelet knows all this. We could perhaps translate 'vanity of vanities,' then, as 'vanity of idols,' or 'idols are wind'!"

87. G. Barton, *Ecclesiastes*, 72; and many other commentators since. Barton draws attention to קדש קדשים in Exod 29:37, עבד עבדים in Gen 9:25, שיר שירים in Song 1:1 and שמי השמים in 1 Kgs 8:27.

The problem in the first reading, of course, is to determine just what being "vapour-like" indicates. Does it mean that things are ephemeral because they have no real substance? Does it mean they are incomprehensible because their meaning cannot be grasped? Does it mean they are ultimately futile because they have no lasting value? Does it mean they are absurd because they are an offense to human reason? There is considerable room for interpretation: the precise implications of the word הבל are as difficult to grasp as is vapour or breath, so that the meaning of this key word, and the motto within which it appears, is itself "vapour-like." In this sense, הבל might be *interpreted* as "ambiguous/ambiguity" (I am *not* offering this as a translation of the word), because, just as a vapour or one's breath cannot be tied down, so the key phrase הבל הבלים and the book it introduces frustrate the reader's (and the commentator's) efforts to find a definitive meaning.

However, the interpretative strategy adopted in this study places the restriction on interpretation that it must conform to the semantic range of the words of the text, either singly or in combination. Therefore, while there are a number of possibilities for translation of הבל and the phrases in which it appears, this strategy demands that the interpretation of this word must display something of the qualities of vapour or breath, even though that be in a somewhat extended or figurative sense.[88] For example, the way in which Fox uses "absurd" is, I suggest, inappropriate as a translation of הבל. He claims that the motto (and the expectation to see it validated) "controls the way we read," and then grants that we "redefine *hebel* in accordance with what we read."[89] But when he translates הבל as "absurd," it seems to be derived totally from the way he has read Ecclesiastes, and to have nothing whatsoever to do with the inherent semantic properties of the word. Fox claims, "while the ephemerality of vapour is relevant to the way Qohelet applies *hebel* in some verses (e.g. 3:19 and 11:10), *no quality of vapour* can be applied to the situations that he calls *hebel*."[90] He then proceeds to define "absurd" in a way that does entail "no quality of vapour":

> The essence of the absurd is a disparity between two phenomena that are supposed to be joined by a link of harmony or causality but are actually disjunct or even conflicting. The absurd is irrational, an affront to reason, in the broad sense of the human faculty that seeks and discovers order in

88. Thus I do not agree with Albertz that "The basic meaning *totally disappears* in the largest category of occurrences (nom. clauses); here *hebel* is *simply* a negative term characterizing human experiences and basic qualities" (*TLOT* 1:352, my emphasis).

89. Fox, *Qohelet*, 168.

90. Ibid., 30, my emphasis.

the world about us. The quality of absurdity does not inhere in a being, act, or event in and of itself (though these may, by extension, be called absurd), but rather in the tension between a certain reality and a framework of expectations.[91]

Certainly "absurd" so defined is an apt description of the world as Fox understands Qohelet to view it, but how can the motto be said to *control* the way we read when its meaning is so clearly *controlled by* the way we read? Rather than the motto controlling the way the book is read, it seems that it provides a gap for the reader to fill in, the gap being restricted only by the semantic range of the word הבל. Good's article on Eccl 1:2–11 is a good example of a reading which appreciates the ambiguity of הבל, and as a result is reticent about too hastily making a decision concerning its interpretation. He explains his approach thus: "I have so far sought to avoid firm conclusions, for the good reason that every expression appears to have more than one possible meaning. The linear mode of interpretation works best if one resists haste in making decisions but, reading with care, ponders possibilities and remains in suspense of conviction."[92] He later refers specifically to the word הבל, saying, "Even the motto with which the poem began is left in the poem *without determinate meaning.* . . . The meaning of *hebel*, then, must be discovered progressively by following it through the rest of Qoheleth's essay . . . we must rest content with hypothesis about *hebel* from this poem."[93] This is precisely the point: the meaning of the key word הבל, and the motto in which it appears, is ambiguous because it may be interpreted in more than one way and thus provides a gap of indeterminacy. However, Good assumes that if the reader suspends judgment, the meaning will become clear as the reading process continues. But this is not the case in Ecclesiastes because the ambiguity of הבל, and other key words, phrases and concepts, is maintained throughout the book.

4.4. *How* הבל *Is Used in Ecclesiastes*

4.4.1. הבל הבל

It is time to turn our attention to an examination of the actual use to which the word הבל is put in the book of Ecclesiastes, to demonstrate

---

91. Ibid., 31. While Fox's basic stance is unchanged in *A Time to Tear Down*, I think it is softened a little by the addition of the line, "Qohelet has taken the term *some distance* from its literal sense" (p. 30, my emphasis). Moreover, he acknowledges that "The basic meaning of *hebel* . . . is *vapor*" (his emphasis), and that this is "the literal sense from which the others are derived" (p. 27).

92. Good, "The Unfilled Sea," 64.

93. Ibid., 71, my emphasis.

this ambiguity. We have already met the expression הבל הבל twice: in the *inclusio* in 1:2 and 12:8. It is used six times in total in Ecclesiastes. In the *inclusio* it appears to be a sweeping statement, "*everything* [or 'all'] is *hebel*," serving as a motto for the book. However, Fox writes, "what is 'all'? It need not encompass absolutely *everything*. 'All' is the sum of events, but this does not encompass everything whatsoever that happens or is done. 'All' is restricted to the sphere of human life."[94] It is not at all clear that this is true in the case of the motto, and there is no reason why the reader should understand it so when first reading 1:2. Moreover, given the fact that the word כל occurs more often than *any* other word in Ecclesiastes,[95] it seems clear that there is much emphasis in the book on "all" or "everything." Indeed, Christianson states, "Because of the all-encompassing referents for הכל, הבל must, it seems, be applied to all things without exception," to the extent that "הכל is here not simply limited to human activity or things under the sun, but to the very activity of God."[96] As will become clear, while I agree with the all-encompassing nature of הכל in relation to what happens "under the sun," I do not agree with Christianson that it includes "the very activity of God," except insofar as that can be observed "under the sun."

On three occasions, in verses with some marked similarities, the expression הכל הבל occurs in the phrase הכל הבל ורעות רוח:

תחת השׁמשׁ	שׁנעשׂו	המעשׂים		כל־ את־	ראיתי	1:14a
	שׁעשׂו	מעשׂי		בכל־ אני	ופניתי	2:11a
תחת השׁמשׁ	שׁנעשׂה	המעשׂה	כי רע עלי	את־החיים	ושׂנאתי	2:17a

ידי ובעמל שׁעמלתי לעשׂות   2:11b

	רוח:	ורעות	הבל הכל	והנה	1:14b
ואין יתרון תחת השׁמשׁ:	רוח	ורעות	הבל הכל	והנה	2:11c
	רוח:	ורעות	הבל הכל	כי־	2:17b

---

94. Fox, *A Time to Tear Down*, 40. However, there seems to be some inconsistency here with his later observations on 1:2. Discussing this verse, Fox states: "The phrase *hakkol habel* provides the subject of *hăbel hăbalim* and resumes the predicate in a de-emphasized form. In the final occurrence of the predicate (*habel*), some weight is given to the subject ('*all* is absurd'), while in the first two occurrences (*hăbel hăbalim . . . hăbel hăbalim*), emphasis is placed on the predicate. In this way, the motto expresses first the intensity of the *hebel*-judgment and then *its universality*" (p. 162, my emphasis).

95. The prefixed ו is used 361 times; ה 301 times; ל 230 times and ב 159 times. כל is the most frequent separate word, occurring 91 times. אשׁר is used 89 times (and the prefixed form שׁ 68–70 times), then כי 87 times.

96. Christianson, *A Time to Tell*, 89.

The linking of these two expressions, in addition to a further four verses where רעות רוח (including one occurrence of the apparently synonymous expression רעיון רוח) is connected to the word הבל, suggest that this expression might aid our interpretation of the word.

Both words, רעות and רוח, contain an element of ambiguity. According to BDB,[97] there are three roots spelled רעה: (1) "pasture, tend or graze"; (2) "associate with"; and (3) "desire, take pleasure in." Four words used in Ecclesiastes come from these roots: רעות (1:14; 2:11, 17, 26; 4:4, 6; 6:9); רעיון (1:17; 2:22; 4:16); מרעהו (4:4); and רעה (12:11). The last of these clearly means "shepherd": it is a common word in the Hebrew Bible which always bears that meaning elsewhere, and "shepherd" makes good sense in 12:11 (although to whom the metaphor "shepherd" refers is another question). מרעהו probably derives from the second root, "to associate with," as something like "companion" or "associate" seems best to fit that context, and the word is occasionally used elsewhere in the Hebrew Bible with that meaning.[98] The first two words, which are our focus here, are taken by the vast majority of commentators to derive from one root, and indeed to be synonymous[99]—though the question why different words are used in the same phrase should not be ignored, and arises in relation to other expressions also (notably, of course, תחת השמש and תחת השמים). Most scholars translate the words along the lines of "strive" or "pursue,"[100] associating this reading with the third root above, and drawing on the parallel between רעה רוח and רדף קדים in Hos 12:2 (Eng. 12:1) and the contrast between יבקש־דעת and ירעה אולת in Prov 15:14.[101] But many read along the lines of "shepherd-ing" or "pastoring,"[102] derived from the first root, and also drawing on

97. BDB, 944–46. Longman finds four roots in these pages of BDB, separating out "to desire" (which "is connected to an Aramaic root (reʿût) found in Ezra 5:17 and 7:18") from "to strive" (*The Book of Ecclesiastes*, 81). Seow notes, "Both words correspond to Aramaic rʿwt and rʿyn 'pleasure, will, ambition, desire' (see Ezra 5:17; 7:18; Dan 2:30; 7:28) and Phoenician rʿt 'desire, intention' . . . but this is probably an Aramaic loanword" (*Ecclesiastes*, 121).

98. E.g. Gen 26:26; 2 Sam 3:8; Prov 19:4.

99. So, for example, Seow writes, "The expression rĕʿût rûaḥ . . . is certainly synonymous with raʿyôn rûaḥ . . . no distinction between the two can be discerned" (*Ecclesiastes*, 121).

100. Thus, e.g., Christianson can write, "I am in agreement with the wide consensus (as witnessed by some modern translations: RSV, NIV, NRSV, NASB) and some linguistic testimony, to translate 'pursuit'" (*A Time to Tell*, 84–85).

101. Seow explains, "The basic meaning here is 'pursuit' or 'striving' (i.e. a striving after something that one desires)" (*Ecclesiastes*, 121).

102. E.g. Crenshaw, *Ecclesiastes*, 68, 73; Ogden, *Qoheleth*, 21; Hubbard, *Ecclesiastes, Song of Solomon*, 62.

Hos 12:2 (Eng. 12:1) and Prov 15:14.[103] Fox, in *A Time to Tear Down*, maintains that "Both essentially retain their well-known Aramaic meanings, 'desire' and 'thought' respectively," and renders the expressions "senseless thoughts."[104] However, both words could derive from a different root altogether, רעע meaning "break." The Syriac, Vulgate and Targum readings seem to be based on this root, and it also lies behind the AV translation "a vexation of spirit."

As Longman notes, "A survey of other commentaries shows a general consensus that these are the options, as well as an appropriate tentativeness in choosing one of the possibilities over the others."[105] What he does not note, however, is that the choice made tends to relate to how הבל is understood, so that the phrase ורעות רוח does not, in fact, serve to clarify the meaning of הבל at all. Thus Longman himself argues that "the phrase reinforces the conclusion that life is *hebel, meaningless.*"[106] Christianson contends: "In relation to הבל, a 'pursuit of wind,' implying as it does a vexatious chore, can have no positive import and complements the sheer negativity of הבל."[107] Fox notes that the literal sense of רעות is probably "pursuit," but translates it as "vexation" because otherwise רעות רוח "would be a neutral phrase, not a negative evaluator that would strengthen a *hebel*-judgment."[108] Ogden and Zogbo, by contrast, interpret the phrase to mean "Human beings can never expect to control the wind and what it does, and in the same way we can never expect to understand all that happens in this world," noting, "This interpretation of the idiom fits with the meaning of 'vanity' which we have discussed above."[109] Fredericks points out that the phrase could be translated "the wind's desire," and

---

103. Of these verses, Crenshaw writes, "in two cases the context is improved by the pastoral rendering (Hos 12:2; Prov 15:14)," explaining: "The first describes Ephraim as herding the wind and pursuing the east wind throughout the day; the second states that 'the mind of one who has understanding seeks knowledge but the mouths of fools feed on folly'" (*Ecclesiastes*, 73).

104. Fox, *A Time to Tear Down*, 45. This represents a move away from his position in *Qohelet*, where he acknowledges that "'pursuit of the wind' is probably its literal meaning," but argues that "the term is a metaphor referring to the emotional effect of the 'pursuer,' i.e., his 'vexation'" (p. 48).

105. Longman, *The Book of Ecclesiastes*, 81.

106. Ibid., 82.

107. Christianson, *Time to Tell*, 85.

108. Fox, *Qohelet*, 48–51 (49). In *A Time to Tear Down* he argues that "the term reᶜut/raᶜyon ruah is clearly a negative evaluator" (p. 48).

109. Ogden and Zogbo, *A Handbook*, 44. In his earlier work, *Qoheleth*, Ogden describes this phrase as "a delightful idiomatic phrase for attempting the impossible" (p. 21).

argues, "This phrase then would be metaphorical just as *hevel* is, connoting the brevity of life and its experiences."[110]

The phrases added to זה הבל[גם־]—namely, ורעה רבה, in 2:21; וענין, רע הוא, in 4:8; and וחלי רע הוא, in 6:2—should also be taken into consideration. It seems very likely that the similarity in appearance especially of רעה רבה to רעות רוח is intentional, and will cause the reader to establish a link between the expressions. This is even more so because of the use of רעה (and the related word רע[111]). However, the question is: Are these intended as near-synonyms, or as a contrast to רעות רוח? There is an alternating pattern in 2:11–26 which the expression in 2:21 disrupts, and probably thereby adds an ironic twist to the verse:

הבל ורעות רוח	הבל		2:11
הבל	גם־זה		2:15
הבל ורעות רוח	הבל		2:17
הבל	גם־זה		2:19
הבל ורעה רבה	הבל	גם־זה	2:21
הבל הוא	הבל	גם־זה	2:23
הבל ורעות רוח	הבל	גם־זה	2:26

The word רוח appears in a higher concentration in Ecclesiastes than anywhere else in the Hebrew Bible.[112] It has a number of closely related meanings. These include "breath," "wind" and "spirit." "Spirit" covers a number of different concepts in much the same way as the word in English: it may refer to the living being of humans or animals,[113] or to human temperaments,[114] or to a divinely given prophetic spirit,[115] or to God's spirit.[116] If רעות/רעיון means "striving," it would be possible to translate רעות רוח as "a striving of spirit"[117] rather than "a striving for wind." However, "wind" fits better the contexts in which the phrase appears, whether רעות/רעיון is read as "striving" or "shepherding," and it also forms an obvious pairing with הבל according to its literal meaning. However, as Seow points out, "throughout the wisdom literature of the Bible, *rûaḥ* 'wind' is frequently a metaphor for things that have no

---

110. Fredericks, *Coping with Transience*, 30.

111. Christianson argues, "In any case it is plausible that an ironic sense lies dormant in the morphological assonance of both רעיון and רעות with the biblical רעה" (*A Time to Tell*, 85 n. 25).

112. For statistics, see R. Albertz and C. Westermann, "רוּחַ *rûaḥ*," *TDOT* 3:1202–20 (1202–3).

113. Cf. Isa 42:5; Zech 13:2; Job 27:3.

114. Cf. Josh 5:1; Judg 9:23; 1 Kgs 10:5.

115. Cf. Num 27:18; 2 Kgs 2:15.

116. Cf. Num 11:17; 1 Kgs 22:24; Mic 3:8.

117. Staples, "The 'Vanity' of Ecclesiastes," 96.

abiding value or are insubstantial,"[118] so that much the same questions arise over the significance of the word רוח as do for the word הבל—and we are no further forward in terms of pinning down the meaning of הבל. (If רעות and רעיון come from the root רעע, "spirit" is more appropriate: "a breaking of spirit," or perhaps with AV, "a vexation of spirit.")

The phrase הבל הבל ורעות רוח occurs in contexts where "the deeds that are done under the sun" are being considered. How, then, are these deeds being viewed? Are they ephemeral in that they have no lasting substance? Are they futile because they ultimately have no value? Are they absurd because something about them offends human reason? Or is the author not specifically describing the deeds at all? Perhaps it is the situation in which these deeds are performed ("an unhappy business" in 1:13–14; lack of [enduring?] "gain" in 2:10–11; the identical death of the wise and the foolish in 2:16–17) that is הבל. The text may be read in any of these ways.

The other occurrence of the expression הבל הבל is in 3:19, near the centre of a passage which states that humans and beasts meet the same fate—death. It is the first of three statements starting with the word הכל:

הכל הבל׃
הכל הולך אל־מקום אחד
הכל היה מן־העפר והכל שב אל־העפר׃

הכל is different here because, while it could mean "all" as it does elsewhere, in the context it seems to refer to "both" humans and beasts.[119] In this context הבל appears to indicate transience, as even some of those commentators who translate it differently elsewhere concede. Thus Crenshaw writes, "the meaning of *habel* would probably be 'fleeting,' 'ephemeral,' or 'transient.' This understanding provides an element of surprise, since the refrain's previous uses had the sense of futility."[120]

---

118. Seow, *Ecclesiastes*, 122. He continues: "Thus, the sages spoke of inheriting wind (Prov 11:29), restraining wind (Prov 27:16), gathering wind (Prov 30:4), windy knowledge (Job 15:2), and windy words (Job 16:3; cf. 6:26; 8:2). In every case 'wind' indicates futility or meaninglessness (see Isa 41:29)." Seow thus covers most of the popular translations of הבל in his description of רוח. The parallel is shown to be even closer by M. V. Van Pelt, W. C. Kaiser and D. I. Block, who write, "Like idols, false prophets are also said to be 'like wind,' or of no real substance" ("רוח," *NIDOTTE* 3:1073–78 [1074]). Albertz and Westermann note, "*rûaḥ* can consequently become a designation of the nothingness . . . senselessness, and uselessness of human action and has thus undergone a shift in meaning similar to that of *hebel* . . . although to a lesser degree" (*TDOT* 3:1205).

119. See also the similar clause at the end of 6:6.

120. Crenshaw, *Ecclesiastes*, 104.

Fox also concedes that "If *hakkol* in 3:19 means 'both' man and beast, then 'ephemeral,' rather than 'absurd,' could be the best translation of *hebel* here."[121] However, Christianson argues, "It seems more likely, however, that Qoheleth reflected that (כי) everything is absurd (הכל הבל, 3:19b) *as a result* of comparing the circumstances of animals to that of humans (3:18–21) and that הבל at 3:19 is therefore more generalized and abstract."[122] Longman translates the expression here, as elsewhere, with "everything is meaningless."[123]

Of the six occurrences of the expression הכל הבל, then, none seems to *demand* a particular translation. In this respect, Christianson's comment is pertinent: "Of the 18 occurrences of הכל 8 stand in (sometimes ambiguous) relation to הבל, and only 1 of these appears to have a clear referent."[124] However, I would stand with the majority of scholars who consider 3:19 to refer to "both" being "transient"—but, the point is precisely that the text *could* be read otherwise, and the other five occurrences give no clear precedent to follow. הכל הבל on these five occasions appears to be a sweeping judgment on "everything" Qohelet has observed, and its translation will depend to a large extent on how the reader understands the rest of the book.

4.4.2. גם־זה הבל

The expression גם־זה הבל (and one occurrence of זה־הבל in 6:2, and of גם־הוא הבל in 2:1) occurs 15 times. It is clearly different from הכל הבל because the use of the demonstrative pronoun indicates that הבל is being applied to something specific. However, in most cases it is unclear precisely what is referred to: as Fox puts it, "it is frequently difficult, sometimes virtually impossible, to identify the antecedents of the pronouns in the *hebel*-judgment. Thus in particular cases it is uncertain exactly what is being judged."[125] In 2:1, גם־הוא־הבל could refer to the masculine noun טוב, which is itself somewhat ambiguous,[126] perhaps

---

121. Fox, *Qohelet*, 42. However, he adds in *A Time to Tear Down*, "It is, however, possible that *hakkol* in 3:19 means 'all' or 'everything'" (p. 39).

122. Christianson, *A Time to Tell*, 88, his emphasis.

123. Longman, *The Book of Ecclesiastes*, 126.

124. Christianson, *A Time to Tell*, 88. Christianson includes among the eight 7:15 where the two words are separated from each other, and where I consider the use of הבל to be quite different, and 9:1 on the basis of an emendation. It is this last which he adjudges to have a clear referent.

125. Fox, *Qohelet*, 38.

126. I believe a key question in Ecclesiastes is "what is *good* for people?" The ambiguity of the word טוב is used to great effect in exploring this question—as will be demonstrated below.

meaning "good" or "pleasure" or "prosperity"; or it might refer to the testing of pleasure.[127] The question also arises whether or not this expression, which appears only once, is synonymous with גם־זה הבל, which is used 13 times. גם־זה הבל in 2:15 could relate to Qohelet's great or excessive wisdom; or to the fact that he will ultimately meet the same fate as the fool; or, if we ignore the Masoretic versification, it might point forward to the observation in v. 16 that there is no more remembrance of the wise than the foolish. In 2:19 גם־זה הבל might refer to all the work which Qohelet did; or to the profit he made from it; or to the fact that someone else will take possession of it. The same applies in 2:21 where again הבל could refer to the "portion" (חלק); or to the fact that someone who did not work for it gets the portion; or to the observation that a person worked with wisdom, knowledge and skill just to give his portion to someone else. However, the addition of the expression ורעה רבה in this instance means that it is more likely the *situation* that is in view rather than הבל specifically referring to the noun חלקו. In 2:23 it must be the situation in which "all their days are full of pain, and their work is a vexation; even at night their minds do not rest" that is described as הבל, and, in contrast to 3:19, "meaningless" or "futile" or "incomprehensible" seems more appropriate than "transient" or "ephemeral." This may suggest that elsewhere גם־זה הבל also refers to a situation rather than a specific noun (although it should be noted that the addition only here of the pronoun הוא [but see 4:8] means that this occurrence of the expression is *not* identical to the others).

In 2:26 it may be the act of sinners gathering to give to the "good" (טוב again) that is described as הבל; or it may be the whole situation described in the verse where God gives wisdom, knowledge and pleasure to the "good" and the task of gathering for the "good" to the "sinner"; or the phrase גם־זה הבל ורעות רוח may serve to balance גם־זה הבל ורעה רבה in 2:21, either to further heighten the contrast between human wisdom and knowledge and that given by God, or to indicate that even the wisdom and knowledge given by God is הבל. The phrase in 2:26 could also serve as a conclusion to the whole of 1:12–2:26, and its ambiguity serves to cast a shadow of doubt over the seemingly positive end to this section of the book.[128]

---

127. Contra Fox, who asserts that "the only available antecedent is the experience of pleasure" (*A Time to Tear Down*, 177).

128. Fox argues that "In 2:18–26, Qohelet complains that the wealth he earned will go to someone else after his death, someone who did not work for it. Qohelet broods on this event, formulating it in various ways and calling it *hebel* four times." He adds, "This is unreasonable, senseless, absurd" (*A Time to Tear Down*, 36).

Precisely the same phrase that occurs at the end of ch. 2 is found again in 4:4 where it could refer either to man's (*sic*) jealousy (or perhaps zeal); or to all work or profit and the skill used in doing or achieving it; or to the situation where this work or profit results from jealousy (or zeal).[129] If Ecclesiastes could be relied upon for adherence to normal grammatical practice, the first could be ruled out because the masculine demonstrative pronoun זֶה does not agree with the feminine noun תבואה. However, there are many grammatical anomalies in the book,[130] besides which the consonants זה appear to be used in Ecclesiastes for *both* masculine and feminine demonstrative pronouns.[131] 4:8 is complicated by the fact that it changes from third to first person halfway through the verse. Is the first person an error, or is it an aside, or is it perhaps Qohelet's way of indicating that he is the person referred to earlier in the verse? And to which part of the verse does הבל relate? Is it טובה that is being described as הבל (although this does not seem to tie in with the demonstrative pronoun זה or the last word of the verse, הוא); or is it Qohelet's depriving himself of טובה that is הבל; or, if the first person section is an aside, does הבל refer to the earlier part of the verse where someone is said not to be satisfied with their wealth; or is it related to the fact that there is no end to all their work; or is it a response to the whole verse introduced by the observation at the beginning of a person who has neither son nor brother?[132]

4:16 is noteworthy because the phrase with which it ends is different from 2:26 and 4:4 (and 6:9): גם־זה הבל ורעיון רוח. The expression רעיון רוח occurs elsewhere only in 1:17, but there too the phrase is different:

רוח	רעיון	הוא	שׁגם־זה		1:17
רוח	ורעיון	הבל	גם־זה	כי־	4:16

There is no apparent difference between this phrase and the more common רעות רוח, but its use may lead the reader to question whether or

129. According to Fox, "In 4:4 . . . the *hebel* is either skilled work or the *fact* that skilled work is motivated by envy" (*A Time to Tear Down*, 37, my emphasis).

130. The most detailed examination of these to date is Schoors, *The Preacher Sought*.

131. Schoors states: "In Qoh the feminine form of the demonstrative pronoun is זה to the exclusion ofזאת (2,2.24; 5,15.18; 7,23; 9,13)," although he argues, "In all these instances, except for 2,2, the pronoun renders the neuter; therefore the LXX always translates it by τουτο, even in 2,2 (ταυτα in 7,23)" (*The Preacher Sought*, 52–54 [52]).

132. Seow unusually interprets הבל here as "an enigma, something that makes no sense" (*Ecclesiastes*, 181). Fox argues: "the formulation of v. 8 ('there is') shows that what is *hebel* is the scenario described in v. 8a" (*A Time to Tear Down*, 37).

not the phrases are synonymous. There are a number of other pertinent questions that arise in 4:16: To whom does "them" at the end of לפניהם refer? Who is "he" in whom those who come after will not rejoice? Is לפניהם to be read spatially as in 2:26 (×2); 3:14; 5:1, 5 (Eng. 5:2, 6); 7:26; 8:12, 13; 10:5, or temporally as in 1:10, 16; 2:7, 9 (the same question arises over precisely the same word in 9:1—the only other time it is used)? The verse illustrates well the use in Ecclesiastes of different words to mean the same thing and the same word to indicate different things, and this exacerbates the problem of establishing what it is that הבל refers to.[133]

In the same way that there appears to be a link between the uses of גם־זה הבל in 2:21 and 2:26, so also a link could be established between the uses of the expression in 4:8 and 4:16, and again the two clauses in which it appears are similar but different:

רבה	ורעה	הבל	גם־זה	2:21
רוח	ורעות	הבל	גם־זה	2:26
רע הוא	וענין	הבל	גם־זה	4:8
רוח	ורעיון	הבל	כי־ גם־זה	4:16

In 5:9 (Eng. 5:10) גם־זה הבל could refer either specifically to תבואה (although it ought in this case to take a feminine demonstrative pronoun) —which might explain why the lover of money is not satisfied with it— or to the situation where the one who loves abundance does not receive any income.[134]

6:2 is the only occasion when זה הבל is used without גם. It occurs in a clause very similar to one which appears in 4:8:

רע הוא	וענין	הבל	זה	גם־		4:8
רע הוא	וחלי	הבל	זה			6:2

The verse is in some respects similar to 2:26,[135] which also focuses on what God gives, and also describes someone losing what they work for to another person. And some similar questions arise in relation to the word הבל: Does it refer specifically to the fact of a stranger enjoying the

---

133. Fox asserts that "In 4:16, *hebel* and *ra'yon ruaḥ* are not predicated of a pursuit or an effort or even a desire—none is mentioned. Rather, Qohelet is evaluating a scenario: the success of wisdom being buried in public fickleness" (*A Time to Tear Down*, 47).

134. Fox specifically notes that here "'This too is absurd' refers to the situation or fact described in the verse as a whole" (*A Time to Tear Down*, 235).

135. Fox notes that "This is essentially the situation called *hebel* in 2:19,21, and 26" (*A Time to Tear Down*, 37).

man's (*sic*) wealth, or to the man's inability to enjoy it himself, or to the whole situation?[136]

In the *BHS* the clause גם־זה הבל ורעות רוח in 6:9 occurs exactly at the centre of the book (to the word, hence the very middle word is הבל). הבל in this verse could refer to הלך־נפש; or to מראה עינים; or to the whole "better than" saying which makes up the first half of the verse.[137] It may also serve as the conclusion to the section from 6:7–9, and perhaps also as a conclusion to the whole of the first half of the book.

The remaining occurrences of the expression גם־זה הבל are all at the end of verses. On a number of occasions up to this point words are added at the end of the expressions גם־זה הבל and הכל הבל, but this does not occur beyond 6:9:

ורעות רוח	הבל	הכל	1:14
	הבל	גם־הוא	2:1
ורעות רוח	הבל	הכל	2:11
	הבל	גם־זה	2:15
ורעות רוח	הבל	הכל	2:17
	הבל	גם־זה	2:19
ורעה רבה	הבל	גם־זה	2:21
הוא	הבל	גם־זה	2:23
ורעות רוח	הבל	גם־זה	2:26
	הבל	הכל	3:19
ורעות רוח	הבל	גם־זה	4:4
וענין רע הוא	הבל	גם־זה	4:8
ורעיון רוח	הבל	גם־זה	4:16
	הבל	גם־זה	5:9
וחלי רע הוא	הבל	זה	6:2
ורעות רוח	הבל	גם־זה	6:9
	הבל	גם־זה	7:6
	הבל	גם־זה	8:10
	הבל	גם־זה	8:14

הבל in 7:6 may refer specifically to the laughter of fools, or to the "better than" saying in v. 5: "It is better to hear the rebuke of the wise than to hear the song of fools . . . but even this is *hebel*."[138] 8:10 is a difficult

136. Here also Fox asserts that "'This' refers to the entire scenario" (*A Time to Tear Down*, 37).

137. Fox acknowledges that "It is difficult to identify the antecedent of 'this' in the *hebel*-judgment" (*A Time to Tear Down*, 246).

138. Fox observes that "Qoh 7:6 is ambiguous. It is unclear whether *hebel* is predicated of the merry noise of fools (in which case the observation is rather trite) or of the rebuke of the wise" (*A Time to Tear Down*, 38). He explains further, "'This too is *hebel*' has four possible referents: (1) The fools' merriment, which is undoubtedly *hebel* in almost any sense of the word. . . . (2) The 'general theme of the

verse which complicates the task of determining to what הבל might refer. Again it may relate specifically to the preceding clause—whoever it is that is forgotten—or it may relate to the verse as a whole.[139] The final occurrence of the expression is in 8:14, where Qohelet describes a situation in which what happens to the righteous would be appropriate for those who commit evil acts, and what happens to the wicked would be appropriate for those who commit righteous acts. It seems clear in this instance that it is the particular *situation* that is being described in this way.[140] Indeed, in every instance גם־זה הבל *could* refer to the situation being described, in most cases this is most likely the way it is being used, and in a few verses it must refer to the situation rather than a specific noun. It seems a fair conclusion, then, that גם־זה הבל is a judgment applied to the various situations Qohelet describes. This means that, as Fox observes, "the use of *hebel* in Qohelet is distinctive" because "nowhere else is *hebel* predicated of an event."[141] Elsewhere, explains Christianson, "Only things, not situations are הבל. The signifieds of הבל outside of Ecclesiastes do *not* include states of affairs within their scope of judgment."[142]

4.4.3. *Other Occurrences in the First Half of the Book*
Only three times in the first half of Ecclesiastes does the word הבל occurs outwith the *inclusio* or the phrases הכל הבל and גם־זה הבל (or גם־הוא הבל, or זה הבל). In 4:7 Qohelet says, "I saw (a) *hebel*." In this instance something like "absurdity" (or "an absurd thing") or "futility" (or "a futile thing") or "incomprehensibility" (or "an incomprehensible thing") seems more appropriate than "ephemerality" (or "an ephemeral thing") or "transience" (or "a transient thing"): first, because it makes more sense to say

passage' (Gordis), in other words the proposition that the wise man's rebuke is better than the fool's merriment.... (3) 'The rebuke of a wise man' in v. 5a.... (4) *Hebel* is used of hollow and ineffective words in 5:6 and 6:11. It may be, however, that the motivation of the *hebel*-judgment is now missing" (*A Time to Tear Down*, 253).

139. Fox takes the הבל statement as introducing v. 11, although he acknowledges that "the exact clause *gam zeh hebel* does not elsewhere introduce a scenario" (*A Time to Tear Down*, 284). This does seem to count rather strongly against his argument here.

140. I agree with Fox that "The only antecedent available for the pronoun in the last sentence is the entire preceding statement, namely the fact that *there are* such occurrences" (*A Time to Tear Down*, 30, his emphasis).

141. Fox, *Qohelet*, 46. We might note that Miller also argues that the use of הבל in Ecclesiastes is unique, but for a different reason: Qohelet's "use of הבל has precedents in its known usage elsewhere, yet he is novel in his employment of it as a literary symbol" ("Qohelet's Symbolic Use of הבל," 454).

142. Christianson, *A Time to Tell*, 81.

that he saw "absurdity" (etc.) than that he saw "ephemerality"; and secondly, because the effect of the passage is lessened if the situation is being described as something insubstantial or passing. The same applies in 6:4 where someone (the subject is unclear: it could be either the "man" or the "stillborn" of the preceding verse) "comes in(to) *hebel* and goes in(to) darkness."[143] The repeated use of חשׁך in the verse further supports a translation along the lines of absurdity/futility/incomprehensibility over transience or ephemerality.[144]

The remaining occurrence of הבל in the first half of the book is in 5:6 (Eng. 5:7), but it is far from clear how this verse should be understood. Commentators adopt different methods of making sense of the verse. Fox suggests two changes to the text, removal of the *waw* before דברים and emendation of ברב to כרב, and renders the verse "for a lot of talk is like a lot of dreams and absurdities. Rather, fear God!,"[145] He maintains that "*Hăbalim* straddles its literal sense of 'vapors' (which come from the mouth) and its figuratives sense of pointless, senseless things—in other words, absurdities."[146] Loader proposes that "a Hebrew word for 'injury' that is almost identical to the word for 'vanity' has dropped out in the course of repeated copyings."[147] Gordis, Ogden and Whitley all recommend reading the verse as it stand in the MT, but each offers a different interpretation. Gordis translates the verse, "In spite of all the dreams, follies and idle chatter, indeed, fear God!," arguing that "ברב is equivalent to 'in spite of the multitude.'"[148] Ogden proposes, "In many dreams, enigmas, and profusion of words."[149] And Whitley suggests, "for in a multitude of dreams and vanities there are *indeed* many words," contending that "the syntactical difficulty of our passage disappears if we recognize that *waw* may have an asseverative or emphatic function."[150]

---

143. Fox says, "In 6:4, *hebel* is an epithet of life (a substitution metaphor)" (*A Time to Tear Down*, 42).

144. However, Seow argues: "The author probably means that the stillborn comes into the world in vain or that it comes *only for a moment*" (*Ecclesiastes*, 212, my emphasis).

145. Fox, *Qohelet*, 209, 212. See also *A Time to Tear Down*, 229, 233.

146. Fox, *A Time to Tear Down*, 233.

147. Loader, *Ecclesiastes*, 60.

148. Gordis, *Koheleth*, 249. He continues, "on the concessive use of the *beth*, cf. Ps 46:3; Isa 1:15, and see BDB p.91a."

149. Ogden, *Qoheleth*, 79.

150. Whitley, *Koheleth*, 50, his emphasis. On the emphatic function of *waw*, see Schoors, *The Preacher Sought*, 124–28. The *waw* in the second ומקרה in 3:19 (Gordis, *Koheleth*, 237); in ולא in 6:10 (Whitley, *Koheleth*, 61), in ועל in 8:2 (Gordis, *Koheleth*, 288) and at the beginning of 11:7 (A. Lauha, *Kohelet* [BKAT 19;

Seow renders the verse, "For vacuous dreams are in abundance, and there are words aplenty. But as for you, fear God!" He explains: "Since *ḥălôm* may be a figure for anything that is illusory and ephemeral and, thus, synonymous with *hebel*, one may take the expression *ḥălōmôt wahăbālîm* as a hendiadys. The two words mean the same thing and only reinforce the idea of emptiness."[151] Perhaps in the end we should with Crenshaw observe the "ambiguous syntax" and admit that "no solution seems entirely satisfactory."[152] As the verse stands, it consists simply of a list with an exhortation to "fear God" attached to the end. Because of the uncertainties of the verse, the translation of הבל must also be uncertain. The link with "words" may play on the literal sense of "breath," but a figurative translation, probably more along the lines of "absurdity" than "transience," is required.

4.4.4. *Occurrences in the Second Half of the Book*
In 6:11, in the second half of the book, there is also a connection between הבל and words: increasing words increases הבל. Here it would be appropriate to render הבל literally, although again it seems probable that there is a play on the word, and the reader is likely to pick up something of the figurative sense, probably along the lines of "absurdity" rather than "transience."

In 8:14, where Qohelet relates (a) *hebel* that is done on earth, both a literal translation and also the sense of transience or ephemerality seem highly inappropriate: the word must bear the sense of something like absurdity, futility or incomprehensibility. This verse uses הבל in two different ways, and in this respect is similar to 4:7–8:

Neukirchen–Vluyn: Neukirchener, 1978], 206) have also been suggested as examples of its emphatic function.

151. Seow, *Ecclesiastes*, 193, 197.

152. Crenshaw, *Ecclesiastes*, 118. Longman argues that any proposals for translation here "must be considered tentative since the prepositions and conjunctions of the verse are amenable to more than one interpretation." He explains, "Any Hebrew grammar will show multiple uses of the conjunctions *kî* and *waw* as well as the preposition *beth*. The *kî* could be causal, temporal, conditional, adversative, concessive, asseverative, resultative, nominalizing, or recitative. The *waw* can serve a coordinative, disjunctive, adversative, alternative, explicative, pleonastic, accompaniment, comparative, emphatic, sarcastic, resumptive, adjunctive, or distributive function. The preposition *beth* 'expresses rest or movement in place or time' and thus has locative, temporal, adversative, instrumental, transitive, agental, causal, and several other meanings. Context often makes the specific stance clear, but such is not the case in our verse" (*The Book of Ecclesiastes*, 155–56).

וְשַׁבְתִּי אֲנִי וָאֶרְאֶה <u>הֶבֶל</u> תַּחַת הַשָּׁמֶשׁ׃   4:7–8
יֵשׁ אֶחָד וְאֵין שֵׁנִי גַּם בֵּן וָאָח אֵין־לֹו
וְאֵין קֵץ לְכָל־עֲמָלֹו גַּם־עֵינָיו [עֵינֹו] לֹא־תִשְׂבַּע עֹשֶׁר
וּלְמִי אֲנִי עָמֵל וּמְחַסֵּר אֶת־נַפְשִׁי מִטּוֹבָה
<u>גַּם־זֶה הֶבֶל</u> וְעִנְיַן רָע הוּא׃

יֶשׁ־הֶבֶל אֲשֶׁר נַעֲשָׂה עַל־הָאָרֶץ אֲשֶׁר   8:14
יֵשׁ צַדִּיקִים אֲשֶׁר מַגִּיעַ אֲלֵהֶם כְּמַעֲשֵׂה הָרְשָׁעִים
וְיֵשׁ רְשָׁעִים שֶׁמַּגִּיעַ אֲלֵהֶם כְּמַעֲשֵׂה הַצַּדִּיקִים
אָמַרְתִּי שֶׁגַּם־זֶה הָבֶל׃

Fox uses 8:14 as a test-case to try out various translations of הבל, and concludes that "none of the qualities usually associated with vapors apply."[153] However, he imposes on the text the need to render both occurrences in the same way, but on a number of occasions in Ecclesiastes the same word is used twice (or more) in one verse with different senses, and the same applies here (and in 4:7–8).

The phrase כל־שבא הבל in 11:8 is something of an enigma, and the use of הבל here is particularly noteworthy in the light of the fact that it was last used in 9:9 (some 37 verses previous[154]), and appears again in 11:10 where many commentators interpret it in a different way than they do here. Crenshaw argues that in 11:8, "The final remark registers unrelieved pessimism: everything that the future holds in Sheol is utterly absurd";[155] but says of 11:10, "The period when you can do these things is brief, fleeting like a breath or a puff of smoke."[156] Fox agrees with Crenshaw when he maintains in relation to 11:8: "Death is absurd and guarantees life's absurdity";[157] but he writes of 11:10,

> In 11:10 the time of youth is called *hebel*. Here alone something is called *hebel* in order to emphasize its precariousness. While youth may be absurd in various ways, that quality is not the point of this statement, for Qoh 12:1 shows that it is the brevity of youth that increases the urgency of seizing the opportunities it offers. "Ephemeral" is therefore the word's primary meaning in this verse. The absurdity of youth (or its futility, triviality, or any other negative quality besides ephemerality) would not be a reason for enjoying it.[158]

153. Fox, *A Time to Tear Down*, 30.

154. 37 being the numerical value of הבל upon which A. G. Wright places so much importance ("The Riddle of the Sphinx: The Structure of the Book of Qohelet," *CBQ* 30 [1968]: 313–34).

155. Crenshaw, *Ecclesiastes*, 183.

156. Ibid., 184.

157. Fox, *Qohelet*, 278.

158. Ibid., 42. This comment is particularly noteworthy in view of Fox's assertion that "Qohelet's thematic statement, 'Everything is *hebel*' implies that there is some

According to Longman, in 11:8, "Qohelet concludes with his character-istic view of the value of life: it is *meaningless*,"[159] but he notes of 11:10, "This may, however, be the one verse where the temporal aspect of the root is emphasized."[160]

Whybray, however, contends that in 11:8 "Qoheleth's intention here is *not* to introduce a note of gloom to negate or qualify the cheerful note struck in v. 7, but to use the backdrop of inevitable death to highlight the positive opportunities for joy in this life."[161] However, he renders הבל with "nothingness or futility" here and, like Crenshaw and Fox, main-tains that in v. 10 it "means what is fleeting or ephemeral rather than 'vanity.'"[162] Ogden interprets the word in 11:8 in this way: "We may know the fact that death is a perpetual state, but what happens at that point and beyond . . . is too much for our limited comprehension";[163] then states of 11:10 that Qohelet uses הבל to comment "on life's ironic dimen-sion."[164] Seow takes a rather different tack, arguing that כל־שבא in 11:8 refers to "*anyone who comes.*" He asserts: "The point is that every human, like anyone or anything else on earth, is *hebel*. Nothing is permanent, so one who has come into this world better enjoy while there is still time."[165] He does not specifically translate הבל in 11:10, but presumably in the light of the way he reads 11:7–10,[166] he would, unlike most other com-mentators, interpret it similarly.

There is a wide scholarly consensus that הבל in 11:10 indicates tran-sience because the author is exhorting readers to enjoy their youth while it last. However, from our survey of the use of הבל throughout the book,

meaning common to the various occurrences of the term," and "for Qohelet there is a single quality that is an attribute of the world. . . . The *hebel* leitmotif disintegrates if the word is assigned several different meanings." However, Fox is forced to concede that on several occasions the occurrences of this word "resist the understanding of *hebel* as absurdity" (*Qohelet*, 35, 36). This position is maintained in *A Time to Tear Down*, but the argument is refined somewhat: "*Hebel* here denotes ephemerality, for that is the only quality of youth that makes pleasure-seeking pressing. At the same time, *it connotes illusoriness and thus absurdity*, because the very brevity that makes it precious also makes it deceptive; and what deceives the mind is absurd" (p. 319, my emphasis).

159. Longman, *The Book of Ecclesiastes*, 260, his emphasis.
160. Ibid., 261–62.
161. Whybray, *Ecclesiastes*, 161, my emphasis.
162. Ibid., *Ecclesiastes*, 163.
163. Ogden, *Qoheleth*, 195.
164. Ibid., 197.
165. Seow, *Ecclesiastes*, 349, my emphasis.
166. See Ibid., 347–50 and 369–71. Miller sees הבל as having the sense of "transience" in both verses ("Qohelet's Symbolic Use of הבל," 448).

it seems that in some cases a translation such as "absurd" or "futile" or "incomprehensible" is more appropriate (but some commentators disagree), while in others it appears to convey more the sense of ephemerality or transience (though some commentators disagree); and in the majority of cases it is not clear which sense it takes.

4.4.4.1. Days of one's Hebel *life.* This is the case also in the phrases in the later chapters where הבל is used in the third, first and second person to describe the days of one's life:

ימי־חיי הבלו		6:12
הבלי	ב ימי	7:15
חיי הבלך	ימי	9:9a
הבלך	ימי	9:9b

Fox says of these verses, "*hebel* refers to human life in general, and it is impossible to determine just what Qohelet has in mind; 'ephemeral' or 'absurd' (or a number of other adjectives) could apply equally well."[167] Longman understands הבל as "meaningless" on each occasion, arguing that "to translate 'transitory' or its equivalent in this verse would be awkwardly redundant."[168] Crenshaw alternates in his translation between "empty" (6:12 and 9:9a) and "brief/fleeting" (7:15 and 9:9b).[169] Ogden only actually translates these expressions in 9:9, and there he offers, "[all] your enigmatic life."[170] Seow translates the phrase in 6:12, "the few days of their fleeting life," arguing that "The word *hebel* here *clearly* refers to the brevity of life."[171] It makes a considerable difference to the interpretation of these verses if הבל is understood to indicate the transient nature of human life, or if it is taken to signify that human life is in some way futile or absurd. It also significantly affects the interpretation if life is said to be meaningless, or vain, or incomprehensible, and so on. Is Qohelet commenting on the brevity of life—an easily observable fact that can hardly be disputed? Is he affirming the mystery of life under the sun whereby people are unable to make sense of life as they observe it? Or is he making the much more radical statement that life is "manifestly irrational or meaningless"? Miller argues that "In these passages, no contextual clues or associated terms are employed. The reader is meant

---

167. Fox, *Qohelet*, 43. Nonetheless, Fox translates הבל as "absurd" on each occasion.

168. Longman, *The Book of Ecclesiastes*, 178. See also pp. 194, 231.

169. Crenshaw, *Ecclesiastes*, 130, 140, 158.

170. Ogden, *Qoheleth*, 153.

171. Seow, *Ecclesiastes*, 233, my emphasis. He writes similarly in relation to both 7:15 (p. 252) and 9:9 (p. 302).

to recognize that any or all of the dimensions of הבל are being alluded to."[172]

4.4.5. *Distribution of* הבל

There are two further points, which are rarely noted, that should be taken into account in relation to this key word, הבל. While it is undoubtedly true that it is a, if not *the* key word in Ecclesiastes, it is not evenly distributed throughout the book, nor is its use consistent. Chart 1 shows the distribution of the word by chapter, but this is a little misleading for the following reasons:

1. Five of the six occurrences in ch. 1 are in the *inclusio*.
2. All three occurrences in ch. 12 are in the *inclusio*.
3. The chapters are of varying lengths so that the five occurrences in the twelve verses in ch. 6 represent a much higher concentration than, for example, the two in the 29 verses of ch. 7.
4. There are *no* occurrences of the word between 9:9 and 11:8, a total of 37 verses, or a sixth of the whole book.

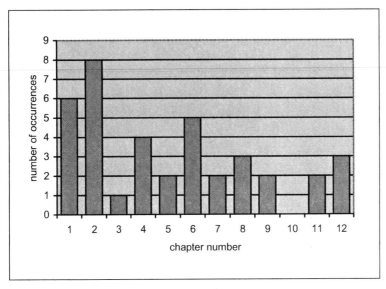

Chart 1. *Distribution of* הבל *by Chapter*

In fact, the "motto" in 1:2 clearly establishes הבל as a key word, but it is then used only once more in that chapter. It is used in its highest frequency when Qohelet reflects on the investigations he undertook in his

---

172. Miller, "Qohelet's Symbolic Use of הבל," 452.

"Solomonic guise." הבל appears only ónce in ch. 3, a chapter which
commences with the poem on "time" then focuses on God more than any
other passage in the whole book. It is then used a few times in each of
chs. 4, 5 and 6. Its use is sporadic in chs. 7, 8 and 9, then disappears
completely from 9:10–11:7, before reappearing once in 11:8 and once in
11:10, and finally three times in the *inclusio* in 12:8. This is shown more
precisely in Chart 2 below:

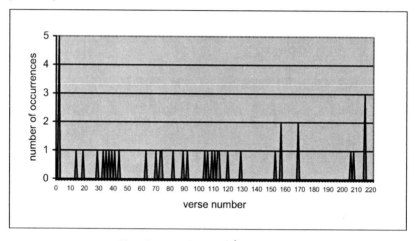

Chart 2. *Distribution of* הבל *by Verse*

הבל הבל is used twice in ch. 1; twice in ch. 2; once in ch. 3, then not
again until the "motto" in 12:8. גם־זה הבל (and equivalents) is (are) used
six times in ch. 2; three times in ch. 4; once in ch. 5; twice in ch. 6; once
in ch. 7; and twice in ch. 8; then not at all in the rest of the book. This
means that all but three occurrences of הבל in the first half of the book
are in the *inclusio* or the expressions הבל הבל or גם־זה הבל (and equivalents); that the sweeping statement הבל הבל effectively ceases as early as
3:19; and that גם־זה הבל occurs often in the early chapters and peters out
in ch. 8. By contrast, four times in the second half of the book הבל is
used in the expression ימי [חיי] הבל, an expression not found in the first
half of the book and where the use of הבל is quite different from the way
it is used in the early chapters. Moreover, on two occasions in the second
half of the book הבל appears twice in a verse (which happens only in the
inclusio in the first half), and on one of these occasions it is used in two
quite different ways.

4.5. *Conclusion*

I believe I have established "beyond reasonable doubt" that the use of הבל in Ecclesiastes is ambiguous (at very least for a modern reader) because in many instances it is unclear precisely what it refers to and because it is often open to more than one interpretation. I hope to demonstrate that this is best explained as a deliberate rhetorical strategy that contributes to the overall intentional ambiguity of the book.[173] I believe I have also shown clearly that the distribution of this "key" word is uneven, with the highest concentration in the early chapters, its use all but petering out towards the end of the book. I have also observed changes in the way הבל is used throughout the book. These observations all have a bearing on how the word functions in helping the reader determine what the book of Ecclesiastes "means."

---

173. Hence I believe Hubbard is misguided when he writes, "In this commentary we shall ordinarily use words like 'mystery,' 'enigma,' or even 'futility' *to avoid the ambiguity* of 'vanity'" (*Ecclesiastes*, 44, my emphasis).

Chapter 5

יתרון IN ECCLESIASTES

5.1. *The Importance of the Word* יתרון

We noted above that there can be little doubt that הבל is a, if not *the* key word in the book of Ecclesiastes. It seems likely that יתרון is also a key word as it appears in a question in 1:3 that rather looks as though it is in some sense "programmatic"[1] for the book. As long ago as 1904, Genung wrote, "Rather than the word *vanity*, the controlling idea of Koheleth's thought . . . [is] profit";[2] and more recently Ogden has claimed, "From the outset, Qoheleth makes clear what his purpose is. He is examining human life and work with a view to ascertaining whether or not there is any 'advantage' (*yitrôn*) in it. The question in 1:3 is the programmatic question for the entire book."[3] The position of this question immediately following the *inclusio* in 1:2 means that it must play an important role in the book,[4] although commentators are divided over, and readers may wonder, whether it should be read as part of Qohelet's words or as part

---

1. Bartholomew states: "positioned where it is, 1:3 is *clearly programmatic*" (*Reading Ecclesiastes*, 241, his emphasis). The word "programmatic" is used by a number of commentators of the question in 1:3, including, Christianson, *A Time to Tell*, 219; Ogden, *Qoheleth*, 28; Salyer, *Vain Rhetoric*, 141. Hubbard describes it as "Koheleth's *guiding question*" (*Ecclesiastes, Song of Solomon*, 45, his emphasis).

2. John F. Genung, *Words of Koheleth* (New York: Houghton, Mifflin, 1904), 214–15.

3. Ogden, *Qoheleth*, 28. Fredericks also considers the concept of "advantage" to be a, if not the key one in Ecclesiastes (*Coping with Transience*, 74). See his extended consideration of the word יתרון in his Chapter 3, and his concluding remarks on p. 97.

4. Salyer says of 1:2–3, "These verses act as a compass for the reader, establishing the north (*hebel*) and south (*yitrôn*) poles from which the other terms gain their latitudinal and longitudinal bearings" (*Vain Rhetoric*, 248). He also provides a list of "major scholars who hold to the centrality of the 'What Profit?' question" (p. 141 n. 54). However, Whybray asserts of 1:3, "this verse, now standing so prominently at the beginning of the book, *oversimplifies and distorts* Qoheleth's own teaching" (*Ecclesiastes*, 38, my emphasis).

of the introduction (along with 1:1–2[5] and perhaps also the "prologue" in 1:4–11[6]—recalling that Qohelet only introduces himself in 1:12). Moreover, while questions beginning מה־יתרון occur two more times (3:9; 5:15), and there are two, seemingly synonymous, uses of מה־[ו]יתר (6:8, 11), these are all in the first six chapters of the book. Furthermore, the word יתרון itself, which appears ten times (1:3; 2:11, 13 [×2]; 3:9; 5:8, 15 [Eng. 5:9, 16]; 7:12; 10:10, 11), is used much more often in the first half of the book (percentage-wise), and is not used at all beyond 10:11. Indeed, the occurrences in 10:10, 11 are in proverbs that look as though they are part of a fairly random collection Qohelet has drawn together rather than written (though this may well be a literary ploy). This raises questions about its "programmatic" role "for the *entire* book." It may well be that יתרון plays a crucial rule in the early chapters after which there is a (possibly gradual) change in emphasis away from the question of what יתרון is to be found "under the sun," and towards instructing the reader how to cope with, among other things, a lack of יתרון.[7]

5.2. *Translation and Interpretation of* יתרון

In terms of translation, there is much more agreement than there is in regard to הבל. Thus מה־יתרון לאדם is rendered "What do people (or 'does man') gain" (RSV, NRSV, NIV, NEB[8]); "What do people get" (NLT);

5.   Rudman notes: "Although commentators on Ecclesiastes largely agree on the editorial nature of the superscription to the book in 1:1, opinion is divided as to whether the prologue to Qoheleth's work begins in vv. 2, 3 or 4" (*Determinism*, 72). The difficulty of establishing the boundaries of the introduction (and the conclusion) add to the ambiguity of the book.

6.   See, e.g., Leo G. Perdue, *Wisdom and Creation: The Theology of Wisdom Literature* (Nashville: Abingdon, 1994), 204.

7.   This raises another issue that cannot be addressed in depth here. While it seems to me that Ecclesiastes resists any attempt to impose upon it (or discover within it) a tidy overarching structure, there are nonetheless clear *trends* within the book. One of these, which has been noted now by a number of scholars, is a progression from a heavy concentration of the first person (to the complete exclusion of any real second person address) in the early chapters, to exclusively second person address at the end of the book (apart from the epilogue[s]). This indicates that progressively examination of life "under the sun" gives way to instruction. Christianson illustrates this nicely with a graph, which he helpfully explains thus: "The graph demonstrates well the shift from experience to advice and an overall strategy in which the reader is invited to partake more and more in the text's story-world" (*A Time to Tell*, 244–45). This, I believe, is a vital clue to the way the book works, and most commentators take far too little account of this feature of Ecclesiastes.

8.   See also, e.g., Davis, *Proverbs, Ecclesiastes, and the Song of Songs*, 170; Fox, *Qohelet*, 60–62.

"What profit has a man" (or equivalent, KJV, REB, NJB[9]); and "what do you have to show for it" (GNB, and "The Message" is similar). Fredericks, Ogden, Seow and Tamez render יתרון "advantage,"[10] while the NJPSV shows the most significant difference when it translates, "What real value is there for a man."[11]

The root יתר is a common enough one in the Hebrew Bible,[12] although the specific word יתרון occurs only in Ecclesiastes (as indeed does the *qitlon* form of the noun[13]). The root is found in all Semitic languages, and, as Kronholm notes, "it is not hard to determine its basic meaning: 'be extra, surplus.' "[14] However, the commentators disagree over the precise implications of the word. Whybray appreciates something of the ambiguity of יתרון when he writes,

> It is derived from the root *ytr*, meaning "to remain over". . . . But the concept of being left over is *susceptible of a number of different connotations*: in post-biblical Hebrew *yitron* can mean "addition," even "redundancy" or "worthlessness" (the state of being surplus to requirements). Consequently it is not a simple matter to determine exactly what Qoheleth intended by it.[15]

So, for example, Crenshaw explains a popular translation when he says, "the word *yitrôn* is possibly a commercial term for what is left after all expenses are taken into account."[16] However Fox disagrees (in *Qohelet*,

9. See also, e.g., Rudman, *Determinism*, 72–75; Salyer, *Vain Rhetoric*, 141; Christianson, *A Time to Tell*, 219. Fox uses "profit" in 1:3 in *A Time to Tear Down*, 112–13, but "adequate gain" in *Qohelet*, 60–62.

10. Fredericks, *Coping with Transience*, 48; Ogden, *Qoheleth*, 28; Seow, *Ecclesiastes*, 100; Tamez, *When the Horizons Close*, 36. Fox states that "Yitron means 'advantage' (when two things are being compared)" (*A Time to Tear Down*, 112; *Qohelet*, 60).

11. This is also the sense that Davis sees in the word when she argues, "His question is not utilitarian but existential: 'What is the human value? Is there any meaning? Will it make me any more of a person?' " (*Proverbs, Ecclesiastes, and the Song of Songs*, 170).

12. It occurs some 223 times in the Hebrew Bible, approximately half of which are verbal forms (Niphal and Hiphil), and half nominal forms. These statistics are discussed in David Latoundji, "יתר," *NIDOTTE* 2:571–54. Latoundji offers all the main translations of יתרון noted above: "surplus, profit, advantage, gain" (p. 572).

13. As Schoors notes, "Qoh employs abstract *qitlon* nouns with a relatively high frequency: ירתון (1,3; 2,11.13; 3,9; 5,8.15; 7,12; 10,10.11), כשרון (2,21; 4,4; 5,10), חשבון (7,25.27; 9,10), חסרון (1,15), שלטון (8,4.8) and זברון (1,11; 2,16). . . . To the list we can add רעיון (Qoh 1,17; 2,22; 4,16) . . . the regular *qittalon* is used by Qoh, too: e.g., זברון (1,11), בטחון (9,4) and חשבנות (7,29)" (*The Preacher Sought*, 63).

14. T. Kronholm, "יתַר," *TDOT* 6:482–91 (482).

15. Whybray, *Ecclesiastes*, 36–37, my emphasis.

16. Crenshaw, *Ecclesiastes*, 59.

at least), noting that "*Yitron* (together with its synonyms *motar* and *yoter*) is commonly translated 'profit,'" and argues, "this translation is problematic because Qohelet, who denies that *yitronot* derive from toil (see especially 1:3; 2:11; 3:9), nevertheless does find profit in that activity and others."[17] However, he concedes that "It is not clear if the notion of adequacy is lexicalized in *yitron* or peculiar to Qohelet's application."[18] A number of other scholars also question the commercial aspect of the term. Davis, for example, argues,

> the fiction that Koheleth is king over Jerusalem implies that he already has every imaginable material asset. Thus we recognize that Koheleth is asking more than the common question of economic self-interest, "What will I get out of this?" His question is not utilitarian but existential: "What is the human value? Is there any meaning? Will it make me any more of a person?"[19]

Ogden maintains that "the original commercial application of *ytr* is absent from Qoheleth's use of his term *yitrôn*," explaining:

> He has assigned it a metaphorical sense to speak of that which is non-material. It might refer, in part, to an inner contentment which abides throughout an enigmatic life, but it seems also to incorporate the possibility of some experience beyond death. . . . [Y]*itrôn* is Qoheleth's special term for *wisdom's reward both here and after death.*[20]

If Fox is guilty of imposing an interpretation upon the word הבל that it cannot bear, Ogden seems here to be packing far too much into a small gap of indeterminacy in relation to the word יתרון. He, like Fox, appears to be reading back his own interpretation of the work as a whole into one key word—and Ogden chooses a positive term through which to channel

17. Fox, *Qohelet*, 60. However, Fox does use the term "profit" in *A Time to Tear Down*, noting that "Outside of comparisons, *yitron* (*as all commentators agree*) means 'profit'" (p. 112, my emphasis). So far as I can see, his previous argument has simply been dropped (because "all commentators agree" against him?).

18. Fox, *Qohelet*, 61.

19. Davis, *Proverbs, Ecclesiastes, and the Song of Songs*, 170. See also, Hubbard, who renders יתרון as "contentment" (like Ogden, *Qohelet*), or "complete satisfaction" (*Ecclesiastes, Song of Solomon*, 45), and Tamez, who writes, "The advantage he seeks is true human fulfillment in the labor process and its fruits, in history, under the sun" (*When the Horizons Close*, 36).

20. Ogden, *Qoheleth*, 25, 29, his emphasis. This position is maintained also in Ogden and Zogbo, *A Handbook*, 5. Murphy expresses the view of a number of commentators when he states simply, "What seems clear is that יתרון is not bound up with an eternal dimension (contra Ogden)" (*Ecclesiastes*, lx). Salyer goes further when he asserts, "interpretations such as Ogden's violate the broader norms of the text in quite flagrant ways" (*Vain Rhetoric*, 267 n. 70).

his optimistic reading of the book, while Fox employs a negative word to emphasise his pessimistic reading. As I made clear earlier, even the ambiguities of Ecclesiastes have to operate within appropriate bounds of interpretation.[21]

A number of commentators understand יתרון to convey a sense of *enduring* or *lasting* gain,[22] advantage,[23] profit[24] or benefit,[25] as opposed to the temporary "reward" that certain activities in life can bring (e.g. the חלק of 2:10). However, here too Fox disagrees (again, at least in *Qohelet*), arguing:

> But how long, by this understanding, must something endure to be a *yitron*? Wealth may endure until the end of one's life—Qohelet expects his own to do so (2:20–23)—and yet fail to be a *yitron*. And if *yitron* meant a gain that endures *beyond* life, the existence of a *yitron* would be precluded by definition for one who, like Qohelet, does not believe in a life beyond death.[26]

There is, though, a danger of circularity in Fox's argument, which uses the deduction that Qohelet does not believe in an afterlife to discount any interpretation that might hint at such a belief. In view of Fox's approach to Qohelet's "contradictions" ("I try to read Qohelet without 'solving' the problems raised by the contradictions"[27]), this is surprisingly dogmatic.

5.3. *How* יתרון *Is Used in Ecclesiastes*

5.3.1. מה־יתרון

Michel devotes a long excursus to the use of יתרון in Ecclesiastes, maintaining that interpretation of this word depends upon how it is used in

---

21. Ogden explains his stance thus: "The semantic field of the term *yitrôn* must be defined broadly enough to include the possibility of an 'advantage' beyond death for the faithful" (*Qoheleth*, 15).

22. A. Schoors refers to "the enduring character of the gain he is searching for" ("Words Typical of Qohelet," in Schoors, ed., *Qohelet in the Context of Wisdom*, 17–39 [25]).

23. Bergant says that Qohelet's conclusion in 2:10–11 is "There is no lasting gain, no tangible dividend" (*Job, Ecclesiastes*, 236).

24. Fredericks, *Coping with Transience*, 75. See below.

25. Ogden and Zogbo argue: "We think it can be defined and perhaps best translated as 'lasting benefit'" (*A Handbook*, 6).

26. Fox, *Qohelet*, 60. It is, perhaps, noteworthy that this paragraph also has disappeared from *A Time to Tear Down*.

27. Fox, *Qohelet*, 28. The question of "the afterlife" is one area in which there are significant differences between *Qohelet* and *A Time to Tear Down*. Compare, for example, Fox's comments in the two books on 3:16–22 and 12:7.

individual passages.[28] It is to this we now turn. The question in precisely the form it appears in 1:3, מה־יתרון, is found only three times in Ecclesiastes, and on each occasion it relates to עמל:

יעמל	שׁ	בכל־עמלו	לאדם	מה־יתרון	1:3
עמל הוא אשׁר	ב	העושׂה	מה־יתרון		3:9
יעמל לרוח	שׁ	לו	מה־יתרון	ו	5:15

The translation "profit" seems particularly appropriate in these verses, but "gain" or "advantage" would also be suitable renderings of יתרון. The question then arises (as it does often in Ecclesiastes) why a different word is used—apparently synonymously[29]—in 6:8, 11 where עמל does not occur:[30]

יעמל	שׁ	בכל־עמלו	לאדם	מה־יתרון	1:3
עמל הוא אשׁר	ב	העושׂה	מה־יתרון		3:9
יעמל לרוח	שׁ	לו	מה־יתרון	ו	5:15
		לחכם מן־הכסיל	מה־יותר		6:8
		לאדם	מה־יתר		6:11

Perhaps the diminishing length of the word from יתרון to יותר to יתר represents the fading of this question at the end of the first half of the book, as new issues come more to the fore in the second half (although there is build up from יתר to יתרון in the second half of the book in 7:11, 12; 10:10, 11, only not in question form). At any rate, "profit" is not a suitable translation in these verses. "Gain" is perhaps the best rendering in 6:11, and 6:8 might be rendered, "what *gain* is there to the wise *more than* to the fool?" or simply, "what *advantage* has the wise over the fool?"

---

28. Michel, *Untersuchungen*, 105–15. Murphy also makes clear that "each case has to be examined for itself" (*Ecclesiastes*, lx). Ogden and Zogbo assert that "its precise meaning can be determined by studying its use in the context of this book" (*A Handbook*, 5).

29. Ogden and Zogbo raise the question of whether these are synonymous, and I think come to the conclusion that there may be some difference in 6:8, leading to their translation "lasting satisfaction" rather than "lasting benefit" (*A Handbook*, 204), though in *Qoheleth* Ogden states, "I would incline to the view that *yôtēr* is here the equivalent of *yitrôn*" (p. 95). Otherwise, commentators generally assume they mean the same thing, and it is notable that Ogden and Zogbo treat מה־יתר לאדם in 6:11 as "Qoheleth's key question reappearing again," returning to the translation "lasting benefit" (*A Handbook*, 210). There does seem to be an inconsistency here.

30. We might also ask why לאדם in 1:3 is replaced with העושׂה (notably without the ל) in 3:9 and just לו in 5:15. These differences are typical of repeated phrases in Ecclesiastes, and raise the question whether or not they are synonymous. This adds to the ambiguity of the book.

It may be, as many commentators suggest, that the "what advantage?" question should also be read in the second half of 6:8:

מה־יותר לחכם מן־הכסיל
מה־לעני יודע להלך נגד החיים׃

Schoors, for example, argues that the sense of מה־יותר carries over from the first half of the verse into the second,[31] for which 5:9 (Eng. 5:10) offers a possible precedent. However, Fox disagrees, maintaining that "The point of the rhetorical question is: since the wise man has no advantage over the fool, there is no value in a poor man knowing how to get along with people."[32]

A similar question to those in 1:3; 3:9 and 5:15 (Eng. 5:16) occurs in 2:22, but here there is no word from the root יתר, rather another unusual word is used, the participle הֹוֶה (which occurs elsewhere only in Neh 6:6):

יעמל	ש	בכל־עמלו	לאדם	מה־יתרון	1:3
עמל הוא	ש	בכל־עמלו וברעיון לבו	לאדם	מה־הוה	2:22
עמל הוא אשר	ב	העושה	מה־יתרון		3:9
יעמל לרוח	ש	לו	ו מה־יתרון		5:15

Schoors argues that "This parallelism clearly shows that הוה replaces יתרון, and that it is used here *to stress the enduring character of the gain he is searching for*,"[33] but the point is precisely that it is *not* clear, and the reader is likely to wonder whether or not the phrases are synonymous.[34] Ogden argues similarly, "Its form, to all intents and purposes, is the same as 1:3, for minor variations are not significant ones, despite the fact that the keyword *yitrôn* is absent."[35] However, this raises two important issues: first, how is the reader to judge (certainly on a first reading) what

31. Schoors, *The Preacher Sought*, 165–66. See also, e.g., Ogden, *Qoheleth*, 95. Longman describes it as an "ellipsis of *advantage* from the first sentence" (*The Book of Ecclesiastes*, 173); so also Seow, *Ecclesiastes*, 214.

32. Fox, *A Time to Tear Down*, 245. See also, e.g., Gordis, *Koheleth*, 261; Crenshaw, *Ecclesiastes*, 120.

33. Schoors, "Words Typical of Qohelet," 25, my emphasis.

34. Isaksson is one of only a few scholars who argue that there is any difference in meaning between the questions in 1:3 and 2:22 (*Studies in the Language of Qoheleth*, 124–25). Schoors quite specifically argues against Isaksson's stance here (*The Preacher Sought*, 185).

35. Ogden, *Qoheleth*, 47. However, in relation to 3:19 Ogden argues: "Does *môtar* convey a concept similar to or distinct from *yôtēr*? Why has Qoheleth used this highly unusual form? On the assumption that a different form probably has a unique significance, we derive from the context clues for its possible interpretation" (p. 61).

counts as significant? Secondly, the absence of what Ogden himself terms "the keyword *yitrôn*" is surely sufficiently significant at least to raise questions for the reader. Thus, for example, Salyer reads this verse rather differently from Schoors when he says, "[Qoheleth] omits his favorite word *yitrôn* ('profit,' 'advantage'), using the ambiguous term *hōweh* ('to happen'), *as a means of accenting the fickle and unknowable nature* of humanity's fate (*miqreh*) which was introduced in 2:14."[36]

5.3.2. *Other Uses of* יתרון

2:11 is a key verse in terms of the meaning of the word יתרון and its function in Ecclesiastes. This is the first occurrence of the word (or, indeed, any word from the root יתר) since the "programmatic question" in 1:3, and on an initial reading of the book it may seem that this provides a definitive answer to the question that was asked there,[37] especially in the light of the reappearance of עמל, which occurs in 2:10 for the first time since 1:3, and תחת השמש. In this context it is clear (and actually pretty obvious anyway) that there is *something* to be gained from one's labours: Qohelet affirms in 2:10, וזה־היה חלקי מכל־עמלי. However, he goes on to say in 2:11:

> ופניתי אני בכל־מעשי שעשו ידי ובעמל שעמלתי לעשות
> והנה הכל הבל ורעות רוח ואין יתרון תחת השמש:

Therefore, there *may* be חלק in or from people's deeds, but, at least in this instance, even if someone has חלק this does not result in יתרון. So whatever יתרון is, it is something other than חלק. Fredericks is one of a number of commentators who compare the transitory nature of חלק with the enduring quality of יתרון,[38] but neither quality is inherent in either

36. Salyer, *Vain Rhetoric*, 290, my emphasis.
37. See, e.g., Bartholomew, *Reading Ecclesiastes*, 241; Christianson, *A Time to Tell*, 219–20; Ogden, *Qoheleth*, 42, 47–48. Salyer states, "v. 11 marks the closure of the gap first introduced by the programmatic 'what profit?' question in 1:3. Qoheleth flatly denies that there is anything to be gained under the sun" (*Vain Rhetoric*, 283, cf. 261).
38. Fredericks argues in relation to 2:10, "achievements are of only transient value. They are valuable (2:10), but only for the moment." He then says of 2:10–11, "a serious reflection on two ostensibly contradictory statements will yield a synthesis that is definitely a candidate for the very theme of Ecclesiastes. . . . There is a reward of pleasure in one's labor . . . but there is no *lasting* profit" (*Coping with Transience*, 52, 74–75, his emphasis). Whybray refers to the contrast in these verses "between the *immediate* satisfaction produced by the pursuit of pleasure for its own sake and the lack of any *lasting* pleasure" (*Ecclesiastes*, 55, his emphasis). Brown says "Qoheleth could find no gain, no lasting legacy," as opposed to "the joy of the toil (v. 10), fleeting and inefficacious" (*Ecclesiastes*, 33). The comparison is also implicit

word. Ogden takes this a stage further by emphasizing the "this-worldly" quality of חלק (which 9:6 specifically informs us does not continue beyond death) as distinct from יתרון, which "is not located in this world."[39]

We face two particular problems in determining the meaning of חלק in Ecclesiastes: first, a number of scholars argue that its use here is "peculiar to Ecclesiastes";[40] and, secondly, commentators are divided over whether it has a positive or negative connotation in the book.[41] The word derives from a common root meaning "divide, distribute," and elsewhere in the Hebrew Bible has the sense of "portion."[42] In Ecclesiastes its meaning seems not to be "portion" as distinct from the whole, but rather one's "lot in life" or "the place of the person in the world."[43] Five of the eight occurrences of חלק involve עמל ("work," 2:10, 21; 5:17, 18 [Eng. 5:18, 19]; 9:9), and another two involve "deeds," from the near-synonym עשׂה (3:22; 9:6; the eighth, 11:2, appears to be a proverbial saying and is rather different from the others, but there is no reason to think its basic

---

in Longman's statement on 2:11 that "there were no *lasting* results from his labors" (*The Book of Ecclesiastes*, 94, my emphasis). See also Farmer's reference to what can be "permanently gained" (*Who Knows What is Good?*, 157); Perry's comment, on 2:10–11, that "The satisfaction of his desires brings pleasure in the present but no lasting value" (*Dialogues with Kohelet*, 79); and Davis's reference to "immediate satisfaction" in 2:10 (*Proverbs, Ecclesiastes, and the Song of Songs*, 179). It is clear that this comparison, whether made explicitly or not, is often drawn, and seems therefore to be an important factor in the way these verses are interpreted—with implications also for the interpretation of יתרון.

39. Ogden, *Qoheleth*, 29, see also p. 42.

40. M. Tsevat, "חלק," *TDOT* 4:447–51 (451). Rudman asserts that "Qoheleth uses the term חלק in a way fundamentally different to its usage elsewhere in the Hebrew Bible" (*Determinism*, 60).

41. Crenshaw argues: "Its essential meaning for him is limitation, a part of something rather than the whole thing. One's portion in life is the share of desirable or undesirable experiences that come along, not as the direct result of good or bad conduct but purely by chance" (*Ecclesiastes*, 82). By contrast, Whybray maintains, "*ḥēleq* . . . is several times used by Qoheleth of the human lot, often, as here, in a positive sense" (*Ecclesiastes*, 55). Provan writes: "The emphasis lies on enjoyment or joy as itself the reward that we may expect from live. . . . Indeed, the 'reward' is itself a gift from God. . . . It is in receiving life as a gift from God and in not striving to manipulate it and exploit it in order to arrive at some kind of 'gain' that mortal beings can find contentment" (*Ecclesiastes, Song of Songs*, 74).

42. חלק is used "to refer to a portion of spoils (Gen 14:24) and food (Lev 6:10). It is, however, more frequently used of land, especially as a portion of the inheritance, as distributed at the conquest (Josh 19:9 . . .), and to be received after the exile (Isa 61:7)" (Cornelis Van Dam, "חלק," *NIDOTTE* 2:161–63 [162]).

43. H. H. Schmid, "חלק, *ḥlq*, to divide," *TLOT* 1:431–43 (432).

meaning is any different). The word seems, then, to be related to one's work or deeds. In addition, five occurrences involve שׂמח ("joy," 2:10; 3:22; 5:17, 18 [Eng. 5:18, 19]; 9:9): indeed, it appears that enjoyment *is* the חלק in these verses,[44] usually enjoyment in one's work (2:10; 5:17, 18 [Eng. 5:18, 19]), or in one's deeds (3:22 and possibly 9:9). On three occasions the verses in which חלק occurs describe the gift of God, but contrary to the claims of a number of commentators,[45] it is *not* חלק which is described as God's gift (in 5:17 [Eng. 5:18] and 9:9 it is "the days of life" that are given; in 5:18 [Eng. 5:19] it is not clear exactly what constitutes "the gift of God"; it may be the *ability* to enjoy the wealth and possessions that God gives and/or to accept one's lot, or the enjoyment of one's work). In three verses the context is explicitly "under the sun," but again it is not specifically חלק that is described as being תחת השׁמשׁ (rather it is the work one does).[46] The word itself is actually neither positive nor negative, but in Ecclesiastes people's חלק usually *involves* finding pleasure in the work or deeds they undertake:[47] this, it seems, is the human "lot" for Qohelet, and adds to the poignancy of the loss of one's חלק in 2:21 and 9:6.[48] By contrast, יתרון seems to be something more than this, some "advantage" beyond one's "lot in life"—or something "in excess" of one's lot in life—and beyond the pleasure one can achieve from what one does.

    If the reader assumed that 2:11 provided the answer to the question in 1:3, 2:13 may come as a surprise, because it starts with the declaration: וראיתי אני שׁישׁ יתרון. As Seow notes,

44. See especially the parallelism between שׂמח מכל־עמלי and חלקי מכל־עמלי in 2:10. This is supported by 3:22. In 5:17–18, "enjoyment in work" may be included in one's חלק, and enjoyment in one's deeds is certainly part of the scenario in 9:6–9. Rudman argues that in 2:21 also "the 'portion' to which Qoheleth refers might well be the pleasure arising from the use of the wealth accrued by the first man" (*Determinism*, 60).

45. Tsevat argues that חלק develops the meaning "'portion in life determined by God,' 'destiny'" (*TDOT* 4:448). Rudman uses this to support his claim that "Although חלק cannot be defined as 'Fate,' it is a concept that illustrates the deterministic nature of Qoheleth's worldview" (*Determinism*, 60). I believe this reads into the word a meaning it does not have *of itself*, i.e., this position derives from how one perceives the word to function in Ecclesiastes.

46. Thus, contra Ogden, there is not an emphasis on חלק as specifically "this worldly" (*Qoheleth*, 42), although this is the implication of 9:6.

47. Fox suggests: "To be precise, a man's portion is the pleasure *potential* in his wealth" (*A Time to Tear Down*, 111, his emphasis). This is helpful so long as one notes that "Pleasure is just one type of portion."

48. There are useful discussions of the use of חלק in Ecclesiastes in Rudman, *Determinism*, 55–60; Fox, *A Time to Tell*, 109–11; and Michel, *Untersuchungen*, 118–25.

Now the author appears to contradict himself: *yēšyitrôn* "there is advantage" in 2:13 stands in stark contrast to *'ênyitrôn* "there is no advantage"
in 2:11. Is there advantage, or is there not? Commentators often gloss
over the problem by calling the advantage over folly "relative."[49] But the
contradiction between 2:11 and 2:13 is far too glaring to be dismissed
so.[50]

In this context "profit" is inappropriate (because there is no pecuniary
advantage in light over darkness), and "advantage" again seems the best
translation. It appears, then, that there *is* advantage to be gained. Indeed,
not only is there an advantage in wisdom over folly, but there is also
advantage in light over darkness. However, the following verses serve to
cast considerable doubt on the value of such an "advantage": the wise
person does have the advantage that he or she does not walk in the dark
like the fool, but this advantage will be wiped out by the darkness of
death.[51] In view of the fact that elsewhere in Ecclesiastes "sight"[52] and
"light"[53] are used as metaphors for life, and "darkness"[54] for death, it
rather seems that for any given individual both the advantage of wisdom

49. Seow is, of course, right that there is no indication in the text that the
advantage is "relative"; thus Fox writes that this is "a superlative affirmation of the
advantage of wisdom over folly," noting that "Light and darkness are polar opposites" (*A Time to Tear Down*, 183). However, Brown states: "By lining up wisdom
and folly side by side Qoheleth finds encouraging that wisdom appears to yield
relative advantage or profit" (*Ecclesiastes*, 34, my emphasis). See also Salyer, *Vain
Rhetoric*, 285.

50. Seow, *Ecclesiastes*, 153. Scholars have debated whether or not the "contradiction" results from quotations from traditional wisdom (in vv. 13–14a) with which
Qohelet disagrees. Compare Gordis, *Koheleth*, 221–22, with Whybray, *Ecclesiastes*,
57–58. See also M. V. Fox, "The Identification of Quotations in Biblical Literature,"
ZAW 92 (1980): 416–31. It may be that this is simply one of the ambiguities of the
book, a point drawn out well by Davidson who, after describing different possibilities, concludes: "Which translation, which particular emphasis is right? We do not
know. Much depends on the overall picture we have in our minds of the author of
the book" (*Ecclesiastes and the Song of Songs*, 4).

51. Thus, for example, Seow argues: "The basic argument of this pivotal section
is that death is a great leveler and so the wise has no advantage over the fool in that
regard. This is, indeed, the point of the entire unit: the wise king (Qohelet-Solomon)
has no real advantage over the ordinary fool; the wise and the fool are alike, as far as
mortality is concerned" (*Ecclesiastes*, 143).

52. Especially the phrase, "seeing the sun," or similar. See 4:3; 6:5; 7:11; 11:7;
12:3(?).

53. See 6:5; 7:11; 11:7; 12:1–2.

54. See 6:4; 11:8; 12:2, 3(?). The passage from 11:7–12:7 is particularly important in this regard, and it is in the early verses of this passage that the symbolic use
of "light" and "darkness" (and also "seeing") comes to a head.

over folly *and* that of light over darkness are wiped out by death.[55] Therefore, there undoubtedly *are* advantages to be gained in life, and this is affirmed in 5:8 (Eng. 5:9); 7:11, 12 and 10:10: however, it is notable that all these verses pose considerable problems for the interpreter so that their precise meaning is far from clear (as a comparison of the commentaries readily reveals[56]), and this raises the question: Just what *is* the "advantage" being described in each verse? The issue for Qohelet seems to be that whatever the advantage, it ceases at death. Perhaps this is why Qohelet affirms *in the abstract* the advantage of "wisdom" over "folly" in 2:13, while questioning at 6:8 the advantage of "the wise *person*" over the "fool," both of whom die.[57] It is notable, then, that the advantages described in 7:11–12 also relate to the abstract notion of wisdom, and that in 7:11 wisdom specifically brings advantage to "those who see the sun" (i.e. those who are alive[58]) and in 7:12 the advantage (of knowledge?) is precisely that wisdom gives life to its possessor.[59] The final

55. However, Longman is one of a number of scholars who maintain that "Symbolic value need not be read into the use of *light* and *darkness*" here (*The Book of Ecclesiastes*, 97). It seems to me much more likely, in a book so dominated by the theme of "death," and deriving from a wisdom tradition that focuses heavily on the theme of "life," that allusions to life and death are intended here. Other commentators agree: see, e.g., Brown, *Ecclesiastes*, 34–35; Crenshaw, *Ecclesiastes*, 84.

56. Whybray says of 5:8 (Eng. 5:9), "This verse has been described, not without reason, as 'An insuperable crux'" (*Ecclesiastes*, 97). Of 7:11 Whybray notes that "Four quite different views have been put forward about the meaning of this verse" (p. 117), and of 7:12, "The meaning of the first half of this verse is disputed" (p. 118). He then states of 10:10, "This verse has been described as linguistically the most difficult in the book, and both ancient and modern translation have rendered it very differently," adding, "The last part (from *but wisdom*) has been described as 'untranslatable,' and its meaning is conjectural" (p. 153). Gordis lists eight different ways in which 10:10 has been read by commentators (*Koheleth*, 321–22).

57. Although, for Gordis, the question in 6:8 is specifically "the man who is wise but poor, as the parallel clause indicates." However, he does acknowledge that (again, notably) the second half of the verse "is a crux" (*Koheleth*, 260). So far as I can see the commentators do not seek to explain why חכם and כסיל are used in 6:8 as opposed to חכמה and סכלות in 2:13, though there may be a hint of this in Ogden and Zogbo: "In 2:13–16 Qoheleth argues that wisdom is *always* an advantage, that it is as different from folly as light is from darkness. Despite this fact both the wise man and the fool die" (*A Handbook*, 204, my emphasis). However, this difference is not explored further.

58. Ogden and Zogbo note "*Those who see the sun* is expressed in TEV as 'everyone who lives.' This is precisely its meaning" (*A Handbook*, 237).

59. Ogden goes too far when he says that in 7:11–12, "Qoheleth forges a link between wisdom in this present and hope of a future. . . . The 'life' it offers must be understood in terms wider than mere present existence" (*Qoheleth*, 109). By con-

clause in 10:10, ‏ויתרון הכשיר חכמה‎, also appears to describe the abstract notion of wisdom as an advantage (although it is far from clear just what the clause means), and the lack of advantage described in 10:11 may be precisely that death is the result (of the snake biting before it is charmed). I suspect that these final two occurrences of ‏יתרון‎ in Ecclesiastes intentionally bring together one affirmation of "advantage" and one denial, but this time in the mundane setting of what appear to be common proverbs addressing wisdom and folly in the activities of daily life: yes, wisdom is an advantage, it means you keep your axe sharpened so that your work is easier and less risky; no, folly does not bring any advantage, the fool (or the one who doesn't exercise wisdom in time) may get bitten by a snake and die![60] This serves to place "wisdom" in its proper context: certainly it brings real advantages, but at best it puts off the day of death when all such advantages will be wiped out, at worst it may come too late to guard one against the vagaries of life.

5.3.3. *Other Words from* ‏יתר‎

3:19 also addresses the issue of death, and also asserts that there is no advantage (and "advantage" seems a good translation here). However, the comparison on this occasion is between people and animals:

‏כי מקרה בני־האדם ומקרה הבהמה ומקרה אחד להם כמות זה כן מות‎
‏זה ורוח אחד לכל ומותר האדם מן־הבהמה אין כי הכל הבל:‎

The question arises again why a different word is used here.[61] Unlike ‏יתרון‎, this word, ‏מותר‎, appears only here in Ecclesiastes and does occur elsewhere in the Hebrew Bible, once in Prov 14:23 and once in Prov 21:5.

---

trast, Brown perceives "a degree of irony" in these verses, arguing that "Wisdom is no better than wealth. . . . Qoheleth is not so much elevating wealth as demoting wisdom" (*Ecclesiastes*, 78).

60. Thus, for example, Fredericks writes: "Of course Qoheleth has his own examples of the protective value of wisdom that could avert death itself. . . . [O]ne should take care when engaging in precarious duties like quarrying and logging" (*Coping with Transience*, 39). Rudman asserts: "Qoheleth evidently *did* believe that wisdom was profitable (2:13; 7:11; 10:10–11), at least in contrast to folly" (*Determinism*, 74, his emphasis). By contrast, Loader argues that in 10:10–11, "wisdom is absolutely meaningless. . . . The argument then runs like this: If an instrument is dull (the ax), it causes trouble that cannot be helped by wisdom, just as an 'object' on which wisdom is supposed to have influence (the snake) can put wisdom out of action" (*Ecclesiastes*, 119). See also Christianson, *A Time to Tell*, 247. "Folly" is not specifically mentioned in 10:11, but the wider context is a consideration of wisdom and folly in various situations.

61. Ogden and Zogbo argue: "here the fact that we have a new form of the root suggests that it means something slightly different. From the context, we conclude

In both these verses מותר is contrasted with מחסור ("lack, poverty"). This confirms the sense of "excess," "profit" or "advantage," and gives no indication of any difference between the use of מותר here and יתרון elsewhere in Ecclesiastes: indeed, most commentators simply treat the words as synonyms (usually without question, in fact). However, if יתרון is a key word that is intended to convey a single concept, it would seem that its effectiveness is lessened—and its ambiguity increases—by the use of the synonyms י[ו]תר and מותר. If, however, an element of ambiguity is intended, the different forms of the word serve to heighten uncertainty over precisely what the word signifies.

יותר appears to be used adverbially in 2:15[62] (so RSV, NRSV and KJV and most commentators, but NIV, NJPSV, NLT, NJB, NEB, REB and GNB, along with a few commentators see יותר here functioning as a noun [or a "predicate adjective"][63] as in 6:8, effectively making it another "what advantage?" question[64]) and 7:16 where it means either "exceedingly" or "excessively." It makes a difference to both verses which of the two words apply—and in both cases it is wisdom that is referred to. In 2:15, Qohelet asks either "why have I been *excessively* wise?"[65] or "why have I been *exceedingly* wise?"[66] The first suggests that he has been more wise

---

that it has the narrower meaning of the *possible advantage* of human beings over animals" (*A Handbook*, 115, my emphasis), as opposed to the sense it has elsewhere of "lasting benefit." This is reflected in their suggested translation, "We all share the same life-spirit, so *in this sense*, human beings are not superior to animals" (my emphasis).

62. Schoors notes that "the participial form יותר is sometimes used as an adverb" (*The Preacher Sought*, 114). 2:15 and 7:16 are the two examples he cites. He observes that it is sometimes regarded as an adverb in 12:9, 12.

63. E.g. Provan, *Ecclesiastes, Song of Songs*, 75; Garrett, *Proverbs, Ecclesiastes, Song of Songs*, 292. Although Crenshaw translates, "so very wise," he explains that "One could then read *yôter* as a predicate adjective: 'Where is the advantage?'" (*Ecclesiastes*, 69, 85). See also Whitley, *Koheleth*, 25.

64. Longman is one of the few commentators to acknowledge these different readings (*The Book of Ecclesiastes*, 98).

65. See Seow, *Ecclesiastes*, 119, 135, 154. Seow is one of the few scholars who explains his translation of יותר, arguing, "The issue is . . . not just having wisdom, which is a 'plus,' but desiring a 'surplus' (*yôtēr*) of it." He also renders the word in precisely the same way here and in 7:16, where many other commentators appear careless in this regard. Hubbard translates, "more wise" (*Ecclesiastes, Song of Solomon*, 85); and Brown, "Why did I excel in wisdom?" (*Ecclesiastes*, 35). See also Bergant, *Job Ecclesiastes*, 238–39.

66. Thus Fox translates here, "so very wise" (*A Time to Tear Down*, 181), as also does Murphy, *Ecclesiastes*, 20; Whybray, *Ecclesiastes*, 59; Tamez, *When the Horizons Close*, 48; Davis, *Proverbs, Ecclesiastes, and the Song of Songs*, 179, and so on. Christianson uses the word "exceedingly" (*A Time to Tell*, 82, 209, 232).

than he ought, perhaps in the hope of gaining greater advantage. The implication that follows may be that it is possible to *be* too wise (which 1:18 would certainly bear out), or perhaps that there is a limit to how much one should pursue wisdom. The second suggests that great wisdom is ultimately futile because it does not save its possessor from the same fate as the fool. The implication that follows is that wisdom is ultimately no better than folly for any given individual, because any advantage is wiped out by death. 7:16 is a deceptively difficult verse (I suspect intentionally so) that has been interpreted in a variety of ways, which may appear only subtly different, but whose differences are highly significant.[67] The relevant clause here, אל־תתחכם יותר, might be rendered "do not be (or perhaps 'make yourself out to be') *exceedingly* wise"[68] or "do not be (or 'make yourself out to be') *excessively* wise."[69] The adverb appears only in Ecclesiastes and in Esth 6:6. In the light of its basic meaning of "left over, excess," and the meaning "more than" in Esth 6:6, the sense in Ecclesiastes is probably "excessively." This fits well with the notion of "excess" implicit in "advantage": excessive wisdom does *not* in the end bring any excess to the given individual who possesses it.

There are two further uses of words from the root יתר, the word ויתר at the start of 12:9 and 12:12. However, commentators are divided about what precisely the role of the words is in these verses—and whether or

---

67. Fredericks writes: "This ticklish assertion has been turned in every direction to make it fit" (*Coping with Transience*, 39 n. 1). Kaiser contends that "Few verses in Ecclesiastes are more susceptible to incorrect interpretations than 7:16–18" (*Ecclesiastes*, 85). W. A. Brindle, after quoting Kaiser, adds, "interpreters of Ecclesiastes tend to view the argument of 7:15–18 in a variety of ways, depending upon whether they are willing to attribute to the author a sense of relativity and 'moderation' in moral conduct" ("Righteousness and Wickedness in Ecclesiastes 7:15–18," *AUSS* 23 [1985]: 243–57 [243]). More recently, Salyer has written, "The juxtaposition of these incongruous admonitions presents yet another blank which results in dueling observations, the final meaning of which is left for the reader to infer" (*Vain Rhetoric*, 340). Compare, for example, Crenshaw, who generally reads Ecclesiastes as a pessimistic work, and renders the verse, "Do not *be* too righteous and do not *be* excessively wise; why should you be ruined?" (*Ecclesiastes*, 140, my emphasis), with Ogden, who is more positive in his interpretation and renders the verse, "Do not *claim* exceptional righteousness or *ardently pursue* wisdom. Why should you invite destruction upon yourself? (*Qoheleth*, 114, my emphasis).

68. So, e.g., Whybray, *Ecclesiastes*, 120.

69. In *Qohelet* (p. 233) Fox renders יותר here "exceedingly"; this was changed to "excessively" in *A Time to Tear Down*, 258. Others who translate "excessively" include Fredericks, *Coping with Transience*, 39, 82; Crenshaw, *Ecclesiastes*, 140; Longman, *The Book of Ecclesiastes*, 195; Seow, *Ecclesiastes*, 252–53. Murphy translates, "wise to excess" (*Ecclesiastes*, 68).

not they function in the same way. There are basically two positions with respect to the meaning of וְיֹתֵר in 12:9:[70]

1.   It is an adverb, as elsewhere in Ecclesiastes, which with שֶׁ means something like, "in addition to" (so NJPSV, RSV, NRSV, NJB, NIV, and a good number of commentators[71]). The first half of the verse would then recall the words of Qohelet earlier in the book and the second half add the new information: "In addition to being wise, Qohelet also taught the people knowledge. . . ." The word עוֹד is then part of the phrase, . . .עוֹד . . . שֶׁ וְיֹתֵר, "in addition to . . . also . . ." Gordis cites parallels to this usage in the Talmud.[72]

2.   It is a conjunction, "in addition," indicating that the following is an addition to the book, which ends at 12:8 (so, implicitly, NEB, REB, NLT, GNB, KJV, and a good number of commentators[73]). Alternatively, it may be understood as a noun, "an addition."[74] This might suggest that an editor is signalling an addition to the original material,[75] or it may be that the author is informing the reader that additional information is being added, perhaps as an explanation, or perhaps as an afterthought. This would be in keeping with Mishnaic usage. It might also mean that the usage in 12:9 and 12:12 is at least very similar.[76]

---

70.   These possibilities are discussed in some detail in Seow, *Ecclesiastes*, 383. N. Lohfink maintains that the issue cannot be resolved ("Zu eigen Satzeröffnungen im Epilog des Koheletbuches," in *"Jedes Ding hat seine Zeit . . .": Studien zur israelitischen und altorientalischen Weisheit* [ed. A. A. Diesel, R. G. Lehmann, E. Otto and A. Wagner; Festschrift for D. Michel; BZAW 241; Berlin: de Gruyter, 1996], 131–48 [131–39]).

71.   So, e.g., Eaton, *Ecclesiastes*, 153; Bergant, *Job, Ecclesiastes*, 290; Garrett, *Proverbs, Ecclesiastes, Song of* Songs, 343; Gordis, *Koheleth*, 351–52; Murphy, *Ecclesiastes*, 123; Crenshaw, *Ecclesiastes*, 189 (but see his comments on p. 190).

72.   However, Seow points out, "the idiom in the two Postbiblical Hebrew texts cited by Gordis is properly *yōtēr min*, not *yōtēr še* as we have in our text" (*Ecclesiastes*, 383).

73.   So, e.g., Seow, *Ecclesiastes*, 383; Ogden and Zogbo, *A Handbook*, 435; Longman, *The Book of Ecclesiastes*, 277; Provan, *Ecclesiastes, Song of Songs*, 226; Whybray, *Ecclesiastes*, 170; Fox, *A Time to Tear Down*, 350.

74.   Longman states, "*yōtēr* must be understood in its nominal, not adverbial, sense" (*The Book of Ecclesiastes*, 277).

75.   Ogden writes, "If we are satisfied that 12:9–14 is an editorial postlude, then we may presume that the term *yōtēr* is the means by which these additions have been signalled" (*Qoheleth*, 208). Loader states, "In verse 9 the writer *expressly says* that the words that follow are an added appendix" (*Ecclesiastes*, 133, my emphasis).

76.   Ogden and Zogbo say of 12:12, "The Hebrew text opens with the same phrase as verse 9. . . . Perhaps it is better if we can render *yother* in the same manner both in verse 9 and here" (*A Handbook*, 440).

A factor in favour of the second reading is the disjunctive *zaqeph gadol* above ויתר in the MT, a feature which suggests that it is to be read as separate from the following. We should note, however, that the pause does not occur in the same place in v. 12. A second factor against the first reading, and in favour of the second, is the absence of the comparative *mem* which is used in Mishnaic Hebrew. We should note again, though, that the *mem* is present in v. 12.

It may be, then, that ויתר serves a different function in the two verses, meaning "in addition" or "moreover" in v. 9, and "in addition *to*" or "more *than*" in v. 12.[77] Such variation in word usage is characteristic of Ecclesiastes, and might suggest, first, that it is the author of the rest of the book who has appended these final verses, and, secondly, that there is one appendix rather than two.

There are, however, two factors that support the first reading above for v. 9. First, the second reading accounts but poorly for the prefixed particle of relation, שׁ. This particle has a wide range of meanings in the Hebrew Bible,[78] often serving merely to link a clause to that which precedes it. Such would need to be the case here, but the verse would make good sense, and be more simple, without it—and its purpose would have been served more effectively by the use of כי as elsewhere in Ecclesiastes.[79] Moreover, in the Mishnah יתר is used with שׁ in the sense of "beyond the fact that . . . ," although it uses the *mem* as well, יתר מש. . . .

The term ויתר in 12:12 is also understood in basically two different ways, roughly corresponding to the two possibilities discussed above for 12:9:

1.   It is an adverb meaning "in addition to," often rendered "beyond" (NEB, REB, GNB, NIV, RSV, NRSV and a good number of commentators[80]). In this case, it would go along with מהמה, and mean "in addition to these [things]."

---

77. Many commentators completely ignore the differences in the use of יתר in 12:9, 12. Thus, for example, Longman uses the disjunctive accent and the presence of the prefixed שׁ rather than מש in 12:9 to argue for the translation "furthermore." He does not then comment on the absence of these in 12:12.

78. This is discussed in Schoors, *The Preacher Sought*, 54–56, 138–49, and Isaksson, *Studies*, 148–61.

79. But see Schoors, *The Preacher Sought*, 134–36; Isaksson, *Studies*, 151–56; Michel, *Untersuchungen*, 200–12.

80. So, e.g., Whybray, *Ecclesiastes*, 173; Murphy, *Ecclesiastes*, 125; Fredericks, *Coping with Transience*, 39–40; Seow, *Ecclesiastes*, 388; Provan, *Ecclesiastes, Song of Songs*, 226; Crenshaw, *Ecclesiastes*, 189.

2. It is a conjunction meaning "in addition," often rendered "fur-thermore" (NJB, NJPSV, KJV and a good number of commenta-tors[81]). The word would then indicate a further comment by the author or editor, either for the first time, or for the second, depending on how ויתר in v. 9 is understood.

In favour of the first option is the commonly attested idiom יתר מן in Postbiblical Hebrew, the absence of a disjunctive pause as in v. 9, and the presence of other such warnings in ancient Near Eastern texts.[82] In favour of the second option is the commonly attested idiom נזהר מן in Postbiblical Hebrew, the absence of the *mem before* יתר, and the lack of clarity over what one is to "be warned" about.[83] As with ויתר in v. 9, recent commentators are fairly evenly divided over how the verse should be read, and there is no clear correlation between their interpretation of the word in v. 9 and in v. 12.

It may be that the use of יתר in 12:9, 12 is intended to pick up on the key word יתרון (and equivalents), and other words from the same root (especially, of course, יֹ[וֹ]תֵר in 2:15; 6:8, 11; 7:11, 16). The differences between the two usages and the uncertainty over their precise meaning (and whether or not they should be understood in the same way) are typi-cal of Ecclesiastes.

5.3.4. *Rhetorical Questions?*

There is one further crucially important issue in relation to the word יתרון that we should consider. Loader is representative of the majority of commentators[84] when he writes of 1:3,

> It is a rhetorical question; it is not designed to gain information but to posit a thesis. The question, "What does man gain?" therefore means that there is no profit at all in all his labor. It is a statement declaring all human toil "under the sun," that is, in life, to be worthless. His interest is focused on what profits humans in life, and his conclusion is that nothing does. At this point already, then, we are told the final conclusion of the

---

81. So, e.g., Fox, *A Time to Tear Down*, 356 (but with the addition of a pause at ויתר); Hubbard, *Ecclesiastes, Song of Solomon*, 251; Gordis, *Koheleth*, 354; Perry, *Dialogues with Kohelet*, 171; Longman, *The Book of Ecclesiastes*, 281.

82. See, especially, Seow, *Ecclesiastes*, 388.

83. See, especially, Fox, *A Time to Tear Down*, 356.

84. E.g., Bartholomew, *Reading Ecclesiastes*, 244; Fox, *A Time to Tear Down*, 165; Tamez, *When the Horizons Close*, 36; Perry, *Dialogues with Kohelet*, 56; Rudman, *Determinism*, 73. Seow states: "This is *clearly* a rhetorical question. A negative answer is implied" (*Ecclesiastes*, 113, my emphasis). See also J. L. Cren-shaw, "The Expression *mi yôdēaʿ* in the Hebrew Bible," *VT* 36 (1986): 274–88.

Preacher's reasoning and conviction. The remainder of the prologue will show how he arrived at this pessimistic conclusion, and the rest of the book will illustrate this theme from all angles.[85]

However, Crenshaw, who reads the verse similarly, acknowledges, "Out of context, the rhetorical question . . . leaves open the possibility of responding that one reaps a bountiful harvest from a diligent labor. But the juxtaposition of this question with the thematic statement in 1:2 rules out any effort to offer specific instances of advantage from toil."[86] This is the point precisely—the reader determines *from the context* whether or not this is a question that demands the answer "no," and different readers understand the context in quite different ways. Thus it should not surprise us to find that Fredericks asserts:

> For Qoheleth the answer is not "there is none," the answer assumed by many who see his thematic *hevel* to mean "vanity, empty, absurd." On the contrary, he says explicitly that there are many advantages to wisdom when one is able to discover it, and that pleasure and enjoyment are good and commendable pursuits to counterbalance one's exhaustive efforts.[87]

Good, Melchert and Wilson all demonstrate convincingly (though from very different perspectives) that the first few verses of the Ecclesiastes can be understood in quite different ways and that this question is an important aspect of that ambiguity.[88] In fact, there is no particular reason why the reader *should* understand 1:3 as a rhetorical question expecting the answer "no," especially in view of the many ambiguities even in the first three verses of the book (as Good, Melchert and Wilson all, I believe, clearly show).

---

85. Loader, *Ecclesiastes*, 20.

86. Crenshaw, *Ecclesiastes*, 60.

87. Fredericks, *Coping with Transience*, 63.

88. Good writes: "The form of the question does not allow us to be sure of its answer. The answer might be positive, that something is left over for the man, and the range of theoretical specifics is very wide" ("The Unfilled Sea," 63). Melchert suggests, "Let us return to the opening verses once more, this time not assuming the text offers a single view," then argues, "Now, verse 3 is not a rhetorical but a real question, asking, 'What value is there or could there be?'" (*Wise Teaching*, 119). L. Wilson asks, "Is this a rhetorical question implying the answer 'no,' or is it a genuine question? Is it answered by v. 2 or by v. 4, or is the verdict left open?" ("Artful Ambiguity in Ecclesiastes 1,1–11," 359). Christianson is heading in this direction when he writes, "In a rhetorical question, however, the answer is only apparent—there is an uncertain tone. . . . Since no answer is given either Qoheleth genuinely does not know it or he relies on the absence of a readerly expectation for an answer" (*A Time to Tell*, 219).

5.4. *Conclusion*

The word יתרון (and related words), then, has (have) *something* to do with "excess" or what is "left over." In most cases, "advantage" is a good translation, providing it includes at times *financial* advantage. However, the *precise* implications of the word are far from clear: questions need to be raised about the synonymity or otherwise of the different nouns used; the function of the adverb/noun יֹת[ר] is unclear in most cases; the translation of many of the verses in which words from the root יתר appear is complicated; and the "programmatic question" in 1:3 is open to different readings. There is much ambiguity surrounding this key word.

Chapter 6

עמל AND עשׂה IN ECCLESIASTES

6.1. *The Importance of the Words* עמל *and* עשׂה

עמל is another important word in Ecclesiastes that is introduced in 1:3. Certainly if we take the total number of occurrences of a word in the book as an indicator, this is clearly a "key" word. It is the next most frequent word after הבל, occurring some 35 times (and only 40 times elsewhere in the Hebrew Bible[1]), and if I am right that עשׂה functions as a near-synonym,[2] words from the two roots together occur more often than any individual word in the book.[3]

---

1. Plus one occurrence of a proper noun, עָמָל, in 1 Chr 7:35.

2. Rudman, for example, notes that עמל "is applied by Qoheleth to any and all human activity" (*Determinism*, 74). However, Fox labels עמל as "unpleasant" and עשׂה as "neutral" (*A Time to Tear Down*, 97). Nonetheless, he states, "At its broadest reach, *ʿamal* covers virtually all human endeavors" (p. 101), and goes on to argue that "Words from the broader and connotationally neutral root ʿSH are used as near equivalents of *ʿamal*" (p. 102). It is notable that after employing the word "ambiguous" several times of עמל, Fox goes on to say that words from the root עשׂה "are subject of the same ambiguity" (p. 103).

3. Leaving aside the relative pronoun (אשׁר [×89] and שׁ [×68–70]), the various uses of the conjunction כי (×87), the preposition מן (×75), the object marker את (×74), the adverb of addition גם (×58), the demonstrative pronoun זה (×43), and the prepositions אל (×23), על (×21) and אם (×21), the most frequent word is כל ("all," ×91), followed by לא (adverb of negation, ×65), עשׂה ("do," ×64), טוב ("good," ×54), חכם ("wise," ×53), ראה ("see," ×51), אדם ("person," ×49), היה ("be," ×49), אין ("not, none," ×44), ידע ("know," ×44), לב ("heart," ×42), אלהים ("God," ×40), עת ("time," ×40), הבל ("vanity," ×38), עמל ("work," ×35), שׁמשׁ ("sun," ×35), תחת ("under," ×34), רבב/רבה ("many, much," ×33), סכל/כסל ("fool," ×33), דבר ("word/deed," ×32), רעה ("bad," ×32), הלך ("go," ×30), אני ("me," ×29), נתן ("give," ×27), יום ("day," ×26), חיה ("live," ×26), מה (interrogative pronoun, ×24), רוח ("wind, spirit," ×24) and אמר ("say," ×20). This includes all words occurring 20+ times in Ecclesiastes. Words from the root יתר ("excess") occur 18 times, from מצא ("find") and שׂמח ("joy") 17 times each, from אכל ("eat"), אחר ("after") and מות ("die") 15 times each (but note that while מות occurs just 15 times, "death" appears in other guises as well, and is a very major theme in the book). These also are important terms in Ecclesiastes. Other significant words include רשׁע ("wicked,"

6.2. עָמָל

6.2.1. *Translation of* עָמָל

Whybray perceives the ambiguity of the word עָמָל when he notes that it

> has several meanings. In general in the Old Testament it has a very nega-
> tive tone: trouble, misfortune, harm. In post-biblical Hebrew, however, it
> simply means "work." There is no doubt that in Ecclesiastes it often has
> this later meaning, which seems to have superseded the earlier ones; but
> in some passages it has additional overtones.[4]

In the context of Eccl 1:3 Whybray favours the neutral term "work" (or
"hard work"), as does Ogden[5]—and both of these commentators present
a positive reading of the book as a whole. (See also NIV, KJV, GNB, NLT.)
Fox notes another difficulty in translating this word:

> A *troublesome ambiguity* encumbers the understanding of the terms for
> "toil" and "work": sometimes they refer to the activity of toiling, some-
> times to the material fruit of that activity, namely earnings or wealth. . . .
> In several occurrences of *ʿamal*, it is nearly impossible to decide which
> sense is most appropriate. . . . And there are passages where he seems to
> vacillate rapidly between the two senses. . . . One may try to identify the
> most appropriate sense in any particular occurrence. . . . But the grounds
> for decision are often extremely slight.[6]

×12), עָנָה ("affliction, business," ×12); צָדַק ("righteous," ×11), יָרֵא ("fear," ×9), חָטָא
("sin," ×8), חֵפֶץ ("lot," ×8), עֹלָם ("enduring, eternal," ×8) and בִּקֵּשׁ ("seek," ×7).
These statistics were generated by computer, and counted by hand—they disagree
with those of Murphy (*Ecclesiastes*, xxix). However, I do agree with Murphy that
the high frequency of "favourite words" is very significant. Christianson says, "If
repetition so offends interpreters, Ecclesiastes is a chief offender. Qoheleth's is a
book of themes—of key words and ideas—and the sensitive reader will no doubt
notice the density of 'like words' that generate such motifs" (*A Time to Tell*, 44). See
also Loretz, *Qohelet und der alte Orient*, 167–80.

    4.   Whybray, *Ecclesiastes*, 37.

    5.   Ogden and Zogbo state that עָמָל "refers to heavy labor, work that is physically
tiring *but nevertheless rewarding*" (*A Handbook on Ecclesiastes*, 24, my emphasis).
A number of commentators use the words "work" or "labour" rather than toil, including, Farmer (*Who Knows What is Good?*, 152–53) and Garrett (*Proverbs, Ecclesiastes, Song of Songs*). S. Schwertner asserts that in Ecclesiastes, "the positive significance of work often stands in the background" ("עָמָל, *ʿāmāl*, toil," *TLOT* 2:924–
26 [926]). B. Otzen argues that Ecclesiastes "comes close to the neutral meaning of
ʿāmal, 'work,' and *ʿāmēl*, 'worker,'" but goes on to say, "But for him the words have
an undertone of frustration, suggesting 'toilsome labor' or, better, the unending
human striving that he can only consider vanity" ("עָמָל," *TDOT* 11:196–202 [200]).

    6.   Fox, *Qohelet*, 55, my emphasis. Reference to "*troublesome* ambiguity" has
disappeared from *A Time to Tear Down*, but nevertheless the word עָמָל is designated
"ambiguous" several times (see, e.g., pp. 100, 101).

Thus NJPSV renders 1:3, "What real value is there for a man in all *the gains* he makes beneath the sun?," adding in a footnote, "Heb. ʿamal usually has this sense in Ecclesiastes."[7] Fox asks, "When Qohelet deprecates toil for not yielding a profit (1:3; 3:9) or for being absurd and senseless (2:11), is it the work or the wealth that is so judged?," and acknowledges that "No syntactic features resolve the question."[8] Nonetheless, he renders עמל in 1:3 (and 2:11; 3:9) as "toil,"[9] which conveys a rather different impression than "the gains," "work" or even "labour."[10] He maintains, "When signifying activity, ʿamal always means onerous, strained labor, 'overdoing' rather than simply 'doing.' This is the usual meaning of ʿamal in Qohelet."[11] In fact, he goes so far as to say, "we could paraphrase *bᵉkol ʿămalo* (1:3) as 'in all his misery.'"[12] Crenshaw translates likewise[13] (see also RSV, NRSV, NEB, REB, NJB), and these two commentators present negative readings of the book as a whole.

It seems highly likely that the negative connotations of the word will come into play for any reader familiar with the other books that now make up the Hebrew Bible. Of the 40 occurrences elsewhere in the Hebrew Bible, 34 are decidedly negative and bear the meaning "sorrow,"

---

7. H. L. Ginsberg argued that in Ecclesiastes the verb almost always means "acquire" or "possess," while the noun has the sense of "possession" or "wealth" (*Koheleth* [Jerusalem: Newman, 1961], 14). However, while this is clearly the sense of the noun in some instances, and may be in a number of others, very few commentators argue for that meaning in 1:3. Nonetheless, Ogden and Zogbo state, "*Toil* is used in this verse as both a verb and a noun, and both describe the act of working, *together with what that work produces*" (*A Handbook*, 24, my emphasis).

8. Fox, *A Time to Tear Down*, 100–101.

9. Rudman quotes Fox (*Qohelet*, 54–55) with approval: "As Fox observes, Qoheleth's use of √עמל . . . is 'a way of showing life's activities in a special perspective, speaking of them as if they were all part of a great wearying task'" (*Determinism*, 74). Murphy writes of the "heavy mood of toil" (*Ecclesiastes*, lx). Tamez describes עמל as "enslaving labor" or "enslaving toil," explaining, "The word ʿamal (labor, work) is a key to Qoheleth's feelings of frustration" (*When the Horizons Close*, 5, 36).

10. But Schwertner argues that "Hebr. shares the notion that work = trouble with many old languages" (*TLOT* 2:925).

11. Fox, *A Time to Tear Down*, 98. Nonetheless, he adds, "I translate 'toil' whenever possible, for this can be understood as a metonymy for earnings where appropriate, but in a few cases, 'wealth' or 'to earn' is required by context" (p. 100).

12. Ibid., 102.

13. Crenshaw writes that עמל "has the nuance of burdensome labor and mental anguish." However, he goes on to acknowledge, "But not always, for it appears that the word also came to designate the fruit of one's labor (wages), and by extension, wealth" (*Ecclesiastes*, 23). See also, e.g., Longman, *The Book of Ecclesiastes*, 65; and David Thompson, "עמל," *NIDOTTE* 3:435–37.

"trouble" or "suffering."[14] However, five of the remaining six occurrences refer to "work" in what appears to be a neutral way (without necessarily carrying overtones of *painful* or *toilsome* work),[15] and in Ps 105:44 (which Otzen says is "from the same late period as Ecclesiastes"[16]) עמל refers to "wealth" or "earnings." It is this more neutral (or even positive) sense of the word that develops in Postbiblical Hebrew (alongside the other meanings found in Biblical Hebrew),[17] and it is also likely to be part of the semantic range of the word as understood by early readers of Ecclesiastes.

6.2.2. *Use of* עמל *in Ecclesiastes*
In a number of verses in Ecclesiastes (2:10, 24; 3:13; 5:17, 18; 8:15; 9:9—all of which, except the first, are verses which issue the "call to enjoyment") the value of עמל as a source of pleasure is affirmed, but is it "work/toil" or the results of that work or toil ("possessions, wealth") that brings joy? In the case of 2:10, either might apply, and it could make quite a difference to the interpretation of the verse: either, ". . . my heart found pleasure from all my work, and this was my portion from all my work" (where "pleasure" is his "portion" from his work),[18] or ". . . my heart found pleasure from all my wealth, and this was my portion from

---

14. Seow observes, "Perhaps the most startling fact about the occurrences of the noun *ʿāmāl* 'toil' in the Bible is its close association with extremely negative terms: *ʾāwen* 'trouble' (Num 23:21; Job 4:8; 15:35; Pss 7:15 [Eng v 14]; 10:7; 55:11 [Eng v 10]; 90:10; Isa 10:1; 59:4; Hab 1:3), *yāgôn* 'grief' (Jer 20:18), *raʿ* 'evil' (Hab 1:13), *šeqer* 'falsehood' (Ps 7:15 [Eng v 14]), *ka ʿas* 'vexation' (Ps 10:14), *šāwʾ* 'lie' (Job 7:3), *sôd* 'destruction' (Prov 24:2), *ḥāmās* 'violence' (Ps 7:17 [Eng v 16]), *ʿŏnî* 'affliction' (Deut 26:7; Ps 25:18), *rîš* 'poverty' (Prov 31:7), and *mirmâ* 'deceit' (Job 15:35; Ps 55:12 [Eng v 11]). Elsewhere, too, the word means pain, misery, or mischief (Gen 41:51; Judg 10:16; Job 3:10; 5:7; 11:16; Pss 73:5,16; 94:20; 107:12; Isa 53:11)" (*Ecclesiastes*, 104). To these might be added Job 3:20 (// מרי נפשׁ, "the bitter in soul"); 16:2 (in the expression מנחמי עמל, "miserable comforters"); 20:22 (// יצר, "distress"); and Ps 140:10 (Eng. 140:9). These are discussed in some detail in Otzen, *TDOT* 11:198–200. According to Otzen, "In the wisdom tradition, a different nuance of *ʿml* [from that found in the Psalms and Prophets] predominates: the affliction, or rather the misery, that is part of the fundamental human condition" (p. 199).

15. Judg 5:26; Jonah 4:10; Ps 127:1; Prov 16:26 (×2). Ps 127:1 is particularly pertinent to the start of Ecclesiastes. Cf. Otzen, *TDOT* 11:197–98.

16. Ibid., 11:201.

17. Ibid., *TDOT* 11:202.

18. So, e.g., Ogden and Zogbo, *A Handbook*, 62 (see also RSV, NRSV, NIV, KJV, NLT, NJB). Murphy translates "toil" in both cases, stating "The mention of 'toil' . . . is ominous, since it often connotes the heavy price that must be paid for any goal" (*Ecclesiastes*, 18). Hubbard, by contrast, says that "The task itself was brimful with joy" (*Ecclesiastes, Song of Solomon*, 76).

all my work" (where "wealth" may be his "portion"),[19] or possibly even "... my heart found pleasure from all my wealth, and this was my portion from all my wealth" (where again "pleasure" is likely to be the "portion").[20] Crenshaw acknowledges this ambiguity, arguing that "Qohelet's fondness for wrenching more than one meaning out of a word appears to be operative in 2:10."[21]

The same issue arises in relation to 2:24; 3:13 and 5:17 (Eng. 5:18), where one is to "see" טוב in עמלו, and 5:18 (Eng. 5:19)[22] where, as in 2:10, one is to שמח in עמלו—again, is it in "work" or "wealth?" NJB translates the expression in 2:24, "enjoying one's achievements," GNB has "enjoy what he has earned," and NJPSV renders, "enjoyment with his means"; while RSV and NRSV translate "enjoyment in his/their toil," NIV opts for "satisfaction in work," and REB reads, "pleasure in return for his labours" (NEB is similar, as is the KJV). Moreover, these distinctions are maintained through all four verses.[23] Most of the commentators render עמל as "work" (or similar),[24] and rarely acknowledge that it could be read otherwise. However, Crenshaw comments on 2:24 that עמל "may refer to wages, making a different point," and translates, "enjoy good things with his earnings."[25]

The contexts in 8:15 and 9:9 are different because although in both cases there is a "call to enjoyment," there is no specific reference to enjoying one's עמל. In 8:15, after commending pleasure, Qohelet says הוא ילונו בעמלו. It is not clear precisely what the pronoun הוא refers to, but it has something to do with "the call to enjoyment" that precedes it. Again, עמל could mean either "wealth" or "work," and again the word is rendered differently in the English versions[26] and mostly as "work" by

19. Rudman acknowledges this possibility (*Determinism*, 58 n. 70).

20. So NJPSV (cf. GNB). Crenshaw acknowledges this possibility (*Ecclesiastes*, 82).

21. Crenshaw, *Ecclesiastes*, 82. Fox notes that "*ʿĀmāl* (noun, twice) is ambiguous in both occurrences" (*A Time to Tear Down*, 180).

22. 5:18 (Eng. 5:19) is a particularly interesting example because enjoying wealth and possessions (עשר ונכסים) is specifically mentioned earlier in the verse, and שמח בעמלו could be read as either parallel to the early advice, or additional to it.

23. Except for NJB's "find contentment in work" in 5:18. NLT reads "satisfaction in work" or equivalent in 2:24; 5:17, 18, but "enjoy *the fruits* of their labor" in 3:13.

24. So, e.g., Farmer, *Who Knows What is Good?*, 159, 161, 170; Gordis, *Koheleth*, 152, 156, 168; Longman, 107, 113, 162. Seow renders "toil" in 2:24; 5:17, 18, but "fruit of their toil" in 3:13 (*Ecclesiastes*, 118, 158, 202).

25. Crenshaw, *Ecclesiastes*, 70, 90.

26. Most versions render עמל here as "work" (or similar), but NJB translates "this comes from what someone achieves," and NJPSV has "That much can accompany him, in exchange for his wealth." REB and NEB read, "this is all that will remain with him to reward his toil."

the commentators.[27] The same ambiguity applies in relation to 9:9, which, after a call to "enjoy life" (רְאֵה חַיִּים) states that הוּא חֶלְקְךָ בַּחַיִּים וּבַעֲמָלְךָ אֲשֶׁר־אַתָּה עָמֵל. Again the antecedent of the pronoun is unclear, and again either "wealth" or "work" could be the sense (although there are fewer advocates of "wealth" in this instance[28]).

Fox argues of these verses where עָמָל is associated with pleasure,

> Even when the word is ambiguous, the meaning of the passage can be clear. When Qohelet affirms the value of ʿamal as a source of benefit, it is clear that what is actually being praised is toil's product, whether ʿamal means "toil" or "wealth." Qohelet nowhere advocates labor for any intrinsic value such as, say, disciplining the spirit or occupying the mind. Toil is a source of pleasure only insofar as it provides the means of pleasure. Thus liśmoaḥ baʿămalo (and variants) does not mean exactly "to take pleasure in his toil," for Qohelet does not preach the "joy of labor."[29]

However, Brown disagrees. He states that "work in and of itself is what Qoheleth has come to value. . . . No longer is enjoyment to be *gained from* one's toil (v. 10); it is recognized as part and parcel of one's work, *discerned within* the labor, an intrinsic joy (v. 24)."[30] In 4:9 עָמָל brings its "reward," and in this instance it seems clear that whatever the reward is, it is found specifically in one's work.[31]

In other passages עָמָל is treated in decidedly more negative terms. In 2:11 it gives no "advantage" (יִתְרוֹן); in 2:18 Qohelet says he hates his עָמָל; in 2:19 he bemoans the fact that עָמָל may be acquired or inherited by a wise person or a fool; in 2:20 he despairs because of his עָמָל; in 2:21 he complains that עָמָל can be lost to one who does not work (עָמַל) for it; in 4:4 עָמָל is said to be the result of jealousy (or possibly zeal[32]); in

27. So, e.g., Fox, *A Time to Tear Down*, 282, 287; Murphy, *Ecclesiastes*, 80, 88.

28. NJPSV translates, "that alone is what you can get out of life and out of the means you acquire under the sun." Crenshaw renders עָמָל here as "wages" (*Ecclesiastes*, 158).

29. Fox, *A Time to Tear Down*, 100.

30. Brown, *Ecclesiastes*, 38, his emphasis. Bergant states: "Here he identifies a possible reward. It is in the *actual toil*, in the doing, in the enjoying and *not* in any anticipated gain" (*Job, Ecclesiastes*, 236, my emphasis).

31. So most commentators (e.g. Fox, *A Time to Tear Down*, 222; Murphy, *Ecclesiastes*, 40). But NJPSV has "their earnings," and Whybray argues, "ʿāmāl here can hardly mean 'toil,' but rather, as frequently in the Old Testament, 'trouble'" (*Ecclesiastes*, 87).

32. The word קִנְאָה in 4:4 might be rendered either "jealousy" (as, e.g., in Num 5:14; Prov 6:34; 27:4) or take its more common sense in the Bible, "zeal" (as, e.g., in Isa 42:13; 63:15; Zech 1:14; 8:2). The word is often used of YHWH. Which nuance is understood here dramatically affects the tone of the verse. A number of commentators unquestioningly adopt the meaning found less frequently elsewhere in the

4:6 rest is said to be better than עמל; in 4:8 Qohelet states that there is no end to one's עמל and complains that עמל has deprived him of pleasure; in 5:14 it is noted that none of people's עמל goes with them beyond the grave, which prompts Qohelet to ask in the next verse what advantage (יתרון) one gains from "working (עמל) for the wind"; in 6:7 he notes that עמל does not bring satisfaction; in 8:17 it is observed that however hard one works (עמל) it does not give insight into God's acts; and 10:15 states that fools' work wearies them.

In all these instances, whether the context is positive or negative, there is no indication that עמל is *itself* positive or negative. Perhaps, then, it is best to view the word itself as neutral, meaning simply "work" or "the results of one's work." It may be that Qohelet is playing on the negative connotations of the word as it appears most often in the Old Testament, while also employing the sense it developed in later usage—the reader being left to decide which applies in any instance. Hence the questions in 1:3 and 3:9 may also be neutral, although the addition to the similar questions in 2:22 and 5:15 of וברעיון לבו and לרוח do give these verses a negative tinge:

	יעמל	ש	בכל־עמלו	מה־יתרון לאדם	1:3
עמל	הוא	ש	בכל־עמלו <u>וברעיון לבו</u>	מה־הוה לאדם	2:22
עמל	הוא	אשר	ב	מה־יתרון העושה	3:9
יעמל <u>לרוח</u>		ש		ו מה־יתרון לו	5:15

But, as with the instances where עמל is associated with pleasure, in these more negative contexts too it is often unclear whether the noun refers to "work" or "wealth." So, although the majority of commentators and English versions render the noun "work" or "toil" in most cases,[33] it would at least be possible in many verses to translate it as "wealth." In 2:11 it could be the "wealth" he worked for that Qohelet considers, concluding that it brought no advantage.[34] There would be a certain irony

---

Hebrew Bible of "jealousy," and interpret the verse in a decidedly negative way. But it could equally be read quite positively, in line with the word's usual sense of "zeal." Crenshaw quotes from the Talmud (*Baba Bathra* 21a) where the word is used in the phrase, "the *rivalry* of scholars increases wisdom" (*Ecclesiastes*, 108). עמל, in this verse, could be translated "wealth" which would fit well with "zeal," and would give an ironic reading with "jealousy."

33. Longman and Seow render the noun עמל by "toil" in every instance. NEB and REB use "labour" and/or "toil" throughout, except in 2:19 where they have "the fruits of my labour." 2:18 is the only verse where NIV translates with "all the things I had toiled for," otherwise it uses "toil."

34. NJPSV renders 2:11 thus: "Then my thoughts turned to all the fortune my hands had built up, to the wealth I had acquired and won—and oh, it was all futile and pursuit of wind; there was no real value under the sun!" Crenshaw also uses

in such a statement, which might fit rather well in the book of Ecclesiastes, and this is even more the case in 2:18 if it is his "wealth" Qohelet now hates.[35] It seems very likely that עמל in 2:19 *is* to be understood as wealth—because "wealth" lends itself to being "controlled" (שׁלט) by someone other than the person who worked for it—and it makes good sense to read the word the same way in both these verses.[36] If this is the case, it might also be that "wealth" is what Qohelet despairs about in 2:20.[37] In 2:21 it may be a person's "work" that is done in (or possibly "for") wisdom, knowledge and skill, but "wealth" would make more sense as the antecedent of the suffix on בו and יתננו.[38] In 2:22 "work"

"wealth" here (*Ecclesiastes*, 69, 83). Fox translates "toil" but acknowledges, "Whether *ma ʿăśim* and *ʿamal* refer to the effort or to its product is uncertain" (*A Time to Tear Down*, 175, 181). Longman uses "toil" (*The Book of Ecclesiastes*, 88), as does Seow (*Ecclesiastes*, 118). "Toil" is also the word used in NIV and NRSV. NEB and REB have "labour and toil," while NJB has "all the effort."

35. This is one of the few verses where Fox renders עמל by "wealth": "And I came to detest my wealth . . ." (*A Time to Tear Down*, 185–87). Crenshaw also uses "wealth" here (*Ecclesiastes*, 69), and Murphy translates, "the fruit of all the toil" (*Ecclesiastes*, 24). NJPSV reads, "So, too, I loathed all the wealth that I was gaining under the sun . . . ," NIV has "all the things I had toiled for," and NJB and NLT are similar. However, Longman again chooses "toil" here (*The Book of Ecclesiastes*, 101). So also Seow (*Ecclesiastes*, 118) and NRSV, while REB and NEB have "labour and toil."

36. Fox translates, ". . . and who will control all my wealth . . ." (*A Time to Tear Down*, 185–87). NJPSV has, ". . . and he will control all the wealth . . ." Murphy again uses "fruit of the toil" (*Ecclesiastes*, 24). Crenshaw renders עמל here with "earnings," noting, "Again *ʿămālî* functions ambiguously, referring to the fruit of one's labor and the toil itself" (*Ecclesiastes*, 70, 88). Seow uses the translation "toil," but explains "it is clearly a metonym [for the benefit of toil, whether it be wealth or other tangibles]" (*Ecclesiastes*, 118, 136). NEB and REB have here "the fruits of my labour," NRSV reads, "all for which I toiled" and NLT "everything I have gained by . . . hard work." Longman has "toil" here also (*The Book of Ecclesiastes*, 101), and NIV and NJB translate with "work."

37. Whybray argues, "it is his *wealth* rather than his toil whose loss through death 'Solomon' regrets" (*Ecclesiastes*, 61). NJPSV reads, "And so I came to view with despair all the gains I had made under the sun." Fox notes "In 2:20, *heʿamal šeʿamalti* is ambiguous," although he holds that "'Toil' seems more appropriate" (*A Time to Tear Down*, 186). Crenshaw renders עמל as "toil" here (*Ecclesiastes*, 70), as do Murphy (*Ecclesiastes*, 24), Longman (*The Book of Ecclesiastes*, 101) and Seow (*Ecclesiastes*, 118), as well as NEB, REB and NRSV. NIV uses "toilsome labour," NJB reads it as "all the effort" and NLT has "hard work."

38. NJPSV renders the verse thus: "For sometimes a person whose fortune was made with wisdom, knowledge, and skill must hand it on to be the portion of somebody who did not toil for it." Crenshaw translates, "For everyone whose earnings were acquired . . ." (*Ecclesiastes*, 70). Fox argues, "In 2:21a, the adverbial phrases

seems to be required because of the linking of עמל and רעיון—as even the NJPSV concedes.

This means that in these verses which focus heavily on עמל, there is one verse where the translation "wealth" seems to be required, and also one which appears to demand the translation "work." It appears, then, that the word is used within a few verses with two different senses, and that the reader is left the task of determining the precise meaning in the remaining verses.[39] The same is true in the rest of Ecclesiastes: "work" is probably the sense in 4:6; 6:7 (but NJPSV has "earnings" here) and 10:15 (all of which have the form of proverbs),[40] while in 4:4 (but NJPSV translates "labor" here); 4:8 and 5:14[41] either "work" or "wealth" would be possible—and the translation "wealth" in 4:4 and 4:8 would again produce the kind of irony we might expect of Ecclesiastes.

The phrase עמל שעמל תחת השמש, or similar (although, typical of Ecclesiastes, the phrase is slightly different each time it occurs, with the exception of 1:3 and 5:17 [Eng. 5:18]), occurs eight times in total in Ecclesiastes. We can trace some development in the way it is used:

תחת השמש	יעמל	שׁ	עמלו	בכל־	1:3
תחת השמש	עמלתי ...	שׁ	עמל	וב	2:11
תחת השמש	עמל	שׁאני	עמלי	את־כל־	2:18
תחת השמש	עמלתי ...	שׁ	עמלי	בכל־	2:19
תחת השמש	עמלתי	שׁ	עמל	כל־ה	2:20
תחת השמש	עמל	שהוא	עמלו ...	בכל־	2:22
תחת־השמש	יעמל	שׁ	עמלו	בכל־	5:17
תחת השמש	עמל	אשׁר־אתה	עמלך	וב	9:9

It occurs first in the "programmatic question," מה־יתרון לאדם בכל־עמלו שׁיעמל תחת השמש. I have argued above that this *may* be read either as a genuine question or as a rhetorical question,[42] but either way it establishes at the very start of the book a key issue that Qohelet then goes on to

'in wisdom, in knowledge, and in skill' modify the activity of toiling, yet the suffix of 'giving it' refers to earnings. ʿ*Amalo* here binds the two ideas most closely" (*A Time to Tear Down*, 186). Longman (*The Book of Ecclesiastes*, 101) and Seow (*Ecclesiastes*, 118) use "toil" here, while NIV and NLT have "work" and NEB, REB, NJB have "labour."

39. Fox states that "Two senses of ʿ*amal* are almost inextricably intertwined in this passage: the toilsome labor itself, and earnings, the material fruits of toil" (*A Time to Tear Down*, 186).

40. NJPSV has "labor" in 4:6 and "exertions" in 10:15.

41. Crenshaw has "wealth" here (*Ecclesiastes*, 119), NJB translates with "achievements." Longman uses "toil" (*The Book of Ecclesiastes*, 161), as do Fox (*A Time to Tear Down*, 237) and Seow (*Ecclesiastes*, 201), along with NEB and REB.

42. Melchert offers examples of both readings (*Wise Teaching*, 114–22).

explore in some detail. It seems at first glance that, following the description of Qohelet-as-Solomon's great works in 1:12–2:10, a specific answer is given to the question in 2:11, where, after describing the deeds he has done (כל־מעשׂי שעשׂו ידי) and the work that he has performed, or the wealth he has worked for (עמל שעמלתי לעשׂות), he states אין יתרון תחת השמשׁ. This is compounded over the next few verses by the observation that wisdom, despite the "advantages" it brings, offers no lasting gain because the wise person dies just like the fool. There then follows in 2:18–22 the most detailed examination of עמל שעמל תחת השמשׁ in the book. In the light of the preceding deliberations (2:11–17) and in view of the fact that he must leave all he has worked for to someone else, Qohelet declares in 2:18 that he hated את־כל־עמלי שאני עמל תחת השמשׁ. The realisation in 2:19 that the one who will have control over כל־עמלי שעמלתי . . . תחת השמשׁ may be a fool, leads him to despair over כל־העמל שעמלתי תחת השמשׁ (2:20). He then describes a specific man (himself prospectively?) who, after working with wisdom, knowledge and skill had to leave his "portion" to one who had not worked for it, and this leads Qohelet to a repetition in a different form of the "programmatic question" that appeared first in 1:3: he asks, "what *is* there for a person בכל־עמלו וברעיון לבו שהוא עמל תחת השמשׁ?"

In ch. 2, then, עמל is portrayed as something very negative, and it therefore gives a decidedly negative answer to the question in 1:3. It is notable that 16 out of a total of 35 occurrences of the word have appeared so far (46 per cent in 18 per cent of the total number of verses in the book), but even more significant is that 14 of these are in 2:10–22 (40 per cent in just 2 per cent of the total number of verses). The appearance of the word is much more sporadic in the rest of Ecclesiastes, with two passages where it occurs a number of times: five times in 4:4–9, and five times also in 5:14–18. The use of עמל, like יתרון (and even to some extent הבל), peters out towards the end of the book, with no occurrences in ch. 7, two in each of chs. 8 and 9, one in ch. 10, then no more in the remaining 29 verses of the book (see Chart 3 [next page]). Again this raises questions about 1:3 functioning as the "programmatic question for the *entire* book."

There is a marked change in the use of עמל at 2:24 because we find here the first of the verses issuing the "call to enjoyment" where עמל is associated with pleasure. Indeed, the remaining two occurrences of the expression עמל שעמל תחת השמשׁ (which we find repeated four times in the five verses 2:18–22), occur in these "calls to enjoyment." In fact, 11 of the remaining 19 occurrences of עמל are in passages featuring the "call to enjoyment." The major exception to this is 4:4–9 where עמל appears in a negative light again. The same is true of 5:14–16 (Eng.

5:15–17), but these verses build up to 5:17–18 (Eng. 5:18–19) where the word is again associated with pleasure—although 5:19 (Eng. 5:20) is decidedly ambiguous, and 6:1–2 is much more negative again. This means that עמל features both in decidedly negative, and much more positive contexts, as well as in a passage that starts negatively and concludes in a positive way, and in one which seems to move from negative to positive and back again.

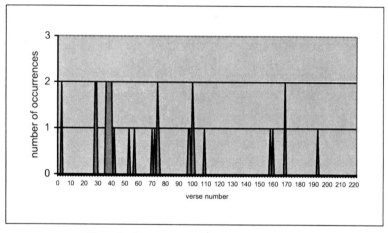

Chart 3. *Occurrences of* עמל *in Ecclesiastes*

6.2.3. Conclusion

I have demonstrated that there are a number of ambiguities surrounding the word עמל: the word may at times mean *either* "work/toil," or the result of such work or toil, "wealth/earnings," and the translation chosen may make a considerable difference to the tone of the verse; עמל may be read in at least some instances as bearing a very negative meaning, "toil" or even "misery," but it could also be read quite neutrally as "hard work" or even positively as "wealth"; and the contexts in which עמל appears may be positive or negative, and may develop from positive to negative or vice versa. Moreover, while there certainly appears to be a development in the way it is used in 2:11–23, leading to very negative conclusions, this is quickly reversed in 2:24 (although there are various ways to read this "reversal"[43]) and from then on it appears more often (but not consistently) in rather positive passages.

---

43. So, for example, for Whybray this is one of the reasons why Qohelet is a "Preacher of Joy" ("Qoheleth, Preacher of Joy," 88–89), and Ogden describes v. 24 in very positive terms as "the climatic statement . . . which puts the thesis of the book" (*Qoheleth*, 14). Salyer writes, "Although the discourse seemed headed in an utterly nihilistic direction in 2:11, the reader now perceives that this is a silver lining

6.3. עשה

6.3.1. *The Translation of* עשה

I commented above on the near-synonymity of עשה and עמל in Ecclesiastes. Vollmar notes that "The semantic field of *ʿśh* is very large, the range of nuances extraordinarily broad" and goes on to point out that "work" is one of its normal meanings elsewhere in the Hebrew Bible.[44] The similarity in meaning of עשה and עמל in this book is suggested by their use together on a number of occasions, where they seem to be used in parallel.[45]

6.3.2. *Use of* עשה *in Ecclesiastes*

That what Qohelet(-as-Solomon) *did* is under consideration in 2:4–11 is demonstrated by the expression הגדלתי מעשי at the start of 2:4; the use of words from the root עשה in 2:4, 5, 6, 8 and 11 (×3); and the words in 2:11, ופניתי אני בכל-מעשי שעשו ידי. However, in the conclusion to the passage in 2:10, words from the root עמל appear with no obvious difference from עשה:

וכל אשר שאלו עיני לא אצלתי מהם
לא־מנעתי את־לבי מכל־שמחה כי־לבי שמח מכל־עמלי
וזה־היה חלקי מכל־עמלי:

And in 2:11 עמל is used in parallel with עשה:

| ופניתי אני בכל־מעשי | שעשו ידי |
| ובעמל | שעמלתי לעשות |

If 2:11 constitutes at least an initial answer to the "programmatic question" in 1:3, then reference here to כל־מעשי שעשו ידי is considered as part of כל־עמלו שיעמל תחת השמש there.[46] A similar parallelism is found in 2:17–18:

to the cloud that is Qoheleth's radical pessimism" (*Vain Rhetoric*, 292), but Crenshaw argues that here "Qohelet's positive counsel rests under a cloud" (*Ecclesiastes*, 90), and Murphy states that his "translation interprets v 24 in line with the many *resigned conclusions* found in the work" (*Ecclesiastes*, 26, my emphasis). Cf. Byargeon, "The Significance of Ambiguity." For Rudman, 2:24–26 point to "a deterministic agenda on Qoheleth's part" (*Determinism*, 130).

44. J. Vollmar, "עשה, *ʿśh*, to make, do," *TLOT* 2:944–51 (945). See also Eugene Carpenter, "עשה," *NIDOTTE* 3:546–52.

45. Fox states, "In Qohelet, *ʿaśah/maʿaśeh* and *ʿamal* are sometimes collocated as near equivalents (2:11; 3:9; 4:4 etc.) or used in equivalent contexts (compare 2:10 and 5:18 with 3:22)" (*A Time to Tear Down*, 103).

46. Vollmar notes, "The typical Old Testament phrase *maʿaśēh yād(ayim)* 'work of the hands' occurs 54× in the MT (15× of Yahweh)" (*TLOT* 2:948).

וְשָׂנֵאתִי אֶת־הַחַיִּים כִּי רַע עָלַי הַמַּעֲשֶׂה שֶׁ נַעֲשָׂה תַּחַת הַשֶּׁמֶשׁ

וְשָׂנֵאתִי אֲנִי אֶת־כָּל־עֲמָלִי שֶׁאֲנִי עָמֵל תַּחַת הַשֶּׁמֶשׁ

However, after a heavy focus on "deeds" (עשׂה) early in the chapter, the focus now turns to "work/wealth" (עמל), because words from the root עמל appear twice in each of the next five verses, while words from the root עשׂה are not used at all. This raises the question of what difference the reader should perceive between the two roots in these verses.

The roots appear together again in 3:9 where it seems that the "programmatic question" of 1:3 is asked in a different form in which העשׂה takes the place of בכל־עמלו:[47]

1:3	מה־יתרון לאדם	בכל־עמלו ש	יעמל
3:9	מה־יתרון העושה ב		אשר הוא עמל

The phrase וראה טוב בכל־עמלו is used in another "call to enjoyment" in 3:12–13, in the midst of a passage focusing on deeds (עשׂה), primarily those done by God. Then in 4:1–9 we find a passage that focuses on deeds/work, using words from the root עשׂה in 4:1, 3 (×2), 4, and עמל in 4:4, 6, 8 (×2), 9. The two occur together in 4:4, again seemingly in parallel:

וראיתי אני את־כל־עמל ואת כל־כשרון המעשה כי היא
קנאת־איש מרעהו גם־זה הבל ורעות רוח׃

At the end of ch. 5 there is a passage that focuses on עמל, but with no words from the root עשׂה (in fact there are no words from this root in the 26 verses from 5:5–6:12 [Eng. 5:6–6:12]). Then from 8:9–9:10 there is a very heavy focus on "deeds" using a large number of words from the root עשׂה (20 out of a total of 64 [31 per cent] in these 19 verses [9 per cent]—see Chart 4) and a few from the root עמל, again with no clear distinction in meaning.

Moreover, just as we find the phrase עמל שעמל תחת השמש repeated eight times, so also the phrase מעשה שנעשה תחת השמש, or something similar (although, again, no two are actually identical), is used six times in the book:

1:14	אֶת־ כָּל־	הַמַּעֲשִׂים	שֶׁ	נַעֲשׂוּ	תַּחַת	הַשֶּׁמֶשׁ
2:11	בְּכָל־	מַעֲשַׂי	שֶׁ	עָשׂוּ יָדַי . . . תַּחַת		הַשֶּׁמֶשׁ
2:17		הַמַּעֲשֶׂה	שֶׁ	נַעֲשָׂה	תַּחַת	הַשֶּׁמֶשׁ

---

47. Fox writes, "Judging from 3:9 . . . a 'doer' may (but need not) 'toil.'" He goes on, "In 9:10, the *ma'áśeh* that is absent from Sheol is the same as the *'amal* that one performs in life (v. 9). Man can get pleasure in his toil (or his toilsome life) (2:10; 5:18) and in his 'works' (3:22; cf. 9:7), and *no practical distinction can be drawn*" (*A Time to Tear Down*, 103, my emphasis).

תחת השׁמשׁ	נעשׂה	אשׁר	הרע	המעשׂה		־את	4:3
תחת השׁמשׁ	נעשׂה	אשׁר		מעשׂה	־לכל		8:9
תחת־ השׁמשׁ	נעשׂה	אשׁר		המעשׂה		־את	8:17

In addition, there are five occurrences of the phrase אשׁר [נ]עשׂה תחת
השׁמשׁ/השׁמים , and the apparently synonymous phrase אשׁר נעשׂה על־הארץ
is used twice, giving 13 specific references to "what is done under the
sun/under heaven/on earth:"

תחת השׁמים		נעשׂה	אשׁר			־כל	1:13
תחת השׁמשׁ		נעשׂוׂ	שׁ	המעשׂים	־כל ־את		1:14
תחת השׁמים		יעשׂוׂ	אשׁר				2:3
תחת השׁמשׁ	ידי . . .	עשׂוׂ	שׁ	מעשׂי	־בכל		2:11
תחת השׁמשׁ		נעשׂה	שׁ	המעשׂה			2:17
תחת השׁמשׁ		נעשׂים	אשׁר				4:1
תחת השׁמשׁ		נעשׂה	אשׁר	הרע המעשׂה		־את	4:3
תחת השׁמשׁ		נעשׂה	אשׁר	מעשׂה	־לכל		8:9
על־הארץ		נעשׂה	אשׁר				8:14
על־הארץ		נעשׂה	אשׁר				8:16
תחת־השׁמשׁ		נעשׂה	אשׁר	המעשׂה		־את	8:17
תחת השׁמשׁ		־נעשׂה	־אשׁר		בכל		9:3
תחת השׁמשׁ		־נעשׂה	־אשׁר		בכל		9:6

Why these variations are introduced is not obvious, but this is clearly an
important theme in the book nonetheless. However, we should note that
these particular phrases do not extend beyond 9:6. In fact, 9:9–10 serve
as the conclusion to this theme and also bring to a close consideration of
the theme of עמל שׁעמל תחת השׁמשׁ when they advise,

ראה חיים עם־אשׁה אשׁר־אהבת כל־ימי חיי הבלך
אשׁר נתן־לך תחת השׁמשׁ כל ימי הבלך
כי הוא חלקך בחיים ובעמלך אשׁר־אתה עמל תחת השׁמשׁ:
כל אשׁר תמצא ידך לעשׂות בכחך עשׂה
כי אין מעשׂה וחשׁבון ודעת וחכמה בשׁאול
אשׁר אתה הלך שׁמה:

There are no more references either to עמל or עשׂה "under the sun."[48]
Thus, although עשׂה is more evenly distributed between the two halves of
the book (32 times in each half, see Chart 4[49]) than is עמל (30 times in

48. There is just one further occurrence of a word from the root עמל, in a
proverb-like saying in 10:15, which does not specify that it is תחת השׁמשׁ. In 10:19,
the root עשׂה is also used in a proverb-like saying (again not specifically תחת השׁמשׁ),
and the other two occurrences within the *inclusio* refer to God's deeds. The two
words from this root in the epilogue are both tinged with irony.

49. This makes עשׂה one of the most frequent words in Ecclesiastes, but this
should be too surprising since, as Vollmar notes, "With 2,627 occurrences, *ʿśh* 'to
make, do' is the third most common verb in the Old Testament" (*TLOT* 2:944).

the first half and 5 in the second), nonetheless consideration of both all but peters out in the last three and a half chapters.

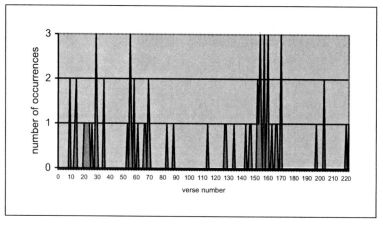

Chart 4. *Occurrences of* עשׂה *in Ecclesiastes*

However, twice in ch. 11 mention is made of what God does (עשׂה), and there are eight references in total in the book to God's deeds (plus an ironic reference to human deeds in 12:14, which picks up on the references to God's deeds):

האלהים	עשׂה	אשר־המעשׂה		את־	3:11
האלהים	יעשׂה	אשר	כל־		3:14a
עשׂה האלהים					3:14b
האלהים		מעשׂה		את־	7:13
האלהים	עשׂה				7:14
האלהים	עשׂה				7:29
האלהים		את־כל־מעשׂה			8:17
אשר יעשׂה האלהים		מעשׂה		את־	11:5
(יבא במשׁפט על כל־נעלם) האלהים	את־כל־מעשׂה				12:14

If this diagram is merged with the one showing references to "deeds done under the sun/under heaven/on earth," it becomes clear that only at one point, 8:17, do the two themes meet. Otherwise passages that deal with deeds done on earth alternate with those that focus on God's deeds:

תחת השׁמים	אשר נעשׂה			כל־	1:13
תחת השׁמשׁ	נעשׂו	שׁ	כל־ המעשׂים	את־	1:14
תחת השׁמים	אשר יעשׂו				2:3
תחת השׁמשׁ...תחת ידי	עשׂו	שׁ	מעשׂי	בכל־	2:11
תחת השׁמשׁ	נעשׂה	שׁ	המעשׂה		2:17
האלהים	אשר־עשׂה	המעשׂה	את־		3:11
האלהים	אשר יעשׂה		כל־		3:14a
האלהים עשׂה					3:14b

	תחת השׁמשׁ	אשׁר נעשׂים			4:1
	תחת השׁמשׁ	נעשׂה אשׁר הרע המעשׂה		את־	4:3
האלהים			מעשׂה	את־	7:13
האלהים		עשׂה			7:14
האלהים		עשׂה			7:29
	תחת השׁמשׁ	נעשׂה אשׁר	מעשׂה	לכל־	8:9
	על־הארץ	נעשׂה אשׁר			8:14
	על־הארץ	נעשׂה אשׁר			8:16
האלהים			מעשׂה כל־	את־	8:17a
	תחת־השׁמשׁ	נעשׂה אשׁר	המעשׂה	את־	8:17b
	תחת השׁמשׁ	נעשׂה־ אשׁר		בכל	9:3
	תחת השׁמשׁ	נעשׂה־ אשׁר		בכל	9:6
האלהים אשׁר יעשׂה			מעשׂה	את־	11:5
האלהים			מעשׂה כל־	את־	12:14

6.3.3. *The Difference Between* עמל *and* עשׂה

This comparison highlights an important difference between the roots עמל and עשׂה—the former is *never* explicitly applied to what God does. In every occurrence of the phrase, עמל שׁעמל תחת השׁמשׁ (and in almost all other occurrences of the root עמל[50]) the verb is active and has as its subject either a specified human individual (or people in general),[51] or it is Qohelet himself,[52] or the reader,[53] and the noun takes a first,[54] second[55] or third[56] person suffix whose antecedent again is a specific human individual, or the antecedent is clear from the context.[57] By contrast, עשׂה is used actively with both human beings[58] and God as subject[59] (or some other specified subject[60]), and the noun with a specified antecedent,[61] but the phrase מעשׂה שׁנעשׂה תחת השׁמשׁ usually uses the verb in the Niphal (and the Niphal of עשׂה occurs in a much higher concentration in Ecclesiastes

---

50. The only exceptions are 4:4(?), 6.
51. 1:3; 2:22; 3:9; 5:15, 17; 8:17.
52. 2:18, 19; 4:8(?).
53. 9:9.
54. 2:10 (×2), 18, 19, 20.
55. 9:9.
56. 1:3; 2:21, 22, 24; 3:13; 4:8, 9; 5:14, 17, 18; 8:15.
57. 2:11, 20; 21; 6:7; 10:15.
58. 2:3, 5, 6, 8, 11 (×2), 12; 3:12, 22; 4:4, 17; 5:5; 6:12; 7:20; 8:3, 4, 10, 11, 12, 16; 9:7, 10 (×3); 12:14.
59. 3:11 (×2), 14 (×2); 7:13, 14, 29; 8:17; 11:5 (×2).
60. 2:2, 11; 10:19.
61. 2:4; 3:11.

than in any other book in the Hebrew Bible[62]), and it is not specified who it is that performs the deeds.[63] The same is true of ומה־שנעשה הוא in 1:9, שם ... שיעשה ... תחת השמש in כל־המעשה in 3:17 and also, crucially, אין־נעשה פתגם מעשה הרעה מהרה in 8:11, and in 8:14:

יש־הבל אשר נעשה על־הארץ אשר
יש צדיקים אשר מגיע אלהם כמעשה הרשעים
ויש רשעים שמגיע אלהם כמעשה הצדיקים
אמרתי שגם־זה הבל:

Vollmar notes that in the Hebrew Bible generally "About one-sixth of occurrences involve an explicitly theological usage with Yahweh as subj.,"[64] and Fox argues:

> In the recurring phrase *hamma ʿăśeh ʿăšer na ʿăśah taḥat haššemeš* (and variants), the *ma ʿăśim* are usually thought to be man's activities, in particular his restless exertions to get rich. I understand the phrase to mean "the events that occur under the sun" and to be equivalent to *ma ʿăśeh ah ha ʾĕlohim*... In other words, "all that happens under the sun" is equivalent to "God's works" or "what God brings to pass," and these are all absurd.[65]

However, in Ecclesiastes words from the root עשה actually occur more than twice as often specifically in relation to people than to God, and in the end it is impossible to state with certainty who is responsible for the deeds "that are done," where the passive form of the verb is used. In short, it is ambiguous.

As both Fox and Rudman[66] note, 8:17 is a crucial verse in this regard, because it explicitly brings together מעשה שנעשה תחת השמש and מעשה האלהים. It reads:

---

62. 14 out of a total of 99 occurrences of the Niphal of עשה are in Ecclesiastes. The only book where it occurs more often is Leviticus, with 16 occurrences. See Vollmar, *TDOT* 2:945.

63. See Bo Isaksson's chapter "Nifal of עשה," in *Studies in the Language of Qoheleth*, 69–74.

64. Vollmar, *TDOT* 2:946.

65. Fox, *A Time to Tear Down*, 104–5. In this Fox is followed by Rudman who argues that "The equivalence of 'the work of God' and 'the work which is done under the sun' is of great importance in understanding the nature of Qoheleth's deterministic worldview" (*Determinism*, 69). See also Murphy, *Ecclesiastes*, 13. Ogden, however, states: "We are left with the impression that this is a reference to all human activity rather than situations in the natural world" (*Qoheleth*, 34). Similarly, Bergant says that "Qoheleth set out to discover the depths and the breadth of all of human endeavor" (*Job, Ecclesiastes*, 234).

66. Fox, *A Time to Tear Down*, 104–5; Rudman, *Determinism*, 60–69.

וראיתי את־כל־מעשׂה האלהים כי לא יוכל האדם למצוא
את־המעשׂה אשׁר נעשׂה תחת־השׁמשׁ
בשׁל אשׁר יעמל האדם לבקשׁ ולא ימצא וגם אם־יאמר
החכם לדעת לא יוכל למצא׃

The verse seems to fall into four parts, an introductory statement and three clauses containing the expression לא [יוכל ל]מצא. The fact that the first occurrence of לא [יוכל ל]מצא appears between את־כל־מעשׂה האלהים and את־מעשׂה אשׁר נעשׂה תחת־השׁמשׁ allows for ambiguity over which clause it relates to. The verse would make sense if either of these two phrases were omitted, but the two sit rather awkwardly together. The reader may initially take לא יוכל האדם למצוא as the conclusion of the first part of the verse, which would give three statements that all use a different form of לא [יוכל ל]מצא, but leaves את־מעשׂה אשׁר נעשׂה תחת־השׁמשׁ in the air:

וראיתי את־כל־מעשׂה האלהים כי <u>לא יוכל האדם למצוא</u>
את־המעשׂה אשׁר נעשׂה תחת־השׁמשׁ
בשׁל אשׁר יעמל האדם לבקשׁ <u>ולא ימצא</u>
וגם אם־יאמר החכם לדעת <u>לא יוכל למצא</u>׃

This seems to be how Fox reads the verse when he translates 8:16–17:

> When I set my heart to gain wisdom and to observe the business that occurs on the earth (my eyes seeing sleep neither by day nor by night), I saw that man cannot grasp anything that God makes happen, that is to say, the events that occur under the sun, for even if a man seeks arduously, he will not grasp (them). And even if the wise man intends to understand, he is not able to grasp (them).[67]

Alternatively, לא יוכל האדם למצוא may be read as the start of the second clause in the verse, but this would leave the opening clause in the air:

וראיתי את־כל־מעשׂה האלהים כי
<u>לא יוכל האדם למצוא</u> את־המעשׂה אשׁר נעשׂה תחת־השׁמשׁ
בשׁל אשׁר יעמל האדם לבקשׁ <u>ולא ימצא</u>
וגם אם־יאמר החכם לדעת <u>לא יוכל למצא</u>׃

This seems to lie behind Loader's reading of 8:16–17:

> When I set my heart on knowing wisdom and seeing all the trouble that is taken on earth, even when man sees no sleep in daytime or at night, then I perceived all the work of God: Man cannot find out what happens under the sun—however man troubles to search it out, he cannot make the discovery. And even if the wise man claims to know, he cannot uncover.[68]

---

67. Fox, *A Time to Tear Down*, 287. Cf., e.g., Gordis, *Koheleth*, 186, NLT and GNB.
68. Loader, *Polar Structures*, 54. See also, e.g., Murphy, *Ecclesiastes*, 80; Crenshaw, *Ecclesiastes*, 153 (who states that "This verse explicitly equates God's work

Perhaps it is intended to relate both ways so that some connection is established between the deeds of God and the deeds that are done under the sun. However, it is not clear what this connection is, and this may be an intentional aspect of the ambiguity of the verse: how *do* God's deeds relate to what is done under the sun? Moreover, the ambiguity is exacerbated by the fact that the כִּי can also be read in different ways,[69] furthering the uncertainty over how the two clauses relate to one another. בְּשֶׁל, too, has been understood in different ways, complicating translation even more.[70] A further possibility is to read the first clause of this verse as the conclusion of 8:16: this is represented in Rudman's translation:

> When I applied my mind to know wisdom, and to see the business which is done upon the earth (my eyes seeing sleep neither by day nor by night), then I saw all the work of God. Surely no-one can find out the work which is done under the sun: for though a man labour to seek it out, yet he shall not find it. Moreover, though a sage claim to know it, yet he shall not be able to find it.[71]

6.3.4. *Conclusion*

I have demonstrated that עָשָׂה, like עָמַל, is ambiguous. The first area of ambiguity involves its synonymity or otherwise with עָמַל: when are words from these roots used with effectively the same meaning, and when should the reader perceive some difference between them? Secondly, the same issue arises in relation to עָשָׂה that we noted with עָמַל: when does the noun refer to the "deed" itself, and when the result of the deed? Thus, for example, Vollmar notes, "*ma ʿᵃśeh* can mean 'work'. . . . In accord with the multidimensional usage of Hebr. noms., *ma ʿᵃśeh* also means the product of work."[72] But thirdly, and most significantly, there is considerable ambiguity over who is responsible for מַעֲשֶׂה שֶׁנַּעֲשֶׂה תַּחַת הַשָּׁמֶשׁ.

with activity on earth"). Seow reads similarly but transposes "even though neither by day nor by night do they sleep" to v. 17 (*Ecclesiastes*, 276–77, 289). See NRSV, NJB, REB, NIV, KJV.

69. Rudman examines the use of כִּי in this verse in some depth (*Determinism*, 60–69). He argues, "The best solution is therefore to understand the particle affirmatively (GKC §159ee)" (p. 67; see also Ogden and Zogbo, *A Handbook*, 312). Fox maintains that "This is a proleptic construction with a precise parallel in Jonah 3:10, where *ki* introduces epexegesis of the direct object" (*A Time to Tear Down*, 289).

70. See, for example, the discussion in Schoors, *The Preacher Sought*, 145–46. Schoors argues for a "causal force," reading אֲשֶׁר בְּשֶׁל as "since." Fox also argues that בְּשֶׁל אֲשֶׁר "introduces a causal clause (as the Aramaic equivalent can do) rather than a final or result clause" (*A Time to Tear Down*, 289).

71. Rudman, *Determinism*, 68. Ogden and Zogbo translate similarly (*A Handbook*, 312). See also NJPSV.

72. Vollmar, *TLOT* 2:948. Fox also notes this point (*A Time to Tear Down*, 103).

Chapter 7

טוב IN ECCLESIASTES

7.1. *The Importance of the Word* טוב

טוב occurs more often in Ecclesiastes than do הבל, יתר and עמל. Indeed, in terms of significant words in this book, the 54 occurrences of יטב/טוב come second only to עשה (×64),[1] and the word טוב is used more frequently here (a total of 52 times in twelve chapters) than in any other book of the Hebrew Bible.[2] Moreover, despite the fact that טוב does not appear until 2:1, it is arguable that the task described in 2:3 introduces a key element in Ecclesiastes[3] (and this might argue in favour of a section running from 1:12–2:3 which introduces the main themes of the book[4]). 2:3 reads:

1. Schoors claims that טוב has "the highest score in the vocabulary of this book," presumably counting actual words rather than words from a particular Hebrew root ("Words Typical of Qohelet," 33).

2. H. J. Stoebe notes that "The word family *ṭôb/yṭb* (excl. proper names) is attested in the Old Testament 741× (738×Hebr., 3×Aram.). . . . *ṭôb* dominates with 559 occurrences: Ps 68×, Prov 62×, Eccl 52×, Gen 41×, 1 Sam 37×, Jer 36×, Deut 28×, 1 Kgs 24×, 2 Chron 23×, Esth 22×, 2 Sam 21×, Isa 13×, 2 Kgs, Job, and Neh 12×, Judg 11×, Ezek 9×, Josh and 1 Chron 8×, Num and Lam 7×, Ezra 6×, Exod, Lev, and Hos 5×, Amos, Mic, and Zech 4×, Ruth 3×, Jonah, Nah, Song Sol, and Dan 2×, Joel and Mal 1×; it does not occur in Obad, Hab, Zeph, and Hag" ("טוב, *ṭôb*, good", *TLOT* 2:486–95 [487]; slightly different statistics appear in I. Höver-Johag, "טוב, *ṭôb*, טוב, *ṭûb*, יטב, *yṭb*," *TDOT* 5:296–317 [304–5]).

3. Thus, for example, Ogden describes טוב as "another central concept" (*Qoheleth*, 39; cf. Ogden and Zogbo, *A Handbook*, 4, 51).

4. This is a position I have long maintained. The only other writer I know who holds this view is Choon-Leong Seow, who, after noting that "It is clear that 1:12 begins a new literary unit," goes on to state: "There are sufficient grounds, therefore, to think that 1:13–2:3 forms a distinctive section marked by the phrase 'under the heavens' at the beginning (1:13) and the end (2:3): that is, the expression 'under the heavens' forms an *inclusio* for the first section. These verses constitute an extended introduction to the entire unit, identifying the problem of the terrible preoccupation (*ʿinyān*) that God has given to humanity, the place of wisdom (*ḥokmâ*), knowledge (*daʿat*), and joy (*śimḥa*) in seeing what is good (*ṭôb*)" (*Ecclesiastes*, 142–43).

תרתי . . . עד אשר־אראה אי־זה טוב לבני האדם אשר יעשו
תחת השמים מספר ימי חייהם:

To my mind the commentators make too little of this question, most
passing over it with little or no comment (rather getting caught up in the
complexities of the earlier parts of the verse which Longman describes as
"very difficult to translate smoothly," although he contends that "its
general sense is quite clear"5). An exception is to be found in Rudman,
who writes: "If there is no 'profit' to be derived from the sentence of hard
labour, one may at least attempt to discover what aspects of that labour
are good, or at any rate, better than others. This is the *real question* that
forms the basis of Qoheleth's investigation into existence (2:3)."6 Perdue
also regards "What is good to humanity in living?" as Qohelet's "essential question."7

A similar question appears near the start of the second half of the
book, in 6:12:8

מי־יודע מה־טוב לאדם בחיים מספר ימי־חיי הבלו

5. Longman, *The Book of Ecclesiastes*, 89. Seow comments about תרתי בלבי,
"All the ancient versions have trouble with the expression" (*Ecclesiastes*, 126); Fox
says of the phrase למשוך ביין את־בשרי that it "has no parallel and is an interpretative
crux" (*Qohelet*, 179); Seow describes the clause ולבי נהג בחכמה as "an awkward
parenthetical comment or gloss" (*Ecclesiastes*, 127), while Fox recommends emending ולא אחז בסכלות to ולאחז בסכלות, which he claims "resolves the awkward
parenthesis" (*Qohelet*, 180; but see *A Time to Tear Down*, 179). Murphy simply
states, "The thought of v. 3 is expressed obscurely" (*Ecclesiastes*, 18).
6. Rudman, *Determinism*, 82, my emphasis; see also pp. 103, 110, 112, 126, 152.
By contrast, Fredericks sees this question in 2:3 (and the similar one in 6:8) as a
variation of the "what advantage . . . ?" question in 1:3 (and 5:11, 16; 6:8) (*Coping
with Transience*, 49). Fredericks refers to טוב and יתרון as "two equivalent phrases
pertaining to advantage" (pp. 51–52).
7. Perdue, *Wisdom and Creation*, 226. Perdue's chapter on Ecclesiastes is
subtitled, "The Tyranny of God and Qoheleth's Quest for the Good."
8. Commentators are divided concerning the function of 6:10–12: Does it serve
as the conclusion to the preceding section (e.g. Eaton, Gordis, Hubbard, Huwiler,
Provan, Tamez); the introduction to the next section (e.g. Bergant, Garrett, Ogden); a
link between the two (Brown, Crenshaw, Davies, Fox, Perry [vv. 9b–11], Salyer); or
the introduction to the second half of the book (Christianson, Longman, Murphy,
Perry [v. 12], Seow, Wright) (and some older commentaries delete some or all of the
verses as a gloss)? However, Whybray states that "Loretz . . . is probably right in his
view that the passage is simply a group of independent short sayings on somewhat
similar themes 'which should not be forced into a logical connection.' It should be
added that as a group they also have no obvious connection with the surrounding
material" (*Ecclesiastes*, 110.)

Some commentators see this question as "the fundamental concern of Israelite wisdom,"[9] though Crenshaw concludes from this that "Qohelet dismisses the essence of the tradition to which he was heir, for he virtually asserts that no person really knows the good."[10] It is my contention that the question of "what is good for people during the few days of their lives"[11] *is* of fundamental concern for Qohelet also,[12] and that here too we meet considerable ambiguity: Qohelet is not simply asking what is "good" for people, but also—implicitly—what it means to call something "good" anyway.

7.2. *Translation of* טוב

Fox's comments about the word טוב are particularly pertinent here:

Ṭob (or *ṭobah*) is the word of positive evaluation Qohelet uses most frequently. It means "beneficial," "efficacious," "virtuous," and "good fortune," "fortunate." . . . Goodness can be of any sort, and it is often difficult to determine just what kind of "goodness" is meant. Elsewhere in the Bible, it rarely refers to the feelings experienced during merrymaking and feasting. Only in Qohelet does "to see good" mean to enjoy oneself . . . .[13]

First, he is certainly correct that this is "the word of positive evaluation Qohelet uses most frequently": hence how it is interpreted and what role it is seen to have in the book is highly significant. There is considerable disagreement over its interpretation and role. Secondly, Fox demonstrates that a range of English words are needed to capture the sense of the word in its various contexts in Ecclesiastes,[14] and, thirdly, he suggests

9. Crenshaw quotes Zimmerli to this effect (*Ecclesiastes*, 131), and identical words appear in Schoors, "Words Typical of Qohelet," 37. See also Tamez, *When the Horizons Close*, 91.

10. Crenshaw, *Ecclesiastes*, 131.

11. We might note, however, that NJPS reads אי־זה as "which of the two" (a reading that would fit well the only other time it occurs in 11:6), and takes טוב to refer to the "better" of the two: "I might learn which of the two was better for men to practice." For discussion of the unusual interrogative pronoun אי־זה, see Schoors, *The Preacher Sought*, 57–58.

12. Farmer says, "It seems to me that 6:12 could be considered the pivot from which two distinct parts of Ecclesiastes swing. Both sections depend upon the question, 'Who *knows* what is *good* for humankind?'" (*Who Knows What is Good?*, 151).

13. Fox, *A Time to Tear Down*, 116. It might be noted that in *Qohelet* (p. 179), Fox offers the literal translation "And see [imperative] good!"

14. Stoebe states that "The scope of *ṭôb* is very broad. Consequently, Eng. translation requires many adjs. in addition to 'good,' according to the various contexts: 'agreeable, pleasant, satisfying, satisfactory, favorable, useful, purposeful, right,

that deciding which sense applies may be difficult. It seems to me that the author of Ecclesiastes is playing on the semantic range of this word so that at times it is not at all clear precisely how טוב should be understood in a particular verse: it is therefore ambiguous and requires the reader to fill in the gap of indeterminacy thus created. Fourthly, it appears that Qohelet sometimes uses the word טוב in a way not found elsewhere in the Hebrew Bible.[15]

7.3. *Use of* טוב *in Ecclesiastes*

7.3.1. ראה טוב

The last point is evident the first time we meet טוב in Ecclesiastes, because it does appear that only in Ecclesiastes does ראה טוב convey the sense "enjoy oneself" (although Ps 34:13 gives a close parallel: מי־האיש החפץ חיים אהב ימים לראות טוב[16]). The combination of ראה and טוב may remind the reader of the repeated phrase וירא אלהים כי־טוב[17] (and I suspect the allusion is intentional) in Gen 1, but here טוב is not the object of the verb, the preposition כי being used to indicate that *it* was good.[18] טוב as the direct object of ראה occurs just four times outside Ecclesiastes,[19] and the form with prefixed ב, as in Eccl 2:1, also four times, though two of these use טוב not טוֹב, and in each of the four it is not "good" itself which is seen, but the "good *of*" something[20]—hence there is *no* direct parallel to the usage in Eccl 2:1. This being said, typically of Ecclesiastes, on no two occasions does the expression occur in identical form in the book itself (note that every occurrence of the verb ראה is different, in addition to different combinations of the verb and טוב), and

---

beneficial, ample, pretty, well-formed, fragrant, friendly, benevolent, joyous, worthy, valiant, true,' etc" (*TLOT* 2:487).

15. Schoors comments: "In the Old Testament the most frequent meaning of the adjective טוב is that of suitability or usefulness of a thing or person: the emphasis here is on the functional aspect, i.e. the fact that something is as it should be, that it answers its essence or task" ("Words Typical," 33). This is affirmed, for example, by Stoebe (*TLOT* 2:487), Höver-Johag (*TDOT* 5:304) and Robert P. Gordon ("טוב," *NIDOTTE* 2.353–57 [353]). But Schoors continues, "This rather common meaning is very rare in Qohelet."

16. See also Job 9:25; Pss 4:7; 128:5.

17. Gen 1:4, 10, 12, 21, 25 (cf. 1:31).

18. See also Gen 3:6; 6:2; 40:16; 49:15; Exod 2:2; Num 24:1; Ps 34:9 (see also the use of הנה־טוב in Gen 1:31; Judg 18:9).

19. Job 7:7; 9:25; Pss 4:7 (Eng. 4:6); 34:13 (Eng. 34:12).

20. Pss 27:13 (לראות בטוב־יהוה); 106:5 (לראות בטובת בחיריך); 128:5 (בטוב ירושלם וראה; וראה ; Jer 29:32 (ולא־יראה בטוב אשר־אני עשה־לעמי).

it is only used in the first half of the book (and it may be significant that the last of these reverses the order of the words and uses the negative form of the verb):

בטוב		וּרְאֵה		2:1
טוב	אֵי־זֶה	אַרְאֶה	אֲשֶׁר־	2:3
טוב	אֶת־נַפְשׁוֹ	וְהֶרְאָה		2:24
טוב		וְרָאָה		3:13
טוב		רָאִיתִי אָנִי	אֲשֶׁר־	5:17 (Heb.)
טובה		וְלִרְאוֹת		5:17 (Heb.)
לֹא רָאָה		וְטוֹבָה		6:6

Most commentators (and NEB, REB, RSV and NRSV[21]) translate וּרְאֵה בטוב in Eccl 2:1 with something like "enjoy yourself."[22] However, Ogden suggests that "we must admit that this is a rather loose translation,"[23] and a number of scholars (as well as NIV, NJB, NLT) attempt to translate the expression more literally.[24] רָאָה (which, like טוב, is used more frequently in Ecclesiastes than anywhere else in the Hebrew Bible) does seem quite often to have the sense of "experience,"[25] and such a reading might fit well in 2:24; 3:13 and 5:17 (Eng. 5:18) which could refer to experiencing enjoyment in one's work/wealth[26] (and 6:6 might be read in a similar way). However, the point in these verses is precisely that this is not the only possible reading: because of the semantic range of the words involved they could also be understood to refer to "seeing good in (or wealth from) one's work."[27]

---

21. GNB translates, "find out what happiness is," while NJPS renders, "Taste mirth!"

22. See, e.g. Fox, *A Time to Tear Down*, 174; Murphy and Huwiler, *Proverbs, Ecclesiastes, Song of Songs*, 185; Isaksson, *Studies in the Language of Qoheleth*, 44; Perry, *Dialogues with Kohelet*, 73; Schoors, *The Preacher Sought*, 177; Seow, *Ecclesiastes*, 126.

23. Ogden, *Qoheleth*, 39.

24. E.g. Crenshaw, *Ecclesiastes*, 69; Fredericks, *Coping with Transience*, 74; Longman, *The Book of Ecclesiastes*, 88; Murphy, *Ecclesiastes*, 16; Ogden and Zogbo, *A Handbook*, 51–52; Provan, *Ecclesiastes, Song of Songs*, 72.

25. See, e.g., BDB, 907; D. Vetter, "רָאָה, rʾh, to see," *TLOT* 3:1176–83 (1178); Jackie A. Naudé, "רָאָה," *NIDOTTE* 3:1007–15 (1008). Some examples are to be found in Jer 5:12; 14:12; 20:18; Pss 16:10; 89:49 (Eng. 89:48); 90:15.

26. See, e.g., Longman, *The Book of Ecclesiastes*, 108, 122, 168; Ogden and Zogbo, *A Handbook*, 81–82, 103–4, 185–86; Perry, *Dialogues with Kohelet*, 84, 91, 107; Seow, *Ecclesiastes*, 139, 164, 208.

27. See Crenshaw, *Ecclesiastes*, 92, 120; Provan, *Ecclesiastes, Song of Songs*, 91, 128; Whybray, *Ecclesiastes*, 63.

טוב might sometimes be best rendered as "joy" or "joyful,"[28] especially when associated with "the heart."[29] In this respect, 7:14 offers the best parallel to וראה בטוב in 2:1 because it contains the only other occurrence of בטוב, and the word there is also preceded by an imperative: היה בטוב probably means "be joyful" (literally "be in joy").[30] It is quite possible that the use of the imperative רְאֵה at the end of the first half of this verse, combined with two occurrences of טוב(ה), plays on the use of the expression ראה טוב elsewhere in the book. 9:7 also offers a parallel, noteworthy because it too commences with the imperative "go!" (but without the final *he*), uses בשמחה and again refers to the heart as being joyful (ושתה בלב־טוב יינך).[31] The verb ייטב in 7:3 may also mean "be joyful," and similarly ייטיבך in 11:9, both of these perhaps referring—as here—to the "heart" being joyful. The expression יטב לב is used six times elsewhere in the Hebrew Bible, and always seems to have this sense.[32] However, this reading of Eccl 7:3 is disputed and will be considered in more detail later.

All this being said, we should note that when ראה is followed by ב- (which it is not in 2:24; 3:13 or 5:17, where ב- follows טוב rather than preceding it) it usually means to "see in," "look at" or "look into" (or equivalent).[33] The other five times ראה ב- appears in Ecclesiastes (3:22; 5:7; 7:15; 11:4; 12:3) accord with this usage. Moreover, of the 22 occurrences of בטוב in the Hebrew Bible, in every case the *beth* functions normally as the preposition "in" or "at" or "with" (or possibly some other English preposition),[34] except where it follows ראה—and hence could

28. Höver-Johag argues: "The striving for the worldly good of joy and contentment is much discussed in Ecclesiastes . . . where *ṭôb* can stand for the 'naive enjoyment of life'" (*TDOT* 5:314, quoting Ellermeier, *Untersuchungen*, 87).

29. See, e.g., BDB, 373–74; Stoebe, *TLOT* 2:489–90; Höver-Johag, *TDOT* 5:307, 314. Some examples are to be found in Deut 28:47; Judg 16:25; 19:69; 1 Kgs 8:66 = 2 Chr 7:10; 1 Kgs 21:7; Esth 5:9; Prov 15:13.

30. See, for example, Seow who translates "enjoy" and suggests, "The expression probably means the same thing as *rĕʾēh ṭôb* in 2:1" (*Ecclesiastes*, 240). This is the usual tack taken by the commentators.

31. לב־טוב occurs only here in the Hebrew Bible, טוב לב occurs nine times, always with this sense (Deut 28:47; Judg 16:25; 2 Sam 13:28; 1 Kgs 8:66; 2 Chr 7:10; Esth 1:10; 5:9; Prov 15:15; Isa 65:14).

32. Judg 18:20; 19:6, 9, 22; Ruth 3:7; 1 Kgs 21:7.

33. See BDB, 907. Of around 100 occurrences of ראה ב- in the Hebrew Bible, the vast majority can readily be explained in this way, and *none* is best explained by translating ראה as "experience" (contra Seow, *Ecclesiastes*, 126; cf. Fox, *A Time to Tear Down*, 176–77).

34. Gen 20:15; Lev 27:10; Deut 23:16; 28:47; 2 Chr 6:41; Neh 9:25, 35; Job 21:13, 25; 36:11; Pss 25:13; 65:4; 103:5; Prov 11:10; Eccl 7:14.

mean something like "look at 'good'" (or "the good . . . ," or "the prosperity of . . .")[35]—and twice when it follows the verb בחר, which regu-
larly takes this preposition.[36] Hence if וראה בטוב in 2:1 is to be rendered
as "enjoy yourself," it *is* unique in the Hebrew Bible. However, on the
basis of the use of these words in Ecclesiastes and the rest of the Hebrew
Bible, it might be better to translate "look into 'good'"—the precise meaning of "good" being left to the reader to work out. This is then picked up
in v. 3 by the implicit question: *What* is "good" for people to do under
the sun during the few days of their lives? This in turn raises the question
whether טוב here should be read with the same nuance as in v. 1. A comparison of the rendering of the relevant parts of these two verses in different English versions (see Fig. 11 [next page]) demonstrates something
of the ambiguity involved.

In each case טוב is rendered differently in the two verses, most often
by some form of "enjoy" in v. 1 and some form of the noun or adjective
"good" in v. 3. This is also the tack taken by many of the commentators,[37]
but Provan may well be correct to emphasise the theme of "goodness" in
these verses and in 2:24 when he writes,

> The quest for what is "good" for human beings in terms of their happiness
> and well-being (Heb. *rᵊʾeh bᵉṭob*, "see the good," in 2:1, and *ʾerʾeh ʾe-zeh
> ṭob*, "see what is good," in 2:3) has thus been successful. There is nothing
> better (*ṭob*) for a person than to eat, drink, and find ways of enjoying (lit.,
> "cause his soul to see good in," v.24, *wᵉherʾa ʾet-napšo ṭob*) his work. It is
> indeed not only good *for* a human being to live in this way. It is also good
> (morally) *that* he or she should live in this way.[38] That which is good in
> itself turns out, unsurprisingly, to be good for those who pursue it.[39]

However, I suspect there is here again deliberate ambiguity which functions to prompt the reader to ask: What *does* it mean to talk about "goodness" in these different contexts?

2:24 is very important in terms of our discussion of טוב in Ecclesiastes. The word is used twice in this verse, the first occurrence in another
construction that is unique to this book (אין טוב) and introduces the first
of the collection of verses issuing the "call to enjoyment." We will return

35. Pss 27:13; 106:5; 128:5; Jer 29:32.
36. Isa 7:15, 16.
37. See, e.g., Fox, *A Time to Tear Down*, 174–79.
38. Longman, however, specifically states that "The context makes it obvious
that the moral sense of 'good' is not intended" (*The Book of Ecclesiastes*, 108).
39. Provan, *Ecclesiastes, Song of Songs*, 77–78. Murphy retains the word "good"
in both verses but emphasises that it is to be understood in terms of "a life of
pleasure" (*Ecclesiastes*, 18); so also Longman, *Ecclesiastes*, 86–87; Seow, *Ecclesiastes*, 118, 126–28.

	2:1	2:3
NIV	to find out what is *good*	what was *worthwhile* for men to do
NLT	Let's look for the *"good things"* in life	the only *happiness* most people find
NJPS	Taste *mirth!*	which of the two was *better* for men to practice
GNB	find out what *happiness* is	the *best way* people can spend their short lives
NJB	see what *enjoyment* has to offer	the *best way* for people to spend their days
NRSV	*enjoy* yourself	what was *good* for mortals to do
REB	*get enjoyment*	what was *good* for mortals to do
NAS	So *enjoy* yourself	what *good* there is for the sons of men to do
NKJV	*enjoy pleasure*	what was *good* for the sons of men to do

Figure 11

"In (all) his work/deeds"	"Seeing good"/ enjoying	Eating and Drinking	"Except"	Preposition +	(Nothing) Better/ Good	Ref.
בעמלו	טוב את־נפשו והראה	ושתה אכל		באדם	אין־טוב	2:24
בחייו	וזה טוב	שתה אכל	כי אם־ ...	בם	טוב	3:12
במעשיו	האדם ממנו			מאשר	אין־טוב	3:22
בכל־עמלו	לראות טובה	ולשתות לאכול		אשר־יפה	טוב	5:17
בעמלו	לו חה אות	ולשתות אכול לאדם	כי אם־	השמש תחת האדם	אין־טוב	8:15

Figure 12

to it shortly. The second occurrence appears in the third occurrence of the expression ‫ראה טוב‬. This is the only time the Hiphil of‫ ראה‬is used in this construction in Ecclesiastes and such a form appears just once elsewhere in the Hebrew Bible in Ps 4:7 (Heb.):

‫רבים אמרים מי־יראנו טוב נסה־עלינו אור פניך יהוה:‬

In Eccl 2:24, Qohelet shows his soul (himself) "good." Again the vast majority of commentators translate along the lines of "find enjoyment,"[40] and a comparison of the verses issuing the "call to enjoyment" indicates that in 2:24; 3:13 and 5:17 the different forms of‫ ראה טוב‬appear to serve the same function as the verb ‫שׂמח‬ (see Fig. 12.)

However, Whybray questions this rendering[41] and the translation "find satisfaction in [his] work" in the NIV and NLT gives the verse a rather different tone. Again the expression "show himself 'good' in his work/ wealth" is open to different interpretations, ranging from hedonistic pleasure-seeking to striving for "the best."

Although the expression ‫וראה טוב‬ in 3:13 is expressed using the Qal rather the Hiphil, and has ‫טוב‬ as the direct object of the verb, it appears to be synonymous with ‫והראה את־נפשׁו טוב‬ in 2:24. The context of the expressions is very similar:

		‫באדם‬	‫טוב‬	‫אין־‬		2:24
‫בי אם־לשׂמוח ולעשׂות טוב בחייו:‬	‫בם‬	‫טוב‬	‫אין‬	‫בי‬	‫ידעתי‬	3:12
‫את־נפשׁו טוב בעמלו‬	‫וחראה‬	‫ושׁתה‬	‫שׁיאכל‬			2:24
‫טוב בכל־עמלו‬	‫וראה‬	‫ושׁתה‬	‫שׁיאכל‬	‫כל־האדם‬	‫וגם‬	3:13
‫היא:‬	‫האלהים‬	‫מיד‬	‫כי‬	‫אני‬	‫ראיתי‬	‫גם־זה‬	2:24
‫היא:‬	‫אלהים‬	‫מתת‬				3:13

The second half of 3:12 which does not have an equivalent in 2:24 is significant because it contains the phrase ‫לעשׂות טוב‬: this might mean that ‫טוב‬ is used three times in 3:12–13 in three different ways. ‫עשׂה טוב‬ occurs once more in Ecclesiastes, in 7:20, where it clearly means "to do good" in an ethical sense:[42]

40. So, e.g., Bergant, *Job, Ecclesiastes*, 240; Crenshaw, *Ecclesiastes*, 90 (but see his translation on p. 70); Fox, *A Time to Tear Down*, 185; Murphy, *Ecclesiastes*, 24; Perry, *Dialogues with Kohelet*, 84; Salyer, *Vain Rhetoric*, 292; Seow, *Ecclesiastes*, 13 (but see his translation on p. 118); Tamez, *When the Horizons Close*, 53–54.

41. Whybray, *Ecclesiastes*, 63 (but see his comments on 3:12 on p. 74).

42. This, at least, meets with general agreement. See, e.g., Brown, *Ecclesiastes*, 81; Crenshaw, *Ecclesiastes*, 142–43; Eaton, *Ecclesiastes*, 115; Ogden, *Qoheleth*, 117; Ogden and Zogbo, *A Handbook*, 257; Schoors, "Words Typical of Qohelet," 33–34; Seow, *Ecclesiastes*, 252.

כי אדם אין צדיק בארץ אשר יעשה־טוב ולא יחטא

The expression appears a further nine times in the Hebrew Bible,[43] and it always has this same sense (indeed, the expression אין עשה־טוב in Pss 14:1, 3; 53:2, 4 (Eng. 53:1, 3) offers a particularly close parallel to the usage here). This would mean that if the majority of English versions and commentators[44] are correct in rendering the phrase in 3:12 as something like "enjoy yourself" (or "fare well"[45]), again this is a usage unique to Ecclesiastes. Whybray explains thus:

> this expression normally means "do good" in the moral sense, and is so used in 7:20. However, *there is little doubt* that here it means to realise happiness (*ʿāśah*, "make, achieve, bring about"), and is equivalent to *rāʾāh ṭôb*, used of enjoyment in 2:1 and 3:13, and to *hĕrāh ĕt-napšô ṭôb* (RSV, "find enjoyment") in 2:24. As indicated by the repetition of the word *ṭôb* three times in this and the following verse . . . and its use elsewhere in the book, Qoheleth's intention here is to lay emphasis on man's possibility of happiness.[46]

However, some English versions and commentators disagree.[47] Fredericks, for example, argues,

> That he is praising righteousness in this latter reference [i.e. 3:12] *should be clear enough*. Though many would see the phrase *ʿasa ṭôb* to be parallel to the Greek *eu prattein*, "to fare well," rather than a moral injunction, it is paralleled most closely later . . . in 5:1 and 7:20. In 5:1, the syntactical equivalent of "to do good" (*ʿăśôt rāʿ ṭôb*) is found, that is, "to do evil" (*la ʿăśôt rāʿ*), where it undoubtedly expresses the opposite moral pole. And in 7:20, to "do good" (*ya ʿśeh-ṭôb*), and never sin, are moral opposites as well.[48]

The way this expression is understood is significant: if it is read with a moral sense it provides precedent in Ecclesiastes for the combination of being joyful and acting in a right way, and this may feed into our reading of טוב elsewhere in the book. However, if it is seen as a (synonymous?) parallel to שמח the emphasis on enjoyment is strengthened (although

---

43. Num 24:13; 2 Chr 24:16; Pss 14:1, 3; 34:15 (Eng. 34:14); 37:3, 27; 53:2, 4 (Eng. 53:1, 3).

44. See, e.g., NLT, NJB, NRSV; Eaton, *Ecclesiastes*, 182; Fox, *A Time to Tear Down*, 192; Longman, *The Book of Ecclesiastes*, 122; Ogden and Zogbo, *A Handbook*, 102; Perry, *Dialogues with Kohelet*, 89, 91; Seow, *Ecclesiastes*, 164.

45. E.g. Crenshaw, *Ecclesiastes*, 98–99. Cf. Murphy, *Ecclesiastes*, 29–30. Rudman translates "fare well" once (*Determinism*, 62), but later renders the expression as "experience pleasure" (p. 74).

46. Whybray, *Ecclesiastes*, 74, my emphasis.

47. See, e.g., NJPS, NIV; Provan, *Ecclesiastes, Song of Songs*, 91.

48. Fredericks, *Coping with Transience*, 88, my emphasis.

one might also say that if עֲשׂוֹת טוֹב is effectively synonymous with שִׂמְחָה,
then it is redundant) and hence there is more of a sense in the book of
carpe diem. In the end, it could be read either way—and thus is ambiguous and requires the reader to supply the precise meaning. This furthers
the sense of uncertainty over what is "good" for people in the book of
Ecclesiastes.

How עֲשׂוֹת טוֹב in 3:12 is read may have a bearing on how one understands רָאָה טוֹב in 3:13. Thus, although the vast majority of scholars
render רָאָה טוֹב something like "find enjoyment"[49] (as we noted that most
do also in 2:24), it is perhaps not surprising that Fredericks, who translates 3:12 as "I know that there is nothing better for them than to rejoice
and *to do good* in one's lifetime," renders v. 13 as "moreover, that every
man who eats and drinks and *sees good* in all his labor—it is the gift of
God."[50] He explains,

> Doing well in Ecclesiastes is primarily accomplished by acting wisely,
> something itemized generously by Qoheleth, and which is surely the
> origin of much of the happiness available in life. It is helpful to see that
> the identical Hebrew phrasing occurs in the "what advantage" question
> and the positive answers provided by Qoheleth. The question as to the
> advantage *in* one's *toil* (*bĕʿāmāl*, or *bĕkol ʿāmāl*; 1:3; 2:22) is answered
> repeatedly by what is in that toil to satisfy the worker (2:24; 3:13; 3:22, in
> his "works"; 5:18; 8:15).[51]

As we will see in more detail later, 5:17 is very similar to the other
"call to enjoyment" verses, including 2:24 and 3:12–13, but does not use
the characteristic expression אֵין טוֹב (and the words אֲשֶׁר־יָפֶה also occur
only here and complicate translation[52]). Instead it appears to provide a
direct answer to the question in 2:3:

---

49. E.g. Brown, *Ecclesiastes*, 44; Eaton, *Ecclesiastes*, 82; Fox, *A Time to Tear Down*, 192; Longman, *The Book of Ecclesiastes*, 122; Ogden and Zogbo, *A Handbook*, 103–4; Perry, *Dialogues with Kohelet*, 89; Seow, *Ecclesiastes*, 164.

50. Fredericks, *Coping with Transience*, 51, my emphasis (but see his translation on p. 66). Crenshaw translates, "experience good in all his toil" (*Ecclesiastes*, 92). See also Huwiler and Murphy, *Proverbs, Ecclesiastes, Song of Songs*, 187–89.

51. Fredericks, *Coping with Transience*, 67. See also Provan, *Ecclesiastes, Song of Songs*, 91.

52. The English versions and commentators are divided over how these words function within the sentence: the options are represented by NRSV, "This is what I have seen to be good: it is fitting to eat . . ."; REB "This is what I have seen: that it is good and proper for a man to eat . . ."; and NJPS, "Only this, I have found, is a real good: that one should eat . . ." Seow explains, "The Masoretes placed the pause on *ʾănî*. This leaves one with the problem of having to explain the syntactically awk-ward and redundant phrase *ṭôb ʾăšer yāpeh*" (*Ecclesiastes*, 208).

עד . . . תרתי   2:3   אשר־ראה אי־זה טוב לבני האדם

5:17 (Heb.)   הנה אשר־ראיתי אני טוב

Of all the verses using the verb ראה alongside the word טוב, only in these two is the verb used in the first person: in 2:3 Qohelet describes how he undertook the search to find out what is good, and in 5:17 he declares what he has seen to be good (although the search seems not to conclude at this point). This suggests that the conclusions he arrives at here are a significant aspect of the book.

From this point in the verse 5:17 continues in very similar vein to 3:13:

3:13   שיאכל ושתה וראה טוב בכל־עמלו

5:17   לאכול־ ולשתות ולראות טובה בכל־עמלו

Precisely the same issues of interpretation occur here as in 3:13, and again the majority of English versions and commentators render the expression ולראות טובה along the lines of "find enjoyment,"[53] though there are some who read otherwise.[54] Either way, there is a play on different senses of the words ראה and טוב. The use of טוב in different senses here is reminiscent of its use in 2:24 and 3:12–13 (and perhaps also 2:1, 3). One might ask whether the feminine form טובה signifies anything different from טוב, but as Fox observes, "There is no discernible difference in meaning between the masculine and feminine."[55]

ראה טוב is used rather differently in 6:6, including being reversed and negated—וטובה לא ראה—but the options for interpretation are very similar to its use in 2:1, 24; 3:13 and 5:17.[56] However, the verse is translated much more diversely, as a comparison of various English versions illustrates:

NEB	and never prosper
NIV	fails to enjoy his prosperity
KJB	never have known the good things of life
KJV	yet hath he seen no good
NKJV	but has not seen goodness
NRSV	yet enjoy no good

53. See, e.g., NJPS, NRSV, NJB, REB, NLT, GNB; Longman, *The Book of Ecclesiastes*, 168; Seow, *Ecclesiastes*, 209. Notably, Fredericks also translates the verse this way (*Coping with Transience*, 43, 66).

54. See, e.g., NIV; Provan, *Ecclesiastes, Song of Songs*, 128.

55. Fox, *A Time to Tear Down*, 116 n. 10. טובה is used ten times in Ecclesiastes (4:8; 5:10, 17 [Eng. 5:11, 18]; 6:3, 6; 7:11, 14; 9:16, 18 [×2]) and its semantic range seems very similar to that of טוב in this book. In 9:18 it is used in two different ways within the same verse, just as טוב is elsewhere.

56. Thus Whybray states that "this expression (*rāʾāh ṭôbāh*) is the same as in 5:18[17], where RSV renders it by 'find enjoyment'" (*Ecclesiastes*, 106).

REB	have no enjoyment
NJPSV	but never had his fill of enjoyment
GNB	never enjoys life
NLT	but not find contentment

Similar diversity is found among the scholars: Provan renders the words literally, "see the good";[57] Ogden explains them thus, "he 'sees' or enjoys no good thing or blessing";[58] Seow offers, "but good he does not see";[59] while Murphy proposes, "without experiencing good";[60] Crenshaw translates, "but does not enjoy the good";[61] Fredericks goes for "enjoy no good";[62] and Longman renders the expression, "does not experience good times";[63] Fox uses "if he did not experience enjoyment";[64] Perry opts for "but did not enjoy himself";[65] Ogden and Zogbo suggest, "but had no worldly goods";[66] and Huwiler proposes, "cannot enjoy prosperity."[67] Certainly there is little distinction in meaning between some of these, but Fig. 13 (including the English versions and commentators) shows the spectrum of terms used, especially for טוב, which ranges from "goodness" through "enjoyment" to "worldly goods," and demonstrates that the different emphases may be significant:

ראה	טוב
see	good
enjoy	the good
known	goodness
had his fill of	the good things
find	good times
experience	blessing
have	prosperity
	worldly goods
	enjoyment
	contentment
prosper	
enjoys	

Figure 13

57. Provan, *Ecclesiastes, Song of Songs*, 130.
58. Ogden, *Qoheleth*, 93.
59. Seow, *Ecclesiastes*, 213.
60. Murphy, *Ecclesiastes*, 45.
61. Crenshaw, *Ecclesiastes*, 120.
62. Fredericks, *Coping with Transience*, 41.
63. Longman, *The Book of Ecclesiastes*, 164.
64. Fox, *A Time to Tear Down*, 241.
65. Perry, *Dialogues with Kohelet*, 108.
66. Ogden and Zogbo, *A Handbook*, 202.
67. Huwiler, *Proverbs, Ecclesiastes, Song of Songs*, 197.

This indicates that there is room for alternative readings, and shows that the words are ambiguous and leave a gap which the commentators and English versions fill in a variety of ways—and so also may the reader of the Hebrew text. Moreover, if this is true for 6:6, it is true also for the other occurrences of ראה טוב (even if there is less diversity among the versions and commentators).

A further question arises concerning the relationship between וטובה לא ראה in 6:6 and לא־תשבע מן־הטובה in v. 3: are these expressions synonymous? There certainly appears to be some parallelism between the two verses which might be demonstrated thus:

אם־יוליד איש מאה ושנים רבוב יהיה ורב שיהיו ימי־שניו		6:3a
ואלו חיה אלף שנים פעמים		6:6a
ונפשו לא־תשבע מן־הטובה		6:3b
וטובה לא ראה		6:6b
וגם־קבורה לא־היתה לו		6:3c
הלא אל־מקום אחד הכל הולך:		6:6c
אמרתי טוב ממנו הנפל:		6:3d

In this case there is less diversity in the translation of טובה, which is generally rendered as "good things,"[68] "goods,"[69] "prosperity"[70] or "wealth"[71] (but NKJV has "goodness") which might support a similar translation in v. 6. However, in the light of Qohelet's propensity for using words in different ways, and the observation that these verses are not in fact parallel in other ways, it might be wise not to place too much significance on the apparent similarity between the two expressions. Besides which, v. 6 might have more impact if it says something different from v. 3, but using similar words.

7.3.2. אין טוב *and the "Call to Enjoyment"*

From the expression ראה טוב, we turn our attention now to אין טוב, and with it the highly significant thread of verses that issue what I shall term "the call to enjoyment" (although even this appellation would not meet with universal approval[72]). The specific expression אין טוב is used four times in Ecclesiastes (2:24; 3:12–13, 22; 8:15), in verses that display

---

68. E.g. ESV, NAS, NJB, NRSV, REB.
69. E.g. NAB.
70. E.g. NIV.
71. E.g. NJPSV.
72. Murphy, e.g., says of 2:24, "the present translation interprets v. 24 in line with the many resigned conclusions found in the work" (*Ecclesiastes*, 26).

marked similarities to each other—which justifies regarding them as a thematic thread in the book. One further verse also bears such similarities (5:17 [Eng. 5:18]), although it does not use אֵין טוב; rather it appears that the words אֲנִי טוב in that verse are a play on the use of אֵין טוב in the other verses. There are two more verses that seem to pick up the same theme (9:7 [+ 8–9]; 11:9 [+ 11:10; 12:1a]), although they do not display the same pattern that is found in the other five.[73] All these are presented in Fig. 14 (next page), the table demonstrating the similarities among the first five.

Ogden maintains, "Insofar as the אֵין טוב form is not known outside Qoheleth, we are left to assume either that the form was not known prior to Qoheleth's use of it, or that such forms were indeed known but are no longer extant."[74] He acknowledges that "An אֵין טוב construction, as opposed to form, occurs in Jer 8:15, reiterated in 14:19" (the line in both is, קַוֵּה לְשָׁלוֹם וְאֵין טוֹב, "We look for peace, but find no good" [NRSV]), adding, "These are the only other examples of this word combination in Old Testament."[75] However, it is at least debatable whether or not the expression should be read differently in Ecclesiastes and Jeremiah. Moreover, the line אֵין־לִי טוֹב כִּי הִמָּלֵט אִמָּלֵט אֶל־אֶרֶץ פְּלִשְׁתִּים (NRSV, "*there is nothing better* for me than to escape to the land of the Philistines"[76]) in 1 Sam 27:1 may offer the closest parallel to the way these words are usually understood in Ecclesiastes. What should be taken into consideration here is that, just like 1 Sam 27:1, so also in Eccl 2:24; 3:12

---

73. Many commentators draw attention to these seven "calls to enjoyment," including: Brown, *Ecclesiastes*, 37; Fredericks, *Coping with Transience*, 65–66; Ogden and Zogbo, *A Handbook*, 79; Perdue, *Wisdom and Creation*, 237; Perry, *Dialogues with Kohelet*, 29–32; Salyer, *Vain Rhetoric*, 162–64; Schoors, "Qoheleth: The Ambiguity of Enjoyment," 35; Tamez, *When the Horizons Close*, 54 and n. 36 on p. 161. Hubbard tabulates six of these (excluding 11:9), which he terms, "Koheleth's Alternative Conclusion" (*Ecclesiastes, Song of Songs*, 91–97). The best known discussion of these verses is Whybray, "Qoheleth, Preacher of Joy," but his clearest statement about this thematic thread of verses is in Whybray, *Ecclesiastes*, where he states, "In a series of passages running throughout the book (2:24; 3:12–13, 22; 5:18; 8:15; 9:7–9; 11:9–12:7) the reader is encouraged to enjoy life to the full. These seven passages clearly form a series; and, in the book as it is now arranged, it is a series which is marked by a steady increase in emphasis" (p. 64).

74. Graham S. Ogden, "Qoheleth's Use of the 'Nothing is Better'-Form," *JBL* 98, no. 3 (1979): 339–50 (339).

75. Ibid., 339 n. 4.

76. So also NKJV, NAS, NIV, NJB, NLT, NJPSV, GNB, REB have "the best thing I can do" (or equivalent). This is a significant point precisely because there is no comparative *mem* in this verse. The כִּי may function in this way, or may play a similar role to כִּי אִם in Eccl 3:12; 8:15.

Figure 14

Eating and Drinking	"Also Every Person"	Ref.	Enjoying and "Doing Good" in his Life	Ref.	Preposition +	(Nothing) Better/Good	First Person Verb +	Ref.
שֶׁיֹּאכַל						טוֹב אֵין		2:24
שֶׁיֹּאכַל	וְגַם כָּל־הָאָדָם	3:13	לַעֲשׂוֹת טוֹב בְּחַיָּיו		בָּם	טוֹב אֵין	וְהִרְאָהוּ	3:12
					בַּאֲשֶׁר	טוֹב אֵין	וְהִרְאִיתִי	3:22
לֶאֱכוֹל־וְלִשְׁתּוֹת					וְ...	טוֹב	אֲנִי רָאִיתִי	5:17
לֶאֱכוֹל וְלִשְׁתּוֹת					מֵהָאָדָם אֲשֶׁר	טוֹב אֵין	זֶה הַשֶּׁמֶשׁ תַּחַת לָאָדָם וְאֵין	8:15

It is his Portion	The Gift of God	First Person Verb +	The (Few) Days of his Life	"In (all) his Work (at which he Works Under the Sun)"	"Seeing Good"/Enjoying	Ref.
				בַּעֲמָלוֹ	וְהֶרְאָה אֶת־נַפְשׁוֹ טוֹב	2:24
	מַתַּת אֱלֹהִים הִיא	רָאִיתִי אֲנִי כִּי		בְּכָל־עֲמָלוֹ	טוֹב וְרָאָה	3:13
הוּא חֶלְקוֹ כִּי					טוֹב וְרָאָה	3:22
...חֶלְקוֹ הוּא	הָאֱלֹהִים נְתַן־לוֹ	אָנֹכִי רָאִיתִי	מִסְפַּר יְמֵי־חַיָּיו	בַּעֲמָלוֹ שֶׁיַּעֲמֹל תַּחַת־הַשֶּׁמֶשׁ	טוֹבָה וְרָאָה	5:17
חֶלְקוֹ הוּא	הָאֱלֹהִים נְתַן־לוֹ		חַיָּיו יְמֵי		טוֹבָה וְרָאָה	8:15

2:24:   There is nothing better for mortals than to eat and drink, and find enjoyment in their toil. This also, I saw, is from the hand of God

3:12–13:   I know that there is nothing better for them than to be happy and enjoy themselves as long as they live; moreover, it is God's gift that all should eat and drink and take pleasure in all their toil.

3:22:   So I saw that there is nothing better than that all should enjoy their work, for that is their lot

5:17 (Heb.):   This is what I have seen to be good: it is fitting to eat and drink and find enjoyment in all the toil with which one toils under the sun the few days of the life God gives us; for this is our lot.

8:15:   So I commend enjoyment, for there is nothing better for people under the sun than to eat, and drink, and enjoy themselves, for this will go with them in their toil through the days of life that God gives them under the sun.

9:7–9:   Go, eat your bread with enjoyment, and drink your wine with a merry heart; for God has long ago approved what you do. Let your garments always be white; do not let oil be lacking on your head. Enjoy life with the wife whom you love, all the days of your vain life that are given you under the sun, because that is your portion in life and in your toil at which you toil under the sun.

11:9–10:   Rejoice, young man, while you are young, and let your heart cheer you in the days of your youth. Follow the inclination of your heart and the desire of your eyes, but know that for all these things God will bring you into judgment. Banish anxiety from your mind, and put away pain from your body; for youth and the dawn of life are vanity.

and 8:15, there is no comparative *mem*; indeed, three different prepositions follow אין טוב in Ecclesiastes,[77] *mem* occurring only once, in 3:22.
Thus, although the majority of English versions and scholars render the
expression, "there is nothing better (than),"[78] this is not, in fact, the most
obvious way to translate the Hebrew words in 2:24; 3:12 and 8:15, which
might be more accurately rendered thus:

> There is nothing good *in* the person who . . . (2:24)
>
> there is nothing good *in* them except . . . (3:12, 13)
>
> there is nothing good *for* a person under the sun except . . . (8:15)

while 3:22 *is* best rendered,

> "there is nothing better *than* . . ."

Fox is one of many commentators who resort to emendation in 2:24,[79]
arguing, "The minor correction of a haplography, from *bᵓdm šy ᵓkl* to
bᵓdm mšy ᵓkl, with a comparative *mem* as in 3:22, *seems hardly in
doubt*."[80] Seow, though, maintains that such an emendation is unnecessary, and that "'there is no good among humanity that they should eat
and drink . . .' is simply elliptical for 'there is no good among humanity

77.   Contra, for example, Longman, who asserts, "*There is nothing better* (ᵓēn-ṭôb
bā-) is a formula that Qohelet uses in three other places (3:12, 22; 8:15) as well as in
the present verse" (*The Book of Ecclesiastes*, 107). The point is that the formula is
different three times; the question is the significance of the differences. Seow
comments, "The parallel statements in the book show that Qohelet expresses the
same sentiment in a variety of ways" (*Ecclesiastes*, 139). He translates "there
is nothing good" in 2:24 and 3:12 and "there is nothing better in 3:22 and 8:15"
(pp. 118, 158–59, 276).
78.   See, e.g., NAS, NIV, NKJV, NLT, NRSV. Also Brown, "'Whatever Your Hand,'"
279; Christianson, *A Time to Tell*, 248; Crenshaw, *Ecclesiastes*, 70, 89, 92 (but see
his translation of 8:15 on p. 153); Eaton, *Ecclesiastes*, 74; Hubbard, *Ecclesiastes,
Song of Solomon*, 94; Longman, *The Book of Ecclesiastes*, 107, 112, 126, 218;
Murphy, *Ecclesiastes*, 24, 29–30, 79–80; Ogden and Zogbo, *A Handbook*, 79–80,
102, 306; Perry, *Dialogues with Koheleth*, 67, 137 (but see his translation of 3:13, 22
on pp. 89, 93); Rudman, *Determinism*, 127; Tamez, *When the Horizons Close*, 54.
79.   Fox states, "It has apparent support in Syr, Vul, and Tg, and Sc, but these
would have been forced by context to supply an 'except' in some form. LXX, however, mechanically imitates the MT" (*A Time to Tear Down*, 189), but only some mss
of the LXX give this reading. See also Crenshaw, *Ecclesiastes*, 89; Huwiler, *Proverbs, Ecclesiastes, Song of Songs*, 186; Longman, *The Book of Ecclesiastes*, 107;
Murphy, *Ecclesiastes*, 24; Whybray, *Ecclesiastes*, 63.
80.   Fox, *A Time to Tear down*, 189, my emphasis. But he translates "there is
nothing good for man but . . ." in 3:12, and "there is nothing good for man under the
sun but . . ." in 8:15.

(except) that they should eat and drink.'" He adds, "The ancient versions probably do not reflect a different reading in the *Vorlage(n)*—i.e. they probably translated the sense of the Hebrew."[81] Loader, by contrast, argues,

> The final part of the poem begins with a statement that strikes some commentators as so strange that they want to change the Hebrew text. For the Preacher says in so many words that it is *not* good for a man to eat and to drink and to afford himself enjoyment for all his toil. Because in another place he says practically the opposite (cf. 3:12, 22), the commentators think something has to be inserted at the beginning to bring the meaning of the sentence into line with later pronouncements. But there is not a single reason for this. The point here is not that the Preacher's pessimism brings him to a conclusion that makes pleasure the most desirable option; the point is to illustrate the incalculability of God's intervention in human life.[82]

However, there is no need to read 2:24 as it stands in the MT in such a way that it contradicts the sentiments of 3:12, 22. This is indicated, for example, by the translation given in the REB,[83] "To eat and drink and experience pleasure in return for his labours, this does not come from any good in a person: it comes from God," which also finds some support among the scholars.[84] Following this line, we might trace a development in this thread of verses,[85] which, typical of Ecclesiastes, expresses similar but subtly different sentiments in different ways each time:

> There is nothing *good* in the person who eats and drinks and "shows himself *good*" in his work—this too I saw is from the hand of God. (2:24)

> I know that there is nothing *good* in them except to be joyful and to "do *good*" in their lives; also all people who eat and drink and "see *good*" in their work—it is the gift of God. (3:12, 13)

> I saw that there is nothing *better* than that a person is joyful in what he does, for that is his portion . . . (3:22)

---

81. Seow, *Ecclesiastes*, 139.

82. Loader, *Ecclesiastes*, 20.

83. See also NJB and NJPS. KJV's "there is no good in them, but . . ." in 3:12 changes to "nothing is better for them than . . ." in NKJV; RSV's "man has no good thing under the sun but . . ." in 8:15 changes to "there is nothing better for people under the sun than . . ." in NRSV.

84. See, e.g., Schoors, "Qoheleth: The Ambiguity of Enjoyment," 40 n. 4.

85. Whybray argues that "these texts are arranged in such a way as to state their theme with steadily increasing emphasis and solemnity" ("Qoheleth, Preacher of Joy," 87).

Consider <u>what I have seen to be *good*</u>: that it is appropriate to eat and drink and "see *good*" in all the work at which one works under the sun the few days of his life which God gives him, for that his portion. (5:17)

I lauded joy because <u>there is nothing *good*</u> for a person under the sun <u>except</u> to eat and drink and be joyful, and it will accompany him in his work the few days of life that God gives him under the sun. (8:15)

2:24 states that there is nothing good *in* the person who eats and drinks and "shows himself good" in his work because this (presumably the eating and drinking and "seeing good") comes from the hand of God. The implication may be that the good comes not from the person him- or herself, but from God. 3:12 appears to contradict 2:24 by acknowledging that there *is* good in people when it says that there is nothing good in them *except* to be joyful and to "do good" in their lives. However, in words almost identical to 2:24, 3:13 reminds the reader that eating and drinking and "seeing good" are God's gift, so that the good in people does come from God. In 3:22 eating and drinking and "seeing good" disappear (so that the *only* "there is nothing better than" verse in the book is actually the one that fits least well in the series in terms of its similarity to the other verses), but the theme of enjoyment is continued—it is described *not* as the gift of God, but as a person's "portion." It is now asserted that there is nothing better for people than to be joyful in what they do: this, it seems, is the best thing people can do. 5:17 combines "this is his portion" with reference to God's giving, and now states the conclusions of the previous verses in a positive way: not "there is nothing good" or "there is nothing good except" or "there is nothing better than," but "what I have seen to be good." However, here it is the "few days of life" that God gives, while eating and drinking and "seeing good" in one's work appear to be described as "one's portion" (and hence equated to being joyful in 3:22?). 8:15 opens by praising joy, using a verb for "praise" which elsewhere in the Hebrew Bible always refers to God,[86] then goes on to assert that there is nothing good *for* people except to eat and drink . . . and *be joyful*. The issue here is not what is good *in* people, but *for* them, specifically "under the sun" (and we might note that the phrase "under the sun" does not feature in 2:24; 3:12, 13; 3:22, occurs once in 5:17 and is used twice in 8:15). Moreover, the phrases "seeing good" and "doing good" are absent, replaced by the word "enjoy" (שׂמח). Hence the emphasis in 8:15 is very much on "joy."

---

86. Cf. 1 Chr 16:35; Pss 63:3 (Eng. 63:2); 106:47; 117:1; 145:4; 147:12. But the only other occurrence of שׁבח in Ecclesiastes, in 4:2, is used for praising the dead.

The development through these passages then leads into the final two verses, 9:17 and 11:9, which express the "call to enjoyment" in the imperative mood.[87] As in 8:15, the emphasis is explicitly on "joy," with no mention of "seeing good" or "doing good." However, there is reference in both verses to "good" in relation to one's heart: 9:7 picks up on eating and drinking in the earlier verses, exhorting the reader to do these בשמחה and בלב־טוב; 11:9 issues a direct exhortation in the imperative, שׂמח, going on to say, ויטיבך לבך. Certainly in 9:7 it appears that בשמחה and בלב־טוב are in parallel and should be regarded as effectively synonymous (and, so far as I can see, this is the position adopted in all the English translations and by all the commentators):

אֱכֹל בְּשִׂמְחָה לַחְמֶךָ
וּשְׁתֵה בְלֶב־טוֹב יֵינֶךָ

The same appears to be the case in 11:9:

שְׂמַח בָּחוּר בְּיַלְדוּתֶיךָ
וִיטִיבְךָ לִבְּךָ בִּימֵי בְחוּרוֹתֶךָ

As we noted above, יטב לב elsewhere in the Hebrew Bible always seems to mean something like "be joyful,"[88] and it occurs once more in Ecclesiastes, in 7:3. It is notable that these three occurrences of the phrase לב טוב/יטב in the book are all different:

ייטב לב (Qal)	7:3
לב־טוב (adjective)	9:7
ויטיבך לבך (Hiphil)	11:9

This raises the question whether or not they are synonymous. ייטב לב in 7:3 is usually taken to refer to the heart being joyful, or glad—for example, NRSV's "the heart is made glad."[89] However, it might also be

---

87. Many themes in Ecclesiastes come to their climax in the imperative mood. Indeed, some follow the development in the book from predominantly first person, through a mixture of first, second and third, to predominantly second person. This is noted by a few commentators (thus, e.g., Brown notes that "his discourse moves noticeably from description to prescription, from autobiographical observation to moral commendation" ["'Whatever your Hand,'" 279]—though I think it is more complex than this suggests), but insufficient attention is given to the way it helps give shape to the book and demonstrates development in Qohelet's reflections.

88. Judg 18:20; 19:6, 9, 22; Ruth 3:7; 1 Kgs 21:7 (in Judg 19:22 the verb is used in the Hiphil, as in Eccl 11:9).

89. See also ESV, NAS, NJB, NJPS, REB; Brown, *Ecclesiastes*, 73–74; Crenshaw, *Ecclesiastes*, 134 (but he acknowledges the alternative reading, and see his translation on p. 132); Farmer, *Who Knows What is Good?*, 175; Murphy, *Ecclesiastes*, 60, 64; Perry, *Dialogues with Koheleth*, 118; Seow, *Ecclesiastes*, 229, 236; Whybray, who acknowledges, but rejects, the alternative reading (*Ecclesiastes*, 114).

read along with NKJV, "the heart is made better."[90] Eaton, for example, argues,

> That *the heart* ". . . may be put right" or ". . . is put right" is the appropriate translation (better than *made glad*), for it means that the inner life may be "better situated" for making right judgments and estimations, "put right" in one's approach to life (*cf.* NIV). A man who has looked death in the face may have his inner life transformed for the better.[91]

The second half of the verse, כִּי־בְרֹעַ פָּנִים יִיטַב לֵב, may introduce a paradox, along with the first reading,[92] or it may indicate that a sad face can actually be good for you, along with the second reading. Either way, I believe there is here an intentional play on the words רַע and טוֹב, again inviting the reader to ponder how "bad" and "good" should be understood.[93]

Although strictly speaking the same could apply in 11:9, the occurrence of יִטַב לֵב there is more consistently translated in line with NRSV's "let your heart cheer you," some such rendering appearing in all the main English versions and most of the commentators.[94] There seem to be good

---

90. See also GNB ("it sharpens your understanding"); NIV ("is good for the heart"); NLT ("has a refining influence on us"); and Bergant, *Job, Ecclesiastes*, 265; Fox, *A Time to Tear Down*, 249, 250; Longman, *The Book of Ecclesiastes*, 180, 183–84; Ogden, *Qoheleth*, 103; Ogden and Zogbo, *A Handbook*, 221; Provan, *Ecclesiastes, Song of Songs*, 140; Dominic Rudman, "The Anatomy of the Wise Man: Wisdom, Sorrow and Joy in the Book of Ecclesiastes," in Schoors, ed., *Qohelet in the Context of Wisdom*, 465–71 (467–68). Stoebe notes that Eccl 7:3 "accents ethics more strongly" (*TLOT* 2:489).

91. Eaton, *Ecclesiastes*, 109.

92. See also the rather strange saying in Prov 14:13.

93. Whybray acknowledges that "each of the four words is ambiguous" (*Ecclesiastes*, 114). Longman states that "Both parts of the verse are enigmatic" (*The Book of Ecclesiastes*, 183). After discussing various readings, Murphy notes that "Interpretation of this verse and others depends on the construal of the entire chapter" (*Ecclesiastes*, 64). Salyer argues, "Qoheleth presents a paradox in these verses whose final *Gestalt* remains open for the reader" (*Vain Rhetoric*, 336). Rudman writes, "The translation of Eccles 7,3 has long been considered problematic, and no fewer than three different interpretations have been offered for this verse." He notes that "interpretations of the final phrase יִטַב לֵב diverge significantly," although he contends: "Ambiguity is (theoretically) avoided by the use of the causal כִּי which precludes the more usual meaning of יִיטַב לֵב" ("The Anatomy of the Wise Man," 465–68).

94. See, e.g., Crenshaw, *Ecclesiastes*, 181; Fox, *A Time to Tear Down*, 316; Fredericks, *Coping with Transience*, 70; Longman, *The Book of Ecclesiastes*, 259; Murphy, *Ecclesiastes*, 111; Perry, *Dialogues with Koheleth*, 155; Seow, *Ecclesiastes*, 347; Whybray, *Ecclesiastes*, 162.

grounds for this in the light of the parallelism we noted above and the apparent development of the verse towards the concluding line:

שְׂמַח בָּחוּר בְּיַלְדוּתֶיךָ
וִיטִיבְךָ לִבְּךָ בִּימֵי בְחוּרוֹתֶךָ
וְהַלֵּךְ בְּדַרְכֵי לִבְּךָ וּבְמַרְאֵי עֵינֶיךָ
וְדַע כִּי עַל־כָּל־אֵלֶּה יְבִיאֲךָ הָאֱלֹהִים בַּמִּשְׁפָּט

However, Provan warns, "That this is not an invitation to hedonism, especially to atheistic hedonism, is already clear from our reading of Ecclesiastes to this point. The language used in 11:9a also indicates this, for *yeṭib leb* ('let your heart give you joy') reminds us of *yiṭab leb* ('is good for the heart') in 7:3 (in the midst of a passage exhorting the adoption of a serious attitude to life,"[95] and Ogden and Zogbo state, "we note that the pleasure spoken of is in the mind or heart (*lev*), so we should not misunderstand Qoheleth. He does not advocate mere entertainment but that kind of joy that satisfies the intellectual as well as other aspects of life." This is borne out by the suggestions they offer for translation of the next part of the verse, either, "live as your mind guides you" or "let your mind guide your life."[96] Nonetheless, the use of טוב or יטב in these exhortations which conclude the thread of verses issuing the "call to enjoyment" does seem to relate to enjoyment rather than any other kind of "good."

A final issue in relation to this series of "call to enjoyment" verses concerns just how they are perceived to function within the book. Indeed, Brown asserts of these verses that "The significance of Qoheleth's commendations within the book as a whole is *the* interpretive crux of Ecclesiastes."[97] He points out that they could be ascribed "entirely to the redactional interpolations of a pious editor set on mitigating the sage's otherwise dour outlook";[98] or viewed (or marginalised) as "authentic but peripheral to the sage's message,"[99] or emphasised (or centralised) "to

95. Provan, *Ecclesiastes, Song of Songs*, 212.
96. Ogden and Zogbo, *A Handbook*, 412.
97. Brown, "'Whatever your Hand,'" 279.
98. Brown says, "Only one scholar to my mind has proposed this possibility, but only for the sake of argument: W. H. U. Anderson makes a case for considering all the 'joy statements' as the product of editorial activity but registers serious misgivings in arguing it ('*Scepticism and Ironic Correlations in the Joy Statements of Qoheleth?* [unpublished diss., Glasgow University, 1997])" ("'Whatever your Hand,'" 279).
99. Again Brown refers to Anderson (*Qoheleth and Its Pessimistic Theology*, 73). One might also quote Fox, who contends that "Qohelet is by no means a 'preacher of joy'" (*A Time to Tear down*, 127), or Schoors, who states, "Qoheleth is not a book with a message of joy" ("Qoheleth: The Ambiguity of Enjoyment," 40).

the point of proclaiming Qoheleth as a "preacher of joy."[100] Ogden is certainly correct when he notes that "The question of emphasis is fundamental in determining Qoheleth's thesis."[101] He goes on to say, "We have already noted above the contrasting conclusions about the book which have marked scholarship in the past. Basically, these have come about because of differing emphases—does one stress the so-called 'vanity'-theme, or the call to enjoyment?" This, it seems to me, is a crucial factor in how one understands the book. Ogden explains his own position thus:

> It will be argued in the commentary to follow that although the *hebel* phrase occurs in many concluding statements, these are points at which the author answers his own programmatic question. They are not the point at

Murphy asserts that the verses issuing the "call to enjoyment" "are not a positive recommendation. They are a concession to human nature" (*Ecclesiastes*, lx).

100. Most notable here is Whybray's "Qoheleth, Preacher of Joy"; but one might also quote Gordis's well-known statement that "For Koheleth, joy is God's categorical imperative for man, not in any anemic or spiritualized sense, but rather as a full-blooded and tangible experience, expressing itself in the play of the body and the activity of the mind, the contemplation of nature and the pleasures of love" (*Koheleth*, 129). Gordis goes on to explain: "That the basic theme of the book was *simhah*, the enjoyment of life, was clearly recognized by Jewish religious authorities who thus explained the custom of reading *Koheleth* in the synagogue on the Feast of Tabernacles, the Season of Rejoicing" (*Koheleth*, 131). Brown himself states that "Qoheleth's seven commendations constitute the book's refrain as much as his *hebel* indictment against the created order serves as its motto and rhetorical frame" ("'Whatever your Hand,'" 279); Salyer says that "this call is in all probability *the* key structural device which guides the reader's sense of the text's development" (*Vain Rhetoric*, 292, my emphasis); and Perdue maintains that "The literary structure of Qoheleth is organized around the sevenfold occurrence of the *carpe diem*" (*Wisdom and Creation*, 237). Fredericks describes this as "a critical theme of Ecclesiastes" (*Coping with Transience*, 64); Choon-Leong Seow states that "The God who put eternity in the human heart has also put in that same heart the response and responsibility of enjoyment. This is Qoheleth's theological ethic in the face of universal *hebel*" ("Theology when Everything is Out of Control," *Int* 55, no. 3 (2001): 237–49 [245]). Provan asserts that "Qohelet's consistent advice throughout the book has been to live joyfully and reverently before God in the midst of what is often a complex world" (*Ecclesiastes, Song of Songs*, 228). Huwiler maintains that "The book addresses two principal questions. The first issue is whether human experience is meaningful, controllable, and predictable. . . . The second question is whether human well-being is possible. To this, the author of Ecclesiastes . . . offers an affirmative answer. It is possible to enjoy the pleasures of eating, drinking, working, and family" (*Proverbs, Ecclesiastes, Song of Songs*, 159). Davis argues that 2:24 "goes to the heart of Koheleth's thought" (*Proverbs, Ecclesiastes, and the Song of Songs*, 182).

101. Ogden, *Qoheleth*, 13.

which he offers his advice on how to live in a society plagued by so many enigmas. That advice comes in the reiterated calls to enjoyment in 2:24; 3:12, 22; 5:17 (18); 8:15, as well as in 9:7–10. We shall be looking not to a secondary element in the book's framework, but to the climactic statement, the call to enjoyment, as that which puts the thesis of the book. Thus the structure assists in our answering the question of the book's thesis. Its thesis, then, is that life under God must be taken and enjoyed in all its mystery.[102]

This stands in sharp contrast to Longman's reading of Qohelet's words. He asks, "What is the theological message of Qohelet's autobiography?," and goes on to answer:

Life is full of trouble and then you die. Some interpreters attempt to mitigate this hard message by appealing to six passages that they interpret as offering a positive view towards life (2:24; 3:12–14; 3:22; 5:17–19 [Eng. 5:18–20]; 8:15; 9:7–10). One must admit, however, that Qohelet only suggested a limited type of joy in these passages. Only three areas are specified—eating, drinking, and work. In addition, Qohelet's introduction to pleasure was hardly enthusiastic. . . . It is more in keeping with the book as a whole to understand these passages as they have been taken through much of the history of interpretation, that is, as a call to seize the day (*carpe diem*). In the darkness of a life that has no ultimate meaning, enjoy the temporal pleasures that lighten the burden (5:18–19 [Eng. 5:19–20]).[103]

Somewhere in the middle we find Hubbard, who notes that a "major issue to be tackled is the relative emphasis to be placed on the two dominant formulas which stitch the Book together: the *vanity verdict* and the *alternative conclusion* which urges Koheleth's students to take daily joy in God's ordinary gifts of food, drink, work, and love." He concludes,

In a sense these two motifs, *vanity* and *joy*, set the rhythm for the Preacher. They are more complementary than contradictory. Each must be heard in terms of the other. *Vanity* marks the limits of our ability to understand and change the way life works. It salutes in its gloomy way the sovereignty of God whose mysteries are to us unfathomable. *Joy* brings relief in the midst of frustration. It announces that God's puzzling clouds of sovereignty carry a silver lining of grace. That grace, expressed in the daily supply of our basic needs, gives us freedom to fear God, not to have God.[104]

Different again is Bartholomew's approach when he maintains that the questions raised in Ecclesiastes are "answered in two ways, that of הבל *and* that of joy," and that "these contradictory answers are invariably

---

102. Ibid., 14.
103. Longman, *The Book of Ecclesiastes*, 35.
104. Hubbard, *Ecclesiastes, Song of Solomon*, 22.

juxtaposed, thereby creating a gap in the reading that needs to be filled."[105] He suggests that "'remembrance of God as creator' potentially fills these gaps," but that the epilogue is "crucial in indicating how the narrator intends us to fill in the gaps. . . . 12:13–14 confirm my reading of 12:1 as the bridge which positively resolves the tension/gap between the *carpe diem* element and the enigma statements."[106]

This all means that the answer to the question "what is 'good' for people to do?" provided by this series of verses is not straightforward. First, on a number of occasions the precise meaning of the word for "good," טוב, is open to different interpretations, particularly in the phrase ראה טוב, which is slightly different every time it is used. Secondly, the seemingly negative answer, "there is nothing good," אין טוב, is complicated by the prepositions which follow it: in 2:24 "there is nothing good *in* the man" (but rather it comes from God); in 3:12–13 "there is nothing good in the man *except*. . ." (but it still comes from God); in 3:22 "there is nothing better than that the man enjoy himself" (which is his lot); in 8:15 "there is nothing good *for* the man under the sun *except*. . ." Moreover, what is "good" is slightly different in 3:22 (it doesn't include eating and drinking and "seeing good"); and 5:17 bucks the trend because there Qohelet states, "Consider what I have seen to be good," rather than "there is nothing good"—but nonetheless, the "good" here is the same as in 2:24; 3:12; 5:17 and 8:15. Finally, scholars disagree about just how these verses function within the overall scheme of the book of Ecclesiastes.

7.3.3 טוב מן *Sayings*

Another frequent use of the word טוב in Ecclesiastes is in "better than" sayings, which Ogden calls *tôb-spruch*,[107] and which, as Stoebe notes, occur "particularly often in wisdom literature,"[108] although Ogden and Zogbo observe that Ecclesiastes "contains almost half of all Old Testament examples of this form,"[109] making it a particular feature of the book. These seem to provide a different kind of answer to the question "what is good for people to do?" in terms of it is *more* good (i.e. better) to do this

---

105. Bartholomew, *Reading Ecclesiastes*, 238.

106. Ibid., 252–53.

107. See Graham S. Ogden, "The 'Better'-Proverb (Tôb-Spruch), Rhetorical Criticism, and Qoheleth," *JBL* 96, no. 4 (1977): 489–505, following G. E. Bryce, "'Better'-Proverbs: An Historical and Structural Study," *SBL Seminar Papers, 1972* (ed. L. C. McGaughy; 2 vols.; Missoula, Mont.: Society of Biblical Literature, 1972), 2:343–54, who in turn follows Walther Zimmerli, "Zur Struktur der alttestamentlichen Weisheit," *ZAW* 51 (1933): 192–95, and others.

108. Stoebe, *TLOT* 2:490. Cf. Höver-Johag, *TDOT* 5:313.

109. Ogden and Zogbo, *A Handbook*, 127.

than that.[110] There are eighteen of these, plus the sayings in 4:17; 7:1b and 9:17 which do not include the טוב element but whose context suggests that they might fulfil a similar function. The better-sayings occur at a number of points throughout the book, but there are clusters around ch. 4 and the start of ch. 7:

3:22	אֵין טוב מֵאֲשֶׁר יִשְׂמַח הָאָדָם בְּמַעֲשָׂיו
4:3	וְטוֹב מִשְּׁנֵיהֶם אֵת אֲשֶׁר־עֲדֶן לֹא הָיָה
4:6	טוֹב מְלֹא כַף נָחַת מִמְּלֹא חָפְנַיִם עָמָל
4:9	טוֹבִים הַשְּׁנַיִם מִן־הָאֶחָד
4:13	טוֹב יֶלֶד מִסְכֵּן וְחָכָם מִמֶּלֶךְ זָקֵן וּכְסִיל
4:17	וְ[טוֹב] קָרוֹב לִשְׁמֹעַ מִתֵּת הַכְּסִילִים זָבַח
5:4	טוֹב אֲשֶׁר לֹא־תִדֹּר מִשֶּׁתִּדּוֹר וְלֹא תְשַׁלֵּם
6:3	טוֹב מִמֶּנּוּ הַנָּפֶל
6:9	טוֹב מַרְאֵה עֵינַיִם מֵהֲלָךְ־נָפֶשׁ
7:1a	טוֹב שֵׁם מִשֶּׁמֶן טוֹב
7:1b	וְ[טוֹב] יוֹם הַמָּוֶת מִיּוֹם הִוָּלְדוֹ
7:2	טוֹב לָלֶכֶת אֶל־בֵּית־אֵבֶל מִלֶּכֶת אֶל־בֵּית מִשְׁתֶּה
7:3	טוֹב כַּעַס מִשְּׂחֹק
7:5	טוֹב לִשְׁמֹעַ גַּעֲרַת חָכָם מֵאִישׁ שֹׁמֵעַ שִׁיר כְּסִילִים
7:8a	טוֹב אַחֲרִית דָּבָר מֵרֵאשִׁיתוֹ
7:8b	טוֹב אֶרֶךְ־רוּחַ מִגְּבַהּ־רוּחַ
7:10	הָיוּ טוֹבִים מֵאֵלֶּה
9:4	לְכֶלֶב חַי הוּא טוֹב מִן־הָאַרְיֵה הַמֵּת
9:16	טוֹבָה חָכְמָה מִגְּבוּרָה
9:17	[טוֹבִים] דִּבְרֵי חֲכָמִים בְּנַחַת נִשְׁמָעִים מִזַּעֲקַת מוֹשֵׁל בַּכְּסִילִים
9:18	טוֹבָה חָכְמָה מִכְּלֵי קְרָב

These are not as straightforward as may initially appear, and they serve to further the questions this book raises about what it means to call something טוב, "good" or "better."

The first better-saying is one we discussed above, and is, notably, expressed in the negative, "there is *nothing* better than," in 3:22. Not only does this introduce the series of sayings in the negative,[111] which may already be a clue that the search for what is "better" will be

---

110. Höver-Johag quite specifically states that "They reply to the anthropocentric question *mâṭôb/yiṯrôn lā'āḏām* (Eccl 1:3; 2:3, 22; 3:9; 5:15b[16b]; 6:8, 12; 10:10f.; etc.)" (*TDOT* 5:313).

111. This point is made by Seow, who writes of the better-sayings in ch. 4, "this series immediately follows the conclusion in Chapter 3 that there is 'nothing better' (*'ên ṭôb*) than to enjoy oneself (3:12, 22). First the author states baldly that there is 'nothing better,' and then he proceeds to give a series of *ṭôb-*sayings. A similar contradiction is evident in 6:10–7:14. . . . [T]he assertion that there is 'nothing better' but to enjoy oneself must be kept in mind as one readers the *ṭôb-*sayings" (*Ecclesiastes*, 186).

somewhat fraught, but it is a construction which does not occur in this precise form anywhere else in the Hebrew Bible. Hence, although the so-called *tôb-spruch* form is common in the Hebrew Bible, and especially in the wisdom literature, its first appearance in Ecclesiastes uses a form unique to the book. Moreover, we have already noted that 3:22 occurs in a series of verses with similar meaning, but again where the precise form אין טוב מ- is unique.

In ch. 4 (and perhaps 5:1–6 [Eng. 5:2–7] should be included with this), it may be that the structure revolves around the use of the first person form of the verb ראה and the better-sayings:

ושבתי אני ואראה	4:1
טוב . . . מ-	4:3
וראיתי אני	4:4
טוב . . . מ-	4:6
ושבתי אני ואראה	4:7
טובים . . . מן-	4:9
טוב . . . מ-	4:13
וראיתי	4:15
(טוב) . . . מ-	4:17
טוב . . . מ-	5:4

This structure implies that the overall theme of ch. 4 is "what is better in light of what I have seen."[112]

4:1–3 explores an example of what is done under the sun (emphasised by the repetition of the phrase אשר נעשים תחת השמש in vv. 1, 3). This specific example is "oppression," conveyed by the use three times of the word עשקים to denote the abstract concept of "oppression," "the oppressed" and "the oppressors." Verse 2 is very close to a better-saying;[113] it is also a rather shocking statement[114] which finds support in the better-sayings in

112. The structure—and indeed the extent—of this section is much disputed among the commentators, as also is its main theme. Huwiler notes that "The segments of the first group (4:1–5:7) are held together by 'better' sayings (4:2–3, 6, 9, 13; 5:5)" (*Proverbs, Ecclesiastes, Song of Songs*, 191). A number of scholars note the role played by these sayings in the structure of the chapter (e.g. Ogden, *Qoheleth*, 65).

113. In fact, Longman says of 4:2: "In this verse Qohelet uses the first of a number of so-called better-than proverbs" (*The Book of Ecclesiastes*, 134). Whybray comments that שבח "is clearly used in a sense similar to that of *tôb*, better" (*Ecclesiastes*, 82).

114. Ogden rather takes the sting out of it by saying, "If Qoheleth's interest is in the possible *yitrôn* after death, then this statement makes good sense" (*Qoheleth*, 67); Eaton does so in another way when he writes, "God-less sorrow leads to suicidal longings" (*Ecclesiastes*, 92). A sharp contrast is provided by Loader's reading: "he praises the advantage the dead have over the living. Yet that is surely no comfort

[טוב] יום המות מיום 6:3 (טוב ממנו הנפל—and see also 6:4–5), and 7:1 (טוב] יום המות מיום
הולד), and the statement in 2:17 (ושנאתי את־החיים), but provides a striking contrast to the statement in 11:7 (וטוב לעינים לראות את־השמש—which
refers metaphorically to life), and the better-saying in 9:4 (in 9:3–4 the
contrast is drawn, as here, between המתים and החיים, leading up to this
proverb):

4:2 ושבח אני את־המתים שכבר מתו מן־החיים אשר המה חיים עדנה:

9:4 לכלב חי הוא טוב מן־האריה המת:

The "piercing irony"[115] of 4:2 is continued in the better-saying of v. 3,
which provides a contrast with the proverb in v. 9:

4:3 וטוב משניהם את אשר־עדן לא היה
4:9 טובים השנים מן־האחד

Which, then, is better:[116] life or death; the one or the two? The obvious
answer is: it depends on the circumstances.[117] The "good," it seems, varies, and what is "good" or "better" at one point, may not be so at another.
In fact, what seems to be "bad" (רע) may actually be "good," or at least
"better" (טוב), at certain times: hence Qohelet's advice in 7:14:

since the Preacher has no expectation of an afterlife. So we have here another
instance of irony, as in the preceding poem—the hardness of life is met with
comforting words that provide no comfort" (*Ecclesiastes: A Practical Commentary*,
48). Cf. Crenshaw's comments: "This preference for the nonexistent over the dead
or the living suits the hatred for life that Qohelet expressed in 2:17. Such loathing of
the conditions under which life must be carried out arises from a vision of the way
things should be in a perfect world" (*Ecclesiastes*, 107). Rudman sees 4:1–3 to support his arguments for determinism in Ecclesiastes: he claims that it is "more likely
that Qoheleth's awareness of the fact that human activity is determined . . . has made
him hate not *his* life, but life or existence in toto. This distinction is supported by
4:1–3" (*Determinism*, 118).

115. Ogden and Zogbo write: "When Qoheleth congratulates people for dying, he
reveals his piercing irony" (*A Handbook*, 126).

116. We might note that instead of "better than" in 4:3, NJPS and NJB both have
"happier than" (an interesting idea for someone who has not yet been born). NAS and
GNB translate "better *off* than," while REB uses "more fortunate than" and NLT "most
fortunate of all." See also Ogden and Zogbo, *A Handbook*, 127.

117. Thus, for example, Ogden and Zogbo state, "Normally life is better than
death, even for Qoheleth, but when he is confronted by the many injustices and evils
of human society, death seems preferable" (*A Handbook*, 126). Whybray states
simply: "There is, however, no doubt that in different moods Qoheleth's attitude
towards life varies" (*Ecclesiastes*, 60).

ביום טובה היה בטוב וביום רעה ראה גם את־זה
לעמת־זה עשה האלהים

This, of course, fits in with the "time-poem" in 3:1–8 (including the claim that there is "a time to give birth and a time to die") and Qohelet's conclusion in 3:11 that God has made everything appropriate *in its time*.[118] But it does raise further questions about what it means to call something "good" or "better"—especially if what is better is actually beyond human grasp, as Seow explains:

> what is better than being alive or dead is not to have come into existence at all and not to have seen the injustices of the world. But that is, in fact, not an option for the humans, inasmuch as they already are living and have already been witnessing life's inevitable tragedies. The alternative of not having lived is not an option that people can choose. The *ṭôb-saying* thus points to the irony of human existence: what is really "better" in this regard is not within the grasp of mortals.[119]

It may be that something of this sense is captured by what Whybray describes as the "tortuous" nature of the argument. He explains:

> First, it is not clear why Qoheleth could not have made his point more simply. Possibly he thought that this step-by-step way of proceeding was more effective rhetorically. In that case he seems to have been generally unwilling to admit that anything was either black or white (cf, 2:13–14; 4:13–16; 9:13–16). Secondly, the point of the "yet" in *not yet been* is not clear. Its presence shows that Qoheleth is not referring—as in 6:3–5 and in Job 3:11–19—to children who are stillborn or who die soon after birth, but to all those who will be born in the future; but since presumably these will cease to be fortunate when they enter the world and *see the evil deeds which are done under the sun*, the comparison does not appear to be a felicitous one. Possibly the insertion of the *yet* is due to Qoheleth's reluctance, mentioned above, to attribute unqualified good to anything at all.[120]

. . . Or perhaps it is another device to draw the reader into exploring just what is "good."

4:4–6 focuses on work, using the roots עמל and עשׂה. It concludes with two sayings which appear to be in some tension, the latter of which is a better-saying that again compares one (handful) favourably with two (hands full; חפנים is a dual). NRSV simply presents the two side-by-side:

---

118. Cf. Eccl 8:5–6; but contrast 9:11–12.
119. Seow, *Ecclesiastes*, 187.
120. Whybray, *Ecclesiastes*, 82.

> Fools fold their hands
>   and consume their own flesh.[121]
> Better is a handful with quiet
>   than two handfuls with toil,
> and a chasing after wind.

This raises the question: Is it or is it not better to toil? However, GNB, NLT and NJPSV seek alternative ways of explaining away the tension that arises:

> *They say that* a man would be a fool to fold his hands and let himself starve to death. *Perhaps so, but* it is better to have only a little, with peace of mind, than to be busy all the time with both hands, trying to catch the wind. (GNB)

> Foolish people refuse to work and almost starve. *They feel* it is better to be lazy and barely survive than to work hard, especially when in the long run everything is so futile. (NLT)

> *True,* the fool folds his hands together and has to eat his own flesh. *But no less truly,* better is a handful of gratification than two fistfuls of labor which is pursuit of wind. (NJPSV)

There is some divergence also in the ways the commentators deal with these verses. Fox, for example, describes these as "Two complementary —not contradictory—proverbs, the first condemning indolence, the second excessive work."[122] Longman observes, "It must be remembered that proverbs do not make unconditional claims. The first could be right in certain situations and the second in other situations."[123] By contrast, Ogden argues that the effect of v. 6 is "to reverse the values of the elements in vv. 4, 5 and to produce a paradoxical statement."[124] Bergant observes that "Qoheleth often quotes a maxim that has captured a bit of conventional wisdom only to follow it with contradictory facts," going

---

121. There is some debate about the precise meaning of this phrase. The vast majority of scholars see it as an indication that the fool destroys himself. However, Seow points out that "The meaning of *wĕʾōkēl bĕśārô* is disputed. It has been proposed that *bĕśārô* means 'his meat' and the aphorism in v. 5 means that the fool does nothing and still is able to eat well. . . . Accordingly, v. 5 supports what is said in v. 4: that effort causes nothing but envy and even fools who are lazy do not become destitute. On the contrary, even fools may eat well" (*Ecclesiastes*, 179). However, while a number of recent commentators discuss this possibility, none that I have found actually support it.

122. Fox, *Qohelet*, 202.

123. Longman, *The Book of Ecclesiastes*, 138.

124. Graham S. Ogden, "The Mathematics of Wisdom: Qoheleth iv 1–12," *VT* 34 (1984): 446–53 (450).

on to assert that "He uses this technique to neutralize the former and emphasize the latter."[125] Perry views them as two different voices in a debate.[126] Murphy reads the two as contradictory, but asks, "Could it be that Qoheleth sees little value in either of them?"[127] Eaton describes v. 6 as "the middle way between the clamourous grasping of v. 4 and the escapism of v. 5."[128] It rather seems that again the reader has to work hard to figure out just what the "good" or "better" actually is in this context.

Where 4:1–3 and 4–6 compare "one" favourably against "two," vv. 7–12 repeatedly indicate that two is better than one, and three better still. While the better-sayings comparing one and two concluded the previous sections, here it seems that the saying comes exactly at the centre. However, after the introductory v. 7, the comparison of "one" and "two" occurs in every verse:

אחד ... שני	4:8
השנים ... האחד	4:9
האחד ... שני	4:10
שנים ... לאחד	4:11
האחד השנים ... המשלש	4:12

And typical of Ecclesiastes, the combination is slightly different each time.

This section continues the theme of work from the previous one. There is a play on the word עמל, which is used three times, possibly with three different senses. Its first occurrence in v. 8, ואין קץ לכל־עמלו, might indicate either "work"[129] or "wealth"[130] (as might possibly be the case in v. 6[131]); the second occurrence is the verb "to work," ולמי אני עמל; and in v. 9 בעמלם probably means "in their work,"[132] but might be "from their

---

125. Bergant, *Job, Ecclesiastes*, 250.

126. Perry, *Dialogues in Koheleth*, 96.

127. Murphy, *Ecclesiastes*, 39.

128. Eaton, *Ecclesiastes*, 93.

129. Murphy renders the word here "toil" (*Ecclesiastes*, 29). See also, among others, Seow, *Ecclesiastes*, 177. Most of the English versions and commentators translate similarly.

130. NJPSV renders the clause, "yet he amasses wealth without limit."

131. NJB renders the second part of the verse, "than two hands full of achievements" (i.e. the result of work), and Fox translates, "than two fistfuls of wealth," explaining, "'*Amal* here means earnings rather than the activity of toiling, for 'fistfuls' is something that can be possessed rather than an action" (*A Time to Tear Down*, 220–21). Most other English versions and commentators use "toil" or similar. See also, e.g., Murphy, *Ecclesiastes*, 40; Seow, *Ecclesiastes*, 177.

132. Seow translates the word "toil" (*Ecclesiastes*, 177). Cf. Murphy, *Ecclesiastes*, 40, and most English version and commentators.

wealth"[133]—Whybray, however, contends, that "*ʿāmāl* here can hardly mean 'toil,' but rather, as frequently in the Old Testament, 'trouble.'"[134] This wordplay is enhanced by the use of three terms (in addition to עמל itself) which may indicate wealth, or the return one gets from working: עשר and טובה in v. 8 and שכר in v. 9. However, ומחסר את־נפשי מטובה is probably parallel to לא־תשבע, so that although טובה does have the sense of "wealth" elsewhere in Ecclesiastes (this is probably the case in 5:10 [Eng. 5:9]), it probably means "good" in a different way here.[135] More-over, the "good reward" or "return," שכר טוב, in v. 9 may be something like companionship *as opposed* to wealth (and this would be borne out by the argument in vv. 10–13)[136]—as Longman notes, "it must be admitted that what Qohelet means by *return* here is ambiguous."[137] Indeed, forms of the word טוב also occur three times in vv. 8 and 9, each with a different meaning (מטובה in v. 8, and טובים and טוב in v. 9), and this once more raises the question: What is "good"? (Verse 8 is further complicated by the unexpected change from third person to first person.[138]) The contrast between the two verses might be demonstrated thus:

v. 8		v. 9
יש אחד ואין שני גם בן ואה אין־לו	one → two	טובים השנים מן־האחד
ואין קץ לכל־עמלו גם־עיניו [עינו] לא־תשבע עשר ולמי אני עמל ומחסר את־נפשי מטובה	Negative → positive	אשר יש־להם שכר טוב בעמלם

133. NJPSV translates here, "they have greater benefit from their earnings."

134. Whybray, *Ecclesiastes*, 87.

135. Ogden and Zogbo explain: "*Pleasure* in this setting does not translate the same Hebrew word for 'pleasure' in 2:1, 10. Here it renders the Hebrew adjective 'good' used as a noun with the sense of 'goods' or 'good things' that money can buy. The problem in this clause is in the fact that the person who is working so hard does not lack material things but lacks the power to be able to enjoy what he has" (*A Handbook*, 136).

136. Thus Ogden and Zogbo explain: "on the basis of examples in verses 10–12, it is clear that Qoheleth is not thinking in material terms; rather he has in mind some social or psychological value. So the term 'benefit' may be closer to Qoheleth's sense" (*A Handbook*, 138). REB renders the clause, "their partnership yields this advantage," which leads straight into vv. 10–12. However, most English versions and commentators translate in the sense of NRSV's "they have a good reward for their toil." Garrett closes out any but the financial return reading: "two can work better than one and so have a larger profit" (*Proverbs, Ecclesiastes, Song of Songs*, 308).

137. Longman, *The Book of Ecclesiastes*, 142.

138. Seow, for example, notes: "The switch from the third person to the first poses a difficult problem for the interpreter. The identity of the speaker is unknown: it is either Qohelet himself or the miser. Not surprisingly, therefore, interpreters sometimes add words to clarify the issue" (*Ecclesiastes*, 181).

While 4:1–3 and 4–6 conclude with a better-saying, and vv. 7–12 have such a saying in the centre, vv. 13–16 start with a better-saying. This saying compares a poor but wise youth favourably against a foolish old king. However, as the section proceeds considerable doubt is cast upon how much the one really is better than the other. In looking at "all the people who go about under the sun," in the middle of the passage, Qohelet realises that ultimately it makes little if any difference: the irony is that the second (the poor, wise youth who follows the foolish old king?) is actually no better than the first. Indeed, Wright concludes his article on this passage by asserting,

> The story in its present context is not primarily about the advantage of wisdom or its vulnerability, or about the transient nature of human achievement and popularity, or about the fact that power makes people foolish, nor does the story primarily illustrate v. 13, although all of those ideas remain in the background for readers rightly to supply as they may wish on a secondary level to explain the causality of the story. *But the primary point of the narrative in its present context is that a "second" is not always an advantage.*[139]

Again the question arises: What is good, or better, in this context?[140] The ambiguity of this passage runs deeper, though.[141]

There is a balance in these verses between the king and the youth: מלך is used twice and מלכות once; ילד also occurs twice and נולד once. However, it is not clear whether it is the same king and the same youth referred to each time, and when explicit reference to either ceases

139. Addison G. Wright, SS, "The Poor But Wise Youth and the Old But Foolish King (Qoh 4:13–16)," in *Wisdom, You Are my Sister: Studies in Honor of Roland E. Murphy, O. Carm., on the Occasion of His Eightieth Birthday* (ed. Michael L. Barré; CBQMS 29; Washington: The Catholic Biblical Association of America, 1997), 142–54 (154), my emphasis.

140. Seow observes: "In the end, then, Qohelet casts doubt on the durability of the things that are better. Even those that are 'better' are not ultimately enduring or reliable" (*Ecclesiastes*, 192).

141. Wright himself observes: "The interpretation of this passage is a very tangled thing. The use of pronouns and the use of verbs with unidentified subjects as well as a very terse style combine to create a number of ambiguities internal to the story" ("The Poor But Wise Youth," 142). Wright outlines the main ambiguities along the same general lines as I do here (quite independently). Longman writes: "The anecdote is surprisingly ambiguous in its second part (vv. 15–16)" (*The Book of Ecclesiastes*, 144). Salyer says: "The story told contains numerous ambiguous details and remains hermeneutically open" (*Vain Rhetoric*, 312). Huwiler suggests: "the ambiguity is so embedded in the narration . . . that it may be preferable to leave the story unclear" (*Proverbs, Ecclesiastes, Song of Songs*, 193). See also, Michael V. Fox, "What Happens in Qohelet 4:13–16," *JHStud* 1 (1997): 1–9.

towards the end of v. 15, it becomes impossible to work out for certain to whom the pronominal suffixes refer. The ambiguity starts in v. 14 where either the king or the youth could be the subject of the two verbs and the pronominal suffix: indeed, Longman asserts, "Due to syntactical diffi- culties, it is *impossible* to be dogmatic about the antecedent of the subject of the subordinate clause (*though he came from* . . .)."[142] Hence we might interpret vv. 13–14 as either,

> Better a poor and wise youth than an old and foolish king who no longer knows to heed warning—for the old king rose from prison to kingship, although he, like the youth, was born poor in his kingdom.[143]

or,

> Better a poor and wise youth than an old and foolish king who no longer knows to heed warning—for the youth rose from prison to kingship (hence deposing the foolish old king) even though he had been born poor in his kingdom (either the youth's kingdom as it became, or the foolish old king's kingdom).[144]

Both readings are grammatically feasible, and the ambiguity may be intentional—especially in the light of the continuing uncertainty in the following verses.

The next difficulty, what Irwin terms "the crux of interpretation,"[145] concerns the expression הילד השני in v. 15. It might be read "the second

142. Longman, *The Book of Ecclesiastes*, 146, my emphasis.

143. Provan notes that "The crucial matter of interpretation relates to the identity of the youth in verse 15," and goes on to argue that the "more natural reading" is "to understand 'he may have come from prison' in verse 14 . . . as referring to the king: The king himself had once been a poor but wise youth, and (a better translation [than NIV's upon which his commentary is based]) 'came out from prison to rule even though in his future kingdom he was born poor'" (*Ecclesiastes, Song of Songs*, 107). See also Garrett, *Proverbs, Ecclesiastes, Song of Songs*, 309.

144. Most of the English versions seem to assume that the youth is the subject of v. 14, and this is made explicit in NIV, NLT and NJPSV. NRSV uses an impersonal form, "*One* can indeed come out of prison to reign, even though born poor in the kingdom"; see also REB. Seow states: "The subject of the verb is unclear, although the undistinguished youngster in v. 13a is probably meant" (*Ecclesiastes*, 184). Fox asserts: "The subject of 'came forth' is the youth, not the old king, for the king's past is irrelevant." He also argues that גם במלכותו.נולד רש should be rendered, "in his rule too a poor man was born" (*A Time to Tear Down*, 225). Ogden and Zogbo take this verse to refer to the youth, but the youth for them is Joseph (*A Handbook*, 144– 46). See also Graham S. Ogden, "Historical Allusion in Qoheleth 4:13–16?," *VT* 30 (1980): 309–15, and Ogden, *Qoheleth*, 70–74.

145. W. A. Irwin, "Eccles. 4,13–16," *JNES* 3 (1944): 255–57 (256). Murphy notes: "In v. 14 the references are vague: the subject of the two verbs, and the person indicated by the suffix in מלכותו" (*Ecclesiastes*, 41).

youth," and a number of commentators read this to mean that where the first youth deposed the foolish king, another youth will come along, win the support of "everyone who goes about under the sun," and depose the first youth.[146] Other commentators find here an unusual, but not unprecedented, Hebrew construction whereby the phrase means either, "the youth, the second" (of the above—i.e. the wise youth as opposed to the foolish king),[147] or "the youth, the successor" (to the king—i.e. the second in line).[148] The introduction of the expression without any prior reference to another youth may serve both to recall the previous verses and to raise questions about who is referred to here.

תחתיו at the end of the verse is also ambiguous. It could be a synonym for תחת השמש at the end of the first half of the verse,[149] but more likely תחת is being used in a different sense to indicate that the youth "succeeds him" as king.[150] However, this leaves open the question whether it is the youth mentioned earlier who succeeds the king, or a second youth who succeeds the first youth. This, of course, is related to how one understands הילד השני earlier in the verse. Then the plural suffix on לפניהם in the first part of v. 16, אין־קץ לכל־העם לכל אשר־היה לפניהם, may refer to the foolish old king and the youth, or to כל־העם.[151] Moreover, כל אשר־היה לפניהם could be read temporally, "all who were before them (in time),"[152] or spatially, "all whom he was over"[153] (which seems to make

146. E.g. Crenshaw, *Ecclesiastes*, 113–14; Fox, *Qohelet*, 207–8; Longman, *The Book of Ecclesiastes*, 145–46; Murphy, *Ecclesiastes*, 41; Seow, *Ecclesiastes*, 185, 191; Whybray, *Ecclesiastes*, 89–90. This is made explicit in REB: "I saw his place taken by *yet another* young man."

147. E.g. Eaton, *Ecclesiastes*, 96. Cf. Irwin, "Eccles. 4,13–16," 256. This is the sense conveyed in most of the English versions (see ESV, NIV, NJB, NLT, NRSV, NJPSV).

148. See Gordis, *Koheleth*, 162, 245. 1 Kgs 22:27 and Ps 60:5 offer near parallels to this construction using a noun where an adjective is used here. However, Gordis argues that there is an exact parallel in the phrases in Hos 2:9, אל אישי הראשון, which he maintains should be translated, "to my husband, who was the first."

149. This is the view taken by Ogden (*Qoheleth*, 73). But one of the grounds for his argument is that a new section begins at v. 15, so that the pronominal suffix does not refer back to v. 14. Perry regards vv. 15–16 as Kohelet's response to the Pessimist (*Dialogues with Kohelet*, 100).

150. So far as I can see, this is the position taken by all the main English versions and most of the commentators.

151. Murphy observes, "לפניהם can be construed as referring to the rulers, but more likely it refers to the people. Hence either translation is possible: '(the people) who lived before them (kings),' or '(the People) whom he led'" (*Ecclesiastes*, 41).

152. See, e.g., Crenshaw, *Ecclesiastes*, 112, 114; Garrett, *Proverbs, Ecclesiastes, Song of Songs*, 309; Ogden and Zogbo, *A Handbook*, 148. So also KJV (but not NKJV), NAS, NIV, NJPSV.

better sense of the singular verb, though העם could be the singular subject of היה even though its sense is plural[154]). לפני is used both temporally[155] and spatially[156] elsewhere in Ecclesiastes.

A further complication is added by the word בו at the end of the next part of the verse, גם האחרונים לא ישמחו־בו: if היה means "he was" rather than "the people were,"[157] then presumably the same "he" is referred to here. In this case the verse could be interpreted, "There was no end to all the people whom he ruled, yet those who come after will take no pleasure in him." But if כל אשר־היה לפניהם is translated as "all who were before them," the singular suffix is more striking and may indicate that "he" is not one of "them"—"There was no end to all the people who were before them [the king and the first youth?], but those who come after will not even rejoice in him [the second youth?]."[158] However, בו could refer to the singular noun, העם, particularly if this is also the subject of the singular verb היה, giving the translation either, "There was no end to all the people whom he ruled, yet those who come after will take no pleasure in them," or "There was no end to all the people who were before them, but those who come after will take no pleasure in them." The sentiments are then very similar to 1:11.

Thus Murphy is surely right when he says, "Any translation, and hence interpretation, of vv. 13–16 is uncertain, because of the vagueness of the text."[159] In fact, though, none of these ambiguities makes any difference to the overall sense of the passage: despite anyone's remarkable rise to power and regardless of their wisdom or folly, such people will still be

---

153. See, e.g., Eaton, *Ecclesiastes*, 96; Fox, *Qohelet*, 208; Whybray, *Ecclesiastes*, 90. So also ESV, NJB, NKJV, NLT, NRSV.

154. LXX, Vulgate and Syriac have the plural verb here.

155. 1:10, 16; 2:7, 9.

156. 3:14 and 8:12, 13; 2:26 and 7:26; 5:1, 5; 10:5. The form לפניהם (with the third person plural suffix) is used elsewhere in Ecclesiastes only in 9:1, but the uncertainties surrounding that verse mean that it is of little help in deciding the meaning of the word in 4:16.

157. Murphy observes that "The subject of היה could be the people . . . or the successor(s) to the throne" (*Ecclesiastes*, 41).

158. Most of the English versions have something like NRSV's "yet those who come later will not rejoice in him," where it is not quite clear whether "him" refers to the youth or the king.

159. Murphy, *Ecclesiastes*, 42. Seow says: "In 4:13–16 we find a tantalizing text. The opening *ṭôb-saying* seems clear enough, but the details which illustrate the saying are rather obscure and confusing" (*Ecclesiastes*, 190). Whybray goes so far as to say, "This passage . . . is one of the most difficult in the book, and has been interpreted in a variety of ways" (*Ecclesiastes*, 88).

forgotten by those who come after—and any "good" that may have been gained will be wiped out.[160] Indeed, Murphy acknowledges this in relation to v. 16 when he writes,

> The text is ambiguous and translations differ. . . . But it is at least clear that Qoheleth is underscoring that a king falls out of favor with succeeding generations. Such is the fickleness of the populace and the fate of royal power: vanity! Since the point of the story is the ephemeral character of popularity, it makes no difference who is identified as the subject of v. 16 (the original youth, or the second who succeeded him).[161]

The ambiguity operates on a different level—it raises questions about who is being referred to throughout the passage, forcing the reader to work hard to try to pin down the references. This may also explain the "historical ring" that Seow claims we find in the passage,[162] and his comment that "Those who find historical allusions in the passage are divided, however, about the nature of the allusions."[163] Perhaps the purpose is to indicate that they cannot precisely be tied down because they refer to everyone.[164] This means that the questions concerning *what* is good can be expanded to include *who* it is good for.

4:17–5:6 (Eng. 5:1–7[165]) is clearly a passage concerned with speech, or, more accurately, restrained speech. This is conveyed by the abundance of words related to speech: five words from the root נדר, which is found only here in Ecclesiastes (5:3 [×3], 4 [×2]); four words from the root דבר (5:1 [×2], 2, 6); two references to "your mouth" (פיך, 5:1, 5); two uses of the word קול (5:2, 5); and one word from the root אמר. There are repeated exhortations to be restrained in what one says:

---

160. This despite Irwin's assertion that "this is one of the difficult passages of a none-too-easy book. Its confusion of pronominal antecedents is characteristic of Hebrew usage at its worst" ("Eccles. 4,13–16," 255).

161. Murphy, *Ecclesiastes*, 43. Similarly, Longman states: "Though we cannot grasp the precise interpretation of this section, the moral lesson is obvious" (*The Book of Ecclesiastes*, 147). Wright also, after listing the various ambiguities in the text, gives a rough outline of the story it tells ("The Poor But Wise Youth," 144).

162. See also Fox, *A Time to Tear Down*, 227–28; Ogden, "Historical Allusion"; and Domonic Rudman, "A Contextual Reading of Ecclesiastes 4:13–16," *JBL* 116 (1997): 57–73.

163. Seow, *Ecclesiastes*, 190. Seow ascribes the same "historical ring" to 10:16–17 and 9:13–15.

164. We might note that Salyer complains that "Although Fox and Wright note the extensive problems this [the ambiguities in 4:13–16] creates for the reader, both attempt to 'resolve' the problems rather than attempt to understand the rhetorical effect this ambiguity has for the reader" (*Vain Rhetoric*, 134).

165. All references in this section follow the Hebrew verse numbering.

אל־תבהל על־פיך	5:1a
אל־ימהר להוציא דבר לפני האלהים	5:1b
יהיו דבריך מעטים	5:1c
כאשר תדר נדר לאלהים אל־תאחר לשלמו	5:3a
את אשר־תדר שלם	5:3b
טוב אשר לא־תדר משתדור ולא תשלם	5:4
אל־תתן את־פיך לחטיא את־בשרך	5:5a
ואל־תאמר לפני המלאך כי שגגה היא	5:5b
למה יקצף האלהים על־קולך	5:5c

Moreover, much speech, or perhaps *un*restrained speech, is associated with fools in 5:2, וקול כסיל ברב דברים; the lack of delight in fools (אין חפץ בכסילים) in 5:3 is probably because they do not fulfil what they vow, that is, they are too ready to speak vows they are unable to carry out; and this is probably the implication of the saying in 4:17, וקרוב לשמע מתת הכסילים זבח, where listening is contrasted with the sacrifice of fools.

Two other features of this passage bear noting. First, there is a greater emphasis on God here than anywhere else in Ecclesiastes—האלהים occurs throughout the passage as indicated below (and there is some debate about whether or not המלאך in v. 5a should also read האלהים[166]):

האלהים	4:17
האלהים	5:1a
האלהים	5:1b
—	5:2
האלהים	5:3
—	5:4
<u>המלאך</u>	5:5a
האלהים	5:5b
האלהים	5:6

Moreover, the passage starts and finishes with imperatives concerned with how people should conduct themselves before God, and has an exhortation not to delay fulfilling vows to God at its very centre (with the word האלהים exactly at the centre of the whole passage):

---

166. LXX and Syriac assume האלהים here, but this is perhaps what one might expect. Fox argues that "The two readings must be granted equal textual claim to validity. From the literary perspective, however, 'to God' seems the preferable reading, for it is the expression used in 5:1, and its repetition gives a tighter structure to the passage" (*Qohelet*, 209). However, it may be a human intermediary between God and humanity that is envisaged, perhaps a temple priest although only in Mal. 2:7 is the term used elsewhere of a priest. This reading is also typical of Qohelet's propensity for using unexpected terms, and is adopted by, among others, Crenshaw, *Ecclesiastes*, 117; Eaton, *Ecclesiastes*, 100; Ogden, *Qoheleth*, 79; and Whybray, *Ecclesiastes*, 96.

4:17   <u>שׁמר</u> רגליך כאשׁר תלך אל־בית האלהים

5:3   כאשׁר תדר נדר לאלהים אל־תאחר לשׁלמו

5:6   את־האלהים <u>ירא</u>

Thus the passage is about careful speech to God. However, in the case of both 4:17 and 5:6 the question arises whether it is simply appropriate respect for God that is called for, or more a sense of being on your guard: Is "watching your feet" about bowing in reverence, or about taking care before a powerful God? Is "fear" simply the appropriate attitude before an awesome God,[167] or is it terror of a transcendent God whose ways are beyond our ken?[168] These two possibilities are important throughout the passage, and are reflected in the contrast between Whybray's and Loader's responses to 5:1. Whybray argues:

> It is quite erroneous to interpret this saying as meaning that prayer is useless because God is unconcerned with human affairs: Qoheleth does not advise his readers not to pray, but rather to remember God's awesome sovereignty and to address him carefully as one would a human superior.[169]

By contrast, Loader contends:

> This is certainly one of the most telling pronouncements that enlightens our study of the Preacher's God-concept. God is the far off remote power; there is a gap between him and human beings. It is not possible to bridge it by way of speech. Prayer is not so much wrong as senseless.[170]

Longman is correct to say that, "Qohelet's tone in this section is hard to determine," and to argue that "The context of the entire book will have to be kept in mind" as we seek to understand the implications of these verses[171] (although we need to build up our concept of "the context of the entire book" by reference to the individual passages in the book such as this one).

---

167. Brown puts it thus: "Simplicity in speech is key, for it reflects the integrity of the speaker and *genuine reverence* for God" (*Ecclesiastes*, 56, my emphasis). He adds later: "Divine reverence or 'fear of God' . . . is entirely real and eminently edifying, for it constitutes the compulsive, moral force behind the fulfillment of duty and the driving rationale behind discriminating, thoughtful speech" (p. 57).

168. Fox uses the word "trepidation" of this passage (*A Time to Tear Down*, 229).

169. Whybray, *Ecclesiastes*, 94. See also Ogden, *Qoheleth*, 77; Eaton, *Ecclesiastes*, 98–99. It is perhaps noteworthy that Crenshaw and Fox who generally take a pessimistic view of Ecclesiastes, are more circumspect in respect of a pessimistic interpretation of this verse. Indeed, Fox concedes that "this unit is remarkable for the conventionality of its content" (*Qohelet*, 209).

170. Loader, *Ecclesiastes*, 58.

171. Longman, *The Book of Ecclesiastes*, 148–49.

Secondly, this is the first section in Ecclesiastes that is cast in the second person.[172] It contains three imperatives (שְׁמֹר, שַׁלֵּם and יְרָא in 4:17; 5:3, 6 respectively); five negative exhortations (אַל־תְּבַהֵל and אַל־תַּמְהֵר אַל־תּוֹצִא in 5:1; אַל־תְּאַחֵר in 5:3; and אַל־תִּתֵּן and אַל־תֹּאמַר in 5:5); five other uses of the second person form of the verb (תֵּלֵך in 4:17; תִּדֹּר twice in 5:3 and once in 5:4; and תְּשַׁלֵּם in 5:4); eight occurrences of the second person singular pronominal suffix (see 4:17; 5:1 [×3], 5 [×4]); and one use of the second person singular pronoun אַתָּה. This makes for a very heavy emphasis on "you" (the reader or the hearer [perhaps "the assembly"], presumably), second only in intensity to 11:9–10. It seems, then, that if this passage does conclude the discussion of "what is good/ better" in ch. 4, having explored various aspects of "the good," Qohelet now finishes by addressing the reader/hearer directly (a trait we have noticed in relation to other themes in the book, and, indeed, a feature of the book as a whole). Perhaps the implication is, having explored what is "good" or "better" (and discovered this to be somewhat problematic), *this* is what I, Qohelet, now recommend to be "good" for you—and, as we will see, *not* good for you.

The saying in 4:17 appears to expand on what it means to "watch your feet when you go to the house of God." The most striking feature of the saying, however, is precisely that as it stands it is not a better-saying because it does not contain the word טוֹב. It does, though, contain the comparative *mem*, and the infinitive absolute (if such it is), קָרוֹב, with which the phrase commences, might suggest either that something is missing or that we should assume an ellipsis of the טוֹב.[173] 9:17, where we find what looks like a better-saying of the same type as in the verses before and after it, but without the טוֹב which both those verses contain, offers a parallel—the difference in this case being precisely that there are better-sayings either side which may give the reader grounds for assuming

---

172. There are no second person verbs as such in the book until this passage, where 10 out of a total of 39 are to be found. However, there is one imperative in 1:10 and two in 2:1, but none of these is addressed to the reader. The three imperatives in this passage make up over a tenth of the total of 28. Aside from one second person suffix in 2:1, where Qohelet addresses himself, the first of these occurs here, too. There are eight in this passage out of a total of 54. We might note, though, Salyer's comment: "although this is the first place in the book where Qoheleth *directly* addresses the reader, the reader is *indirectly* addressed by the rhetorical questions which abound in the first third of this book (cf. 1:3; 2:2, 12, 15, 19, 22, 25; 3:9, 21, 22; 4:8, 11)" (*Vain Rhetoric*, 152 n. 90).

173. However, Seow argues: "But apart from the need to assume an ellipsis, the syntax of the verse is awkward, with the juxtaposition of an infinitive absolute and a prefixed infinitive construct" (*Ecclesiastes*, 194).

it should be read similarly. This is less the case here where the last such saying was in 4:13, and the next is in 5:4. Thus, even if this is the conclusion the reader comes to, he or she will need to work hard to arrive at that conclusion. A number of English translations do read it as a better-saying along similar lines to NRSV's "to draw near to listen *is better* than to offer the sacrifice of fools."[174] However, the infinitive absolute could continue the sense of the finite imperative verb שְׁמֹר with which the verse began,[175] giving a reading like that found in the NAS, "Guard your steps as you go to the house of God *and draw near* to listen rather than to offer the sacrifice of fools."[176] Gordis suggests yet another possibility:[177] he argues on the basis of the use of קָרֹב in Pss 75:2; 119:151 and Job 17:2 that the word may have the sense "praise, glorify," and could be read here as an adjective meaning "it is more praiseworthy."[178] This line is followed in the translation in NJPSV, "*more acceptable* is obedience than the offering of fools." NJPSV also takes שְׁמַע to mean "obey"[179] rather than "hear" or "listen": the former would bring the sentiments of Eccl 4:17 very close to those expressed in 1 Sam 15:22:[180]

ויאמר שמואל החפץ ליהוה בעלות וזבחים כשמע בקול יהוה
הנה שמע מזבח טוב להקשיב מחלב אילים׃

174. See, e.g., ESV, GNB, NJB, REB; also Murphy, *Ecclesiastes*, 44–45; Ogden and Zogbo, *A Handbook*, 151.

175. So also Longman, *The Book of Ecclesiastes*, 149. But Seow notes: "The infinitive absolute of *qrb* is not attested anywhere, however, and the comparative *min* in *mittēt* makes this reading problematic" (*Ecclesiastes*, 194).

176. See also NIV, NKJV.

177. Another possibility is put forward by Perry who maintains that God is the subject of קָרוֹב, which along with the following infinitive should be rendered, "and [he is] near to hearing"—"omission of God's name as the subject of the verb is not uncommon. . . . Alternatively, the subject is carried over from the previous word *ʾelohim*" (*Dialogues with Kohelet*, 102). Perry's argument is unconvincing, and in any case does not produce a good reading.

178. See also Garrett, *Proverbs, Ecclesiastes, Song of Songs*, 310; Seow, *Ecclesiastes*, 194; and Fox, who explains that "*Qarob* apparently means 'near to God's favor,' 'acceptable'. . . . Though it is not elsewhere used of actions, in 1 Kgs 8:59 words of prayer are said to be "near to the Lord" meaning acceptable to him" (*A Time to Tear down*, 230).

179. See also REB; Brown, *Ecclesiastes*, 55; Farmer, *Who Knows What is Good?*, 167; Ogden and Zogbo, *A Handbook*, 151.

180. Numerous commentators draw the connection with this verse: e.g. Brown, *Ecclesiastes*, 55; Crenshaw, *Ecclesiastes*, 115; Davis, *Proverbs, Ecclesiastes, and the Song of Songs*, 192; Farmer, *Who Knows What is Good?*, 167; Murphy, *Ecclesiastes*, 50. Seow warns against making too much of this comparison for much the reasons I give here (*Ecclesiastes*, 194).

However, "hear" or "listen" provides a more striking contrast with the unrestrained words that Qohelet warns against in the rest of the passage, and it is not sacrifice as such which is criticised, but the particular kind of sacrifice offered by fools (that is, too many words). Nonetheless, the question remains: Is this something Qohelet is saying is "better," or not?

Matters are further complicated by the last part of the verse, which appears to offer an explanation of the preceding saying. The grammar is straightforward, but most commentators struggle with its meaning. It might be translated, "for they do not know to do evil," and the most obvious reading of the phrase is "for they do not know *how* to do evil." This is often rejected because, as Barton argues, "it is obviously contrary to Q.'s thought."[181] Various attempts have been made to get round this difficulty by emending the text or postulating a different meaning for the *lamed*,[182] but if we are to remain true to the MT (particularly when there is no good textual evidence for doing otherwise), perhaps we should follow Fox when he says, "Since the MT is clear and grammatically feasible, I translate the sentence literally without understanding its point."[183] This would mean that there is some uncertainty here about how "to do evil" (לעשׂות רע) should be understood (and, indeed, Ogden and Zogbo make the fair point that "evil" may not be the best way to translate רע anyway[184]), rather than the questions over the meaning of "good" we met

181. G. Barton, *Ecclesiastes*, 125.

182. Fox explains these suggestions, but concludes, "An emendation would be in order if that would solve the problem, but none proposed so far is persuasive" (*A Time to Tear Down*, 230–31). Seow, however, argues that "There is, in fact, no need to emend the text" because the phrase "*yādā' la'ăśôt rā'* means 'to know of doing evil,' that is, 'to recognize doing evil.' It does not mean 'to know *how to* do evil'" (*Ecclesiastes*, 194–95). Much the same position is taken by Longman, *The Book of Ecclesiastes*, 150–51; Ogden, *Qoheleth*, 76; Whybray, *Ecclesiastes*, 93—but he concedes that the phrase "would normally mean 'they do not know how to do evil,'" adding "but in the context this meaning is highly improbable." This may be possible, but does not readily remove the struggle at least the modern reader has in making sense of the text as it stands in the light of the usually meaning of ידע elsewhere in the Hebrew Bible generally and Ecclesiastes specifically, and it may well be that ancient readers too would have had to work hard to figure out what it meant. Davis states: "The Hebrew reads, 'For they do not know *how to do evil*'; and this is exactly what Koheleth means. If they are 'good,' according to the conventional definition of that term it is simply because they are not even smart enough to be wicked!" (*Proverbs, Ecclesiastes, and the Song of Songs*, 192).

183. Fox, *A Time to Tear Down*, 231.

184. They explain, "The majority of uses of this adjective (as distinct from the form *rasha'*) in Qoheleth carry the idea of something disastrous and painful, not of moral failure and evil." They conclude, "Therefore the fool here is not doing something morally outrageous but something stupid" (*A Handbook*, 152).

earlier.[185] Nonetheless, it does seem that the following verses give advice for avoiding such "evil" and thus approach the question of "what is good" from the other side.

By contrast with 4:17, 5:4 clearly is a better-saying, and its translation is straightforward. Indeed, I can find no significant variation in translation among the English versions and commentators. What is more difficult to understand is why there is so much weight placed on fulfilling vows. This emphasis is achieved by repeating effectively the same thing three times in different words:

לשלמו	לאלהים אל־תאחר	כאשר תדר נדר
שלם		. . . את אשר־תדר
תשלם	משתדור ולא	טוב אשר לא־תדר

"Vowing" is emphasised by using five words from the root נדר, and "fulfilling" is emphasised by three different forms of the verb שלם, each placed at the end of the clause, including the imperative issuing a direct command to the reader, "what you vow, *fulfil!*" which is particularly stark because of its unusual construction and the abruptness with which it appears in the verse. Verse 3 bears a striking resemblance to Deut 23:22 (Eng. 23:21), and indeed Eccl 5:3–5 may well allude directly to Deut 23:22–24 (as many commentators observe[186]):

אל־תאחר לשלמו	לאלהים	תדר נדר	Eccl 5:3
לא תאחר לשלמו	אלהיך	תדר נדר ליהוה	Deut 23:22

Might it be that Murphy is correct to note "a subtle difference between Deuteronomy and Ecclesiastes?" He continues, "In the former the emphasis is on making vows, rather than on not making them; while in Ecclesiastes it is the other way around: the preference is not to make them lest they be unfulfilled"[187] (but Longman goes too far when he claims that Qohelet "encourages them not to make vows in the first place"[188]). This would figure if Eccl 5:1b is an ironic allusion to Deut 4:35–40 in general and v. 39 in particular:

185. Murphy says the phrase אינם יודעים לעשות רע is "ambiguous" (*Ecclesiastes*, 46).

186. E.g. Fox, *A Time to Tear Down*, 232. He also notes, "Hasty vows are warned against in Prov 20:25 and Sir 18:22f., and payment of vows is demanded in Num 30:3 and Ps 50:14b." It may also be that there is an allusion also to Ps 115:3, ואלהינו בשמים כל אשר־חפץ עשה.

187. Murphy, *Ecclesiastes*, 50.

188. Longman, *The Book of Ecclesiastes*, 153. (See also Crenshaw, *Ecclesiastes*, 117.) Indeed, Perry argues that "Some have used these verses to prove that K discourages vows, but the case seems to be the opposite" (*Dialogues with Kohelet*, 103–4).

Eccl 5:1   כי   האלהים בשמים <u>ואתה</u> על־הארץ
Deut 4:39   כי   יהוה הוא האלהים בשמים ממעל ועל־הארץ בתחת

(The following verse, Deut 4:40, notably includes the phrase אשר ייטב
לך.) This raises the question whether Eccl 5:1 is a confirmation of such
sentiments, or whether it calls them into question, "God is in heaven, but
you are on earth." On the one hand, Longman states, "We take this statement not as an assertion of divine power, but of divine distance, perhaps
even indifference," although he concedes that "the tone of the verse is
once again ambiguous, and the verse could conceivably be read two
ways."[189] On the other hand, Brown asserts, "'God is in heaven,' and the
gulf that separates the creature from the creator mandates sparseness of
speech that reflects integrity and proper reverence. . . . God's transcen-
dence is far from connoting divine indifference to human conduct and
petition."[190]

Following on from the statement in 3:22, which starts "there is nothing
better for people," it does seem clear that better-sayings are an important
feature in this passage from ch. 4, and it may also be that the passage
concludes with the second person passage in 4:17–5:6, which includes
one clear example of a better-saying, and one seemingly incomplete
better-saying. But at the end of this section of the book, the reader is still
left with many questions about what actually is better: Is life or death to
be preferred? Is one better, or two, or perhaps three? Is it better to work
or to rest? Is it better to be young, wise and poor than old, foolish and
king? Is it better to be the king's successor? And actually, if there is
something better to be achieved, for whom is it better? It certainly seems
that in 4:17–5:6 Qohelet advises the reader that it is better to be careful
in speech before God than to rush into vows that one is unable to keep—
but is this because God is distant and unpredictable, or is it out of due
respect for an awesome God?

The highest concentration of better-sayings in Ecclesiastes (and,
indeed, as Ogden and Zogbo point out, in the whole of the Hebrew
Bible[191]) is to be found in 7:1–8. It is undoubtedly significant, as many
commentators observe, that this series of sayings follows the question in
6:12, מי־יודע מה־טוב לאדם בחיים,[192] just as the earlier series followed on
from 3:22. The passage revolves around these better-sayings: it opens
and closes with two sets of two short better-sayings (thus forming an

189. Longman, *The Book of Ecclesiastes*, 151.
190. Brown, *Ecclesiastes*, 56.
191. Ogden and Zogbo, *A Handbook*, 214.
192. See, e.g., Ogden and Zogbo, *A Handbook*, 214; Murphy, *Ecclesiastes*, 62;
Seow, *Ecclesiastes*, 242.

inclusio[193]), and in between these are three further better-sayings each with supporting statements. This might be represented thus:

proverb	*(inclusio)*	מַשֶּׁמֶן טוב	טוב שֵׁם	v. 1
proverb		מִיּוֹם הִוָּלְדוֹ:	וּ(טוֹב) יום המות	
proverb		מֵֽלֶכֶת אֶל־בֵּית מִשְׁתֶּה	טוב ללכת אֶל־בֵּית־אֵבֶל	v. 2
explanation		בַּאֲשֶׁר הוא סוף כָּל־הָאָדָם וְהַחַי יִתֵּן אֶל־לִבּוֹ:		
proverb		מִשְּׂחֹק	טוב כַּעַס	v. 3
explanation		כִּי־בְרֹעַ פָּנִים יִיטַב לֵב:		
explanation		לֵב הַחֲכָמִים בְּבֵית אֵבֶל וְלֵב כְּסִילִים בְּבֵית שִׂמְחָה:		v. 4
proverb		מֵאִישׁ שֹׁמֵעַ שִׁיר כְּסִילִים:	טוב לִשְׁמֹעַ גַּעֲרַת חָכָם	v. 5
explanation		כִּי כְקוֹל הַסִּירִים תַּחַת הַסִּיר כֵּן שְׂחֹק הַכְּסִיל וְגַם־זֶה הָבֶל:		v. 6
explanation		כִּי הָעֹשֶׁק יְהוֹלֵל חָכָם וִיאַבֵּד אֶת־לֵב מַתָּנָה:		v. 7
proverb	*(inclusio)*	מֵרֵאשִׁיתוֹ	טוב אַחֲרִית דָּבָר	v. 8
proverb		מִגְּבַהּ־רוּחַ:	טוב אֶרֶךְ־רוּחַ	

It thus appears that, as Ogden and Zogbo state, "This series of 'better' sayings . . . provides us with Qoheleth's answer to the question in 6:12."[194] But what kind of an answer does it provide. Seow argues:

> The effect of the overall presentation is to show that it is indeed true that no one—not even the sages, the teachers who propounded the *ṭôb-sayings* —knows what is really *ṭôb* "good" or "better" for humanity in general. Each saying may contain an element of truth, but the sum total of these many words is "vanity"—just so much empty talk.[195]

He explains:

> The author employs a rhetoric of subversion. He deliberately presents each proposition in aphoristic style, and then carries the argument to its logical conclusion in order to show that the proposition is of dubious value. In this way, he undermines any confidence in the reliability of the "good advice," such as the advice that one typically gets in the didactic wisdom tradition.[196]

Murphy's approach is similar when he argues that "Qoheleth is dialoguing with traditional wisdom, and modifying it."[197] Fox, however, states

---

193. But Ogden and Zogbo maintain that "verse 8 with its double 'better' saying *clearly* starts a new subsection" (*A Handbook*, 229, my emphasis).

194. Ogden and Zogbo, *A Handbook*, 214.

195. Seow, *Ecclesiastes*, 242–43.

196. Ibid., 244.

197. For a slightly different approach, see Perry, *Dialogues with Kohelet*, 118–19.

that Qohelet is "serious about the advice itself and does *not* undermine its validity" (emphasis added), pointing out that "The weakness of this approach [that is, Murphy's, and the same would apply to Seow] is its arbitrariness in separating out traditional wisdom from Qohelet's."[198] Longman argues:

> There is a link with the question posed at the end of 6:10–12, "who knows what is good for people during the few days of their meaningless life?" That question was rhetorical, indicating that Qohelet felt that there was nothing absolutely good. By the use of the "better-than proverb," however, Qohelet does indicate that some things are better than others. That is, he gives expression to what he believes are relative values.[199]

Provan goes further and asserts that "Qohelet has never deviated from his conviction that some ways of being are better than others. . . . The point is now underlined in the opening verses of ch. 7, as numerous 'good' things (*ṭob*) are described and often compared to 'better' (also *ṭob*) things."[200] Huwiler contends, "In this section Qohelet *qualifies* the negative conclusion of 6:12, which was that knowledge about what is good in life is unavailable to humans. Here Qohelet makes claims about what is good."[201] Clearly the commentators disagree about the significance of this passage, how it relates to 6:12, and in what ways it might answer the question, "what is good?"

Crenshaw describes the first of these sayings as "an exquisite example of chiastic alliteration."[202] This is certainly true. The play on the words שֵׁם and שֶׁמֶן, and on the meaning of טוֹב is typical of Ecclesiastes. However, the literary artistry and the comfortable sentiments serve to heighten the effect of the shocking statement that follows in the second half of the verse (with which we might compare 4:2–3, which we considered above). It would appear that the sense of the first טוֹב carries over into this half of the verse, but its omission serves to speed up the clause and to give it a balanced parallelism in place of the chiasmic arrangement of the first half of the verse. Both halves thus revolve around the comparative *mem*, but in different ways. Both halves also play on the word טוֹב, the first by using it in two different senses, the second seemingly by assuming the sense of a better-saying but without the actual use of the word טוֹב.

198. Fox, *A Time to Tear Down*, 250.
199. Longman, *The Book of Ecclesiastes*, 179.
200. Provan, *Ecclesiastes, Song of Songs*, 139.
201. Huwiler, *Proverbs, Ecclesiastes, Song of Songs*, 199.
202. Crenshaw, *Ecclesiastes*, 133. This is observed by many commentators.

The question arises how the two proverbs in this verse relate to each other. Seow argues that in the second proverb Qohelet challenges the validity of the first (well-known) adage:[203] "He does so by carrying the assumption of the saying to its absurd conclusion: if one's name (memory) is better than the present possession of good, then the day of death is better than the day of birth."[204] This would raise questions about the validity of the first saying—is a "good" name *really* so "good?" However, Fox states simply that "This verse is a proverb of ration: just as a reputation is preferable to good oil so is the day of death preferable to the day of birth."[205]

Verse 2 displays similar precision in the way it is constructed. It consists of two halves—a better-saying and a supporting statement—each of nine words and 28 letters. Moreover, the two elements being compared in the first half are also precisely the same length (in terms of words and letters), as are the two halves of the supporting statement introduced by באשר:

טוב   ללכת אל־בית־אבל
מ־   לכת אל־בית משתה
באשר   הוא סוף כל־האדם
        והחי יתן אל־לבו:

Like the comparisons in the first verse, there is only one word which is different in the two halves of the better-saying here, and this draws particular attention to these words: אבל and משתה. This offers support to the statement in the second half of v. 1,[206] but seems surprising in the light of the verses which issue the "call to enjoyment" where eating and drinking are lauded. Indeed, in 2:24; 3:13 and 8:15, eating and drinking are part of what is described as "given by God"; 8:15 also asserts that there is no good for people *except* to eat, drink and enjoy themselves; and 9:9 exhorts the reader to eat and drink. Seow discusses two possible ways of reading the verse, then concludes:

> In either case, one is left a little uncomfortable and unsure as to what really is *tôb* "good." One is made to ponder if one can really know what is *tôb* "good," after all. That is precisely the point that the text is making:

---

203. Longman contends that "While the first proverb of the verse is traditional, the second is not" (*The Book of Ecclesiastes*, 182).

204. Seow, *Ecclesiastes*, 244.

205. Fox, *A Time to Tear Down*, 251.

206. Thus Ogden and Zogbo assert that "The second of the two 'better' sayings in this verse [v. 1] sets the tone for the next three verses. These explain what Qoheleth means by the saying in the second half of verse 1" (*A Handbook*, 218).

no one really knows what is *ṭôb* for humanity in general and at all times. One can accept what is true and good at any given moment and in a given situation. The clichés about what is "good" or "better" for humanity are just so many words that dissipate as quickly as mist before life's inconsistencies. Even the cleverly constructed and memorable sayings that humans are wont to repeat are, like human beings themselves, all "vanity." They usually come up empty. They are unreliable.[207]

Verse 3 displays similar balance:

טוב כעס
מ־ שׂחק
כי־ ברע פנים
  ייטב לב:

This saying, too, is rather surprising, especially in view of the use of these words elsewhere in the book. The use of כעס in 1:18; 2:23; 5:16; 7:9 and 11:10 seems to imply that this is *not* something desirable—although, of course, "better" does not *necessarily* imply "desirable," but perhaps the point is that the words "good" and "better" are identical in Hebrew:[208]

1:18 כי ברב חכמה רב־כעס ויוסיף דעת יוסיף מכאוב
2:23 כי כל־ימיו מכאבים וכעס ענינו גם־בלילה לא־שכב לבו
5:16 גם כל־ימיו בחשׁך יאכל וכעס הרבה וחליו וקצף
7:9 אל־תבהל ברוחך לכעוס כי כעס בחיק כסילים ינוח:
11:10 והסר כעס מלבך והעבר רעה מבשׂרך

And while laughter, שׂחק, is treated negatively in 2:2, לשׂחוק אמרתי מהולל, it is stated in 3:4 that there is a time for it, and in 10:19 the assertion is made לשׂחוק עשׂים לחם (although this and the other statements in 10:19 may well be double-edged). I commented above on the play on טוב/יטב in 7:3.

An explanation of v. 3 is then given in v. 4, again in a verse that is carefully balanced, and again in a statement that is surprising in the light of the "call to enjoyment" verses:

לב חכמים בבית אבל
ולב כסילים בבית שׂמחה:

This is particularly striking here because of the word שׂמחה—attention is drawn to this word because it disrupts the parallel between this verse and v. 2:

---

207. Seow, *Ecclesiastes*, 246.

208. Indeed, Seow argues, "If taken seriously, the proverb here contradicts Qohelet's own teachings elsewhere in the book" (*Ecclesiastes*, 246).

טוב ללכת אל־   בית־אבל   מלכת אל־   בית משתה
לב הכמים ב   בית אבל   ולב כסילים ב   בית שמחה

Seow maintains that "in vv. 3–4 [Qohelet] caricatures the teachings of traditional sages, and exaggerates their general advice in extreme terms. . . . The sayings are perhaps deliberately ludicrous. By their sheer absurdity, Qohelet challenges the audacity of anyone to tell others what is good."[209] By contrast, Provan argues, "Qohelet has previously written of such things as joy and eating and drinking as aspects of the good life as it is received from God (e.g. 2:24–26). We are not to think, therefore, that these things in themselves are being criticized here. It is, rather, the *pursuit* of them as part of a frivolous and trivializing way of life that is under consideration."[210] Longman, though, asserts that "It is important to feel the tension between this verse and the *carpe diem* passages that appear throughout the book."[211]

Verse 5 introduces some of its own surprises in the light of what precedes it: on the one hand, the verse is surprising because of how *un*surprising are its sentiments when compared to the earlier verses;[212] on the other, it lacks the careful balance of the verses that go before. The symmetry of the two halves of this better-saying is disrupted in two ways: the singular חכם is compared to the plural הכסילים (which may indicate that the rebuke of *even one* wise person is worth more than the singing of *many* fools); and the infinitive verb לשמע in the first half is paralleled by a noun and participial verb, איש שמע, in the second. These make the line sound rather awkward by comparison to the smooth flow and balanced parallelism of the earlier sayings.[213] The lack of intricate structuring

209. Ibid., 246.

210. Provan, *Ecclesiastes, Song of Songs*, 139.

211. Longman, *The Book of Ecclesiastes*, 184. He goes on to argue, "These tensions lead to the conclusion . . . that Qohelet is a confused wise man who doubts the traditions of his people."

212. Ogden and Zogbo note that "Many of these 'better' sayings seem to go against our normal expectations" (*A Handbook*, 214). However, they go on to say of this verse, "again we have a reversal of what we expect; a song is more pleasant than criticism" (p. 224). Nonetheless, the preference for "the criticism of a wise person" over "the song of fools" is unsurprising in its own right (see, e.g., Prov 13:1; 15:31; 17:10; 25:12), and therefore perhaps surprising in this series. Seow argues that "Unlike the other *ṭôb-sayings* presented so far, this one does not appear to be a parody" (*Ecclesiastes*, 247; see also Whybray, *Ecclesiastes*, 115). Brown observes that "The proverbs that comprise roughly the first half of ch. 7 range from the typically conventional (e.g. vv. 1a, 5–6, 8–9, 11–12) to the radical and enigmatic (e.g. vv. 1b–4, 13)" (*Ecclesiastes*, 71).

213. Fox calls this a "lopsided comparison" which he tries to correct by emendation (*A Time to Tear Down*, 252–53).

continues in v. 6, which serves as an effective explanation of v. 5b (although שׁיר כסילים changes to שׂחק כסיל), and in v. 7. The general sense of v. 7 is clear enough (even though there are some difficulties in translation), but it is a decidedly awkward verse when compared with the intricacy and careful balance in vv. 1–4. Moreover, it is difficult to see how it fits in its context. As Ogden and Zogbo explain,

> This verse presents considerable difficulties to the interpreter and translator. Not only are there several words whose meaning is difficult to determine, but the relationship of the verse to what comes before and what follows also is not easy to establish. How does this verse fit with the rest of the chapter? Does it flow naturally from what comes before it, or, as some claim, does it have a kind of independent status?[214]

This means that the verses which present somewhat contentious ideas are quite straightforward and flow beautifully, while the uncontentious statements are awkward and tax the reader's interpretative skills. The "good" or "better" that appears straightforward on one level may, it seems, be more complex on another.

This passage concludes with another two brief better-sayings, the first of which is not quite so neatly balanced as the second:

טוב	אחרית דבר
מ-	ראשׁיתו
טוב	ארך־רוח
מ-	גבה־רוח:

The words אחרית and ראשׁיתו are ambiguous because it is unclear what "beginning" and "end" is intended. דבר could be translated "word,"[215] in which case the sentiments seem to be similar to 4:17–5:6 and to 8:1–6 and 10:12–14. 12:12–13 is also pertinent, although typical of Ecclesiastes, it uses two different words for "end" neither of which is the word used here. However, דבר could also be read as "thing" or "matter," in which case there might be another allusion to a person's death and birth along similar lines to 7:1b,[216] or simply a reference to "endings" generally.[217]

---

214. Ogden and Zogbo, *A Handbook*, 226–27. Ogden and Zogbo discuss the difficulties in some detail, exploring the different options for translation. They are not directly relevant to our study here of the word טוב, but do illustrate the ambiguity of this verse. Fox suggests that something has dropped out, explaining, "4QQoh[a] has space for fifteen to twenty letters after 7:6. . . . Although these letters are lost, the arrangement of the lines on the fragment indicates that something once stood before 7:7" (*A Time to Tear down*, 254).

215. This is the reading followed by the LXX, which uses λόγων.

216. So, e.g., Farmer, *Who Knows What is Good?*, 175; Longman, *The Book of Ecclesiastes*, 187.

The second half of v. 8 is perhaps surprising for its conventional nature. The difficulty here again is working out just how it fits in this context:[218] yes, it may be better to be patient than proud, but in what circumstances is this the case? Perhaps it is used ironically: it is better to be patient in waiting for the end of your life (which is, after all, better than its beginning), than to be proud, say, of what you achieve in your life.

7:9–14 continue to address the question of "what is good?," but with only one of the better-sayings that were so much a feature of the earlier verses. Like the conclusion to 4:1–5:6 (Eng. 4:1–5:7), this passage also concludes in the second person, with two direct exhortations to the reader in v. 9 (אל־תבהל) and v. 10 (אל־תאמר), and the repeated imperative ראה in vv. 13 and 14.

The first exhortation uses twice the word כעס, which appeared in the better-saying in v. 3, and at least stands in tension with that saying:[219]

7:3   טוב כעס משחק כי־ברע פנים ייטב לב:
7:9   אל־תבהל ברוחך לכעוס כי כעס בחיק כסילים ינוח:

The question arises again: Is it, or is it not, better to be angry? Are there times when anger is at least a relative "good," even if at other times it should be avoided?[220] Or is it perhaps *rushing* to anger that is warned against—maybe fools are too quick to get angry,[221] while a wise person

---

217. So, e.g., Ogden and Zogbo (*A Handbook*, 230), who translate, "It is better to finish a task than to begin it."

218. Ogden and Zogbo (*A Handbook*, 230) assert: "we can note a slight connection. To get to the 'end' of a task you must be 'patient.' And at the 'beginning' of a project or task you are tempted to be over-confident ('proud') about your ability and success."

219. Whybray suggest that the word "is used here in a different sense from that which it has in v. 3" (*Ecclesiastes*, 116–17), as do Crenshaw (*Ecclesiastes*, 137), Murphy (*Ecclesiastes*, 65) and Ogden and Zogbo (*A Handbook*, 232), while Fox argues that the context is different (*Qohelet*, 230). However, Longman simply states that "Qohelet contradicts himself concerning *anger*" (*The Book of Ecclesiastes*, 188). Seow not only notes a contradiction between v. 3 and v. 9, but argues that v. 9 also modifies v. 8: "It is fools who are 'patient' . . . in this sense: they nurture their seething anger in secret. Qohelet thus undermines in v. 9 what is said about patience in v. 8. Is patience always better? Is it really better in the case of the fool? The universal applicability of the *ṭôb-sayings* in v. 8 is thus called into question, at least where anger is concerned" (*Ecclesiastes*, 248).

220. Thus Fox argues: "Neither verse makes a statement about anger in all circumstances, and the present verse does not condemn irritation flatly, but only hasty vexation" (*A Time to Tear Down*, 254).

221. Thus Perry translates, "Then do not be quick to put on an angry face" (*Dialogues with Kohelet*, 118).

knows the right time for anger? Or might it be that fools "nurture" anger (playing on the word בְחֵיק),[222] while the wise reserve it for an appropriate situation. Once more, a fairly short, simple, pithy saying proves to be far from straightforward.

The second exhortation seems to address the common matter of "harking back to the 'good old days.' "[223] It seems like good advice, perhaps warning against living in the past, and might be compared with 7:14, which may warn against living for the future.[224] It may also relate to v. 8a and v. 1b, especially if it is understood to deny that the former days were better;[225] but it might stand in some tension with these verses if it is read to say, "Even though the former days were better, it is not wise to ask why this was."[226] It is also possible, as Crenshaw argues, that Qohelet is referring to the confidence the wisdom tradition placed in the "insights that earlier teachers gained," such that "Verse 10 criticizes traditional wisdom as it appears in 7:8–9."[227] However, the most significant point for our discussion is the fact that it exhorts the reader *not* to say that something is better than something else, which is rather ironic in the light of the significance of better-sayings in vv. 1–8. Moreover, this is picked up in the next verse by a saying which is not in fact a better-saying, even though that might be what the reader would have expected: in this context the saying טובה חכמה מֵנַחֲלָה would seem appropriate, but instead the text reads, טובה חכמה עִם־נחלה. Brown is surely correct to say that "this proverb *deliberately* breaks from the typical 'better-than' pattern that characterizes the proverbs of verses 1, 2, 3, 5, and 8."[228] Seow argues

---

222. Fox writes, "More to the point is the image of a baby snuggling in its father's arms. The fool coddles his vexation, nurtures it, lets it grow, while all along, of course, it is gnawing at him" (*Qohelet*, 230).

223. NLT makes this explicit when it renders the verse, "Don't long for 'the good old days,' for you don't know whether they were any better than today." Davis also argues along these lines (*Proverbs, Ecclesiastes, and the Song of Songs*, 201–2).

224. Thus, for example, Brown states: "Regardless of whether the present is fraught with less favorable conditions, the present constitutes the immediate realm of the living from which one cannot and should not try to escape. The present moment carries a morally binding force all its own. Wisdom informs the living of *these* days, not the reliving of the 'former days.' All one can seize is the present, not the past or, for that matter, the future" (*Ecclesiastes*, 77).

225. Fox, for example, maintains that "Qohelet . . . rejects the notion that the present is worse than the past" (*Qohelet*, 230). See also Longman (*The Book of Ecclesiastes*, 189).

226. This is basically the reading followed by Fox, *Qohelet*, 230–31. See also Provan, *Ecclesiastes, Song of Songs*, 141.

227. Crenshaw, *Ecclesiastes*, 137.

228. Brown, *Ecclesiastes*, 77–78, my emphasis.

similarly: "it is striking that Qohelet does not say that wisdom is 'better than' material possessions. Having encountered the 'better than'-proverbs in vv. 1–10, one certainly expects him to use a 'better than' form. But he does not." Seow concludes that "The slight shift in form is part of Qohelet's subversive strategy. We realize that he is saying, after all, that wisdom is only as good as inheritance—and both are in the end unreliable. This is finally how we are to understand the *ṭôb-sayings*: what is *ṭôb* is still ephemeral and unreliable."[229]

The English versions adopt different approaches to the verse: REB renders the verse as a better-saying, "Wisdom *is better than* possessions,"[230] RSV translates literally, "Wisdom is good with an inheritance,"[231] but NRSV modifies this to "Wisdom is *as good as* an inheritance,"[232] and NJPSV goes a step further when it renders the clause, "Wisdom is as good as a patrimony, *and even better*,"[233] while NIV opts for "Wisdom, *like an inheritance*, is a good thing."[234] Similar diversity is found among the commentators. The matter is complicated by the first half of the following verse, which seems to be parallel to v. 11 and has also engendered a range of interpretations:

7:11 טובה חכמה עם־נחלה ויתר לראי השמש׃
7:12 כי בצל החכמה בצל הכסף ויתרון דעת החכמה תחיה בעליה׃

Thus Garrett, after observing, that v. 12 is "a highly abbreviated line" which "has caused a great deal of speculation and discussion," argues that "The easiest solution is to take those who have both wisdom and an inheritance (v. 11) as the implied subject. Thus, 'For [those who possess, both are] in the shadow of wisdom, [they are] in the shadow of money.'"[235] Longman, after describing the verse as "enigmatic" and "cryptic" offers a different translation, but the overall sense is similar: "For *to be* in the shadow of wisdom *is to be* in the shadow of money."[236] Both commentators take this to be a positive comment about wisdom and money,

229. Seow, *Ecclesiastes*, 249.

230. עם might function as a comparative in 2:16a. See also Tamez, *When the Horizons Close*, 97.

231. See also ESV, NAS, NKJV; Crenshaw, *Ecclesiastes*, 133; Garrett, *Proverbs, Ecclesiastes, Song of Songs*, 321; Longman, *The Book of Ecclesiastes*, 181; Perry, *Dialogues with Kohelet*, 118.

232. See also NJB, GNB; Murphy, *Ecclesiastes*, 60; Odgen and Zogbo, *A Handbook*, 235–36; Seow, *Ecclesiastes*, 230.

233. See also NLT.

234. See also Provan, *Ecclesiastes, Song of Songs*, 141–42.

235. Garrett, *Proverbs, Ecclesiastes, Song of Songs*, 321.

236. Longman, *The Book of Ecclesiastes*, 181.

understanding "shadow" as indicating protection.[237] Ogden takes this much further when he argues:

> If we were to ask in what specific manner wisdom could be likened to an inheritance, we find in v. 12 that wisdom and "money" (*kesep*)—the latter we presume is equivalent to "inheritance" in v. 11—both provide "shade" or "protection" (*ṣēl*). . . . It will be obvious why Qoheleth draws on the inheritance concept for illustrative purpose; he believes that wisdom offers some hope of dealing more adequately with the question of death and beyond.[238]

Seow, however, renders the line, "wisdom is as a shadow and money is as a shadow," and argues that "one should understand [Qohelet] to emphasize *not* the protective power of wisdom and money, but their unreliability."[239]

It is clear that interpretation of 7:11 and 12 is not a straightforward matter. Questions arise concerning: why the preposition עם is used rather than the comparative *mem* as earlier in the chapter; whether wisdom and an inheritance alike are being viewed positively or negatively; whether wisdom is simply being likened to an inheritance or in some way contrasted with it (i.e. "*but* wisdom is an advantage . . ."); how the glaring gaps in v. 12a should be filled in order to make sense of the line; what precisely is the "advantage" referred to, and so on. Again this generates considerable ambiguity with regard to the question of just what is "good" or "better" in the book of Ecclesiastes.

7:13–14 are important verses in relation to the significance of the word טוב in this book. The wordplay on טוב is typical of Ecclesiastes and illustrates the difficulty of pinning down the precise meaning of the word in any given instance (and we should note also the play on the words רעה and ראה). The use of expressions not found elsewhere in the Hebrew Bible, היה בטוב[240] and על־דברת ש-, adds further to the sense of indeterminacy. The incomplete parallelism between טוב and רעה is particularly

---

237. Indeed, Longman maintains that "it is *clear* that what is meant is protection, presumably from the hard realities of life" (*The Book of Ecclesiastes*, 190, my emphasis). This is the understanding of most commentators: so, for example, Ogden and Zogbo assert that "this verse means '*As* the protection of wisdom, *so* is the protection of money'" (*A Handbook*, 237).

238. Ogden, *Qoheleth*, 109. Longman describes this as "a particularly tortuous understanding of the verse with the intention of reading Qohelet as a positive, orthodox wise man" (*The Book of Ecclesiastes*, 190).

239. Seow, *Ecclesiastes*, 249–50, my emphasis.

240. See Ps 25:13 and Job 21:13 for reasonably close parallels involving the word בטוב. The closest parallels using both the word טוב and the verb היה are to be found in Eccl 7:10; 8:12 and Jer 44:17.

noteworthy, especially when the clause about ‏רעה‎ leads straight into a
statement which affirms that God makes both:

‏ביום טובה היה   בטוב‎
‏וביום רעה   ראה‎
‏גם את־זה לעמת־זה‎
‏עשה האלהים‎

The ascription of both to God further calls into question the whole enterprise of seeking to establish what is "good" as opposed to what is "bad."
Moreover, the implications of the question about the work of God in
v. 13, ‏מי יוכל לתקן את אשר עותו‎, may be that, even if one can discern
the "straight" from the "crooked" (= the good from the bad?), there is not
much he or she can do to change it.

The final line of v. 14 is part of a series of similar clauses which run
through the book that question human ability to know anything about the
future, but how exactly it relates to the preceding lines is unclear. As
Murphy explains,

> The connection between the experience of good and evil and human
> ignorance of the future (so the usual translation . . .) is not clear. God has
> made both the good and the evil day to keep humans from finding out the
> future? That has little, if any meaning. . . . Perhaps in v. 14 it means that
> humans know not whether their portion will be good or bad, but the point
> is expressed very obscurely.[241]

Murphy argues that "it is possible to recognize an idiom in 'find after'"
and translates the second half of the verse, "God made them both so that
no one may find fault with him."[242] This reading is not certain, however,
and is made less likely by the similarity of the sentiments here to other
verses in the book.[243] But even amongst those who agree that the line
refers to the future, there is disagreement both on the question of what
"the future" refers to (someone's own future,[244] or the future after they
die[245]) and what the implications of the statement are: Fox, for example,

241. Murphy, *Ecclesiastes*, 66.
242. Ibid., 60–61. This reading is reflected also in NAB and NJPSV. See also Perry
(*Dialogues with Kohelet*, 125–27). Crenshaw discusses this possibility, but concludes, "It is not clear how this reading of Eccl 7:14 improves the meaning"
(*Ecclesiastes*, 139).
243. See 3:22; 6:12; 8:7; 10:14; 11:2. Thus, for example, Fox comments, "similar
sentences in 3:22; 6:12; and 10:14 speak unambiguously of man's ignorance of the
future" (*A Time to Tear Down*, 259).
244. See Longman, *The Book of Ecclesiastes*, 192; Seow, *Ecclesiastes*, 240.
245. See Hubbard, *Ecclesiastes, Song of Solomon*, 167; Huwiler, *Proverbs,
Ecclesiastes, Song of Songs*, 201; Ogden and Zogbo, *A Handbook*, 244–45.

interprets the verse to imply that "God keeps man off balance";[246] Loader contends that "God as the overruling supreme Power is pictured in even grimmer terms here," concluding "The only conceivable posture one can adopt is a kind of mindless acceptance or mute resignation";[247] Rudman sees this as an example of "a deterministic worldview in which all human actions and emotions are controlled by the deity";[248] whereas Seow argues that "It is this mysterious 'activity of God' that the reader is called to 'see,' to recognize for what it is";[249] and Provan goes so far as to say "The crucial thing to be remembered about the universe is that *God* has created it (vv. 13–15). . . . [I]n the end we must remember that the universe is not a predictable machine but a personally governed and complex space."[250] Bergant acknowledges that "v. 14 is very difficult to understand and allows for a diversity of interpretations!"[251]

Thus 7:1–14 picks up from the question in 6:12, מי־יודע מה־טוב לאדם, and launches into a series of better-sayings that may appear initially to provide a positive response to this question. However, it soon becomes apparent that determining just what Qohelet actually considers to be "good" or "better" is far from easy, and the reader is left to work out how these better-sayings are being used, and what the implications are of the various plays on the word טוב and the concluding advice which ascribes both the good and the bad to God. There is considerable ambiguity surrounding the use of the word טוב, and many gaps of indeterminacy emerge which require some involvement on the reader's part in determining just what is "good" or "better."

The word טוב occurs just twice in the next section of the book (7:15–22), but nonetheless this is a significant passage in consideration of the meaning of this word. טוב itself is used in two different ways, one with a moral sense (v. 20), the other not (v. 18). But a number of other words are used which explore possible meanings of "goodness"—טוב, צדק, חכם and ירא אלהים—and of "badness"—חטא, רעה, רשע and סכל. There is a confusing interchange between these words such that the distinction between ethical and non-ethical is decidedly blurred. One might argue that, ethical implications side, there is still a comparison between opposites, the "good" on one side, and the "bad" on the other, but doubt is cast on the usefulness of such categorisation.

246. Fox, *A Time to Tear Down*, 259.
247. Loader, *Ecclesiastes*, 85.
248. Rudman, *Determinism*, 177.
249. Seow, *Ecclesiastes*, 251.
250. Provan, *Ecclesiastes, Song of Songs*, 151.
251. Bergant, *Job, Ecclesiastes*, 267.

7:15b is presented in the form of two balanced antithetical phrases, each element of which—apart from the introductory יֵשׁ—seems to be the opposite of its counterpart:

יֵשׁ צדיק אבד   בצדקו

וְיֵשׁ רשע מאריך   ברעתו׃

It seems that a counter-example is being given to traditional doctrine, because where one might have expected יֵשׁ צדיק מַאֲרִיךְ צדקו (along the lines of, e.g., Exod 20:12; Deut 4:40 and Prov 3:1–2) and רש רשע אֹבֵד ברעתו (along the lines of, e.g., Pss 37:10; 55:23; Prov 7:24–27), the verbs are used the other way around.[252] Might Qohelet be attempting to shock the reader by presenting facts contrary to accepted wisdom[253]—or is there, perhaps, a double twist to the verse?

The balance of the verse is disturbed by the last word, ברעתו. The effect of the conciseness and repetition of the first phrase is quite striking: of the four words, two are from the same root, צדק, one is the introductory יֵשׁ, and the other is the one on which the whole phrase turns, אבד. This construction is typical of the better-sayings in 7:1–4. However, the effect is lost somewhat in the second phrase because a different root is used for the final word. To have gained the full effect of the statement, we might have expected an unambiguous word for "evil" from the root רשע, as earlier in the verse, but רעה is used instead. In the previous verse רעה seems to be used without moral connotations to indicate "adversity," hence 7:15b might be rendered, "there is a righteous person who perishes in his righteousness, and there is a wicked person who prolongs his life in his adversity." This might be understood to mean that while there *are* righteous people who die before their time despite their righteousness, there are also wicked people who live longer but experience adversity all their days. This could be understood as a vindication of traditional wisdom in the light of the apparent anomaly of wicked people out-living righteous people. 8:12–13 might be read in a similar way:

אשר חטא עשה רע מאת ומאריך לו

כי גם־יודע אני אשר יהיה־טוב ליראי האלהים אשר יראו מלפניו׃

וטוב לא־יהיה לרשע ולא־יאריך ימים כצל

אשר איננו ירא מלפני אלהים׃

---

252. Brown asserts, "Traditionally, righteousness is the salutary sphere of moral agency, but no longer within Qoheleth's purview. It seems that righteousness and wickedness have traded places in the absurd scheme of things" (*Ecclesiastes*, 80).

253. Thus Longman argues: "The two case studies present us with a paradox, and Qohelet surely wanted his listener/reader to be shocked by what he said. He saw the *righteous perishing* and the *wicked living long*. This is the polar opposite of what some strands of biblical teaching indicate" (*The Book of Ecclesiastes*, 194).

7:15b is, in fact, ambiguous (and this despite the fact that the English versions and commentators treat רשע and רעה as synonymous; NAS's "there is a righteous man who perishes in his righteousness and there is a wicked man who prolongs his life in his wickedness" is typical[254]), but at least the attentive reader may wonder why the balance of the final phrase is upset by the use of this different word at the end: Is there any difference between "badness" and "evil?"

Verse 16 raises similar issues: the verse is understood in different ways by the commentators,[255] and this might be illustrated by comparing Crenshaw and Fox, who generally read Ecclesiastes as a pessimistic work, with Ogden and Whybray, who are more positive in their interpretation. On the one hand, Crenshaw renders the first part of the verse, "Do not *be* too righteous and do not *be* excessively wise";[256] and Fox translates it, "Do not *be* very righteous nor *become* exceedingly wise";[257] on the other hand, Ogden offers the translation, "Do not *claim* exceptional righteousness or *ardently pursue* wisdom";[258] and Whybray contends that the verse argues against *self*-righteousness and *pretensions* to wisdom.[259] Similar differences appear in the English translations: for example NIV translates, "Do not be overrighteous, neither be overwise,"[260] while NJPSV goes for, "So don't overdo goodness and don't act the wise man to excess, or you may be dumbfounded."[261] Murphy comes to the conclusion that "v. 16 must be a bitter and ironic admonition,"[262] but Seow asserts that "The problem is overconfidence in human ability to

---

254. Seow at least distinguishes between "wicked ones" and "badness," but he makes no further comment (*Ecclesiastes*, 252).

255. Kaiser contends that "few verses in Ecclesiastes are more susceptible to incorrect interpretation than 7:16–18" (*Ecclesiastes*, 85). Brindle, after quoting Kaiser, adds, "interpreters of Ecclesiastes tend to view the argument of 7:15–18 in a variety of ways, depending upon whether they are willing to attribute to the author a sense of relativity and 'moderation' in moral conduct" ("Righteousness and Wickedness," 243).

256. Crenshaw, *Ecclesiastes*, 140, my emphasis. See also Longman, *The Book of Ecclesiastes*, 192, 195–96.

257. Fox, *Qohelet*, 233, my emphasis.

258. Ogden, *Qoheleth*, 114, my emphasis.

259. Whybray, *Ecclesiastes*, 120. See also G. R. Castellino, "Qohelet and His Wisdom," *CBQ* 30 (1968): 15–28. Longman ascribes this approach to "Interpreters who want to guard Qohelet's piety or orthodoxy" (*The Book of Ecclesiastes*, 195).

260. See also GNB, NAB, NAS, NKJV, NLT, REB.

261. See also NRSV. ESV, NJB, RSV come somewhere in between, referring to *making* yourself too wise.

262. Murphy, *Ecclesiastes*, 70.

attain extreme righteousness and wisdom, the ability to achieve perfection on one's efforts and natural ability."[263]

The problem for the interpreter comes in the form of four apparently parallel admonitions in vv. 16–17, which, in fact, are not parallel. They might be compared thus, pairing the phrases which appear initially to be directly parallel to each other (and where one might usually expect antithetic parallelism):

$$
\begin{array}{cc}
הרבה & אל־תהי צדיק \\
הרבה & אל־תרשע
\end{array}
$$

$$
\begin{array}{c}
ואל־תתחכם \\
ואל־תהי סכל
\end{array}
$$

By comparing these phrases in this way it readily becomes apparent that they are not so carefully matched as we might have expected were Qohelet simply warning the reader away from extremes of righteousness, wisdom, wickedness and folly. Had this been the intention, the verses could have been constructed so that they presented clear and unambiguous parallels.

The first point to note is that the translation of הרבה with "overly" or "excessively" (or similar) goes beyond the sense of the Hebrew word, which means "greatly" and does not express the judgment implicit in "overly."[264] This word occurs fifteen times in Ecclesiastes and is not generally translated in this way anywhere else. However, the word יתר often does indicate an excess of something, and there would, therefore, be justification in rendering יותר here as "excessively" or "overmuch." The same may apply in 2:15, למה חכמתי אני אז יותר, which also refers to wisdom, and is also set in a context where doubt is being cast on the value of wisdom.

The second point is the use of the verb היה in אל־תהי צדיק הרבה and אל־תהי סכל. Of the six admonitions in the form . . . אל־ת in this passage, only two of these use היה. Whybray argues, "the elliptical form (*'al-t°hi saddiq*) rather than the simple verbal form *'al-tisdaq* (compare the parallel *'al-tirsaʿ* in v.17) suggests that the meaning is 'Do not *claim* to be a saddiq,' that is, a righteous person"[265] (and, indeed, elsewhere Whybray asserts that the meaning of this admonition "is a matter of crucial

263. Seow, *Ecclesiastes*, 169.

264. See Ogden and Zogbo, *A Handbook*, 249.

265. Whybray, *Ecclesiastes*, 120. See also Ogden and Zogbo (*A Handbook*, 249), who state that "the peculiar Hebrew of this command must be appreciated." They render the phrase, "Don't be too sure of your righteousness" or "Don't think of yourself as so righteous."

importance for the understanding of Qohelet's teaching as a whole"[266]). However, Fox counters, "Qohelet's words as they stand do not refer merely to a pretense of righteousness. He could have expressed that idea by a prohibition such as *ʾal toʾmar saddiq ʾani*."[267] Fox is certainly correct that had the intention been *unambiguously* to say "do not *claim* to be greatly righteous," this could have been achieved in much clearer fashion. Whybray is also correct that the more complicated structure could be seen as elliptical. We should note, though, that if this phrase is to be read as an ellipsis, so then is the phrase וְאַל־תִּהִי סָכָל, which could also have been rendered more simply.[268] Perhaps the point is that nothing is stated clearly and simply, so that multiple interpretations are possible.[269]

The clause וְאַל־תִּתְחַכַּם יוֹתֵר in v. 16b raises the question why the author has used the Hithpael form of the verb. Of the six admonitions in the form אַל־תְּ . . . in this passage, only here is the Hithpael used. If the intention was unambiguously to say, "do not be excessively wise," this would have been simply expressed by the use of the Qal, as in the question in 2:15. The reader might conclude, then, either that this is not what was intended, or that the phrase is designed to be ambiguous. The Hithpael of חכם is used elsewhere in the Hebrew Bible only in a difficult phrase in Exod 1:10, הָבָה נִתְחַכְּמָה לוֹ פֶּן־יִרְבֶּה. The sense seems to be "let us act wisely," or "let us display wisdom." If the latter applies, the phrase in Eccl 7:16 might be translated, "do not display excessive wisdom," which could be understood to mean that one should not seek to display greater wisdom than he or she possesses, or that people should not flaunt their wisdom.[270] Whybray cites 2 Sam 13:5 as an example of a Hithpael verb used to indicate feigning of something one does not possess,[271] but

---

266. R. N. Whybray, "Qoheleth the Immoralist? (Qoh 7:16–17)," in Gammie and Brueggemann, eds., *Israelite Wisdom*, 191–204 (191). Salyer states that "It is not too much to say that 7:16–17 has greatly influenced the final *Gestalt* which readers have made of Qoheleth's character" (*Vain Rhetoric*, 339).

267. Fox, *Qohelet*, 235. See also Seow, *Ecclesiastes*, 253.

268. Longman uses this point against Whybray's reading (*The Book of Ecclesiastes*, 196).

269. Contra Whybray, who says, "If then the connotations of 16a and 16b are similar in that they both warn against certain human pretensions, why did not Qoheleth use the same grammatical construction to express his meaning? It was the limitations of the Hebrew language which prevented him from doing this *if his meaning was to be unambiguous*" ("Qoheleth the Immoralist?," 196, my emphasis).

270. Thus Ogden and Zogbo offer the translations "do not pretend to be wise" and "don't try to make yourself appear wise [when you aren't]" (*A Handbook*, 250).

271. See also *GesK*, 54d. Perry also argues this line (*Dialogues with Kohelet*, 128), as does Hubbard (*Ecclesiastes, Song of Solomon*, 168–70). Seow argues that "The Hithpael form of *ḥkm* in classical Hebrew never means 'to pretend to be wise'

Fox counters by using Exod 1:10 to indicate that the Hithpael does not imply a pretence at wisdom. Again it seems that a more complicated form has been adopted which, far from clarifying its meaning, allows the phrase to be read in different ways.

אל־תרשע רבה seems unambiguous, and is the only one of these four phrases which appears to be clear and concise. Is there some reason why only the statement not to be very wicked is clear when the others are not? Is the reader to draw the conclusion that of the four admonitions made here, only the call not to be very wicked is unequivocal? However, the implications of this phrase are not so straightforward. The reader may wonder whether the admonition not to be *very* wicked implies that a small degree of wickedness is acceptable. Fox, for example, argues that "by warning against acting *very* wickedly, Qohelet seems to be recommending a *little* wickedness."[272] The implications of Gordis's "Golden Mean" interpretation, which is followed by many commentators,[273] are similar: he argues that we find here "the Aristotelian principle of ethics with which Koheleth is familiar."[274] However, Crenshaw disputes this argument: "The ancient curse in Deut 27:24 ('Cursed be whoever slays his neighbour in secret') does not suggest that it is all right to do so in public. In the same way, Qohelet's warning against excessive wickedness does not endorse moderate evil."[275] It may be, then, that rather than *recommending* a little evil, Qohelet is conceding the fact that people do commit some evil acts, and is warning against more than this level of wickedness. Such realism would be in line with the sentiments expressed in v. 20. However, I must agree with Murphy that, "The intent of the admonitions in vv. 16–17 is elusive."[276]

Verse 18 draws these verses together by asserting what is "good" in all this. It does not take the form of a better-saying,[277] but rather a טוב אשר

or 'to imagine oneself wise.' In Sir 10:26, the verb means 'to show oneself wise' not in the sense of pretense but pretentiousness (so NAB: 'flaunt not your wisdom'). The issue there is not hypocrisy but boasting" (*Ecclesiastes*, 253). However, although Fox does not agree with Whybray's reading, he does say that "*tithakkam can* mean 'pretend to wisdom'" (*A Time to Tear Down*, 260, my emphasis).

272. Fox, *Qohelet*, 235. See also Longman, *The Book of Ecclesiastes*, 196.

273. See, e.g., Bergant, *Job, Ecclesiastes*, 268–69; Longman, *The Book of Ecclesiastes*, 196; Salyer, *Vain Rhetoric*, 299.

274. Gordis, *Koheleth*, 178. Murphy argues that this is a "red herring": "Qoheleth is not advocating in vv. 16–18 a 'middle way.' The view that he has adopted the Greek notion of avoiding excess, that virtue stands in the middle . . . is a common misreading of these verses" (*Ecclesiastes*, 72).

275. Crenshaw, *Ecclesiastes*, 141.

276. Murphy, *Ecclesiastes*, 69.

277. Contra Ogden, *Qoheleth*, 115.

saying which we find elsewhere only in 5:4, 17 (Eng. 5:5, 18). The first half of the verse consists of two admonitions conveying the same idea, one in a positive way and one in the negative form familiar from the preceding verses, . . . אל־תּ. However, it is not clear precisely what is being referred to. Some commentators assume that "this" and "that" refer to righteousness and wickedness in the previous two verses.[278] If this is the case, Qohelet would be recommending that we grasp hold of righteousness, but presumably in moderation, and that we should not cast off wickedness, although in this regard, too, we should practise moderation. This reading, however, selects only two of the four admonitions,[279] and it might be better to take "this" and "that" as referring to the counsel of each of the two verses as a whole.[280] If we read the phrase in this way it serves to emphasise the advice offered in the preceding verses—however they are understood. It would not, therefore, do anything to clarify the interpretation. Tamez argues that the phrase basically means "to 'hedge one's bets,' prudently keeping options open even when one does not fully agree with them."[281] Such sentiments might tie in well with the advice offered in 11:6 where it is stated that "you" do not know whether "this" or "that" or both of them are good:

בבקר זרע את־זרעך ולערב אל־תנח ידך
כי אינך יודע אי זה יכשר הזה או־זה ואם־שניהם כאחד טובים׃

Of the second half of the verse, Crenshaw maintains that "The optimism in the final clause does not agree with Qohelet's experience in 7:15. . . . If the observation is authentic, it *must be full of irony*."[282] However, this very much depends on how a rather ambiguous clause is understood. There are two particular issues. The first concerns the word יצא, the usual meaning of which in the Hebrew Bible is "to come forth from," though on occasion this could be rendered "get away from" or

---

278. E.g. Crenshaw, *Ecclesiastes*, 142.

279. Perry considers "this" and "that" as referring to righteousness and wisdom in v. 16 (*Dialogues with Kohelet*, 125); Huwiler regards the antecedents as "self-destruction" (v. 16) and "premature death" (v. 17) (*Proverbs, Ecclesiastes, Song of Songs*, 206).

280. See, e.g., Fox, *Qohelet*, 236; Longman, *The Book of Ecclesiastes*, 197; Ogden and Zogbo, *A Handbook*, 252; Provan, *Ecclesiastes, Song of Songs*, 142; Whybray, *Ecclesiastes*, 121. Garrett oddly comes to this conclusion: "the two things to be maintained are, on the one hand, devotion to God and the teachings of wisdom and, on the other hand, enjoyment of the good things of life" (*Proverbs, Ecclesiastes, Song of Songs*, 324).

281. Tamez, *When the Horizons Close*, 99.

282. Crenshaw, *Ecclesiastes*, 142, my emphasis.

"escape."[283] If such is the case in 7:18, it would seem to imply that the one who fears God escapes the dangers mentioned in vv. 16–17, which would be a very positive claim. However, some commentators perceive here a meaning of יצא which is not attested elsewhere in the Hebrew Bible, but does appear in the Mishnah. Thus Whitley argues,

> It is to be noted that יצא connotes "what is due" in Ben Sira; for example
> ושׂית אבלו כיוצא בו (and arrange his mourning as his due, 38:17; cf. also
> 10:27). So in Mishnaic Hebrew the verb conveys the sense of "fulfilling
> one's duty": thus אם כיון לבו יצא (If he directs his mind [to the Shema]
> he fulfils his obligation, Bera 2:1). Hence, we may render here: "he gives
> due attention to both of them."[284]

If the word is read in this way, it simply serves to emphasise that the "person who fears God" follows the advice in vv. 16–17. However, Crenshaw seems to read יצא in the opposite sense when he writes: "In *Ber.* 2:1 . . . the idiom *ysʾ* means to be *released* from the power of an obligation. The same sense of *ysʾ* appears to be found in Sir 38:17."[285] In this case the meaning is little different from the usual biblical meaning. Murphy simply states, "The translations of the final three words are varied *and all of them uncertain*."[286]

By contrast with the ambiguities of vv. 15–18, v. 20 seems remarkably straightforward, and, indeed, Perry argues that "The formulaic ring of this saying gives it the sound of a traditional view."[287] However, it is separated from these verses by a verse whose relevance in this context is very difficult to discern.[288] Moreover, the sentiments of v. 20 itself are deeply ironic in the light of the emphasis in the earlier verses of this chapter (not to mention 4:1–5:6 [Eng. 5:7]) on what is good: actually there is no-one who does "good" and does not sin, anyway! This is probably the only verse in the book where טוב unambiguously takes a moral sense[289] (but Seow argues, "In this context, *ṣaddîq* also is not a religious term, it refers to one who is always correct—the opposite of the fool. . . . The one who 'does only good' is one who is always correct and

---

283. E.g. Gen 39:12, 15; 1 Sam 14:41; Jer 11:11.

284. Whitley, *Koheleth*, 67.

285. Crenshaw, *Ecclesiastes*, 142, my emphasis.

286. Murphy, *Ecclesiastes*, 68, my emphasis.

287. Perry, *Dialogues with Kohelet*, 129.

288. This point is made by many commentators, including, Longman (*The Book of Ecclesiastes*, 197). Fox states: "This saying is irrelevant in its current place," and moves it to follow v. 12 (*A Time to Tear Down*, 256).

289. See, for example, the discussion in Schoors, "Words Typical of Qohelet," 33–34.

does not make mistakes"[290]). However, we should consider whether the expression טוב לפני האלהים has moral implications, and we shall return to this shortly.

First we will look briefly at the remaining verses where better-sayings are used: these are 6:3, 9 and 9:16–18. There is another play on the word (ה)טוב in 6:3 and 6 where, as discussed earlier, the possibly synonymous phrases לא־תשבע מן־הטובה and וטובה לא ראה appear either side of the "better"-saying טוב ממנו הנפל. There is considerable irony in the claim that a stillborn child is better (off?) than a man who has a hundred children and lives many years, and the comparison is based precisely on the observation about the man that ונפשו לא־תשבע מן־הטובה. This comes at the end of a long passage (that may start with another occurrences of the verb שבע in 5:9,[291] אהב כסף לא־ישבע כסף[292]) which reflects on the "goods" and mostly "bads" of wealth.[293] Indeed, this passage could be divided into sections that consider wealth in this way:

> what is "bad" in relation to wealth (5:9–16 [Eng. 5:10–17])
> what is "good" in relation to wealth (5:17–19 [Eng. 5:18–20]—one of the "calls to enjoyment" discussed above)
> what is "bad" in relation to wealth (6:1–2)
> what is *not* "good" in relation to wealth (6:3–6)

If this is sustainable (as I believe it is), it would mean that in one way or another the discussion of what is "good" and, conversely, what is "bad" for people extends from 3:22 at least until 7:20. It is then worth observing that the highest concentrations of words from the roots רעע and רשע are to be found in ch. 8,[294] and טוב occurs again in 8:12, 13, 15 and 9:2 (×2), 4, 7. Consideration of "good" and "bad" (and related concepts) is an important aspect of Qohelet's deliberations throughout 3:22–9:7.

In this passage from 5:9–6:6, a highly significant contrast is drawn in two very similar lines which highlight the "good" (following on from

---

290. Seow, *Ecclesiastes*, 142.

291. A number of commentators regard 5:9–6:9 as a distinct section. See especially D. C. Fredericks, "Chiasm and Parallel Structure in Qoheleth 5:9–6:9," *JBL* 109 (1989): 17–35 (18 n. 5), and others whom he mentions.

292. This provides a further example of a phrase that appears in different forms in Ecclesiastes: לא־תשבע מן־הטובה 6:3; לא־ישבע כסף 5:9; לא־תשבע עשר 4:8. These seem to be synonymous, which may help in interpreting these verses, or raise again the question why a different expression is used.

293. 5 out of 9 occurrences of the word עשר are in this passage. Other words related to wealth, such as אכל, רב/רבה and עמל occur here often as well, in addition to a number of uses of the word רעה/רע.

294. 7 out of a total of 32 words from the root רעע are in ch. 8; 5 out of a 12 words from the root רשע are in ch. 8.

הנה אשר־ראיתי אני טוב אשר־יפה in 5:17 [Eng. 5:18]) and the "bad" (following on from יש רעה אשר ראיתי in 6:1), and whose similarity draws into sharp focus the key element that is different:[295]

לאכל ממנו	והשליטו	כל־האדם אשר נתן־לו אלהים עשר ונכסים	5:18
			(Heb.)
אשר יתן־לו האלהים עשר ונכסים...ולא־ ישליטנו האלהים לאכל ממנו			איש 6:2

The main difference (in addition to the potentially significant contrast between כל־האדם and איש, and the addition in the middle of 6:2 that I have left out[296]) is precisely who is and who is not השלט לאכל ממנו, "empowered (by God) to enjoy (or it might be 'consume')" the riches and wealth that they are given (also by God). This seems to be what lies behind the clause ונפשו לא־תשבע מן־הטובה in 6:3. There is then in 6:3 a very effective literary reversal, combined with a play on the word (ה)טוב, which captures the astonishing reversal that makes the stillborn better (off) than the man of many years who has many children:

That is to say, if you are not satisfied with "the good" then even a stillborn child is "more good" than you. This certainly adds impetus to the drive to discern what is good, but it also raises the question whether "good" results from what God gives, and "bad" from what he withholds. Does good arise when God empowers one to enjoy the good things of life, and conversely does bad come about when God does not so empower?[297]

---

295. Seow writes: "These verses [6:1–2] are problematic for the interpreter because they seem to negate what has been said in 5:18–20 (Heb vv. 17–19). This appears all the more so because the vocabulary and style in 6:1–2 suggest that this section is intended to mirror 5:18–19 (Heb. vv. 17–18) in some way" (*Ecclesiastes*, 224).

296. Few commentators address these differences; Seow, however, list them as follows, carefully explaining what he understands to be their significance (in what I find a very persuasive way, see *Ecclesiastes*, 224–25):

5:18–19 (Heb vv. 17–18)	*6:1–2*
all people	a person
God has given	God gives
God has authorized	God does not authorize
this is the gift of God	this is vanity

297. Rudman says of this: "human beings are dependent on God for the *ability* to make use of the material wealth that they acquire. . . . This is a fundamentally new idea in the Hebrew Bible. For whereas God is shown to bestow riches on the sage in

Here, as so often elsewhere in Ecclesiastes, commentators respond to this question in different ways. Thus, for example, Tamez argues, "Qoheleth shows us an arbitrary God, the cause of this inability to enjoy. God gives the gift of riches, but to some people he doesn't give the ability to enjoy them. In Qoheleth's time God was seen as the source of both good and bad things. He does not understand this absurd activity of God."[298] On the other hand, Seow asserts, "As a general rule, God has permitted humans (*kol-hāʾādām*) to enjoy what they have, given them material possessions, and authorized them to partake of what they have as their portion. This is the manifestation of God's gift to humanity. Yet there are instances when that gift is not evident, when the same God who gives material possessions may not give certain individuals the ability to enjoy them."[299] It depends, it seems, on where the emphasis is placed; in other words, on what is centralised and what is marginalised. Is the "good" that God does give (in general to "all people") the key point, or is it more significant (and more reflective of the kind of God whom we should "fear") that for some seemingly inexplicable reason that God withholds such "good" on occasion?

There is widespread agreement concerning the translation of the better-saying in 6:9:

טוב מראה עינים מהלך־נפש

Crenshaw asserts that "The meaning of this 'better saying' is elusive, despite the ease of translation."[300] The expression מראה עינים occurs once more in Ecclesiastes, in an exhortation to readers to enjoy their lives in 11:9:

שׂמח בחור בילדותיך ויטיבך לבך בימי בחורותך והלך בדרכי לבך
ובמראי עיניך

Seow comments about 11:9 that "The meaning of the first half of the saying is clear enough from the usage of the idiom elsewhere; it has to do with enjoying the pleasures of the moment";[301] he explains that although "*marʾēh ʿênayim* normally refers to vision, the ability to see (Lev 13:12; Isa 11:3) . . . here it refers to the experiencing of what the eyes see—what

---

Proverbs, the implications of God being responsible for the ability of the individual to make a choice as to whether such wealth is used points more strongly to a deterministic outlook on life" (*Determinism*, 143).

298. Tamez, *When the Horizons Close*, 87.

299. Seow, *Ecclesiastes*, 225.

300. Crenshaw, *Ecclesiastes*, 129.

301. Seow, *Ecclesiastes*, 228. Perry, following Gordis, expresses this in the concise phrase, "a joy at hand" (*Dialogues with Kohelet*, 108).

one has."[302] Murphy also notes that "The key to the meaning of v. 9a is the word מראה, which can denote either the action of seeing or the object seen," but he goes on to disagree with Seow when he states, "Our translation opts for the straightforward action of seeing (the meaning it seems to have in 11:9),"[303] explaining that "Seeing is superior to desire because it implies some kind of possession. . . . The one who sees something has an object in view, whereas the one who is locked into desire, by definition, has not attained the desired."[304] Farmer reads differently again, interpreting "to have seeing eyes" as to "be wise."[305] So, while translation of this expression may be straightforward, its precise meaning is not.

Longman argues that the second part of the saying "is the clearest as to its meaning and harks back to 6:7, where the same Hebrew word, there translated 'appetite,' appears."[306] He translates it as "roving desire." However, Seow notes that

> mēhălok-nāpeš probably has more than one meaning. On the one hand, hălok-nāpeš (NRSV: "the wandering of desire") alludes to the voracious appetite of those who are discontented with their lives. . . . On the other hand, the use of the verb hālak, recalls remarks about the destiny of mortals: they "go" in darkness (v. 4) and all "go" to the one place (v. 6). Indeed, Qohelet regularly uses the verb hālak to speak of death (1:4; 2:14; 3:20; 6:4, 6; 9:10; 12:5). Elsewhere in the Bible, too, hālak, may be so used.[307]

He translates the second part of the saying, against the majority of commentators and English translations, as "the passing of life." Hubbard,[308] Loader[309] and Whybray[310] argue similarly, but Longman asserts that "The biggest problem with their approach . . . is that it requires a different translation of nepeš, desire, than it did just two verses before."[311] To my mind this is insufficient argument in the book of Ecclesiastes. Ogden and Zogbo helpfully note that "This saying brings together four terms that are used elsewhere in 6:1–8: better ('good' in verses 3, 6), sight ('seen' and 'enjoy' in 1, 5, 6), wandering ('go,' 'goes' and 'conduct [himself]' in 4,

302. Seow, Ecclesiastes, 214. See also Ogden and Zogbo, A Handbook, 206.
303. Murphy, Ecclesiastes, 49.
304. Ibid., 54.
305. Farmer, Who Knows What is Good?, 172.
306. Longman, The Book of Ecclesiastes, 174.
307. Seow, Ecclesiastes, 215.
308. Hubbard, Ecclesiastes, Song of Solomon, 155.
309. Loader, Ecclesiastes, 69–70.
310. Whybray, Ecclesiastes, 108–9.
311. Longman, The Book of Ecclesiastes, 174.

6, 8) and *desire* (Hebrew *nefesh* in 3 [and 7])."[312] We have already observed the different ways in which טוב is used: the same holds true for ראה and הלך, and might also be the case with נפשׁ.

It seems, then, that in this verse a number of words which are already familiar from earlier verses in this chapter (and in earlier chapters also) come together in a way that allows for easy *translation* on a literal level, but that the precise meaning is unclear. Moreover, even among those who are pretty much agreed on the meaning, there is disagreement about how Qohelet views the proverb, especially in the light of the verse's conclusion: גם־זה הבל ורעות רוח. Many compare the proverb to the saying in English, "A bird in the hand is worth two in the bush";[313] Hubbard, for example, quotes this proverb as a parallel to Eccl 6:9, then states that "The Preacher would surely apply this verse to all the treasures that his friends were vainly striving after."[314] A number of commentators also regard v. 9 as Qohelet's answer to the question in v. 8.[315] Others, though, challenge the position that this is a proverb of which Qohelet approves: Murphy, for example, asserts that "Qoheleth rejects this 'better' saying."[316] A crucial issue here is what the concluding clause refers to: thus Longman explains that "the antecedent to *this* is ambiguous. Some believe it refers only to the second half of the proverb,[317] others to the whole.[318] It could conceivably characterize the whole section."[319] So, even if one could be reasonably confident about what the proverb *means*—that is, just what Qohelet is saying is "better" than what—a problem remains in determining his attitude to the saying. Once again, working out "what is good for people" according to Qohelet is no simple task.

The sayings in 9:16–18 all have to do with wisdom, and all seem to portray "wisdom" as something that is "good" or "better":

מגבורה		טובה חכמה	9:16
מזעקת מושל בכסילים	בנחת נשמעים	דברי חכמים	9:17
מכלי קרב		טובה חכמה	9:18

However, none is completely straightforward. Verse 16 concludes a passage which tells a tale about a poor wise man who was not remembered, presumably because he was poor. This verse then opens with a

312. Ogden and Zagbo, *A Handbook*, 206.
313. See, e.g., the comment in Longman, *The Book of Ecclesiastes*, 175.
314. Hubbard, *Ecclesiastes, Song of Solomon*, 154–55.
315. E.g. Provan, *Ecclesiastes, Song of Songs*, 139.
316. Murphy, *Ecclesiastes*, 54; see also Ogden and Zagbo, *A Handbook*, 206.
317. See, e.g., Whybray, *Ecclesiastes*, 109.
318. See, e.g., Ogden, *Qoheleth*, 95–96.
319. Longman, *The Book of Ecclesiastes*, 175.

better-saying which compares "wisdom" favourably against "might," but continues severely to modify the comparison by pointing out that a *poor* wise man is not heeded—which may offer support to the saying in 7:11, טובה חכמה עם־נחלה, discussed above. The saying of three words is balanced, or more accurately *counter*-balanced, by two further clauses of three words each, which shift the focus from "wisdom" to "poor" to "nobody," thus effectively demolishing the "good" of the better-saying:[320]

טובה חכמה מגבורה

וחכמת המסכן בזויה

ודבריו אינם נשמעים

So how much better is wisdom after all? And how does this saying tie in with the apparent affirmation of a poor wise youth in 4:13? Is wisdom of any use if it is unaccompanied by wealth—or not?

The better-saying in v. 18 seems to be synonymous with the one in v. 16, but it too is modified[321]—this time using a play on the word טובה whereby wisdom is "more good" than weapons of war, but "much good" is destroyed by just one sinner:[322]

טובה חכמה מכלי קרב וחוטא אחד יאבד טובה הרבה

Again the question arises as to just how "good" wisdom really is if "much good" (presumably resulting from wisdom) can be so easily

320. Loader comments: "The advantage of wisdom over strength is well attested in general wisdom circles (see Prov 21:22; also 20:18; 24:5–6), but the Preacher stresses the unfortunate side of the story. Only half a line is given to the advantage of wisdom, but a full line, embracing two parallel pronouncements, is devoted to the disadvantages" (*Ecclesiastes*, 114).

321. Although some commentators propose a major break between v. 18a and v. 18b, linking v. 18b with 10:1; see, for example, Garrett, *Proverbs, Ecclesiastes, Song of Songs*, 334.

322. There is much disagreement about how the word "sinner" should be rendered (e.g. "sinner" in RSV became "bungler" in NRSV) and whether or not it refers to the ruler of the previous verse (so, e.g., Seow, *Ecclesiastes*, 311). The main area of discussion revolves round whether or not it has ethical or religious connotations here, but there is also debate about whether or not it might be understood as one "sin" (e.g. "sin" in NJB; "slip" in NAB; "error" in NJPSV; "mistake" in REB) rather than "sinner" (so, e.g., ESV, GNB, NAS, NIV, NKJV, NLT). Whybray writes: "Elsewhere in the book (2:26; 7:20, 26; 8:12; 9:2) it is certainly or probably used in its moral or religious sense, which may well have been its original meaning here; but in its present context, in which it is contrasted with wisdom, it probably means one who misses, or is lacking: in this case, lacking in sense (for this meaning, cf. Prov 8:36)" (*Ecclesiastes*, 149). This will be discussed further below.

undone. Qohelet's attitude to wisdom generally is ambivalent.[323] He claims to be wiser than any before him in Jerusalem (1:16; 2:7) and wisdom remains with him throughout his investigations (1:13; 2:3; 7:23), yet wisdom is far from him (7:23) and he seeks it (1:17; 7:25). Wisdom is as advantageous over folly as light is over darkness (2:13–14)—it brings life to the one who possesses it (7:12), it gives considerable strength to the wise person (7:19), it makes one's face shine (8:1), it enables one to know "the time and way" (8:5), it helps one succeed (10:10) and the words of the wise bring them favour (10:12). But Qohelet asks why he has been so wise because wise and fool die alike and neither is long remembered (2:15–16). He asks whether the wise do have any advantage over the fool (in a rhetorical question expecting the answer "no"?) (6:8). He advises against acting too wisely (7:16). He asserts that the wise do not know "the work of God" (8:17), nor is "bread to the wise" (9:11) and he states that wisdom brings much sorrow (1:18). Qohelet lauds the poor wise youth over the foolish old king (4:13), yet seems to suggest that wisdom is good when it is accompanied by wealth (7:11) and is unheeded when dispensed by a poor person (9:13–16). Finally, it is unclear just how "good" Qohelet thinks are the actions associated with the wise in the better-sayings in ch. 7 (7:4, 5, 7, 10, 11–12[?]). The sentiments of the better-sayings along with the modifying clauses in 9:16 and 18 fit very well within this ambivalence.

9:17, though seems to sit rather awkwardly in this context: it appears very positive about wisdom and it does not consist of a better-saying plus modifying statement.[324] It might be that the sense of the better-saying in the previous verse is continued in v. 17, as we find also in 7:1. However, in 7:1 the saying which omits טוב follows directly from a saying in which it is used, and both are in the same verse. 4:17, on the other hand, may provide an example of a verse where טוב is presupposed without there being a better-saying immediately preceding it. However, there are other explanations for 4:17 which do not require טוב to be supplied or assumed, and the same applies here. *GesK* (116e) cites a number of examples from the Hebrew Bible where the Niphal participle has the

323. Fox states that "Qohelet both affirms and denies the value of wisdom," adding, "but on balance he unquestionably prefers it to ignorance" (*A Time to Tear Down*, 93).

324. Although Longman does describe it as a better-saying (*The Book of Ecclesiastes*, 235–36), and Ogden and Zogbo assert, "though lacking the Hebrew word 'better', it is obvious from the form that this is a 'better' saying" (*A Handbook*, 352). ESV, GNB, NAB, NAS and NLT have a better-saying here; NIV, NJB, NKJV, NRSV, NJPSV and REB do not. We might note that RSV uses a better-saying, but this has changed in NRSV.

sense of the Latin gerundive. If this applies here, 9:17 could be read, "the words of the wise spoken in quiet are worthy to be heard more than the shouting of a ruler among fools."[325] But it should be noted that even if טוב is not read from v. 16, מן is sometimes used alone to signify superiority of one thing over another,[326] so that it may be best rendered "*better than*" even without the טוב. An alternative adopted by some commentators is to move the disjunctive accent to בנחת and to read the verse, "the words of the wise spoken in quiet are heard more than the shouting of a ruler among fools."[327] This would display an ironic twist typical of Qohelet: though a ruler shouts, if it be among fools it will be heard less than the words of the wise, however softly spoken.

7.3.4. טוב לפני האלהים

We return now to consider whether the term טוב לפני האלהים has moral implications. The phrase occurs in 2:26 and 7:26, and in both verses it is contrasted with חטא:

2:26   כי לאדם שטוב לפניו   נתן חכמה ודעת ושמחה
ולחוטא   נתן ענין לאסוף ולכנוס

7:26   טוב לפני האלהים ימלט ממנה
וחוטא ילכד בה

Indeed, in 2:26 there is a very careful balance to the verse (with the exception of the concluding phrase, גם־זה הבל ורעות רוח, which may be highly significant) which means that not only is there antithetic parallelism between טוב לפני האלהים and חטא, but טוב לפני האלהים surrounds חטא:

לאדם שטוב לפניו נתן
חכמה
ודעת
ושמחה
ולחוטא נתן
ענין
לאסוף
ולכנוס
לתת לטוב לפני האלהים

---

325. Cf. Whybray, *Ecclesiastes*, 149.

326. *GesK*, 133b cite Gen 29:30; 37:3; Deut 14:2; 1 Sam 2:29; Hos 6:6; Job 7:15 and Eccl 2:13 as examples.

327. Cf. Fox, *A Time to Tear Down*, 297; Longman, *The Book of Ecclesiastes*, 236. Murphy renders the verse, "The calm words of the wise are better heeded than the cry of a ruler among fools," stating that "There is an inherent ambiguity here: are the words spoken calmly or heard calmly?" He asserts, "More likely the former" (*Ecclesiastes*, 96–97).

This is a beautifully structured verse which very effectively compares the wisdom, knowledge and joy given by God to the טוב לפני האלהים with the business of gathering and heaping given to the חוטא, before adding the lovely twist at the end, that all this giving ends up with the חוטא giving to the טוב לפני האלהים (and the question remains whether there is a double twist introduced by the addition of גם־זה הבל ורעות רוח, which disrupts the chiasmus). But to whom does the verse refer? Who are טוב לפני האלהים and חטא? Crenshaw argues, "Qohelet's predecessors used *tob* and *hoteʾ* as ethical terms for good and bad people. Here, the two terms mean simply 'fortunate and unfortunate, lucky and unlucky.'"[328] Murphy agrees with this position when he renders לאדם שטוב לפניו, "To whomever he pleases," explaining that "No moral connotation is to be given to the terms טוב, 'good,' and חטא, 'one who misses the mark.'"[329] Seow's approach is slightly different when he maintains, "The *hōṭeʾ* is what one may call 'a bungler' or 'a loser' in contemporary parlance. The *hōṭeʾ* is displeasing. In contrast to the *hōṭeʾ*, the one who is *ṭôb* is the smart one, the one who does everything right." Nonetheless, he also denies that these are religious or ethical categories. Ogden and Zogbo claim that "Throughout wisdom writing *sinner* is equivalent to 'fool,' and *good* is the equal of 'wise.'"[330] Fox asserts, "Certainly the *hoteʾ* and the man who is 'good before God' are not simply sinner and saint," but he emphasises that "the concept of *hoteʾ* is not diluted to the point of being merely an 'unfortunate' man," and concedes, "here the usual connotations of sinfulness are in play."[331] On the other hand, while Whybray notes that "Most commentators, on the basis of a few passages elsewhere in the Old Testament (Judg 20:16 [Heb.]; Job 5:24; Prov 8:36; 14:21; 19:2; 20:2; Isa 65:20) and of usages of the same root in cognate languages, maintain that the word here means 'to fail, miss, fall short' and lacks any religious or ethical connotations. (In some of the above cases this meaning is dubious.)," he then goes on to point out,

---

328. Crenshaw, *Ecclesiastes*, 90.

329. Murphy, *Ecclesiastes*, 24, 26. Murphy maintains that this position is "today generally recognized." One might note, for example, the almost identical comments in Schoors, "Words Typical of Qohelet," 38–39.

330. Ogden and Zagbo, *A Handbook*, 354.

331. Fox, *A Time to Tear Down*, 189–91. I think the last point is a move away from the position he held in *Qohelet*. Nonetheless he says there something very similar to these words in *A Time to Tear Down*: "*ḤṬʾ* always denotes offensiveness to someone. Since the offense in question is usually of a moral nature (even in Qohelet: 7:20; 8:12; 9:2), the translation 'sinner' is usually accurate, but not always so" (p. 190).

On the other hand, there are 231 occurrences of the verb in the Old Testament in which it means "to sin," together with 356 occurrences of nouns cognate with it where the meaning is undoubtably "sin." Of the other occurrences in Ecclesiastes (7:20, 26; 8:12; 9:2, 18), only in 9:18 is this meaning improbable. The present verse in itself offers no evidence that the meaning of *ḥôṭeʾ* is other than the usual one.[332]

Similarly, Eaton writes, "In 2:26 'wisdom' is explicitly set over against 'the sinner' in terms that are clearly moral. It is doubtful, therefore, whether the moral element can be excluded from the word sinner here."[333] Tamez simply notes that "Here, in v. 26, Qoheleth follows the line of traditional wisdom";[334] Huwiler describes the verse as "an affirmation of retribution";[335] and Fredericks refers to the "transfer of the sinner's property to the righteous mentioned in 2:26."[336]

Longman (who opts for the amoral reading) notes that 2:26 "gives Qohelet's understanding of how God deals with people," but acknowledges that "It is a difficult text to interpret and can be read in one of two ways, but in the final analysis *context must determine its meaning.*"[337] But this verse illustrates well the way in which commentators interpret verses in Ecclesiastes to support their own theories regarding its meaning, so that the reader who seeks direction from different commentaries may get hopelessly caught up in hermeneutic circles spiraling both up and down. As Davidson explains,

> Verse 26 is an interesting example of the problems we face when we try to enter into Koheleth's mind. If we think that behind all Koheleth's questions there is a man who remains firm in the faith of his fathers, or if we think of him as a man who expresses and enters into the doubts of other people in order to help them through to a more certain faith, then we can read this verse as expressing such faith. . . . If, however, we see Koheleth, as this commentary does, as a man trying to come to terms with his own doubts, a man who has serious reservations about the faith in which he has been brought up, then we can read this verse differently.[338]

Thus, for example, on the one hand Loader writes: "Verse 26 links wisdom with enjoyment: God gives them to whomever he wants. . . .

332. Whybray, *Ecclesiastes*, 64.
333. Eaton, *Ecclesiastes*, 132–33.
334. Tamez, *When the Horizons Close*, 55.
335. Garrett, *Proverbs, Ecclesiastes, Song of Songs*, 185.
336. Fredericks, *Coping with Transience*, 90.
337. Longman, *The Book of Ecclesiastes*, 109.
338. Davidson, *Ecclesiastes and the Song of Solomon*, 20–21.

God is bound to no rule, and wisdom has nothing to do with whether a person is fortunate or unfortunate. It all depends on God's unpredictable and totally arbitrary pleasure";[339] while on the other hand, Garrett argues that "this verse does not present God as capricious but does relate to the biblical idea of the *grace* of God. To believe that one's life is ruled by impersonal fate is intolerable; to believe that life is controlled by a personal God is a comfort."[340]

We might note that חטא in Ecclesiastes does seem usually to indicate "sin" in the same sense it normally has elsewhere in the Hebrew Bible. So in 8:12 it is stated that חטא עשׂה רע, and v. 13 uses רשׁע as a parallel to חטא in v. 12; in 7:20 צדיק is equated with the person who יעשׂה טוב ולא יחטא; and in 9:2 טוב and חטא in the second half of the verse parallel צדיק and רשׁע in the first half of the verse. The use of לחטיא in 5:5 is also in keeping with the usual biblical sense. However, in 9:18 and 10:4 חטא is used twice in a passage that focuses on wisdom and folly, and in 9:18 חוטא seems to be contrasted with חכמה in the same way that words from the roots סכל and כסל are elsewhere in that passage. An important aspect of the ambiguity of Ecclesiastes is the uncertainty over what precisely such words as טוב and חטא (and צדק, רשׁע, רע—even חכם and סכל/כסל) mean: What is it that makes a person "good" (in God's eyes, or other-wise), and what is it that makes a person a "sinner"? The different interpretations of 2:26 serve well to illustrate this particular ambiguity, and precisely the same issues arise in relation to the use of לפני האלהים טוב and חוטא in 7:26. Thus, for example, Murphy argues: "The terms טוב, 'good,' and חוטא, 'errant,' are best understood as in 2:26, not as moral qualifications, but as designations of human beings in terms of the inscrutable divine will. Some will fall victim to this type of woman, but others will not, as God pleases. . . . [T]he concern of 7:26 is not morality but the mysterious actions of God."[341] By contrast, Provan states that "The *good man, walking on the right path* and embracing wisdom rather than folly, will 'escape' (*mlt*) her 'snare'. . . . The *sinner*, on the other hand, has no motivation to avoid the trap and thus falls straight into it."[342] Hubbard simply points out the ambiguity: "Both '*he who pleases*' (lit. 'one who is good') and the '*sinner*' (lit. 'one who misses the mark') are somewhat ambiguous. The words may mean 'fortunate' and 'unfortu-nate' and put the whole outcome in God's unpredictable hands or they

339. Loader, *Ecclesiastes*, 32.
340. Garrett, *Proverbs, Ecclesiastes, Song of Songs*, 296.
341. Murphy, *Ecclesiastes*, 76.
342. Provan, *Ecclesiastes, Song of Songs*, 154.

may have strong moral connotation depicting the behavior of the two types of persons."[343]

In the light of this discussion of טוב לפני האלהים and חוטא there is considerable irony in the comparison of the "good person" and the "sinner" in 9:2: "As are the good, so are the sinners" (NRSV). However exactly the words טוב and חטא are understood, in both 2:26 and 7:26 there is clear advantage to the טוב לפני האלהים over the חוטא, though in 9:2 טוב and חטא seem to be equated, presumably because, as 9:2 states and 9:3 reiterates, לכל מקרה אחד. The implication seems to be that any advantage the "good" may have enjoyed during life is wiped out by death. As the text stands in *BHS*, this is further highlighted by the fact that there is an extra occurrence of the word טוב in v. 2 which disrupts the pattern of matched pairs—presumably presenting the extremes which indicate that everyone who falls between these poles is included in the compass of the verse:

הכל כאשר לכל מקרה אחד
לצדיק ולרשע
<u>לטוב</u>
ולטהור ולטמא
ולזבח ולאשר איננו זבה
כטוב כחטא
הנשבע כאשר שבועה ירא:[344]

This is explained in different ways. Gordis suggests that לטוב ought to be combined with the next word so that לטוב ולטהור is paired with ולטמא, the first element being longer than the second to balance the next pair where the second element, לאשר איננו זבח, is longer than the first, ולזבח.[344] This position is represented in NJPSV's translation, ". . . for the good and pure, and for the impure." Fox proposes, on the basis of the LXX,[345] that ולרע should be added to provide a pair for לטוב,[346] and this is the line most English translations follow.[347] However, both these

---

343. Hubbard, *Ecclesiastes, Song of Solomon*, 176.

344. Gordis, *Koheleth*, 300. See also Provan, who explains, "It may be that the combination of 'good and clean' is intended to clarify that it is not simply ritual cleanness to which Qohelet refers, but moral cleanness" (*Ecclesiastes, Song of Songs*, 180). Likewise Perry, *Dialogues with Kohelet*, 143.

345. But Murphy states: "The textual tradition for לטוב is uncertain. MT reads it, but LXX omits it. Syriac and Vulgate add 'and the evil'" (*Ecclesiastes*, 89). Many other commentators draw attention to the *addition* in LXX of καὶ τῷ κακῷ.

346. Fox, *A Time to Tear Down*, 292. He explains, "LXX-Qoh is too mechanical to have added a word for the sake of literary balance." Cf. Brown, *Ecclesiastes*, 91; Seow, *Ecclesiastes*, 299.

347. See, e.g., ESV, GNB, NAB, NIV, NJB, NLT, NRSV, REB.

solutions ignore the fact that טוב appears later in the list with a pair, and there seems no good reason either for repeating it, or for providing it with a different pair from the one later in the verse—thus NAS and NKJV retain the word without supplying a matching pair. Therefore, we may conclude either that לטוב is an error and ought to be removed,[348] or that it is intended to disrupt the list. Considering the plays on the word טוב earlier in the book, the latter is a distinct possibility. It raises very sharply the question: What really is "good" in the light of the fate which befalls *everyone*, however good or bad they are? This is borne out by the emphasis on "badness" in the very next verse:

זה רע בכל אשר־נעשה תחת השמש כי־מקרה אחד לכל
וגם לב בני־האדם מלא־רע והוללות בלבבם בחייהם ואחריו אל־המתים׃

It may be that this repetition of רע (used in two different senses) in v. 3 mirrors the repetition of טוב in v. 2, giving the contrast between the "good" which appears to be neutralised by death and the "bad" which is so dominant a feature of life under the sun. And these sentiments recall the statements Qohelet makes particularly in 7:20 and 8:11, but also in 7:29:

7:20   כי אדם אין צדיק בארץ אשר יעשה־טוב ולא יחטא
8:11   אשר אין־נעשה פתגם מעשה הרעה מהרה על־כן מלא
       לב בני־האדם בהם לעשות רע
7:29   לבד ראה־זה מצאתי אשר עשה האלהים את־האדם ישר
       והמה בקשו חשבנות רבים

The contrast between the "good" and the "bad" in 9:2–3 then leads into the striking better-saying in v. 4, כי־לכלב חי הוא טוב מן־האריה המת: it is *more* good (i.e. better) to be alive than dead, however "bad" life may be (for at least the living have *some* hope). As we noted above, this stands in considerable tension with the better-saying in 4:3 and the verse that leads up to it:

4:2   ושבח אני את־המתים שכבר מתו מן־החיים אשר המה חיים עדנה׃
4:3   וטוב משניהם את אשר־עדן לא היה
      אשר לא־ראה את־המעשה הרע   אשר נעשה תחת השמש׃
9:3   זה רע בכל   אשר־נעשה תחת השמש . . .
9:4   לכלב חי הוא טוב מן־האריה המת׃

By contrast, 11:7 is much more positive—here "seeing the sun" appears to be a metaphor for life, and Qohelet states that it is "good" ומתוק האור:
וטוב לעינים לראות את־השמש.

---

348. Thus Murphy argues that לטוב is "redundant in view of the כטוב כחטא in v. 2b" (*Ecclesiastes*, 89); cf., e.g., Longman, *The Book of Ecclesiastes*, 225; Ogden and Zogbo, *A Handbook*, 320.

Again the question arises: Is it, or is it not, good or better to be alive? 9:2–4 seems to indicate that it is better to be alive regardless of how bad life is. By contrast, 4:2–3 appears to suggest that there are circumstances in which it is better to be dead, or even better never to have lived at all. So what is "good" or "better?"

The other side of the coin is the question: What is "bad"? The vast majority of English versions and commentators simply render the two occurrences of רע in 9:3 by "evil,"[349] (and, indeed, Longman argues that "The use of *rāʿ* here *must* be moral"[350]) but this fails to take into account the semantic range of the word and makes no distinction between רע and רשׁע. NJPSV gives a different slant to this verse when it translates, "That is the *sad* thing about all that goes on under the sun: that the same fate is in store for all. (Not only that, but men's hearts are full of *sadness*, and their minds of madness, while they live; and then—to the dead!)"[351] Similarly, Provan translates, "This is the *miserable* thing in all that is done under the sun . . . the human heart knows its full measure of *misery*,"[352] and this is the line taken also by Ogden and Zogbo, who argue: "*An evil (rāʿ) may also be expressed as an adjective '[this is] sad' or 'calamitous.'* . . . [W]e should recognize Qoheleth's normal word usage here and treat *rāʿ* as the adjective describing a situation that is painful or distressing."[353] Such a reading of רע in this context is certainly possible, and has implications for its opposite, טוב—might it be better on occasion to render טוב as "happy"/"happiness" (the thing that is "good" for people in the midst of the sadness of life under the sun is "happiness" [even if the same fate befalls the happy and the sad in the end])? The important point here is that to understand רע as "sad" or "sadness" makes good sense *in some instances*, and to render טוב as "happy" or "happiness" (or, indeed, "joy") also fits particularly well *in some instances*, but neither gives a sufficient understanding of the words as they are used throughout Ecclesiastes. There is more to "good" and "bad" than "happy" and "sad," but these words may well, *on occasion*, best capture the *significance* of the words in a particular context. In other words, each word carries a degree of indeterminacy such that the precise meaning it conveys needs to be

---

349. E.g. ESV, NAS, NIV, NJB, NKJV, NRSV. See also Brown, *Ecclesiastes*, 91; Eaton, *Ecclesiastes*, 125–26; Loader, *Ecclesiastes*, 108; Longman, *The Book of Ecclesiastes*, 225; Murphy, *Ecclesiastes*, 91; Perry, *Dialogues with Kohelet*, 138; Seow, *Ecclesiastes*, 296.

350. Longman, *The Book of Ecclesiastes*, 227, my emphasis.

351. NLT translates: "It seems so *tragic* that one fate comes to all . . ."

352. Provan, *Ecclesiastes, Song of Songs*, 181.

353. Ogden and Zogbo, *A Handbook*, 321.

determined by the context in which it is used. What is "good" or "bad" for people in their lives under the sun? Well, it largely depends on the context—and how one reads that particular context.

A further twist is added to this question in 8:12–13, where Qohelet states that he *knows*[354] that it will be "good" for the one who fears God, and "not good" for the wicked, because they do not fear God:

כי גם־יודע אני אשר
יהיה־טוב ליראי האלהים אשר ייראו מלפניו
וטוב לא־יהיה לרשע ולא־יאריך ימים כצל אשר איננו ירא מלפני אלהים

Commentators struggle greatly with this verse, especially in view of its apparent contradiction in the succeeding verse:

יש־הבל אשר נעשה על־הארץ אשר
יש צדיקים אשר מגיע אלהם כמעשה הרשעים
ויש רשעים שמגיע אלהם כמעשה הצדיקים
אמרתי שגם־זה הבל:

Thus Crenshaw argues in relation to v. 12,

> The second half of the verse presents a view that Qohelet does not otherwise endorse, in language normally used for his own insights. The *ki gam-yodea* *'ani* (yet I know) introduces a subordinate clause that extends to verse 14. Either this affirmation of traditional belief about the fate of sinners and good people is a secondary gloss or it constitutes a concession to tradition that Qohelet boldly undercuts in verse 14. In this instance, the verdict "gloss" seems justified.[355]

He goes on to claim that "Qohelet strikes down the traditional belief of 8:12b–13 with a crushing blow." A number of scholars[356] take an approach similar to that adopted by Loader when he asserts, "when the author says in verse 12b, 'yet I know,' he uses a different form of the Hebrew verb from that used when he offers his own opinion. What he is doing is this: he cites the anticipated answer to the first part of his

354. This is particularly striking in the light of the fact that Qohelet only 5 times claims to know something (1:17; 2:14; 3:12, 14; 8:12). By contrast 19 times Qohelet either says people do not know (4:13, 17; 6:5; 8:5, 7; 9:1, 5, 10, 12; 10:14, 15; 11:2, 5 [×2] 6 [all these in ch. 11 are in the second person, "*you* do not know"]), or asks the (rhetorical?) question, "who knows?" (2:19; 3:21; 6:12; 8:1).

355. Crenshaw, *Ecclesiastes*, 155–56.

356. E.g. Davidson, *Ecclesiastes and the Song of Solomon*, 60; Longman, *The Book of Ecclesiastes*, 219–20; Murphy, *Ecclesiastes*, 85; Schoors, *The Preacher Sought*, 135. Perry ascribes the two contradictory views here to the two different voices which he finds in dialogue throughout the book (*Dialogues with Kohelet*, 137).

argument in advance in order to torpedo it in the last part."[357] Some English translations also take this approach, most notably the GNB which offers this rendering:

> Oh yes, I know what they say: "If you obey God, everything will be all right, but it will not go well for the wicked. Their life is like a shadow and they will die young, because they do not obey God." But this is nonsense. Look at what happens in the world: sometimes righteous men get the punishment of the wicked, and wicked men get the reward of the righteous. I say it is useless.[358]

However, as Fox points out, there is nothing that clearly marks these words out as the opinion of anyone other than Qohelet. Fox's own view is that Qohelet simply presents the contradictions in all their shocking reality.[359] Likewise Seow notes that "Qohelet accepts the orthodox doctrine of retribution, but he points to a contradiction of it in reality. He does not deny that there are all sorts of contradictions in the world."[360] Ogden's conclusion is more positive, but some similarity can be seen when he states, "we conclude that Qoheleth basically supports the traditional view about divine justice, but this does not mean that he cannot also bring before it some serious questions which must be faced."[361] Whybray similarly sees v. 14 as recording "inexplicable exceptions and no more,"[362] and Fredericks asserts that "it is only a *temporary* situation that justice is not apparent. . . . Qoheleth is consoled by the fact that 'everything is temporary.'"[363] Again it seems to be a matter of what one regards as the "centre" of Qohelet's discussion here, and what is viewed

---

357. Loader, *Ecclesiastes*, 101.

358. NJPSV puts vv. 12b–13 in quotes: "For although I am aware that 'It will be well . . .'"

359. Fox, *Qohelet*, 252–53. See also Bergant for a similar view (*Job, Ecclesiastes*, 273–74).

360. Seow, *Ecclesiastes*, 288. Brown puts it like this: "even in Qoheleth's topsy-turvy world, rife with contradiction, the sage refuses to let go of his faith in holy reverence" (*Ecclesiastes*, 89).

361. Ogden, *Qoheleth*, 137–38. Garrett simply states, "It is a word of faith in the face of apparently contradictory evidence" (*Proverbs, Ecclesiastes, Song of Songs*, 329), and Tamez contends that "Verses 12 and 13 are a vehement affirmation of faith in the face of the gross injustice practiced by sinners" (*When the Horizons Close*, 108).

362. Whybray, *Ecclesiastes*, 137. This seems also to be how REB understands the text when it adds "sometimes" to v. 14, "There is a futile thing found on earth: *sometimes* the just person gets what is due to the unjust . . ."

363. Fredericks, *Coping with Transience*, 89. See Farmer for a similar view (*Who Knows What is Good?*, 182).

as "marginal." In this respect Hubbard's comments are particularly revealing:

> The reflection of verse 14 drags us back to the nagging fact that justice at times seems topsy-turvy. *"There is"* (Heb. *yēsh*) seems to make this the exceptional situation, not the normal one described in verses 12–13. It is as though the Preacher gestured to an odd series of events *on the margin* of the scene that could readily be overlooked, had he not pointed us to something that *"there is"* over there. [364]

On the other hand, Davidson marginalises vv. 12b–13 by treating them as a quote which provides the grist for the mill of Qohelet's argument against a doctrine of retribution:

> The Good News Bible is, I believe, right in putting the second half of verse 12 and the whole of verse 13 in quotation marks. . . . Here Koheleth is taking issue with the widely held view that the wicked perish and come to an early sticky end, while people who obey God, prosper and live to a ripe old age. Don't believe it, he says; that is nonsense. Life does not work out like that. [365]

In fact, the apparently traditional theology presented in vv. 12b–13 and the observations in v. 14 are simply juxtaposed, leaving a gap for readers to fill in as they try to work out for themselves what is the connection between them. Thus, as they seek to advise Bible translators in relation to vv. 12–13, Ogden and Zogbo concede:

> Translators, then, have a very difficult choice to make. They can either interpret the passage as Qoheleth's strong affirmation, or as a quotation that raises an insoluble problem. . . . Since this text is really ambiguous, the translator may choose to put one interpretation in the text and the other in a footnote. We can choose, for example, to translate the clause as Qoheleth's firm belief, but add a footnote stating that some understand this to be a quotation from traditional wisdom, which Qoheleth then goes on to question. [366]

. . . and, of course, what you choose to put in the text and what is relegated to the footnote indicates clearly what is considered "central" and what "marginal." This raises in very stark terms the question: What does Qohelet mean by stating that it will be "good" for the God-fearer when he also observes that what should fall to the righteous goes instead to the wicked and vice versa?

---

364. Hubbard, *Ecclesiastes, Song of Solomon*, 194, my emphasis.
365. Davidson, *Ecclesiastes and the Song of Solomon*, 60.
366. Ogden and Zagbo, *A Handbook*, 300.

7.4. *Conclusion*

In summary, it is clear that טוב is a significant word in Ecclesiastes. Moreover, it is arguable that the issue raised in 2:3,

תרתי . . . עד אשר־אראה אי־זה טוב לבני האדם אשר יעשׂו תחת
השׁמים מספר ימי חייהם:

is a key one in this book. Certainly it features as a key element throughout much of 3:22–9:7 (just over 100 verses out of a total of 222 in the middle of the book, running from the 66th through to the 167th verse). But just what does טוב *mean*? Just what is "good" for people to do in the few days of their lives under heaven? And what does it mean to call something "good" anyway? These questions are left without definitive answer precisely because of the ambiguous ways (and there are numerous such ways) in which this word (and related words) is (are) used in Ecclesiastes. Ironically, whatever precisely טוב means (and whatever precisely its opposite here, רע, means), the book ends by asserting that God will bring every deed to judgment, *whether good or evil*:

כי את־כל־מעשׂה האלהים יבא במשׁפט
על כל־נעלם אם־טוב ואם־רע:

Chapter 8

תחת השמש IN ECCLESIASTES

8.1. *A Different Kind of Ambiguity*

The phrase תחת השמש is a key one in Ecclesiastes, appearing some 29 times.[1] Although the expression is not used anywhere else in the Hebrew Bible,[2] there seems to be no dispute about its *translation*, "under the sun." However, תחת השמש is ambiguous because it can be *interpreted* in more than one way. Fox explains the ambiguity thus:

> There are two ways in which "under the sun" might be intended: restrictively and inclusively. In the first, the purpose of the phrase would be to modestly restrict the application of Qohelet's observations to this world *alone*, excluding other domains that are beyond human ken. In this case, Qohelet would be holding out the possibility of a different situation elsewhere, namely in the heavens. . . . If the sense of "under the sun" is inclusive, Qohelet's purpose is to underscore the *breadth* of his observations, claiming that such-and-such is true in the *entire* world "under the sun," not just a part of it.[3]

1. Longman observes, "Perhaps only the *hebel* refrain is more widely known than Qoheleth's phrase *under the sun*" (*The Book of Ecclesiastes*, 66).
2. Commentators are divided on the original source of this expression. Thus, for example, Lohfink describes the phrase as "intellectual jargon in a Greek mode…(in normal Hebrew, they wrote 'under the heavens')" (*Qoheleth*), but Seow stands with many other commentators when he states that "The idiom is well attested in Semitic texts, so there is no need to explain this expression as a grecism" (*Ecclesiastes*, 105).
3. Fox, *A Time to Tear Down*, 165, his emphasis. L. Wilson also draws attention to the different readings of the phrase in an article entitled "Artful Ambiguity in Ecclesiastes 1,1–11"; see p. 359. However, in a personal note, Wilson states: "I wonder if this phrase is 'ambiguous' in the sense that *hebel* is ambiguous. I argue that *hebel* is meant to be ambiguous, and that the reader should not opt for one or other of its poles of meaning, but retain both. Yet the phrase 'under the sun' is different. It might mean 'on earth' as opposed to 'in heaven,' or it might mean something like 'leaving God and his heavenly realities' out of the picture (I suspect it means the first). However, I do not think that it is designed to mean both—it is one or the other, and it is a matter of which of the possible meanings can be established in the light of how the phrase is used in the book."

Fox acknowledges that the first sense is "the traditional understanding of the phrase," which "makes Qohelet out to be pious and modest in his claims and even hints at hopes for a better life above and beyond this one,"[4] but he argues that "The inclusive function is more likely," explaining, "Since most of the facts that Qohelet observes 'under the sun' can hardly be imagined to exist in any other domain but human life, there is no need for him to exclude other domains of reality."[5] Hubbard also writes that the term "under the sun" pictures "the *universality* of the Preacher's perspective," adding "Anywhere one goes, the uncertainty, injustice, futility, and fixity of life will be evident."[6] Similarly, Crenshaw states, "the phrase 'under the sun' reinforces the universal sweep of the thematic statement and its rationale," though he goes on to say, "Nothing falls outside the area circumscribed by *taḥat haššāmeš, except Sheol and heaven.*"[7] By contrast, Longman maintains that "Qohelet's frequent use of the phrase *under the sun* highlights the restricted scope of his inquiry," arguing that "His worldview does not allow him to take a transcendent yet immanent God into consideration in his quest for meaning."[8] Ogden and Zogbo say that "under the sun" "is an important [phrase] for this book because it sets the limits within which Qoheleth is investigating the problem of 'lasting benefit.'" They add, "Later on he will conclude that there is no lasting benefit here on earth, by which he may be suggesting

---

4. Thus, for example, Matthew Henry writes, "There is a world above the sun, for the glory of God is its light, where there is work without labour and with great profit, the work of angels; but he speaks of the work *under the sun*, the pains of which are great and the gains little… The fruit of our labour in heavenly things is *meat that endures to eternal life*, but the fruit of our labour for the world is only *meat that perishes*" (*A Commentary of the Whole Bible* [6 vols.; Iowa Falls, Iowa: World Bible Publishers, n.d.], 3:982, original emphasis).

5. Fox, *A Time to Tear Down*, 165.

6. Hubbard, *Ecclesiastes, Song of Songs*, 46, his emphasis.

7. Crenshaw, *Ecclesiastes*, 59, my emphasis.

8. Longman, *The Book of Ecclesiastes*, 66. Longman states that "In the Bible this viewpoint is unique to Qohelet." Similarly, Fredericks writes, "These phrases identify the parameters of his search and observations of 'everything': 'under the sun' (nearly 30 times); 'under heaven' (three times); and 'on the earth' (six times). This is the scope of his observation and experiences, and he has resigned himself to knowing or discovering nothing else" (Fredericks, *Coping with Transience*, 92). Fredericks does, though, go on to compare the temporary nature of everything "under the sun" with "the eternal as the gift of God, put in man's heart" (*Coping with Transience*, 93). Likewise, Mills says, "it has to be noted that Qohelet's knowledge and evaluation are always limited to what is under the sun… Here is a specifically human assessment" (*Reading Ecclesiastes*, 52).

that there is one beyond this life."[9] Seow takes a somewhat different tack when he says that "the expression 'under the sun' is temporal, referring to the experiences in the realm of the living—this world of light and life, as opposed to the world of darkness in the netherworld."[10] Davis's approach is different again. She argues:

> The question is one of faith. . . . The faith that such engagement requires, and at the same time deepens, is faith that there is a stable reality *beyond* this world of our immediate perceptions and experiences. Like the New Testament writers, Koheleth knows that we will never have full relief from puzzles, frustrations, and trouble (see John 16:33) as long as we are "under the sun." Koheleth never presumes to make positive statements about the nature of reality "beyond the sun," yet the admonition to "fear God" (5:7; 12:13) implies that that ultimate reality always conditions his thought.[11]

Similarly, Eaton equates "under the sun" specifically with the earthly realm,[12] claiming that "If our view of life goes no further than 'under the sun,' all our endeavours will have an undertone of misery"; but that "There is another realm altogether, the Preacher will contend later (5:2), when he will speak of God who may be approached and worshipped (5:1–7)."[13] Farmer also suggests that "Qohelet seems to hint that a distinction can be made between what happens on earth, 'under the sun,' and what happens elsewhere."[14] Ogden, understands Qohelet to use "under the sun" to refer to "this worldly existence" as opposed to what happens after death, although he acknowledges that Qohelet, "like all

9. Ogden and Zogbo, *A Handbook on Ecclesiastes*, 24.

10. Seow, *Ecclesiastes*, 111.

11. Davis, *Proverbs, Ecclesiastes, and the Song of Songs*, 166. This approach characterises many popular works on Ecclesiastes. For instance, Roland Cap Ehlke writes, "This is the first key thought of Ecclesiastes: everything under the sun is, in and of itself, meaningless. Solomon's [*sic*] repeated use of this concept implies that there is something 'beyond the sun.' Somewhere out there is something or someone not subject to this meaningless world. That someone, of course, is God" (*Ecclesiastes, Song of Songs* [People's Bible Commentary; St Louis, Mo.: Concordia, 1992], 4–5); R. C. Sproul Jr. argues similarly, "We have explored how life 'under the sun' is foolishness, devoid of meaning. And now this: we turn our attention to purpose, how life 'beyond the sun' is replete with meaning and significance" (*Vanity and Meaning: Discovering Purpose in Life* [Grand Rapids: Baker Book House, 1995], 45–46); a short book entitled *Beyond the Sun: A Guide to Understanding Ecclesiastes* (Greenville, S.C.: Bob Jones University Press, 2001) is authored by Coart Ramey.

12. Eaton, *Ecclesiastes*, 44–45.

13. Ibid., 57–58.

14. Farmer, *Who Knows What is Good?*, 150.

other wisdom teachers, must remain tentative about that which resides outside the sphere of empirical research."[15]

8.2. תחת השמים *and* תחת השמש

A further complication is added by the use just three times of the expression תחת השמים, once in each of the first three chapters (1:13; 2:3; 3:1). This phrase *is* used elsewhere in the Hebrew Bible, but apart from Ecclesiastes it is always in the form מתחת השמים[16] or תחת כל־השמים.[17] These are subtle differences (which are not, so far as I am aware, pointed out by the commentators), but they do mean that the precise form the expression takes in Ecclesiastes is unique to this book in the Hebrew Bible, so that there are no exact parallels with which to compare it. Its use in Ecclesiastes raises the question why a different term is used on these few occasions and whether any different nuance is intended. If it were simply an exact synonym, used for literary variation, one might expect it to be used more often and distributed more evenly.[18] Again the commentators are divided. Fox reasons thus:

> Though emendation to "sun" is not necessary, it does have a good claim to a Hebrew origin, being attested by Syr, Jerome, Tg, and most of the LXX tradition. The interchange between the functional synonyms *šemeš* and *šamayim* may have occurred in the transmission of texts or in the process of translation.[19]

This would remove the question altogether. However, Longman (along with most recent commentators) takes the opposite position:

> The phrase *under heaven* is a rough synonym for "under the sun," for it is similarly used in the book of Ecclesiastes (cf. 1:3). Some Hebrew manuscripts and a number of versions replace "under heaven" with the more common "under the sun," but this is probably an overcorrection caused by the more common occurrence of the latter phrase in the book.[20]

15. Ogden, *Qoheleth*, 29.

16. Gen 1:9; 6:17; Exod 17:14; Deut 7:24; 9:14; 25:19; 29:20; 2 Kgs 14:27. In most cases these refer to people or their names being "blotted out from under heaven."

17. Gen 7:19; Deut 2:25; 4:19; Job 28:24; 37:3; 41:11; Dan 9:12.

18. It should perhaps be noted that תחת השמש is not evenly distributed throughout the book: most notably it is completely absent from the final 39 verses, but there is also a 38-verse absence throughout ch. 7 and into ch. 8

19. Fox, *A Time to Tear Down*, 171.

20. Longman, *The Book of Ecclesiastes*, 80. Hubbard says "'*under heaven*' is virtually a synonym for '*under the sun*'" (*Ecclesiastes, Song of Songs*, 61) and Perry also describes the phrases as "synonymous" (*Dialogues with Kohelet*, 57).

Webb concedes, "It could be that the two expressions are simply synonymous, but it is more likely, in my judgment, that there is a subtle difference." He argues that "by life 'under the sun' we are meant to understand
human existence viewed primarily with reference to the earth as the envi-
ronment in which men and women live. In contrast . . . the expression
'under heaven' carries the additional nuance of the divine government of
the world in which human beings live."[21] Similarly, Lohfink says (in
relation to 1:13) that, "It may not be by accident that Qoheleth does not
say 'under the sun' here, but rather 'under the heavens.' He is already
drawing the reader here toward God, about whom the text will immediately speak."[22] Seow also maintains that the two expressions have different nuances, but he explains the difference thus:

> Qoheleth clearly knows the more common expression "under the heav-
> ens" and he uses it, but his preference is for "under the sun." This distinc-
> tion is perhaps not without nuances. Whereas "under the heavens" refers
> to the universality of human experiences everywhere in the world (i.e. it
> is a spatial designation), "under the sun" refers to the temporal universe
> of the living (cf. 8:9, where "under the sun" is defined temporally: "a time
> when . . ."). In other words, "under the heavens" simply means the cos-
> mos (a term of universality), whereas "under the sun" is a term for "this
> world" as opposed to the netherworld (see 9:6). The this-worldliness of
> the expression "under the sun" explains its recurrence in Ecclesiastes.[23]

By contrast, Crenshaw represents the majority of commentators when he
writes, "A variant (*taḥat haššāmāyim*) occurs three times in Ecclesiastes
(1:13; 2:3; 3:1), but there seems to be no difference in meaning between
the two expressions."[24]

In Ecclesiastes, where, I believe, language is manipulated very
cleverly, careful readers are likely to wonder why the author employs a

---

21. Webb, *Five Festal Garments*, 95. T. M. Moore argues similarly: he says of
his reading of the book, "This interpretation of the purpose of Ecclesiastes largely
hangs on one's understanding of the phrases 'under the heavens' and 'under the
sun.' Most—but not all—commentators take these phrases as essentially equivalent,
merely different ways of saying the same thing. I see them instead as opposing
phrases, used throughout the book to set the discussion either in an earthbound or in
a God-oriented frame of reference" (*Ecclesiastes*, 11).

22. Lohfink, *Qoheleth*, 46.

23. Seow, *Ecclesiastes*, 105.

24. Crenshaw, *Ecclesiastes*, 60. Murphy also writes that "the expression is varied
in 1:13; 2:3; 3:1" (*Ecclesiastes*, 7) while Ogden and Zogbo state that "*Under heaven*
is a variation of the phrase 'under the sun'... [T]he meaning of the two phrases is
identical" (*A Handbook*, 42). Whybray describes the terms as "equivalent" (*Ecclesiastes*, 110) and Hubbard uses the description "sister-phrase" (*Ecclesiastes, Song of
Songs*, 46).

unique term when another was available, and why a unique form of the expression found elsewhere in the Hebrew Bible is used on a few occasions, and to ask themselves whether there is any difference in meaning between the two. In support of Seow's argument, it certainly appears to be true that the immediate contexts in which תחת השמים is used in 1:13 and 3:1 emphasise respectively the universality of Qohelet's explorations and the universality of the statement that "for everything there is a time"; hence "everywhere" or "anywhere" (in the sense of "*wherever* such-and-such occurs," indicating the representative comprehensiveness of Qohelet's enquiries without implying that he actually saw what happened *everywhere*) might be appropriate paraphrases:

> [I] applied my mind to seek and to search out by wisdom all that is done *everywhere* . . . (1:13)

> For everything there is a season, and a time for every matter *everywhere*. (3.1)

It is also the case that the use of מתחת השמים and especially תחת כל־ השמים elsewhere in the Hebrew Bible emphasise universality. But the paraphrase "everywhere"/"anywhere" would not work in a number of the verses where תחת השמש is used, while something like "in this world" would. For example:

> Enjoy life with the wife whom you love, all the days of your vain life that are given you *in this world*, because that is your portion in life and in your toil at which you toil *in this world*. (9:9)

If this distinction could be maintained, there clearly would be grounds for arguing that תחת השמש might emphasise *this* world rather than *everywhere*, with the further implication that there may be another world or realm where things are different. However, while "in this world" would be an appropriate paraphrase for every use of תחת השמש, it is not at all evident that it should be understood "temporally" as Seow argues. In some verses the temporal aspect of "this world" does seem to be the main issue (5:18 [Eng. 5:19]; 6:12; 8:9; 9:9), but in other verses the universality of a particular observation of something that happens in "this world" appears to be emphasised (1:14; 3:16; 4:1; 9:3). In the majority of cases תחת השמש seems simply to indicate that what is described is an observable feature of the way life is "in this world" with no necessary implication either of the universality of what is being observed nor of its temporality (especially in contradistinction to some notion of "the eternal"). Moreover, while universality is emphasised when תחת השמים is used in 1:13 and 3:1 (and, indeed, in both contexts there is an emphasis on God's activity), temporality seems to be more to the fore in 2:3 (and God is notably absent from this section of the book):[25]

> I searched with my mind how to cheer my body with wine—my mind still guiding me with wisdom—and how to lay hold on folly, until I might see what was good for mortals to do *under heaven* during the few days of their life. (2:3)

Thus it is difficult to sustain any clear distinction between the two expressions תחת השמש and תחת השמים, both indicating "this world" with the precise implications varying according to context. Nonetheless, the use of these two expressions may well be intended to raise questions in the readers' minds about just what they mean, and whether or not they should be interpreted differently.

It should be noted that השמים occurs just once more in Ecclesiastes. We read in 5:1 [Eng. 5:2], האלהים בשמים ואתה על־הארץ. This clause may intentionally reflect Deut 4:39 so as to emphasise the distinction in Ecclesiastes between the human and divine realms:[26]

ואתה על־הארץ	האלהים בשמים	כי Eccl 5:1 (Heb)
ועל־הארץ מתחת	בשמים ממעל האלהים הוא כי יהוה	Deut 4:39

---

25. It is notable that Moore, who makes a distinction between the meanings of "under the heavens" and "under the sun" refers to only two occurrences of the former, and takes no account whatsoever of its use here (see *Ecclesiastes*, 10–12).

26. Seow, for example, writes: "This is an attempt to correct any misunderstanding about God's immanence and to emphasize the distance between God and humanity. God and mortals do not belong to the same realms" (*Ecclesiastes*, 198–99). Fox refers to "The vast disparity between God's lofty station and man's earthbound lowliness" (*A Time to Tear Down*, 231). Needless to say, the implications of this clause have been interpreted quite differently; as Whybray notes, "this lapidary statement has been interpreted in quite different ways: as being entirely in accordance with the main Old Testament tradition and as completely 'heretical' and a deliberate denial of Dt. 4:39's 'Yahweh is God in heaven above and on the earth beneath.'" Whybray himself argues that "The former view is nearer the truth" (*Ecclesiastes*, 94). See also, e.g., Eaton, *Ecclesiastes*, 98–99; Lohfink, *Qoheleth*, 75; Ogden and Zogbo, *A Handbook*, 154–55; Provan, *Ecclesiastes, Song of Songs*, 116; Tamez, *When the Horizons Close*, 76). Contrast, for example, Longman, who, after acknowledging "that the tone of the verse is once again ambiguous, and the verse could conceivably be read two ways," states, "We take this statement not as an assertion of divine power, but of divine distance, perhaps even indifference" (*The Book of Ecclesiastes*, 151). See further Davidson, *Ecclesiastes and the Song of Solomon*, 34–35; Loader, *Ecclesiastes*, 58. Farmer simply says, "As a reason this is rather obscure," explaining, "Perhaps it implies that God is too exalted to be bothered by a lot of unnecessary babbling from earthbound mortals. Or perhaps it means that God in heaven is able to see what our needs are without hearing a lot of words from us about them" (*Who Knows What is Good?*, 167).

If the term תחת השמש is effectively synonymous with תחת השמים, this might be taken to indicate, in view of 5:1, that תחת השמש designates specifically the human realm (אתה על־הארץ) as opposed to the divine realm (האלהים בשמים). תחת השמש would also then be paralleled by the expression על־הארץ as it is used in 5:1 [Eng. 5:2] and 8:14, 16; 11:2.[27] 8:14–17 seem to support this contention because על־הארץ is used once in v. 14, תחת השמש twice in v. 15, על־הארץ once in v. 16 and תחת השמש once in v. 17 with no apparent difference in meaning. This use of three different, but at least roughly synonymous, expressions adds to the ambiguity: readers are left to work out for themselves whether or not the three are completely synonymous and what is the precise nuance of each in different verses. It should be observed that the use of על־הארץ in 10:7; 11:3 and 12:7 is rather different, because in each of these verses something takes place "upon the ground" rather than "on earth"; this may serve to heighten the ambiguity of the expression.

8.3. *Use of* תחת השמש *in Ecclesiastes*

In order to establish more clearly the contexts in which the phrase "under the sun" and its near-equivalents are used, Fig. 15 (next page) demonstrates that with only one exception the phrase תחת השמש is always used with the near-synonyms עשה and עמל, or with the first person use of the verb ראה, and that two of the three seemingly synonymous occurrences of תחת השמים and two of the three seemingly synonymous occurrences of על־הארץ function in the same way. Moreover, the "universal" aspect of the expressions is shown by the frequent use of the word כל.

This appears to indicate that, whatever the precise implications of these phrases, they refer particularly to the realm that the author observes in which human work and deeds are performed; and that these observations are comprehensive. Moreover, "seeing the sun" is used elsewhere in Ecclesiastes as a metaphor for life: in 6:5 the stillborn child is described as not seeing the sun; in 7:11 "those who see the sun" may describe "the living"; and in 11:7 "seeing the sun" seems to indicate life in contrast to the "darkening of the sun" in 12:3, which probably pictures approaching death. תחת השמש (along with תחת השמים and על־הארץ) thus indicates the world people experience while they are alive, the observable world of work and other human activity.

---

27. Thus Crenshaw writes of 8:14: "Here Qohelet uses ʿal-hāʾăreṣ instead of *taḥat haššāmeš*, but the meaning is the same" (*Ecclesiastes*, 156). So also, e.g., Eaton, *Ecclesiastes*, 44; Longman, *The Book of Ecclesiastes*, 220; Ogden and Zogbo, *A Handbook*, 304. Murphy, though, argues that "'under the sun'/'under the heavens' has more than the pale meaning of 'on the earth'" (*Ecclesiastes*, 7).

תחת השמש or equivalent	עמל	עשה	כל	ראה	
תחת השמש	עמלו שיעמל		בכל־		1:3
תחת השמש		שנעשה הוא שיעשה ...			1:9
תחת השמש		המעשים שנעשו	את־כל־	ראית	1:14
תחת השמש	ובעמל שעמלתי...	בכל־ מעשי שעשו ידי			2:11
תחת השמש		המעשה שנעשה			2:17
תחת השמש	עמלי שאני עמל		את־כל־		2:18
תחת השמש	עמלי שעמלתי ...		בכל־		2:19
תחת השמש	העמל שעמלתי		כל־		2:20
תחת השמש	עמלו ... שהוא עמל		בכל		2:22
תחת השמש				ראית	3:16
תחת השמש		העשקים אשר נעשים	את־כל־	ואראה	4:1
תחת השמש		המעשה הרע אשר נעשה	את־		4:3
תחת השמש				...ואראה	4:7
תחת השמש				...ראיתי	4:15
תחת השמש				ראית	5:12
תחת השמש	עמלו שיעמל		בכל־	...ראיתי	5:17
תחת־השמש	עמלו שיעמל		בכל־	...ראיתי	5:18
תחת השמש				ראית	6:1
תחת השמש		לכל־ מעשה אשר נעשה		...ראיתי	8:9
תחת השמש	בעמלו ...				8:15*
תחת־השמש		המעשה אשר נעשה	את־	...וראיתי	8:17
תחת השמש		אשר־נעשה	בכל		9:3
תחת השמש		אשר־נעשה	בכל־		9:6
תחת השמש	ובעמלך אשר אתה עמל				9:9*
תחת־השמש				ורא̇ה	9:11
תחת השמש				...ראיתי	9:13
תחת השמש				ראית	10:5
תחת השמים		אשר נעשה	כל־		1:13
תחת השמים		אשר יעשו		...אראה	2:3
על־הארץ		אשר נעשה			8:14
על־הארץ		אשר נעשה			8:16

Figure 15
(Asterisk indicates two occurrences of תחת השמש.)

   The precise implications of the phrase תחת השמש in any given context need to be worked out, or perhaps supplied, by the reader—and different readers understand these implications differently. Thus, for example, Leupold explains that

the very important expression "under the sun" must be carefully evaluated, for the correct appreciation of this phrase is one of the major safeguards of the message of the entire book... Each time the phrase occurs it is as though the author had said, "Let us for the sake of argument momentarily rule out the higher things." If one follows his suggestion one obviously has earthly things pure and simple to reckon with; nothing more."[28]

This has been a very popular approach to the book, well expressed by Hendry in the third edition of the *New Bible Commentary*. For Hendry, Ecclesiastes

> is in reality a major work of apologetic or "eristic" theology. Its apparent worldliness is dictated by its aim: Qoheleth is addressing the general public whose view is bounded by the horizons of this world; he meets them on their own ground, and proceeds to convict them of its inherent vanity. This is further borne out by his characteristic expression "under the sun," by which he describes what the New Testament calls "the world" (Gk. *kosmos*). His book is in fact a critique of secularism and of secularized religion.[29]

Indeed, Garrett observes that "Conservative Christians have generally assumed that the purpose of Ecclesiastes is to show the futility of the world over against eternity; that is, the book is evangelistic."[30] However, this is also an ancient reading, found, for example in Gregory Thaumaturgos' paraphrase of Ecclesiastes[31] and in a rather different form in

28. Leupold, *Exposition of Ecclesiastes*, 42–43.

29. G. S. Hendry, "Ecclesiastes," in *New Bible Commentary* (ed. D. Guthrie; 3d ed.; Leicester: InterVarsity, 1970), 570. The article by Michael A. Eaton in the latest edition of the *New Bible Commentary* is more nuanced, though it too sees the book as "an evangelistic tract, calling secular people to face the implications of their secularism" (from the section of the Introduction entitled, "Purpose and Abiding Message," in the electronic version of *New Bible Commentary: 21st Century Edition* [ed. D. A. Carson et al.; 4th ed.; Leicester: InterVarsity, 1994]). See also Eaton's commentary, *Ecclesiastes*, 44–45, and Paul N. Benware, *Survey of the Old Testament* (Everyman's Bible Commentary; Chicago: Moody Press, 1998), 160–61; Ehlke, *Ecclesiastes, Song of Songs*, 4–5.

30. Garrett, *Proverbs, Ecclesiastes, Song of Songs*, 271. He adds, "This was the view of the Reformers and Puritans (Whitaker, Pemble, Cocceious, Matthew Poole, Matthew Henry), and John Wesley. In like manner, Ralph Wardlaw used Ecclesiastes to point to the cross."

31. Οὐδὲ γὰρ ἔχει τις εἰπεῖν ὄφελός τι τούτοις προσηρτημένον, ἅπερ ἄνθρωποι περὶ γῆν ἕρποντες, καὶ σώμασι καὶ ψυχαῖς ἐκτελέσαι σπεύδουσι, τῶν μὲν προσκαίρων ἡττημένοι, ἀνωτέρω δὲ τῶν ἄστρων τῷ γενναίῳ τῆς ψυχῆς ὄμματι, οὐδ' ὁτιοῦν κατιδεῖν βουλόμενοι ("Nor can anyone say that there is any use connected with the things which human beings, crawling on the earth, are striving to achieve by physical and mental effort. They have given themselves over to transitory things, not wanting to look—with the soul's noble eye—at anything higher than the stars"; text and translation from John Jarick, *Gregory Thaumaturgos' Paraphrase of Ecclesiastes* [Septuagint and Cognate Studies 29; Atlanta: Scholars Press, 1990], 9). Jarick comments that here "Gregory supplies a contrary expression not present in the

rabbinic texts.[32] Moreover, it is a reading that finds support, explicitly or implicitly, among a number of recent commentators. Thus Longman basically adopts the same argument when he states that "Qohelet's worldview does not allow him to take a transcendent yet immanent God into consideration,"[33] but argues, "A second voice is heard at the beginning of the book (1:1–11) and at the end (12:8–14), placing a frame around Qohelet's speech and providing the perspective through which we should read his opinion."[34] According to Longman, this second voice, "affirms that Qohelet sought to find truth, although nowhere does he ever clearly state that Qoheleth found truth. What truth Qohelet found was truth 'under the sun.' Indeed, apart from God, which is one of the meanings I believe this phrase has, there is no meaning, no reason to do more than to pursue the simple pleasures of life (eat, drink, and enjoy work)." The frame narrator then "turns his son [the narratee] toward the central truths of revealed religion."[35] Ogden reads Ecclesiastes (and especially the words of Qohelet) very differently from Longman, but he arrives at a similar conclusion when he maintains that while "Qoheleth concludes that there is *no* advantage to man 'under the sun' (2:11)…that is to say, *yitrôn* is not located in this world,"[36] there is nevertheless "an awareness that the time and experience of this world are not the only dimensions with which we have to do, and that *yitrôn* is bound up with that 'eternal' dimension."[37]

original book—namely the phrase ἀνωτέρω τῶν ἄστρων…and thus introduces a perspective quite unknown to the original author" (p. 10).

32. See *Shab.* 30B and *Qoh. Rab.* 1:3, and the discussion of these passages in Ruth N. Sandberg, *Rabbinic Views of Qohelet* (Lewiston, N.Y.: Mellen Biblical Press, 1999), 24–25. Sara Japhet and Robert B. Salters discuss Rashbam's interpretation of the phrase, *The Commentary of R. Samuel Ben Meir Rashbam on Qoheleth* (Jerusalem: Magnes, 1985), 44–46.

33. Longman, *The Book of Ecclesiastes*, 66.

34. Ibid., 37.

35. Ibid., 284. Brown is one of a number of commentators who argue that this "frame narrative" serves to "blunt the book's subversive edge in order to bring it into the biblical mainstream" (*Ecclesiastes*, 10). Webb disagrees with both: "Overall, the effect of the voice we hear in the epilogue is to inculcate respect for Qohelet and to guide us to the conclusion the frame narrator wants us to draw from his teaching. I have tried to argue that this is not an artifical conclusion to the book, but one that emerges naturally from Qohelet's own train of thought" (*Five Festal Garments*, 102; see his discussion of Longman in n. 32 on that page). I agree that the closing "frame" is not "an artifical conclusion"; in fact, it is highly ambiguous as this sample of opinions demonstrates.

36. Ogden, *Qoheleth*, 29.

37. Ibid., 24.

By contrast, Bergant writes, "The phrase 'under the sun'…is a figurative way of speaking of the place where the human drama unfolds. Life must be lived here on earth and all hopes must be realized here as well,"[38] adding that he "has expressed no hope in an afterlife."[39] Similarly, Garrett states, "The Teacher tells his readers how to live in the world as it really is instead of living in a world of false hope. In short, *Ecclesiastes urges its readers to recognize that they are mortal*."[40] Further, Fox asserts,

> Qohelet does not exclude the possibility that beyond the sphere of events "under the sun" or within the divine intellect there might be a resolution of absurdities, but he (unlike the author of Job) does not affirm or even suggest that there is one. Such a resolution is simply of no use to Qohelet, any more than the unknowable possibility of an afterlife is the solution to the problem of mortality for the living.[41]

8.4. *Conclusion*

So, תחת השמש is an expression unique to Ecclesiastes in the Hebrew Bible which indicates the observable realm which people inhabit and where they work and do other things. It appears to be used synonymously with the term תחת השמים (though some dispute this), which does appear elsewhere in the Hebrew Bible (in the forms מתחת השמים and תחת כל־השמים), and the common phrase על־הארץ. But there is considerable disagreement among the commentators over its implications. Does it emphasise the universality of Qohelet's explorations (this is what life is like *everywhere*), or does it indicate that there may be another realm where things are different (this is what life is like *in this realm*)? On these questions the commentators disagree and it makes a significant difference to their overall understanding of the book of Ecclesiastes—or, perhaps, their understanding of the book of Ecclesiastes has a significant bearing on how they interpret this expression. Either way, תחת השמש is ambiguous.

---

38. Bergant, *Job, Ecclesiastes*, 231.
39. Ibid., 291. A number of other commentators quite specifically deny that Ecclesiastes offers any hope of an afterlife: so, e.g., Crenshaw, *Ecclesiastes*, 26; Murphy, *Ecclesiastes*, lxvii–lxviii.
40. Garrett, *Proverbs, Ecclesiastes, Song of Songs*, 278, his emphasis.
41. Fox, *A Time to Tear Down*, 35.

Chapter 9

CONCLUSION

this ambiguous reality
which is called existence
—Simone de Beauvoir[1]

Page, in a book entitled *Ambiguity and the Presence of God*, mentions Ecclesiastes only once when she writes,

> "Vanity of vanities," says Ecclesiastes in the Old Testament, "all is vanity." He has seen change, inequality and injustice in this life and has no hope after death, so he recommends that people should enjoy their work and recreation under God as they can. Anything more is emptiness and the chasing of wind. A similarly disillusioned conclusion could emerge from the recognition of Ambiguity [*sic*] in every aspect of human and natural possibility.[2]

1. De Beauvoir, *The Ethics of Ambiguity*, 25. A comparison of Ecclesiastes with *The Ethics of Ambiguity* indicates some fascinating parallels between the thought of de Beauvoir and Qohelet. Of course, much has been written on Ecclesiastes and existentialism (and de Beauvoir states, "From the very beginning, existentialism defined itself as a philosophy of ambiguity" [p. 9]), and I suspect Qohelet might have found something of a kindred spirit in de Beauvoir. One crucial difference between the two works, however, is that de Beauvoir refuses to allow God to feature in her assessment of the ambiguous nature of the human condition: "The first implication of such an attitude is that the genuine man will not agree to recognize any foreign absolute. When a man projects into an ideal heaven that impossible synthesis of the for-itself and the in-itself that is called God, it is because he wishes the regard of this existing Being to change his existence into being; but if he agrees not to be in order to exist genuinely, he will abandon the dream of an inhuman objectivity. He will understand that it is not a matter of being right in the eyes of a God, but of being right in his own eyes. Renouncing the thought of seeking the guarantee for his existence outside of himself, he will also refuse to believe in unconditioned values which would set themselves up athwart his freedom like things" (p. 14). I have no doubt that Qohelet is not an existentialist in any way comparable to the twentieth-century existentialists—but perhaps if he'd lived 2000 years later, things might be different.

2. Page, *Ambiguity and the Presence of God*, 23.

However, it is precisely the ambiguous nature of life "under the sun" that is captured by the ambiguity in Ecclesiastes. It has often been suggested that whatever else the author of Ecclesiastes is, that author is at least a realist,[3] and a key element in that realism—which has not sufficiently been taken into account—is the portrayal by means of ambiguous text of a world which is itself subject to hugely varied interpretation. Just as people come to the world with different presuppositions and "read" it differently, so readers come to the world of Ecclesiastes and respond to in it different ways. Crenshaw takes a first step towards acknowledging this aspect of the book when he says,

> Qohelet bares his soul in all its twistings and turnings, ups and downs, and he invites readers to accompany him in pursuit of fresh discovery. But the contradictions suggest more than the result of time's passage. They express the ambiguities of daily existence.[4]

Ellul goes somewhat further, arguing that when we read Ecclesiastes, we "enter an extremely ambiguous universe, in which we can never be sure we have fathomed the author's intention."[5] The same might be said of life under the sun: it, too, is extremely ambiguous, and people can never be sure they have fathomed *its* Author's intention—however hard they may seek, however wise they may be, however much they may claim to know. Salyer expresses this at some length, concluding:

> by characterizing the text's rhetoric as a vain rhetoric, I hint at a subtle effect of Qoheleth's extensive use of a rhetoric of ambiguity. Through the constant use of strategies of indirection, the implied author has constructed a text which constantly frustrates the reader, and ultimately, allows the reader no closed *Gestalten* or sure answers. It often leaves the reader in a state of perplexity, confusion or indecision. By so doing, the implied author has consciously constructed a text which would recreate the same sense of *hebel* at a literary level which he experienced in real life. The "Riddle of the Sphinx" is merely a means of recreating in the reader the iterative experience of life's existential conundrums. Vain rhetoric therefore describes the abiding literary experience of reading the book of Ecclesiastes in a performative sense. The illocutionary force of the implied author's various gapping techniques and strategies of indirection is to recreate in the reader life's penchant for absurdity and ambiguity.[6]

---

3. For example, Whybray states: "Whether he was a pessimist or an optimist, therefore, will remain a matter of opinion; what is certain is that he was a realist" (*Ecclesiastes*, 28). This is also a position argued recently by Miller (*Symbol and Rhetoric in Ecclesiastes*, 173–74).

4. Crenshaw, *Ecclesiastes*, 49.

5. Ellul, *Reason for Being*, 117.

6. Salyer, *Vain Rhetoric*, 396.

Take, for example, the cycles of nature described in 1:4–7: are they dependable phenomena which provide an element of security and predictability to life, or are they part of a monotonous cycle of endless repetitions from which there is no escape? According to 3:1–8, everything under the sun has its time: are people then but pawns in a cosmic chess game over which they have no real control (as 7:13 and 14 seem to assert) and whose rules they can never fully comprehend (as 8:17 may imply), or are they free to explore the limits and limitations of life (as Qohelet does throughout; cf., e.g., 1:13, 17; 2:1, 3, 10, 12; 7:25; 8:9; 9:1), and express and enjoy themselves within these necessary restrictions (as perhaps is advised in the "calls to enjoyment" in 2:24; 3:12–13, 22; 5:17–18; 8:15; 9:7–9; 11:9–10)? Is work (or is it "toil"?) a necessary evil to provide the means for survival and what little pleasure people can glean in the few days of life available to them (as, e.g., in 2:18–23), or is it given to enrich life and provide creative activity (as may be indicated in 2:24; 5:17 and 9:9)? Is wisdom a benefit which enables its possessor more fully to appreciate the complexities of the world and to live a more fulfilling life as a result (as suggested by verses such as 2:13–14a, 24; 7:11–12, 19; 8:1; 9:17–18; 10:2–12), or is it an extra burden that gives greater insight into the injustices and anomalies of life, but which does not provide any ultimate return (which seems to be argued in 1:18; 2:14b–16, 21; 7:13–18; 8:16–17; 9:10–11, 13–16; 10:1)? Is death a blessed release from life under the sun (4:2), or is it the final irony which casts its shadow over all the pleasures of life (as 9:10 suggests and perhaps is implied in 11:8; 12:7–8), or is it the supreme injustice because it takes no account of good or evil (as Qohelet complains in 2:14b–16; 9:2–3), or is it simply one of the necessary limits within which people have to operate (as may be intended in 3:2; 11:8 and perhaps 12:7)? In an ambiguous world people are confronted by endless data, which they read differently (not only from other people, but also at different times in their own lives) according to the interpretative strategy they bring to bear upon them. The writer of Ecclesiastes observes this world very carefully, and records these observations in language that captures the world's ambiguous nature.

Not only is the ambiguous nature of the text of Ecclesiastes a reflection of life under the sun, so too are the patterns that can be observed in the book. There are undoubtedly patterns and structures in Ecclesiastes, which tempt the reader to seek the one overall pattern that explains the way the book is put together.[7] So also life under the sun: here too there

---

7. A. G. Wright, "The Riddle of the Sphinx," offers a useful summary of outlines of the book's structure proposed pre-1968. Also useful in this regard is Ellermeier's

are patterns and structures that tease people into trying to find *the* solution that explains it all, to search for "grand narratives." One of the features of postmodernism is the realisation that no such solution is to be found;[8] one of the features of my reading of Ecclesiastes is the claim that no such solution to the structure of Ecclesiastes is to be found.[9] We can certainly discover trends in the book, for example a development from first person to second person address, or from observations about what happens under the sun to statements about the limitations of human knowledge, but none of these provides a sufficient explanation of the book's structure. Similarly, trends can be discerned in the world—for example, that those who act wisely or righteously *tend* to benefit in some way as a result (thus, e.g., 8:12b–13; and most of ch. 10), or that power is frequently on the side of an oppressor while the oppressed have no-one to comfort them (e.g. 4:1; 5:7)—but none of these trends provides a sufficient governing principle for life. We can also discover structures within Ecclesiastes, but any attempt to structure the whole book in similar fashion is ultimately frustrated. Attempts are still made, and will no doubt continue to be made, to find *the* structure of Qohelet, but any overall structure to the book involves some degree of manipulation of the text to make it fit a particular pattern.[10] Similarly, life under the sun eludes

study, *Qohelet*, 131–41. For more up-to-date resumés, see Schoors, "La structure litteraire de Qoheleth"; Crenshaw, *Ecclesiastes*, 34–49; Diethelm Michel, *Qohelet* (Darmstadt: Wissenschaftliche Buchgesellschaft, 1988), 21–45; Murphy, *Ecclesiastes*, xxxv–xli. Schoors edited a volume of papers arising from a conference in Leuven in 1997 (the *Colloquium Biblicum Lovaniense*) devoted to Ecclesiastes: in his introduction Schoors observes, "It is striking that the much debated question of the structure of Qohelet was more or less absent from the programme. It was only obliquely touched upon in the discussion of the exegesis of certain pericopes. There seems to be a certain weariness in examining again and again ingeniously built structures" (*Qohelet*, 13).

8. As Barry Smart (*Postmodernity* [London: Routledge, 1993]) notes, "It has been suggested that the postmodern political condition is premised upon the demise of 'grand narratives'" (p. 101). More precisely: "Our explanations, assumptions and values, along with the grand narratives of liberalism and socialism which derive from the complex eighteenth-century configuration known as 'The Enlightenment,' are found wanting when we try to make sense of contemporary conditions" (p. 26).

9. To this extent I agree with the much quoted passage from F. Delitzsch's nineteenth-century commentary: "All attempts to show, in the whole, not only oneness of spirit, but also a genetic progress, an all-embracing plan, and an organic connection, have hitherto failed, and must fail" (*Commentary on the Song of Songs and Ecclesiastes* [trans. M. G. Easton; Edinburgh: T. & T. Clark, 1877]).

10. In my work for my (unpublished) Ph.D. thesis, "The Ambiguity of Qohelet" (University of Stirling, 1996), I undertook extensive analysis of the text of

our efforts to discern an overall pattern in which everything has its appropriate place. No matter how simple or sophisticated our philosophy, there will always be those aspects of life that defy explanation and refuse to fit our scheme. Of course, such aspects of life (and Ecclesiastes) may be pushed to the margin, but it is only as we allow the voices from the margin[11] to speak and to challenge our own presuppositions that we truly begin to understand the world (and Ecclesiastes) in all its plurality and ambiguity.[12]

Of course, it may be argued that there is one certainty both for the writer of Ecclesiastes and in the world: that death is the end of life under the sun.[13] However, even this is ambiguous. The text within the *inclusio* starts with (an ambiguous) reference to the coming and going of generations (1:4, 11), and ends with a description of approaching death

Ecclesiastes (using various computer programmes to assist) in order to elucidate the structure of the book. I came to the very firm conclusion that, while there are many carefully structured passages within the book, and a number of important trends in the development of the book (and there *is* clear development), it eludes any attempt to find a definitive structure. The huge amount of repetition of words, phrases and themes invites the search for structure, but the text will not submit to any nice, neat pattern—leading, I suspect, to some frustration among those (like me) who seek such a pattern (unless they "squeeze" the text to "make it fit," as, I believe, a number have done).

11. *Voices from the Margin* (London: SPCK, 1991) is the title of a collection of essays on biblical topics by Latin American, Asian and black biblical scholars. R. S. Sugirtharajah, the editor, explains in his introduction (p. 2) that the titles indicates two things. First, "it highlights the struggles and exegetical concerns of those who are on the periphery of society." Secondly, "it points to the marginalization of Asian, Latin American, black and other biblical scholars by mainline biblical scholarship."

12. *Plurality and Ambiguity* (London: SCM, 1987) is the title of a book by David Tracy in which he argues, "Every discourse, by operating under certain assumptions, necessarily excludes other assumptions. Above all, our discourses exclude those others who might disrupt the established hierarchies or challenge the prevailing hegemony of power. And yet the voices of the other multiply." He continues: "But only by beginning to listen to those other voices may we also begin to hear the otherness within our own discourse and within ourselves. What we might then begin to hear, above our own chatter, are possibilities we have never dared to dream" (pp. 78–79).

13. Perhaps Qohelet would agree with de Beauvoir, who writes about "this ambiguity of their condition, which is the most fundamental of all: that every living movement is a sliding toward death." She goes on, "But if they are willing to look it in the face they also discover that every movement toward death is life. In the past people cried out, 'The king is dead, long live the king'; thus the present must die so that it may live; existence must not deny this death which it carries in its heart; it must assert itself as an absolute in its very finiteness; man fulfills himself within the transitory or not at all. He must regard his undertakings as finite and will them absolutely" (*The Ethics of Ambiguity*, 127).

(12:1–7). But the final words of this description *could* hint at the possibility of something beyond death, a hint that *might* also be found in 3:21, but stands in some tension with 9:10. Moreover, at least in the canonical form of the book (and, I would maintain, also by the author's design) there is an epilogue that takes the reader beyond the *inclusio* surrounding Qohelet's description of life—and death—under the sun. Qohelet, whose words are recorded in 1:2–12:8,[14] is now described in the third person, and perhaps also in the past tense: Qohelet *was* a wise person, who *taught* the people knowledge and *sought* to find pleasing words. In the epilogue readers are taken beyond the world described by the person (or, more probably, persona[15]) Qohelet so that they are privy to the perspective of the omniscient author, who then addresses the readers directly in the imperatives of the second half of the epilogue. The confident assertion with which the epilogue, and the book, closes, that God will bring (possibly future as also in 3:17 and 11:9) all deeds into judgment, raises again the question whether life "under the sun" is all there is. Qohelet examined thoroughly every aspect of this world, but perhaps—and here lies the final great ambiguity of the book—the author finally takes the readers beyond Qohelet's world, beyond the realm under the sun where everything is characterised by הבל. The epilogue to Ecclesiastes might then serve a similar purpose to the prologue to Job, which takes its readers outside the world Job knows and gives them privileged information to which Job, his three companions and Elihu do not have access. However, two crucial differences should be noted: first, God features as a speaking character in Job but is notably silent in Ecclesiastes; secondly, Job commences with explicit acknowledgement

---

14. I agree here with Fox who states, "the words of Qohelet (1:3–12:7), the motto (1:2–12:8), and the epilogue (12:9–14) are all the creation of the same person, the author of the book, who is not to be identified with Qohelet, his persona. In other words, the speaker we hear referring to Qohelet in the third person in 1:1–2; 7:27 (*'amar haqqohelet*); and 12:8, who comes to the fore in the epilogue (12:9–14), and whose 'I' we hear just once in the suffix of *beni* in 12:12—this speaker is the 'teller of the tale,' the frame narrator of the 'tale' of Qohelet. This narrator looks back and, using the common stance of wisdom teacher, tells his son about the sage Qohelet, transmitting to him Qohelet's teaching, then appreciatively but cautiously evaluating the work of Qohelet and other sages. The body of the book is formally a long quotation of Qohelet's words" (*Qohelet*, 311). Cf. Fox, *A Time to Tear Down*, 363–77.

15. As Fox explains, "Since there is an implied author mediating Qohelet's words, we cannot simply identify Qohelet with the author. Qohelet is a persona, a character created in the work who may be a close expression of the author's attitudes, but whose words cannot be assumed to be inseparable from the ideas of his creator." Fox goes on to assert that "Qohelet may be recognized as a persona even if one regards him as based on an historical character" (*Qohelet*, 315).

of another realm but Ecclesiastes gives only the faintest ambiguous hints that there may be something beyond life under the sun.

However, Ecclesiastes, even without the epilogue, is not simply a dis-interested representation of an ambiguous world—even were such a thing possible. A crucial element in the interpretative strategy that the author brings to bear on the "text" of the ambiguous world explored in the book is that there is a God. Moreover, there are three main character-istics of this God to which attention is drawn—none of which the author can have discerned by simple observation of the world.[16] First, God gives.[17] Thirteen times (or 14 if the "one shepherd" in 12:11 refers to God) the root נתן is used with God as subject (1:13; 2:26 [×2]; 3:10, 11, 13; 5:17, 18 [×2]; 6:2; 8:15; 9:9; 12:7); on three further occasion God's giving is described without using the verb נתן (2:24; 5:19; 9:7); and once God's *not* giving is referred to, again without using the verb נתן (in 6:2).

Secondly, God acts.[18] The root עשׂה is used eleven times in connection with God (3:11 [×3], 14 [×2]; 7:13, 14, 29; 8:17; 11:5 [×2]); but we are also informed that God "seeks" (3:15); "tests" (3:18, if indeed this is what the verb means); and "judges" (3:17; 11:9; 12:14). Perhaps the reference to "your creator" in 12:1 could be included in this category.

Thirdly, God is to be worshipped.[19] God acts, according to 3:14, in order that people might fear him. "Fearing God" is mentioned six times in total (3:14; 5:6; 7:18; 8:12, 13; 12:13); and those who are "good" in God's sight (2:26; 7:26) may be equivalent to those who "fear" him

---

16. However, it may be that this statement betrays a twenty-first century CE perspective on the interpretative strategy in Ecclesiastes. It may be that the existence of God was considered by the author to be an obvious, perhaps unavoidable, conclusion to draw from observation of a world in which there are many things that could not be explained other than as "given by God." It may also be the case that the author believed he or she could discern God's activity in the world—even if that activity was beyond understanding. Clearly such a God is to be "feared"—however precisely one understands that term in this context.

17. What God gives and does not give is the primary focus of 5:17–6:2, where one of three main clusters of occurrences of the word אלהים appears. However, this is an important feature of discussion relating to God throughout the book.

18. This is the main theme of the latter part of ch. 3 where there is a greater concentration of occurrences of the word אלהים than anywhere else in the book. What God "does" is important elsewhere, and the important themes of God's "giving" and "judging," and "fearing" God also occur in ch. 3. This is a critical passage for determining how God is represented in Ecclesiastes. It is also one of the most ambiguous parts of the whole book.

19. Worship of God is the main theme of 4:17–5:6, where there is another cluster of occurrences of the word אלהים.

(7:18; 8:12). In addition, the passage 4:17–5:6, which instructs the reader concerning appropriate ways to worship, explicitly mentions God six times.[20]

However, none of these divine characteristics is unambiguous. Certainly God's giving is associated with the "call to enjoyment" (cf. 2:24, 26; 3:13; 5:17, 18 [×2]; 8:15; 9:9), which seems to be positive (unless, of course, it is ironic). But the giving (of "business," NRSV) in 1:13 and 3:10 is somewhat more negative; "the sinner" comes off rather badly from God's giving in 2:26; and there is considerable irony in the giving of wealth without the ability to enjoy it in 6:2. Moreover, the "giving" in 3:11 and 5:19 is highly ambiguous and it is not at all obvious whether these are positive or negative.

God makes things beautiful (or appropriate?) in their time (3:11); what God does endures forever (3:14); God seeks out what is past (? 3:15); God makes people upright (7:29); and he judges the righteous and the wicked and all deeds, whether good or bad (3:17; 11:9; 12:14). But an important characteristic of God's deeds to which Qohelet draws attention is that people cannot make them out (3:11; 8:17; 11:5). Moreover, it seems that he acts in order that people will fear him (3:14); and human beings are unable to change what God does (7:13), even though he causes both the good and bad times (7:14). The statement of what God does in 3:18 is ambiguous and rather obscure.

Commentators are divided on just what "fear of God" implies in Ecclesiastes. So, for instance, Crenshaw argues,

> In many contexts within Proverbs, fear before the deity is presented as the correct attitude of a religious person, translatable by something like "to be religious." Qohelet's concept differs greatly, for in a few instances fear of God comes very close to terror before an unpredictable despot.[21]

Elsewhere Crenshaw writes that "fear" takes on a "wholly new meaning" in Ecclesiastes.[22] However, Whybray argues,

> the idea that Qoheleth's concept of the "fear of God" is essentially different from its usual meaning in the Old Testament (devotion to God,

20. These three categories include 39 out of the 40 explicit references to God in Ecclesiastes.

21. Crenshaw, *Ecclesiastes*, 99–100. Other commentators who adopt a similar view of the meaning of "fear" in this context include Davidson, *Ecclesiastes and Song of Solomon*, 24; Loader, *Ecclesiastes: A Practical Commentary*, 41.

22. James L. Crenshaw, *A Whirlpool of Torment* (Philadelphia: Fortress, 1984), 82. Cf. Crenshaw, "The Eternal Gospel (Eccl 3,11)," in *Essays in Old Testament Ethics* (ed. James L. Crenshaw and John T. Willis; New York: Ktav, 1974), 23–55, where he describes it as "cold terror." See also Murphy, "Recent Research," 134.

worship of God, or willing obedience to his commandments) is an idea derived from particular interpretation of Qoheleth's thought in general rather than from his actual use of the phrase.

He concludes, "His meaning is that God rightly demands 'fear' from men in the sense of recognition of his essential difference from his creatures."[23] Similar questions are raised about the meaning of the phrase "the one who pleases God" (NRSV), literally, "the good before God": does "good" have ethical connotations here (and elsewhere in Ecclesiastes), or does it mean simply those who are "fortunate" or "lucky?" In addition to such semantic questions, we might also ponder the motivation for the instruction about worship in 4:17–5:6: Should one take care to adopt the appropriate attitude out of reverence, or is the advice motivated by the fear of an unknown and distant God?

The author of Ecclesiastes is also an enigma. Is the author a king, or a wise person, or perhaps a counsellor—or none of these? Indeed, is the author to be equated with the main "speaker" in the book, Qohelet (or is it *the* qohelet—הקהלת in 12:8) or not? And if not, what attitude does the author take to Qohelet? Are Qohelet's words endorsed, or perhaps softened by the epilogue, or does the author distance him or herself from what Qohelet says? What is the author's own theology and philosophy of life? The answers to these and other questions concerning the author are far from clear. Perhaps this is a reflection also of the Author of life. Just as the relationship between the reader of Ecclesiastes and its author is abstruse, so also the relationship between humanity and God. Is it ever possible to be quite sure what the author/Author intends at any point? Is the author/Author toying with the reader by giving hints of answers to the questions life poses; by providing clues to structures and patterns which never quite work out; by speaking with different, perhaps even contradictory, voices? Does the author/Author approve of what Qohelet says, or of the words of the wise, or even of the instruction to fear God? One might well ask if such questions are not the response of a reader who is to a greater or lesser extent a child of the modern and postmodern age, and could not be the intention of the author of Qohelet. This is probably true. The question remains open how much ambiguity was

23. Whybray, *Ecclesiastes* 75. Elsewhere Whybray writes, "The evidence suggests that for Qoheleth the designation "he who fears God" is the highest accolade of moral virtue that can be bestowed" ("Qoheleth the Immoralist?," 201). Eaton agrees with Whybray when he writes that this "fear" is "not a craven terror in the face of the monstrous or the unknown, but rather the opposite, reverence and awesome regard for God" (*Ecclesiastes*, 82). Norbert Lohfink writes, "the 'fear of God' is the greatest human possibility" ("The Present and Eternity: Time in Qoheleth," *Theology Digest* 34 [1987]: 236–40 [239]).

intended by the person or people who wrote the book we know as Ecclesiastes.

What this particular reader has attempted to do is to probe the text of Ecclesiastes for ambiguities so as to explore the ways in which it might, with the imposition of very different interpretative strategies, yield "meaning." My conclusion is that the text of Ecclesiastes is highly ambiguous, and the intentions of its author are often far from clear. The observation that this ambiguity occurs throughout the book, that it affects words and phrases which are crucial to the reader's understanding of the work, that it operates at the formal as well as the textual level, and that consensus on almost every aspect of the book—author, setting, structure, meaning . . . even its right to be included in the Hebrew Bible—has eluded commentators throughout its history,[24] while it has nonetheless continued to fascinate its readers who have consistently found it realistically to address the world they know, leads me to conclude that it is a carefully crafted work in which ambiguity is an integral part *by design*. It is thus a very accurate reflection of life under the sun: it too is highly ambiguous, and the intentions of its Author (or Creator) are also often unclear.

When I first took an interest in Ecclesiastes as an undergraduate, about twenty years ago, "Ecclesiastes Studies" was something of a quiet

---

24. This takes us back to Salter's quote at the start of Chapter 2 in this book. Many other commentators have made similar observations. Seow provides an excellent example: "There is perhaps no book in the Bible that is the subject of more controversies than Ecclesiastes. From the start, its place in the canon was called into question largely because it was perceived to be internally inconsistent and partly because it appears to be unorthodox. Down at least to the fifth century of the common era, there were voices of doubt regarding the canonicity of the book. Even in modern times there have been some who have wondered about its authority. Nevertheless, through the ages the book has fascinated interpreters and inspired writers, even musicians. Hundreds of commentaries, both ancient and modern, have been written on it. Indeed, the book has rightly been regarded as one of the most remarkable little books in world literature.

"There has been little on which commentators agree, however. The book has been dated anywhere from the tenth century B.C.E. to the first century C.E. Interpreters have variously judged the author of the book to be utterly pessimistic or thoroughly optimistic; some say he is the quintessential skeptic, while others perceive him to be a paragon of piety. Some have detected commonalities between Ecclesiastes and Greek philosophy, others find affinities with Mesopotamian, Egyptian, or even Buddhist thought. A majority of scholars find absolutely no structure to the book, although in recent years some have discerned evidence of a careful, even intricate structure. Perhaps there are some things about the book that will always remain elusive and incomprehensible—a veritable testimony to the message of Ecclesiastes that everything is *hebel* 'vanity,' literally 'a breath'" (*Ecclesiastes*, ix).

backwater. It was not to remain so. Over the last twenty or so years a large number of commentaries and other books and articles—not to mention doctoral theses, a good indication of current interest—have appeared on this book. But why? Part of the explanation is probably that the previous lack of interest generated a vacuum that had to be filled. But the interest is not restricted to those in the academic arena who might be aware that such a vacuum even existed—the book has attracted considerable popular interest as well. I believe that much of the interest arises from Ecclesiastes' particular appeal to those affected, all be it unconsciously, by postmodernism.[25] Society today, as never before, is aware of the ambiguous nature of the world. It is no longer satisfied with a previous generation's "metanarratives," nor indeed does it seek any overarching worldview to give structure to life. In this post-structuralist, deconstructionist world order, certainty and security seem to be things of the past. In modern society ambiguity was marginalised in favour of producing coherent meaning. Postmodern society is content to live with ambiguity, and to permit (even encourage) a plurality of different voices and meanings.

Ecclesiastes was a problem for a previous "scientific" generation. It refused to fit into a neat mould. Whatever consistent meaning was discerned in the book was only given voice by pushing to the margins other voices crying out to be heard. Such plurality, such discord, such lack of consistent meaning, such unstructuredness . . . such ambiguity appeals to a postmodern reader, and accords well with the world seen through postmodern eyes.

Different people with different presuppositions will continue to read the world differently, and will come to different conclusions about the intentions of its Author. Indeed, the commentators and readers of this "text" have throughout known history disagreed, and will no doubt continue to disagree, about its Author (if such is even accepted), its setting, its structure and its meaning. Such is life. Such also is the book of Ecclesiastes.

> *Ambiguity is the warp of life, not something to be eliminated. Learning to savor the vertigo of doing without answers . . . and making do with fragmentary ones opens up the pleasures of recognizing and playing with pattern, finding coherence within complexity, sharing within multiplicity.*

> —Mary Catherine Bateson[26]

25. Salyer says, "Perhaps, more than we know, the book of Ecclesiastes is the most timely of biblical books for a postmodern consciousness" (*Vain Rhetoric*, 399).

26. Mary Catherine Bateson, *Peripheral Vision: Learning Along the Way* (New York: HarperCollins, 1994).

BIBLIOGRAPHY

Aaron, David H. *Biblical Ambiguities: Metaphor, Semantics, and Divine Imagery*. Leiden: Brill, 2001.

Abrams, M. H. *The Mirror and the Lamp: Romantic Theory and the Critical Tradition*. Repr., New York: W. W. Norton, 1958 (originally published 1953).

Adam, A. K. M. *Handbook of Postmodern Biblical Interpretation*. St Louis, Mo.: Chalice, 2000.

—*Postmodern Interpretations of the Bible: A Reader*. St Louis, Mo.: Chalice, 2001.

Aichele, G. Jr. *The Limits of Story*. Philadelphia: Fortress, 1985.

Alter, Robert. *The World of Biblical Literature*. London: SPCK, 1992.

Alter, Robert, and Frank Kermode. *The Literary Guide to the Bible*. London: Fontana, 1987.

Anderson, William H. U. *Qoheleth and its Pessimistic Theology: Hermeneutical Struggles in Wisdom Literature*. Lewiston, N.Y.: Edwin Mellen, 1997.

Bal, Mieke. *Narratology: Introduction to the Theory of Narrative*. 2d ed. Toronto: University of Toronto Press, 1997 (1995).

Barr, James. *The Bible in the Modern World*. Reissue, London: SCM Press, 1990 (1973).

—*Biblical Words for Time*. London: SCM Press, 1962.

Barthes, Roland. *Image, Music, Text*. London: Fontana, 1977.

Bartholomew, Craig G. *Reading Ecclesiastes: Old Testament Exegesis and Hermeneutical Theory*. AnBib 139. Rome: Editrice Pontificio Istituto Biblico, 1998.

Barton, George A. *Ecclesiastes*. ICC. Edinburgh: T. & T. Clark, 1912.

Barton, John. *The Cambridge Companion to Biblical Interpretation*. Cambridge: Cambridge University Press, 1998.

—"Classifying Biblical Criticism." *JSOT* 29 (1984): 19–35.

—*Reading the Old Testament: Method in Biblical Study*. 2d ed. London: Darton, Longman & Todd, 1996 (1984).

Barucq, A. *Ecclésiaste*. VS 3. Paris: Beauchesne, 1968.

Bateson, Mary Catherine, *Peripheral Vision: Learning Along the Way* (New York: HarperCollins, 1994).

Bateson, F. W. *English Poetry: A Critical Introduction*. London: Longmans, 1950.

Beal, Timothy K. "C(ha)osmopolis: Qohelet's Last Words." Pages 290–304 in *God in the Fray: A Tribute to Walter Brueggemann*. Edited by Tod Linafelt and Timothy K. Beal. Minneapolis: Augsburg Fortress, 1998.

Beardslee, William A., and David J. Lull, eds. "Introduction." Pages 1–6 in idem, *Old Testament Interpretation from a Process Perspective*. Semeia 24. Chico, Calif.: Scholars Press, 1982.

Beauvoir, Simone de. *The Ethics of Ambiguity*. New York: Citadel, 1976.

Benware, Paul N. *Survey of the Old Testament*. Everyman's Bible Commentary. Chicago: Moody Press, 1998.

Bergant, Dianne. *Israel's Wisdom Literature: A Liberation–Critical Reading*. Minneapolis: Fortress, 1997.

—*Job, Ecclesiastes*. Old Testament Message 18. Wilmington, Del.: Michael Glazier, 1982.

—"Vanity (*Hebel*)." *The Bible Today* 22 (1984): 91–92.

Bible and Culture Collective, The. *The Postmodern Bible*. New Haven: Yale University Press, 1995.

Bishop, E. F. F. "A Pessimist in Palestine." *PEQ* 100 (1968): 33–41.

Bolton, F. J. "The Sense of the Text and a New Vision." Pages 87–90 in Crossan, ed., *The Book of Job and Ricoeur's Hermeneutics*.

Brenner, Athalya, and Carole Fontaine, eds. *Wisdom and Psalms*. A Feminist Companion to the Bible, Second Series. Sheffield: Sheffield Academic Press, 1998.

Brindle, W. A. "Righteousness and Wickedness in Ecclesiastes 7:15–18." *AUSS* 23 (1985): 243–57.

Brown, William P. *Character in Crisis: A Fresh Approach to the Wisdom Literature of the Old Testament*. Grand Rapids: Eerdmans, 1996.

—*Ecclesiastes*. Interpretation. Louisville, Ky.: John Knox, 2000.

—*Seeing the Psalms: A Theology of Metaphor*. Louisville, Ky.: Westminster John Knox, 2002.

—"'Whatever Your Hand Finds to Do' Qoheleth's Work Ethic." *Int* 55, no. 3 (2001): 271–84.

Bryce, G. E. "'Better'-Proverbs: An Historical and Structural Study." Pages 343–54 in volume 2 of the *SBL Seminar Papers, 1972*. Edited by L. C. McGaughy. 2 vols. Missoula, Mont.: Society of Biblical Literature, 1972.

Burkes, Shannon. *Death in Qoheleth and Egyptian Biographies of the Late Period*. SBLDS 170. Atlanta: Society of Biblical Literature, 1999.

Byargeon, R. W. "The Significance of Ambiguity in Ecclesiastes 2,24–26." Pages 367–72 in Schoors, ed., *Qohelet in the Context of Wisdom*.

Caneday, A. B. "Qoheleth: Enigmatic Pessimist or Godly Sage?" *GTJ* 7 (1986): 21–56.

Carson D. A. et al., eds. *New Bible Commentary: 21st Century Edition*. 4th ed. Leicester: InterVarsity, 1994.

Castellino, G. R. "Qohelet and His Wisdom." *CBQ* 30 (1968): 15–28.

Ceresko, Anthony R. *Introduction to Old Testament Wisdom: A Spirituality for Liberation*. Maryknoll, N.Y.: Orbis, 1999.

Childs, B. S. *Introduction to the Old Testament as Scripture* (London: SCM Press, 1979)

Chouraqui, André. *La Bible, traduite et présentée par André Chouraqui*. Paris: Desclée de Brouwer, 1975.

Christianson, Eric S. "Qoheleth the 'Old Boy' and Qoheleth the 'New Man': Misogynism, the Womb and a Paradox in Ecclesiastes." Pages 109–36 in Brenner and Fontaine, eds., *Wisdom and Psalms*.

—*A Time to Tell: Narrative Strategies in Ecclesiastes*. JSOTSup 280. Sheffield: Sheffield Academic Press, 1998.

Clemens, D. M. "The Law of Sin and Death: Ecclesiastes and Genesis 1–3." *Themelios* 19 (1994): 5–8.

Clements, R. E. "Beyond Tradition-History." *JSOT* 31 (1985): 95–113.

Clifford, Richard J. *The Wisdom Literature*. Interpreting Biblical Texts. Nashville: Abingdon, 1998.

Clines, David J. A.

—"Methods in Old Testament Study." Pages 23–45 in vol. 1 of *On the Way to the Postmodern*.

—*On the Way to the Postmodern, 1968–1998*. Vols. 1 and 2. JSOTSup 292/293. Sheffield: Sheffield Academic Press, 1998.

—"Possibilities and Priorities of Biblical Interpretation in an International Perspective." Pages 46–47 in vol. 1 of *On the Way to the Postmodern*.

—"The Pyramid and the Net: The Postmodern adventure in Biblical Studies." Pages 138–57 in vol. 1 of *On the Way to the Postmodern*.

—"Story and Poem: The Old Testament as Literature and as Scripture." Pages 225–37 in vol. 1 of *On the Way to the Postmodern*.

—"Varieties of Indeterminacy." Pages 126–37 in vol. 1 of *On the Way to the Postmodern.*

—*What Does Eve Do to Help? And Other Readerly Questions to the Old Testament.* JSOTSup 94. Sheffield: JSOT Press, 1990.

—ed. *The Dictionary of Classical Hebrew*, vol. 2 (Sheffield: Sheffield Academic Press, 1995).

Cochrane, A. C. "Joy to the World = The Message of Ecclesiastes." *The Christian Century* 85 (1968): 27–35.

Collini, Stefan, ed. *Interpretation and Overinterpretation: Umberto Eco.* Cambridge: Cambridge University Press, 1992.

Cotterell, Peter, and Max Turner. *Linguistics and Biblical Interpretation.* London: SPCK, 1989.

Crenshaw, J. L. *Ecclesiastes.* OTL. London: SCM Press, 1988.

—"The Eternal Gospel (Eccl 3,11)." Pages 23–55 in *Essays in Old Testament Ethics.* Edited by James L. Crenshaw and John T. Willis. New York: Ktav, 1974.

—"The Expression *mi yôdēaʿ* in the Hebrew Bible." *VT* 36 (1986): 274–88.

—"Qohelet in Current Research." *HAR* 7 (1983): 41–56.

—"The Shadow of Death in Qoheleth." Pages 205–16 in Gammie et al., eds., *Israelite Wisdom.*

—*A Whirlpool of Torment.* Philadelphia: Fortress, 1984.

Crossan, John Dominic, *Cliffs of Fall: Paradox and Polyvalence in the Parables of Jesus.* New York: Seabury, 1980.

—ed. *The Book of Job and Ricoeur's Hermeneutics.* Semeia 19. Chico, Calif.: Scholars Press, 1981.

Culler, Jonathan. "In Defence of Overinterpretation." Pages 109–23 in Collini, ed., *Interpretation and Overinterpretation.*

—*On Deconstruction: Theory and Criticism After Structuralism.* UK ed. London: Routledge & Kegan Paul, 1983 (1982).

—*Structuralist Poetics: Structuralism, Linguistics and the Study of Literature.* London: Routledge & Kegan Paul, 1975.

Culley, Robert C., and Robert B. Robinson, eds. *Textual Determinacy: Part One.* Semeia 62. Atlanta: Scholars Press, 1993.

Dancy, John. *The Divine Drama: The Old Testament as Literature.* Cambridge: Lutterworth, 2001.

Davidson, Robert. *Ecclesiastes and the Song of Solomon.* The Daily Study Bible. Louisville, Ky.: Westminster John Knox, 1986.

Davies, Philip R., ed. *First Person: Essays in Biblical Autobiography.* The Biblical Seminar 81. London: Sheffield Academic Press, 2002.

Davis, Ellen F. *Proverbs, Ecclesiastes, and the Song of Songs.* Westminster Bible Companion. Louisville, Ky.: Westminster John Knox, 2000.

Deemter, Kees van, and Stanley Peters, eds. *Semantic Ambiguity and Underspecification.* CSLI Lecture Notes 55. Stanford, Calif.: CSLI Publications, 1996.

Delitzsch, F. *Commentary on the Song of Songs and Ecclesiastes.* Translated by M. G. Easton. Edinburgh: T. & T. Clark, 1877.

Dell, K. J. "Ecclesiastes as Wisdom: Consulting Early Interpreters." *VT* 44 (1984): 301–29.

Derrida, Jacques. *Of Grammatology.* Translated by Gayatri Chakravorty Spivak. Baltimore: The Johns Hopkins University Press, 1976.

—*Positions.* Translated by Alan Bass. Chicago: University of Chicago Press, 1981.

Detweiler, Robert. *Derrida and Biblical Studies.* Semeia 23. Chico, Calif.: Scholars Press, 1982

Dulles, Avery. *Models of Revelation.* New York: Doubleday, 1983.

Eagleton, Terry. *Literary Theory: An Introduction.* Oxford: Blackwell, 1983.

Eaton, Michael A. *Ecclesiastes.* TOTC. Leicester: InterVarsity, 1983.

Eco, Umberto. "Interpretation and History." Pages 23–43 in Collini, ed., *Interpretation and Overinterpretation.*

—"Overinterpreting Texts." Pages 45–66 in Collini, éd., *Interpretation and Overinterpretation*.

Ehlke, Roland Cap. *Ecclesiastes, Song of Songs*. People's Bible Commentary. St Louis, Mo.: Concordia, 1992.

Eliot, T. S. *The Use of Poetry and the Use of Criticism*. London: Faber & Faber, 1933.

Ellermeier, F. *Qohelet*. Vol. 1, Part 1. Herzberg: Jungfer, 1967.

Ellul, Jacques. *Reason for Being: A Meditation on Ecclesiastes*. Grand Rapids: Eerdmans, 1990.

Empson, William. *Seven Types of Ambiguity*. 2d ed. London: The Hogarth Press, 1991 (1930).

Exum, J. Cheryl, and Stephen D. Moore. *Biblical Studies/Cultural Studies: The Third Sheffield Colloquium*. Gender, Culture, Theology 7. Sheffield: Sheffield Academic Press, 1998.

Farmer, Kathleen A. *Proverbs and Ecclesiastes: Who Knows What is Good?* ITC. Grand Rapids: Eerdmans; Edinburgh: Handsel Press, 1991.

Fish, Stanley. "Interpreting the *Variorum*." Pages 235–40 in Newton, ed., *Twentieth-Century Literary Theory*; repr. from *Critical Inquiry* 2 (1976): 478–85.

—*Self-Consuming Artifacts: The Experience of Seventeenth-Century Literature*. Berkeley: University of California Press, 1972.

—"Why No One's Afraid of Wolfgang Iser." *Diacritics* 11, no. 1 (1981): 2–13; reproduced in extended form on Pages 68–86 of his *Doing What Comes Naturally: Change, Rhetoric, and the Practice of Theory in Literary and Legal Studies* (Oxford: Clarendon, 1989).

Fontaine, Carole R. "Ecclesiastes." Pages 153–55 in *The Women's Bible Commentary*. Edited by Carole A. Newsom and Sharon H. Ringe. London: SPCK, 1992.

—"'Many Devices' (Qoheleth 7.23–8.1): Qoheleth, Misogyny and the *Malleus Maleficarum*." Pages 137–68 in Brenner and Fontaine, eds., *Wisdom and Psalms*.

Forman, C. C. "The Pessimism of Ecclesiastes." *JSS* 3 (1958): 336–43.

Fox, Michael V. *Ecclesiastes*. The JPS Bible Commentary. Philadelphia: The Jewish Publication Society, 2004.

—"Frame-Narrative and Composition in the Book of Qohelet." *HUCA* 48 (1977): 83–106.

—"The Identification of Quotations in Biblical Literature." *ZAW* 92 (1980): 416–31.

—"Job 38 and God's Rhetoric." Pages 53–61 in Crossan, ed., *The Book of Job and Ricoeur's Hermeneutics*.

—"Qohelet 1:4." *JSOT* 40 (1988): 109.

—*Qohelet and His Contradictions*. Bible and Literature Series 18. Sheffield: Sheffield Academic Press, 1989.

—"On Reading Contradictions." Pages 1–26 in idem, *A Time to Tear Down*.

—*A Time to Tear Down and a Time to Build Up: A Rereading of Ecclesiastes*. Grand Rapids: Eerdmans, 1999.

—"The Uses of Indeterminacy." Pages 173–92 in Robert B. Robinson and Robert C. Culley, eds., *Textual Determinacy: Part Two*.

—"What Happens in Qohelet 4:13–16." *JHStud* 1 (1997): 1–9.

Fox, M. V., and B. Porten. "Unsought Discoveries: Qoh 7:23–8:1a." *HS* 19 (1978): 26–38.

Fredericks, Daniel C. "Chiasm and Parallel Structure in Qoheleth 5:9–6:9." *JBL* 109 (1989): 17–35.

—*Coping with Transience: Ecclesiastes on Brevity in Life*. The Biblical Seminar 18. Sheffield: JSOT Press, 1993.

Fretheim, Terence E., and Karlfried Froehlich. *The Bible as Word of God: In a Postmodern Age*. Minneapolis: Fortress, 1998.

Freund, Elizabeth. *The Return of the Reader: Reader-Response Criticism*. New Accents. London: Methuen, 1987.

Gadamer, Hans Georg. *Truth and Method*. London: Sheed & Ward, 1975.

Gammie, J. G. et al., eds. *Israelite Wisdom: Theological and Literary Essays in Honor of Samuel Terrien*. Missoula, Mont.: Scholars Press, 1978.

Garrett, Duane A. *Proverbs, Ecclesiastes, Song of Songs*. The New American Commentary 14. Nashville: Broadman Press, 1993.

Genung, John F. *Words of Koheleth*. New York: Houghton, Mifflin, 1904.

Ginsberg, H. L. *Koheleth*. Jerusalem: Newman, 1961.

Ginsburg, Christian D. *Coheleth, Commonly Called Ecclesiastes*. New York: Ktav, 1970.

—*Koheleth*. Jerusalem: Newman, 1961.

Gnuse, Robert, *The Authority of the Bible: Theories of Inspiration, Revelation and the Canon of Scripture*. New York: Paulist Press, 1985.

Goldingay, John. *Models for Scripture*. Grand Rapids: Eerdmans, 1994.

Good, Edwin M., "The Unfilled Sea: Style and Meaning in Ecclesiastes 1:2–11." Pages 59–73 in Gammie et al., eds., *Israelite Wisdom*.

Gordis, Robert. *Kohelet: The Man and his World; A Study in Ecclesiastes*. 3d ed. New York: Ktav, 1968.

Gray, Martin. *A Dictionary of Literary Terms*. York Handbooks. Harlow, Essex: Longman, 1984.

Greimas, A.-J. *Structural Semantics*. Translated by D. McDowell, R. Schleifer and A. Velie. Repr., Lincoln: University of Nebraska Press, 1983 (1966).

Green, Georgia M. "Ambiguity Resolution and Discourse Interpretation." Pages 1–26 in Deemter and Peters, eds., *Semantic Ambiguity*.

Haden, N. Karl. "Qoheleth and the Problem of Alienation." *Christian Scholars Review* 17 (1987): 52–66.

Hawkes, Terence. *Structuralism and Semiotics*. New Accents. London: Methuen, 1977.

Hawthorn, Jeremy. *Unlocking the Text: Fundamental Issues in Literary Theory*. London: Edward Arnold, 1987.

Heidegger, Martin. *Being and Time*. New York: Harper, 1962.

—*Poetry, Language and Thought*. New York: Harper & Row, 1971.

Hendry, G. S. "Ecclesiastes." Pages in *New Bible Commentary*. Edited by D. Guthrie. 3d ed. Leicester: InterVarsity, 1970.

Henry, Matthew. *A Commentary of the Whole Bible*. 6 vols. Iowa Falls: World Bible Publishers, n.d.

Hirsch, E. D. *The Aims of Interpretation*. Chicago: University of Chicago Press, 1976.

Hirst, Graeme, *Semantic Interpretation and the Resolution of Ambiguity*. Studies in Natural Language Processing. Cambridge: Cambridge University Press, 1987.

Holm-Nielsen, S. "The Book of Ecclesiastes and the Interpretation of it in Jewish and Christian Theology." *ASTI* 10 (1975–76): 38–96.

—"On the Interpretation of Qoheleth in Early Christianity." *VT* 24 (1974): 168–77.

Holub, Robert C. *Reception Theory: A Critical Introduction*. New Accents. London: Routledge, 1984.

House, Paul R., ed. *Beyond Form Criticism: Essays on Old Testament Literary Criticism*. Winona Lake, Ind.: Eisenbrauns, 1992.

Hubbard, David A. *Ecclesiastes, Song of Solomon*. The Communicator's Commentary, 15B. Dallas: Word Books, 1991.

Husserl, Edmund. *The Idea of Phenomenology*. The Hague: Nijhoff, 1964.

Ingram, Doug. "The Ambiguity of Qohelet: A Study of the Ambiguous Nature of the Language, Syntax and Structure of the Masoretic Text of Qohelet." Ph.D. diss., University of Stirling, 1996.

—*Ecclesiastes: A Peculiarly Postmodern Piece*. Grove Biblical Series B34. Cambridge: Grove Books, 2004.

Irwin, W. A. "Eccles. 4,13–16." *JNES* 3 (1944): 255–57.

Isaksson, Bo. "Nifal of עשה." Pages 69–74 in *Studies in the Language of Qoheleth*.

—*Studies in the Language of Qoheleth with Special Emphasis on the Verbal System*. AUUSSU 10. Uppsala: Almquist & Wiksell, 1987.

Iser, Wolfgang. *The Act of Reading: A Theory of Aesthetic Response*. Baltimore: The Johns Hopkins University Press, 1978.

—"Indeterminacy and the Reader's Response." Pages 226–31 in Newton, ed., *Twentieth-Century Literary Theory*; reprinted from Pages 2–45 in *Aspects of Narrative: Selected Papers from the English Institute*. Edited by J. Hillis Miller. New York: Columbia University Press, 1971.

—"Talk like Whales." *Diacritics* 11, no. 3 (1981): 82–87.

James, Kenneth W. "Ecclesiastes: Precursor of Existentialists." *The Bible Today* 22 (1984): 85–90.

Japhet, Sara, and Robert B. Salters. *The Commentary of R. Samuel Ben Meir Rashbam on Qoheleth*. Jerusalem: Magnes, 1985.

Jarick, J. *Gregory Thaumaturgos' Paraphrase of Ecclesiastes*. Septuagint and Cognate Studies 29. Atlanta: Scholars Press, 1990.

—"The Hebrew Book of Changes: Reflections on *hakkol hebel* and *lakkol zeman* in Ecclesiastes." *JSOT* 90 (2000): 79–99.

Jauss, Hans Robert. "Literary History as a Challenge to Literary Theory." Pages 221–26 in Newton, ed., *Twentieth-Century Literary Theory*.

Jefferson, Ann, "Structuralism and Post-Structuralism." Pages 92–121 in Jefferson and Robey, eds., *Modern Literary Theory*.

Jefferson, Ann. and David Robey. *Modern Literary Theory: A Comparative Introduction*. 2d ed. London: B. T. Batsford, 1986 (1982).

Jenni, Ernst, and Claus Westermann, eds. *Theological Lexicon of the Old Testament*. Translated by M. E. Biddle. 3 vols. Peabody, Mass.: Hendrickson, 1997.

Jobling, David. *The Sense of Biblical Narrative: Structural Analyses in the Hebrew Bible*. 2 vols. JSOTSup 7, 39. Sheffield: Sheffield Academic Press, 1986.

Jobling, David, Tina Pippin and Ronald Schleifer, eds., *The Postmodern Bible Reader*. Oxford: Blackwell, 2001.

Johnson, Barbara. *The Critical Difference*. Baltimore: The Johns Hopkins University Press, 1980.

Kaiser, Walter C. Jr. *Ecclesiastes: Total Life*. Everyman's Bible Commentary. Chicago: Moody Press, 1979.

—*Toward an Exegetical Theology: Biblical Exegesis for Preaching and Teaching*. Grand Rapids: Baker Book House, 1981.

Keegan, Terence J. "Biblical Criticism and the Challenge of Postmodernism." *BibInt* 3, no. 1 (1995): 1–14.

Kidner, Derek. *The Message of Ecclesiastes: A Time to Mourn, and a Time to Dance*. Leicester: InterVarsity, 1976.

Knopf, C. S. "The Optimism of Koheleth."*JNL* 49 (1982): 195–99.

Lauha, A. *Kohelet*. BKAT 19. Neukirchen–Vluyn: Neukirchener, 1978.

Lavoie, Jean-Jacques. *La pensée du Qohélet: Étude exégétique et intertextuelle*. Quebec: Fides, 1992.

Lee, Peter K. H. "Re-reading Ecclesiastes in the Light of Su Tung-p'o's Poetry." *Ching Feng* 30 (1987): 214–36.

Leupold, H. C. *Exposition of Ecclesiastes*. Grand Rapids: Baker Book House, 1952.

Levine, E. *The Aramaic Version of Qohelet*. New York: Sepher-Hermon, 1978.

Levison, John R., and Priscilla Pope-Levison, eds. *Return to Babel: Global Perspectives on the Bible*. Louisville, Ky.: Westminster John Knox, 1999.

Loader, J. A. *Ecclesiastes: A Practical Commentary*. Translated by John Vriend. Text and Interpretation. Grand Rapids: Eerdmans, 1986 (originally published 1984).

—*Polar Structures in the Book of Qohelet*. New York: de Gruyter, 1979.

Lohfink, Norbert. "The Present and Eternity: Time in Qoheleth." *TD* 34 (1987): 236–40.

—*Qoheleth*. Translated by Sean McEvenue. A Continental Commentary. Minneapolis: Fortress, 2003.

—"Zu eigen Satzeröffnungen im Epilog des Koheletbuches." Pages 131–48 in *"Jedes Ding hat seine Zeit...": Studien zur israelitischen und altorientalischen Weisheit*. Edited by A. A. Diesel, R. G. Lehmann, E. Otto and A. Wagner. Festschrift for D. Michel. BZAW 241. Berlin: de Gruyter, 1996.

Longman, Tremper, III. *The Book of Ecclesiastes*. NICOT. Grand Rapids: Eerdmans, 1998.

—*Literary Approaches to Biblical Interpretation*. Foundations of Contemporary Interpretation 3. Leicester: Apollos, 1987.

—"The Present and Eternity: Time in Qoheleth." *TD* 34 (1987): 236–40.

Loretz, O. *Qohelet und der alte Orient: Untersuchungen zu Stil und theologischer Thematik des Buches Qohelet*. Freiburg: Herder, 1964.

Lumbala, Francois Kabasele. "An African Perspective." Pages 81–86 in Levison and Pope-Levison, eds., *Return to Babel*.

Lux, R. " 'Ich, Kohelet, bin König...' Die Fiktion als Schlüssel zur Wirklichkeit in Kohelet 1:12–2:26." *EvT* 50 (1990): 331–42.

Maclean, Ian. "Reading and Interpretation." Pages 122–44 in Jefferson and Robey, eds., *Modern Literary Theory*.

McKenna, John E. "The Concept of *Hebel* in the Book of Ecclesiastes." *SJT* 45 (1992): 19–28.

McKim, Donald K., ed. *The Authoritative Word: Essays on the Nature of Scripture*. Grand Rapids: Eerdmans, 1983.

McKnight, Edgar V. *The Bible and the Reader: An Introduction to Literary Criticism*. Philadelphia: Fortress, 1985.

—*Post-Modern Use of the Bible: The Emergence of Reader-Oriented Criticism*. Nashville: Abingdon, 1988.

Melchert, Charles F. *Wise Teaching: Biblical Wisdom and Educational Ministry*. Harrisburg, Pa.: Trinity Press International, 1998.

Michel, Diethelm. *Qohelet*. Darmstadt: Wissenschaftliche Buchgesellschaft, 1988.

—*Untersuchungen zur Eigenart des Buches Qohelet*. Berlin: de Gruyter, 1989.

Miller, Douglas B. "Qohelet's Symbolic Use of הבל." *JBL* 117, no. 3 (1998): 437–54.

—*Symbol and Rhetoric in Ecclesiastes: The Place of* Hebel *in Qohelet's Work*. Atlanta: Society of Biblical Literature, 2002.

—"What the Preacher Forgot: The Rhetoric of Ecclesiastes." *CBQ* 62 (2000): 215–35.

Mills, Mary E. *Reading Ecclesiastes: A Literary and Cultural Exegesis*. Aldershot: Ashgate, 2003.

Miscall, P. D. *The Workings of Old Testament Narrative*. Philadelphia: Fortress, 1983.

Moore, Stephen D. *Poststructuralism and the New Testament*. Minneapolis: Fortress, 1994.

Moore, T. M. *Ecclesiastes: Ancient Wisdom when All Else Fails. A New Translation and Interpretive Paraphrase*. Downers Grove, Ill.: InterVarsity, 2001.

Morgan, Robert, with John Barton. *Biblical Interpretation*. The Oxford Bible Series. Oxford: Oxford University Press, 1988.

Murphy, Roland. *Ecclesiastes*. WBC 23A. Dallas: Word, 1992.

—"On Translating Ecclesiastes." *CBQ* 53 (1991): 571-79.

—"Qohelet Interpreted: The Bearing of the Past on the Present." *VT* 32 (1982): 331–37.

—"Recent Research on Proverbs and Qoheleth." *CR:BS* 1 (1993): 119–40.

Murphy, Roland, and Elizabeth Huwiler. *Proverbs, Ecclesiastes, Song of Songs.* NIBC. Carlisle: Paternoster, 1999.

Newsom, C. A. "Job and Ecclesiastes." Pages 227–50 in *Old Testament Interpretation—Past, Present, and Future: Essays in Honor of Gene M. Tucker.* Edited by J. L Mays, D. L. Petersen and K. H. Richards. Nashville: Abingdon, 1995.

Newton, K. M., ed. *Twentieth-Century Literary Theory: A Reader.* Houndsmills: Macmillan, 1988.

Norris, Christopher, *Deconstruction: Theory and Practice.* New Accents. London: Methuen, 1982.

Ogden, C. K., and I. A. Richards, *The Meaning of Meaning.* New York: Harcourt, 1923.

Ogden, Graham. "The 'Better'-Proverb (Tôb-Spruch), Rhetorical Criticism, and Qoheleth." *JBL* 96, no. 4 (1977): 489–505.

—"Historical Allusion in Qoheleth 4:13–16?" *VT* 30 (1980): 309–15.

—"The Mathematics of Wisdom: Qoheleth iv 1–12." *VT* 34 (1984): 446–53.

—*Qoheleth.* Readings: A New Biblical Commentary. Sheffield: Sheffield Academic Press, 1987.

—"Qoheleth's Use of the 'Nothing is Better'-Form." *JBL* 98, no. 3 (1979): 339–50.

—"'Vanity' it Certainly is Not." *BT* 38 (1987): 301–7

Ogden, Graham S., and Lynell Zogbo. *A Handbook on Ecclesiastes.* UBS Handbook Series. New York: United Bible Societies, 1997.

Olsen, Stein Haugom. *The Structure of Literary Understanding.* Cambridge: Cambridge University Press, 1978.

Page, Ruth. *Ambiguity and the Presence of God.* London: SCM Press, 1985.

Pennacchini, Bruno. "Qohelet ovvero il libro degli assurdi." *Euntes Docete* 30 (1977): 491–510.

Perdue, Leo G. *Wisdom and Creation: The Theology of Wisdom Literature.* Nashville: Abingdon, 1994.

Perry, T. A. *Dialogues with Kohelet.* Pennsylvania: The Pennsylvania State University Press, 1993.

Peter, C. B. "In Defence of Existence: A Comparison Between Ecclesiastes and Albert Camus." *Bangalore Theological Forum* 12 (1980): 26–43.

Peterson, Eugene H. *Five Smooth Stones for Pastoral Work.* Grand Rapids: Eerdmans, 1980.

Pippin, Tina, ed. *Ideological Criticism of Biblical Texts.* Semeia 59. Atlanta: Scholars Press, 1992.

Poesio, Massimo. "Semantic Ambiguity and Perceived Ambiguity." Pages 159–201 in van Deemter and Peters, eds., *Semantic Ambiguity.*

Polzin, Robert. *Biblical Structuralism: Method and Subjectivity in the Study of Ancient Texts.* Philadelphia: Fortress, 1977.

Provan, Iain. *Ecclesiastes, Song of Songs.* The NIV Application Commentary. Grand Rapids: Zondervan, 2001.

Ramey, Coart. *Beyond the Sun: A Guide to Understanding Ecclesiastes.* Greenville, S.C.: Bob Jones University Press, 2001.

Ransom, J. C. *The New Criticism.* Norfolk, Conn: New Directions, 1941.

Reed, E. D. "Whither Postmodernism and Feminist Theology." *FT* 6 (1994): 15–29.

Richards, I. A. *Principles of Literary Criticism.* New York: Harcourt, 1924.

Ricoeur, Paul. "Metaphor and Symbol." Pages 45–69 in *Interpretation Theory: Discourse and the Surplus of Meaning.* Fort Worth: Texas Christian University Press, 1976.

Rimmon, Shlomith. *The Concept of Ambiguity: The Example of James.* Chicago: University of Chicago Press, 1977.

Robey, David. "Anglo-American New Criticism." Pages 73–91 in Jefferson and Robey, eds., *Modern Literary Theory: A Comparative Introduction*.

Robinson, Robert B., and Robert C. Culley, eds. *Textual Determinacy: Part Two*. Semeia 71. Atlanta: Scholars Press, 1995.

Rorty, Richard. "The Pragmatist's Progress." Pages in 89–108 in Collini, ed., *Interpretation and Overinterpretation*.

Rudman, Dominic. "The Anatomy of the Wise Man: Wisdom, Sorrow and Joy in the Book of Ecclesiastes." Pages 465–71 in Schoors, ed., *Qohelet in the Context of Wisdom*.

—"A Contextual Reading of Ecclesiastes 4:13–16." *JBL* 116 (1997): 57–73.

—*Determinism in the Book of Ecclesiastes*. JSOTSup 316. Sheffield: Sheffield Academic Press, 2001.

Salters, R. B. "Exegetical Problems in Qoheleth." *IBS* 10 (1988): 44–59.

Salyer, Gary D. *Vain Rhetoric: Private Insight and Public Debate in Ecclesiastes*. JSOTSup 327. Sheffield: Sheffield Academic Press, 2001.

Sandberg, Ruth N. *Rabbinic Views of Qohelet*. Lewiston, N.Y.: Mellen Biblical Press, 1999.

Saussure, Ferdinand de. *Cours de Linguistique Générale*. Paris: Payot, 1922; English translation by Wade Baskin. *Course in General Linguistics*. New York: Philosophical Library, 1959.

Sawyer, John F. A. *The Fifth Gospel: Isaiah in the History of Christianity*. Cambridge: Cambridge University Press, 1996.

Schleifer, Ronald. *A. J. Greimas and the Nature of Meaning: Linguistics, Semiotics and Discourse Theory*. London: Croom Helm, 1987.

Schoors, Antoon. *The Preacher Sought to Find Pleasing Words: A Study of the Language of Qoheleth*. OLA 41. Leuven: Peeters, 1992.

—"Qoheleth: The Ambiguity of Enjoyment." Pages 35–41 in *The Bright Side of Life*. Edited by Ellen van Wolde. *Concilium* 2000, no. 4. London: SCM Press.

—"La structure litteraire de Qohelet." *Orientalia Lovaniensia Analecta* 13 (1982): 91–116.

—"Words Typical of Qohelet." Pages 17–39 in Schoors, ed., *Qohelet in the Context of Wisdom*.

—ed. *Qohelet in the Context of Wisdom*. BETL 136. Leuven: Leuven University Press, 1998.

Schwartz, Matthew J. "Koheleth and Camus: Two Views of Achievement." *Judaism* 35 (1986): 29–34.

Scott, R. B. Y. *Proverbs, Ecclesiastes: A New Translation with Introduction and Commentary*. AB 18. New York: Doubleday, 1965.

Selden, Raman, and Peter Widdowson. *A Reader's Guide to Contemporary Literary Theory*. 3d ed. New York: Harvester Wheatsheaf, 1993.

Seow, Choon-Leong. *Ecclesiastes: A New Translation with Introduction and Commentary*. AB 18C. New York: Doubleday, 1997.

—"Theology when Everything is Out of Control." *Int* 55, no. 3 (2001): 237–49.

Shapiro, Rami. *The Way of Solomon: Finding Joy and Contentment in the Wisdom of Ecclesiastes*. San Francisco: HarperSanFrancisco, 2000.

Shead, Andrew G. "Reading Ecclesiastes 'Epilogically.'" *TB* 48, no. 1 (1997): 67–91.

Sheppard, G. T. "The Epilogue to Qoheleth as Theological Commentary." *CBQ* 39, no. 2 (1977): 182–89.

Sherwood, Yvonne. *A Biblical Text and its Afterlives: The Survival of Jonah in Western Culture*. Cambridge: Cambridge University Press, 2000.

Smart, Barry. *Postmodernity*. London: Routledge, 1993.

Sneed, Mark. "[Dis]closure in Qohelet: Qohelet Deconstructed," *JSOT* 27 (2002): 115–26.

Sommer, Benjamin D. *A Prophet Reads Scripture: Allusion in Isaiah 40–66*. Stanford, Calif.: Stanford University Press, 1998

Song, Choan-Seng. "An Asian Perspective." Pages 87–92 in Levison and Pope-Levison, eds., *Return to Babel*.

Spangenberg, I. J. J. "A Century of Wrestling with Qohelet: The Research History of the Book Illustrated with a Discussion of Qoh 4,17–5,6." Pages 61–91 in Schoors, ed., *Qohelet in the Context of Wisdom*.

Spanos, William V. "Breaking the Circle: Hermeneutics as Dis-closure." Pages 196–202 in Newton, ed., *Twentieth-Century Literary Theory*.

Sproul, R. C., Jr. *Vanity and Meaning: Discovering Purpose in Life*. Grand Rapids: Baker Book House, 1995.

Staples, W. E. "The 'Vanity' of Ecclesiastes." *JNES* 24, no. 2 (1943): 95–104.

Sternberg, Meir. *The Poetics of Biblical Narrative: Ideological Literature and the Drama of Reading*. Bloomington: Indiana University Press, 1985.

Sugirtharajah, R. S., ed. *Voices from the Margin*. London: SPCK, 1991.

Tamez, Elsa. "A Latin American Perspective." Pages 75–80 in Levison and Pope-Levison, eds., *Return to Babel*.

—*When the Horizons Close: Rereading Ecclesiastes*. Eng. ed. Maryknoll, N.Y.: Orbis, 2000 (originally published 1998).

Thiselton, Anthony C. *New Horizons in Hermeneutics: The Theory and Practice of Transforming Biblical Reading*. Grand Rapids: Zondervan, 1992.

Tidball, Derek. *That's Life! Realism and Hope for Today from Ecclesiastes*. Leicester: InterVarsity, 1989.

Tracy, David. *Plurality and Ambiguity*. London: SCM, 1987.

VanGemeren, Willem A., ed. *New International Dictionary of Old Testament Theology and Exegesis*. 5 vols. Carlisle: Paternoster Press, 1996.

Vanhoozer, Kevin J. *Is There a Meaning in This Text? The Bible, the Reader and the Morality of Literary Knowledge*. Leicester: Apollos, 1998.

Voelz, James W. *What Does This Mean? Principles of Biblical Interpretation in the Post-Modern World*. 2d ed. St Louis, Mo.: Concordia.

Wal, A. J. O. Van der. "Unique Statement in Israel's Wisdom Tradition." Pages 413–424 in Schoors, ed., *Qohelet in the Context of Wisdom*.

Walsh, J. T. "Despair as a Theological Virtue in the Spirituality of Ecclesiastes." *BTB* 12 (1982): 46–49.

Webb, Barry G. *Five Festal Garments: Christian Reflections on the Song of Songs, Ruth, Lamentations, Ecclesiastes and Esther*. New Studies in Biblical Theology 10. Leicester: Apollos, 2000.

Whitelam, Keith W. *The Invention of Ancient Israel: The Silencing of Palestinian History*. London: Routledge, 1996.

Whitley, Charles F. *Koheleth: His Language and Thought*. BZAW 148. Berlin: de Gruyter, 1979.

Whybray, R. N. *Ecclesiastes*. OTG. Sheffield: Sheffield Academic Press, 1989.

—*Ecclesiastes*. Grand Rapids: Eerdmans; London: Marshall, Morgan & Scott, 1989.

—"Ecclesiastes 1:5–7 and the Wonders of Nature." *JSOT* 41 (1988): 105–12.

—"Qoheleth as a Theologian." Pages in 239–65 in Schoors, ed., *Qohelet in the Context of Wisdom*.

—"Qoheleth, Preacher of Joy." *JSOT* 23 (1982): 87–98.

—"Qoheleth the Immoralist? (Qoh 7:16–17)." Pages 191–204 in Gammie et al., eds:, *Israelite Wisdom*.

Willey, Patricia Tull. *Remember the Former Things: The Recollection of Previous Texts in Second Isaiah*. SBLDS 161. Atlanta: Scholars Press, 1997.

Wilson, G. H. "The Words of the Wise: The Intent and Significance of Qoheleth 12:9–14." *JBL* 109 (1984): 175–92.

Wilson, L. "Artful Ambiguity in Ecclesiastes 1,1–11." Pages 357–65 in Schoors, ed., *Qohelet in the Context of Wisdom.*

Wimsatt, W. K., and M. C. Beardsley. "The Affective Fallacy." Pages 21–40 in idem, *The Verbal Icon.*

—"The Intentional Fallacy." Pages 3–18 in idem, *The Verbal Icon.*

—*The Verbal Icon: Studies in the Meaning of Poetry.* Repr., London: Methuen, 1970 (1954).

Wright, A. G. "Additional Numerical Patterns in Qoheleth." *CBQ* 45 (1983): 32–43.

—"The Poor But Wise Youth and the Old But Foolish King (Qoh 4:13–16)." Pages 142–54 in *Wisdom, You Are my Sister: Studies in Honor of Roland E. Murphy, O. Carm., on the Occasion of His Eightieth Birthday.* Edited by Michael L. Barré, SS. CBQMS 29. Washington: The Catholic Biblical Association of America, 1997.

—"The Riddle of the Sphinx: The Structure of the Book of Qohelet." *CBQ* 30 (1968): 313–34.

Wright, J. Stafford. "Ecclesiastes." Pages 1137–97 in *The Expositor's Bible Commentary*, Vol. 5. Edited by Frank E. Gaebelein. Grand Rapids: Zondervan, 1991.

Zimmerli, Walther. "Zur Struktur der alttestamentlichen Weisheit." *ZAW* 51 (1933): 192–95.

INDEXES

INDEX OF REFERENCES

Index of References

289

3:12	165, 177–79, 183, 185–87, 192–94, 246		212	4:8a	118
		4:1–5:7 Eng.	219	4:9	155, 162, 165, 194–96, 199, 200
		4:1–5:7	195		
		4:1–5:6	219, 231		
		4:1–9	162		
3:13	153, 154, 165, 173, 174, 177–80, 185–87, 215, 268, 269	4:1–3	195, 196, 199, 201	4:10–13	200
				4:10–12	200
		4:1	162, 163, 165, 195, 255, 258, 265	4:10	199
				4:11	199, 208
				4:12	199
				4:13–16	197, 201, 204, 205
3:14	62, 119, 165, 204, 246, 268, 269	4:2–3	195, 214, 245	4:13–14	202
		4:2	187, 195, 196, 264	4:13	12, 79, 194, 195, 201, 209, 237, 238, 246
3:14a	164, 165	4:3	140, 162, 163, 165, 194–96, 244, 256		
3:14b	164, 165			4:13a	202
3:15	268, 269			4:14	202, 203
3:16–22	134		159	4:15–16	201, 203
3:16	255, 258	4:4–9		4:15	195, 202, 203, 258
3:17	55, 166, 267, 268, 269	4:4–6	197, 199, 201		
		4:4	72, 112, 118, 120, 132, 155, 158, 161, 162, 165, 195, 198, 199	4:16	112, 118–20, 132, 203, 205
3:17a	85			4:17–5:6	205, 212, 218, 268–70
3:18–21	116				
3:18	76, 269				
3:19	76, 109, 115–17, 120, 122, 128, 142			4:17	165, 194, 195, 206–209, 211, 238, 246
		4:5	198, 199		
3:19b	116	4:6	112, 156, 158, 162, 165, 194, 195, 198, 199	5	30, 128, 162
3:20	235			5:1–7 Eng.	205
3:21	61, 76, 208, 267			5:1–7	252
				5:1–6	195
3:22–9:7	249	4:7–12	199, 201	5:1	61, 66, 119, 178, 204–208, 212, 256, 257
3:22	138, 139, 161, 162, 165, 174, 179, 182, 183, 185–87, 192–95, 208, 212, 223, 232, 264	4:7–8	123, 124		
		4:7	121, 199, 258		
		4:8	67, 76, 87, 114, 117–20, 156, 158, 162, 165, 180, 199, 200, 208	5:2	66, 205, 206, 252
				5:2 Eng.	61, 119, 256, 257
4	30, 128, 194, 195,			5:2–7 Eng.	195

INDEX OF AUTHORS